SLEEP

This hay fever medication is making me sleepy every day. I was sleepy drawing the cover. I'm sleepy writing this. I hope I'm not still sleepy when this book comes out.

—Tite Kubo

BLEACH is author Tite Kubo's second title. Kubo made his debut with ZOMBIEPOWDER., a four-volume series for WEEKLY SHONEN JUMP. To date, BLEACH has been translated into numerous languages and has also inspired an animated TV series that began airing in the U.S. in 2006. Beginning its serialization in 2001, BLEACH is still a mainstay in the pages of WEEKLY SHONEN JUMP. In 2005, BLEACH was awarded the prestigious Shogakukan Manga Award in the shonen (boys) category.

BLEACH
Vol. 50: THE SIX FULLBRINGERS
SHONEN JUMP Manga Edition

STORY AND ART BY
TITE KUBO

Translation/Joe Yamazaki
Touch-up Art & Lettering/Mark McMurray
Design/Yukiko Whitley, Kam Li
Editor/Alexis Kirsch

Printed in the U.S.A.

Published by VIZ Media, LLC
P.O. Box 77010
San Francisco, CA 94107

10 9 8 7 6 5 4 3 2 1
First printing, November 2012

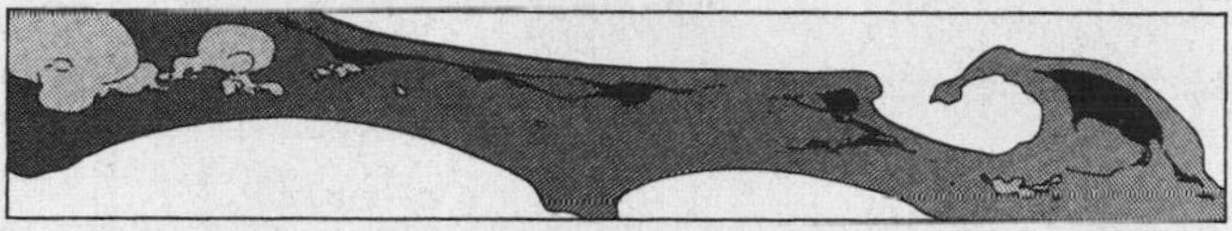

Time always approaches from behind
Growling and flowing past our eyes

Stand your ground
No matter how much time shows its fangs
In order to wash you away to a beautiful past

Do not look forward
Your hopes creep up behind you
Only existing in dark turbid waters

BLEACH50 The Six Fullbringers

Shonen Jump Manga

STARS AND

Orihime Inoue

Chad Yasutora

Ichigo Kurosaki

plot

When high school student Ichigo Kurosaki meets Soul Reaper Rukia Kuchiki his life is changed forever. Soon Ichigo is a soul-cleansing Soul Reaper too, and he finds himself facing off against ex-Soul Reaper Aizen and his dark ambitions. In exchange for his Soul Reaper powers, Ichigo is finally able to defeat Aizen and seal him away!

With the long battle over, Ichigo says goodbye to Rukia and returns to a normal life. But one day, his friend Uryu is attacked and Ichigo is confronted by a mysterious man named Kugo Ginjo. Ginjo and his allies say they want to help Ichigo regain his powers. Then suddenly Chad appears...

BLEACH ALL

沓澤ギリコ

Giriko Kutsuzawa

銀城空吾

Kugo Ginjo

Riruka Dokugamine

毒ヶ峰リルカ

STORIES

BLEACH 50

The Six Fullbringers

Contents

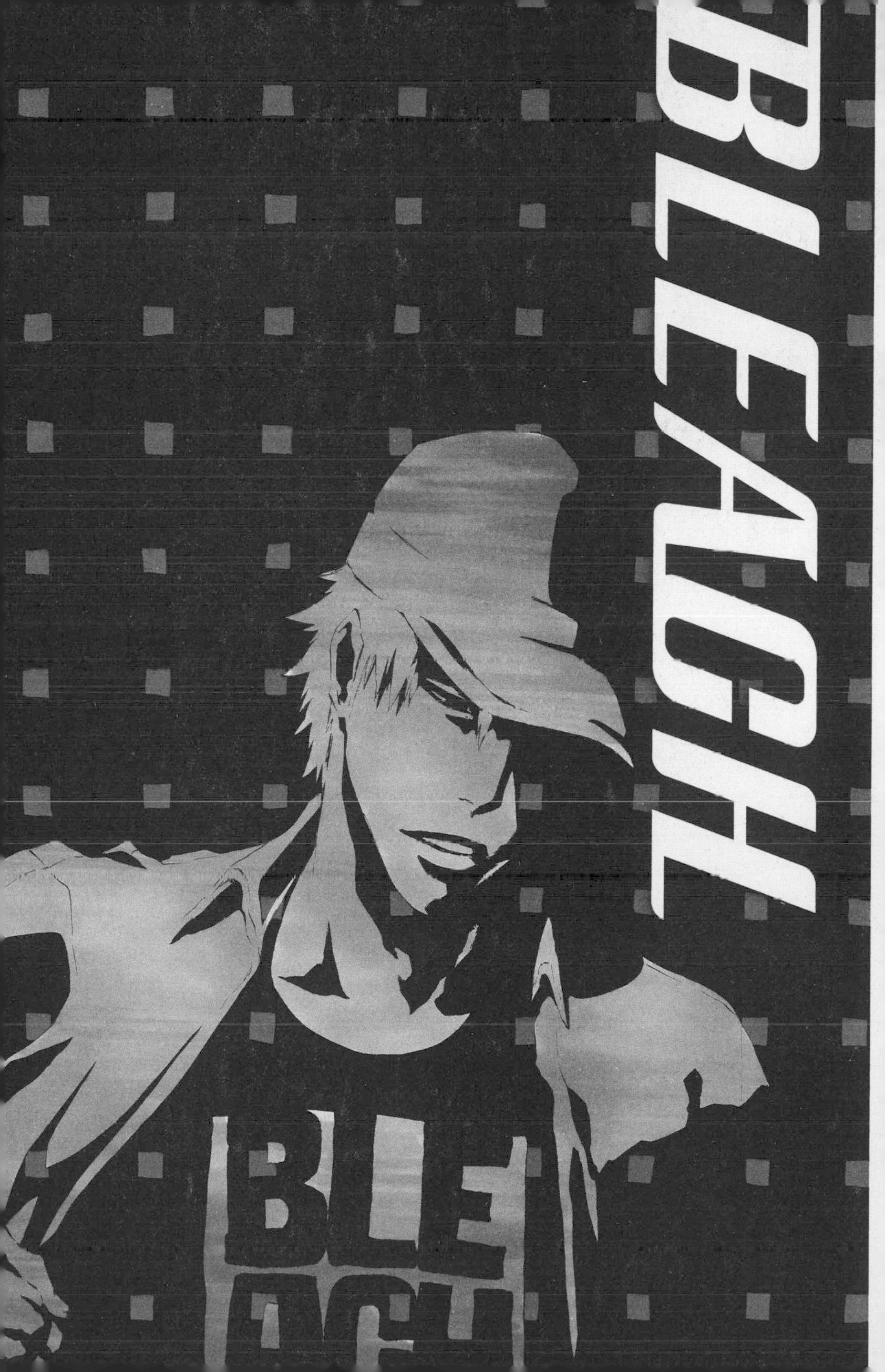
BLEACH
BLE

BLEACH
ブリーチ

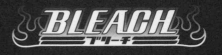

READ THIS WAY

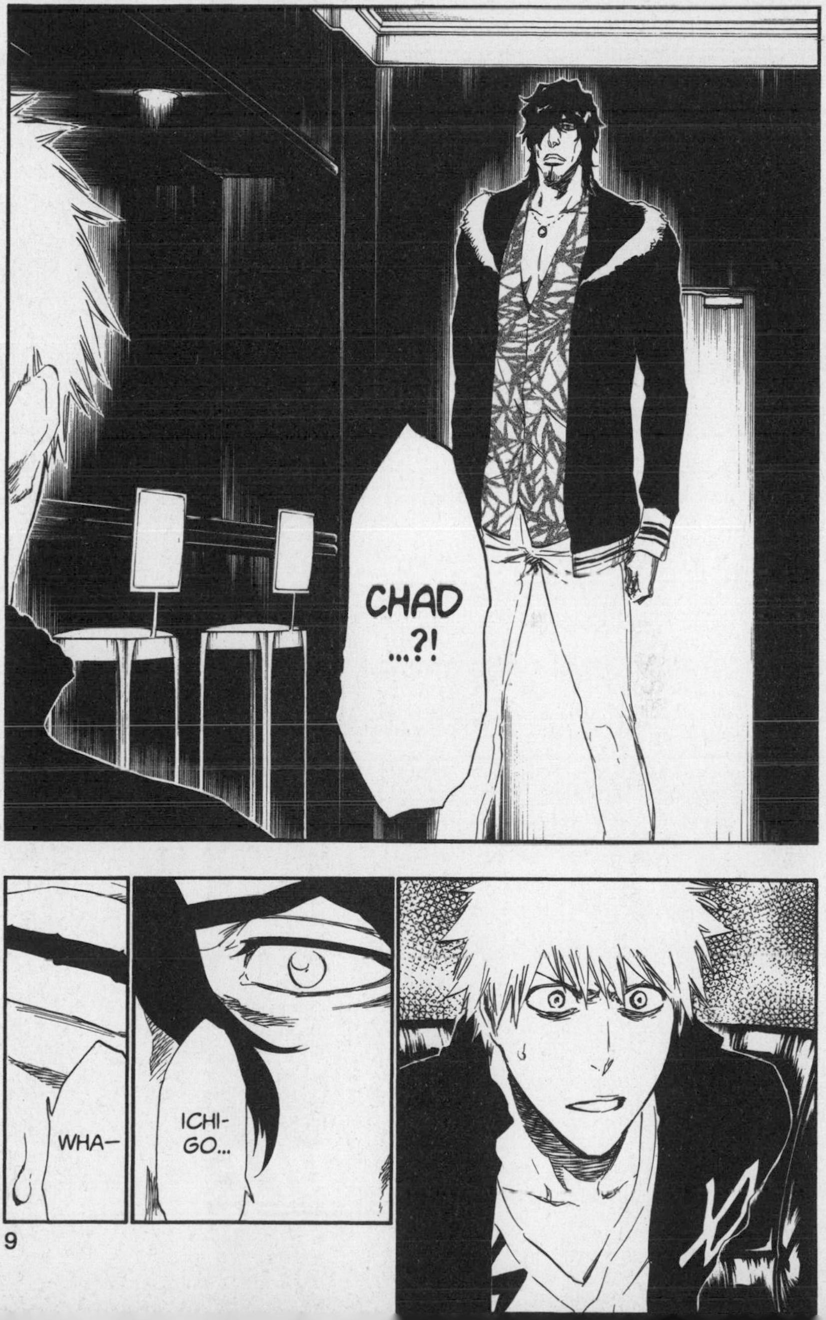
CHAD ...?!
ICHI-GO...
WHA—

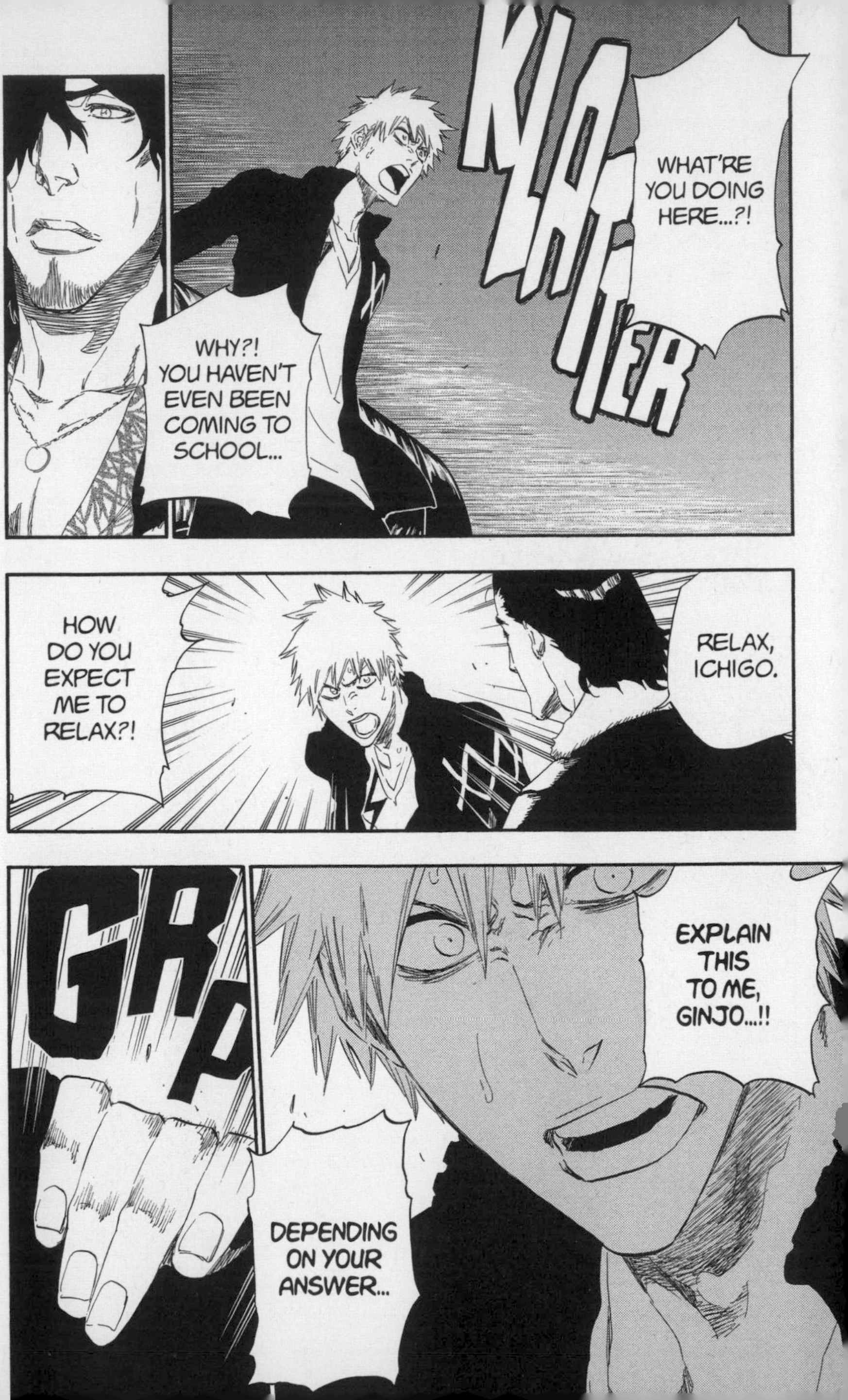
KLATTER
WHAT'RE YOU DOING HERE...?!
WHY?! YOU HAVEN'T EVEN BEEN COMING TO SCHOOL...
RELAX, ICHIGO.
HOW DO YOU EXPECT ME TO RELAX?!
EXPLAIN THIS TO ME, GINJO...!!
DEPENDING ON YOUR ANSWER...
GRAB

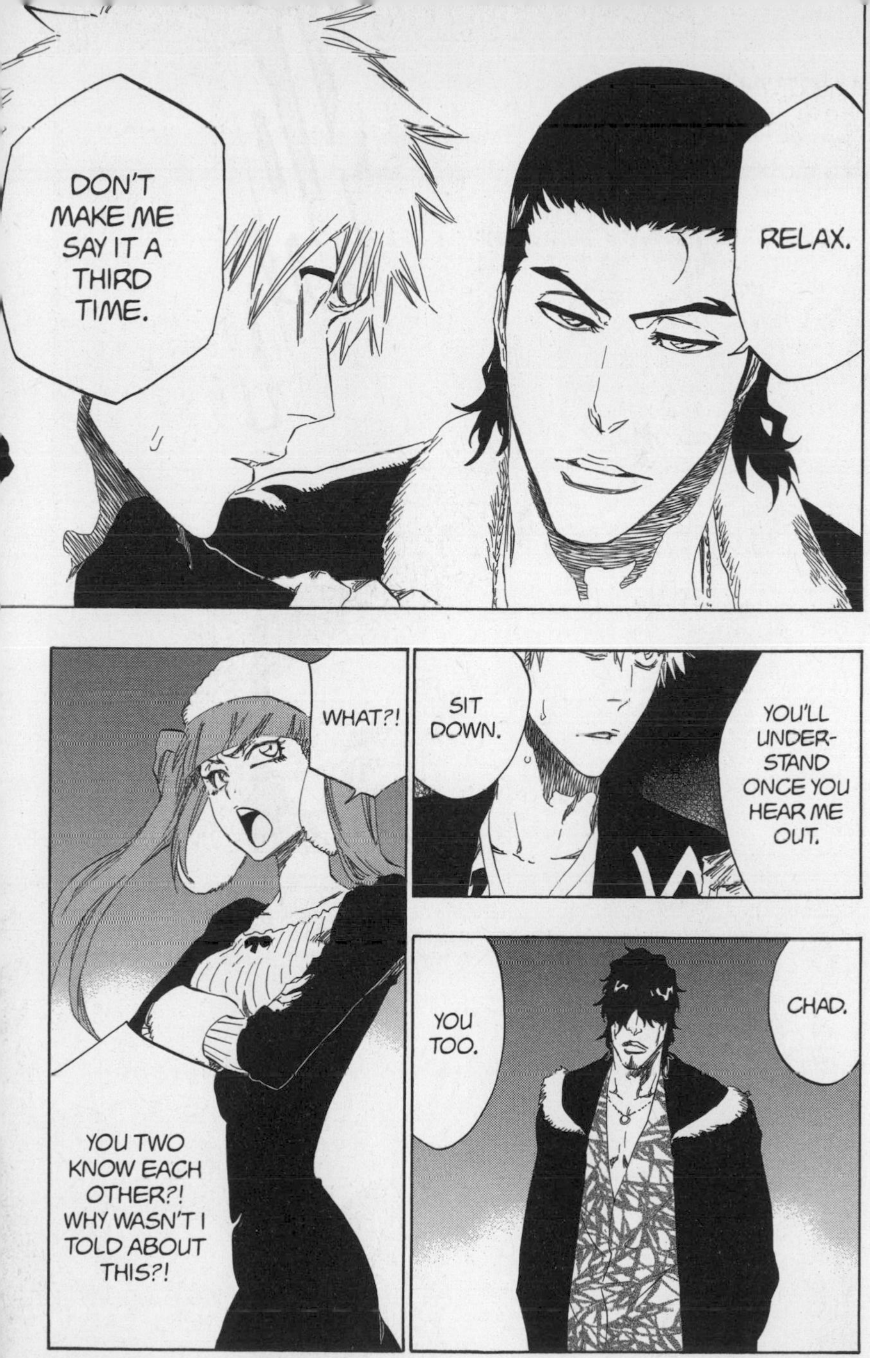
RELAX.
DON'T MAKE ME SAY IT A THIRD TIME.
YOU'LL UNDERSTAND ONCE YOU HEAR ME OUT.
SIT DOWN.
CHAD.
YOU TOO.
WHAT?!
YOU TWO KNOW EACH OTHER?! WHY WASN'T I TOLD ABOUT THIS?!

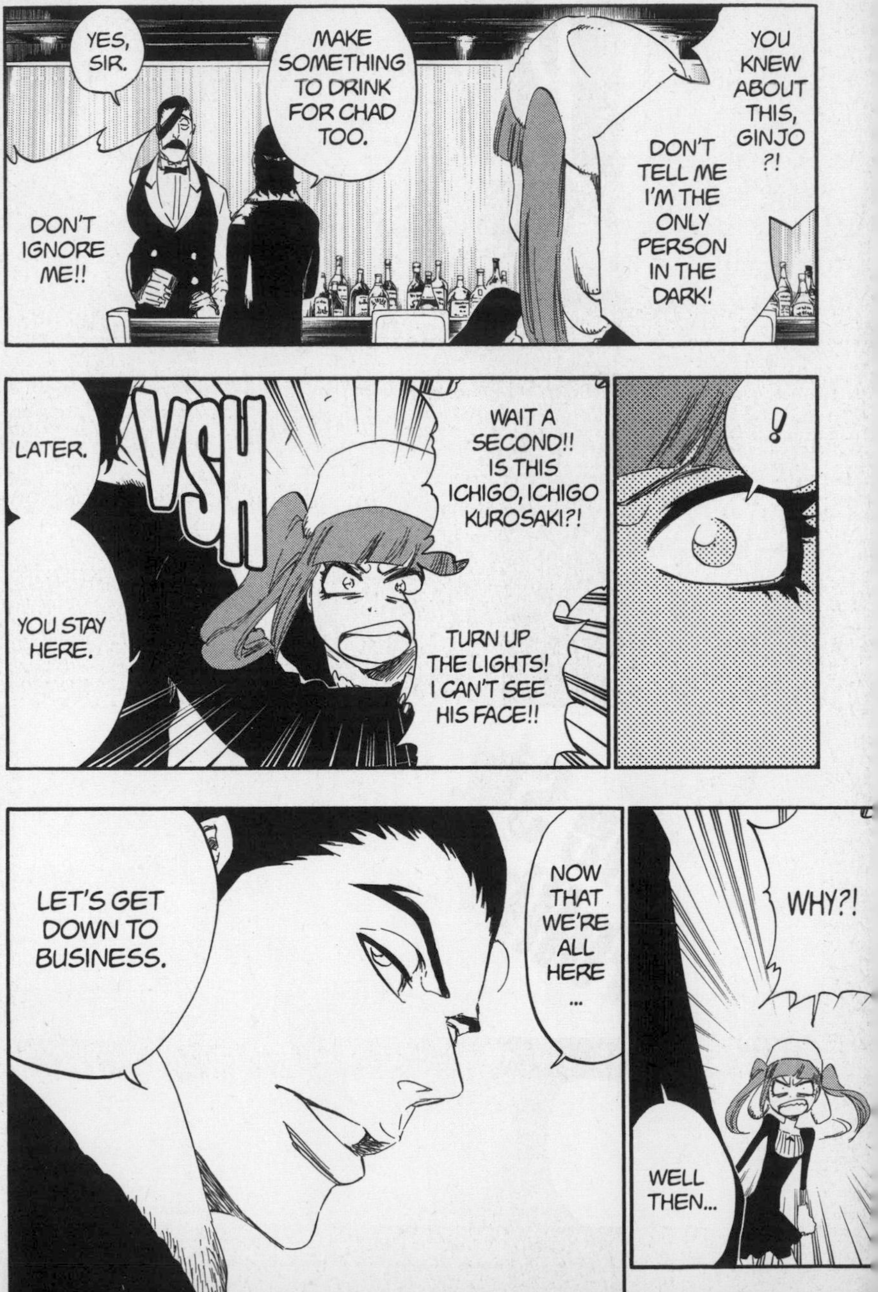
YOU KNEW ABOUT THIS, GINJO?!
DON'T TELL ME I'M THE ONLY PERSON IN THE DARK!
MAKE SOMETHING TO DRINK FOR CHAD TOO.
YES, SIR.
DON'T IGNORE ME!!
!
WAIT A SECOND!! IS THIS ICHIGO, ICHIGO KUROSAKI?!
TURN UP THE LIGHTS! I CAN'T SEE HIS FACE!!
VSH
LATER.
YOU STAY HERE.
WHY?!
WELL THEN...
NOW THAT WE'RE ALL HERE ...
LET'S GET DOWN TO BUSINESS.

BLEACH

433.

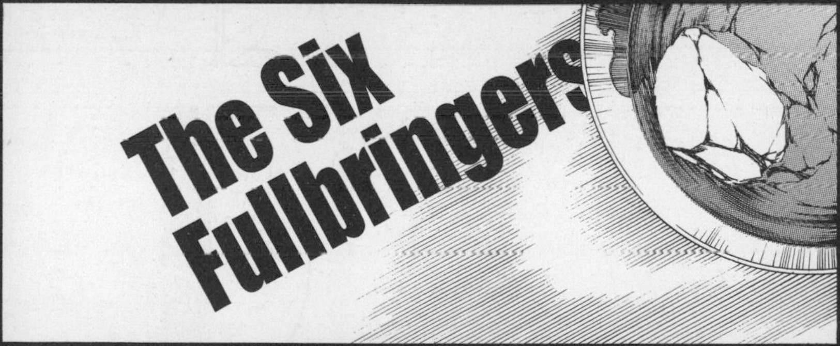
The Six Fullbringers

IF SO...

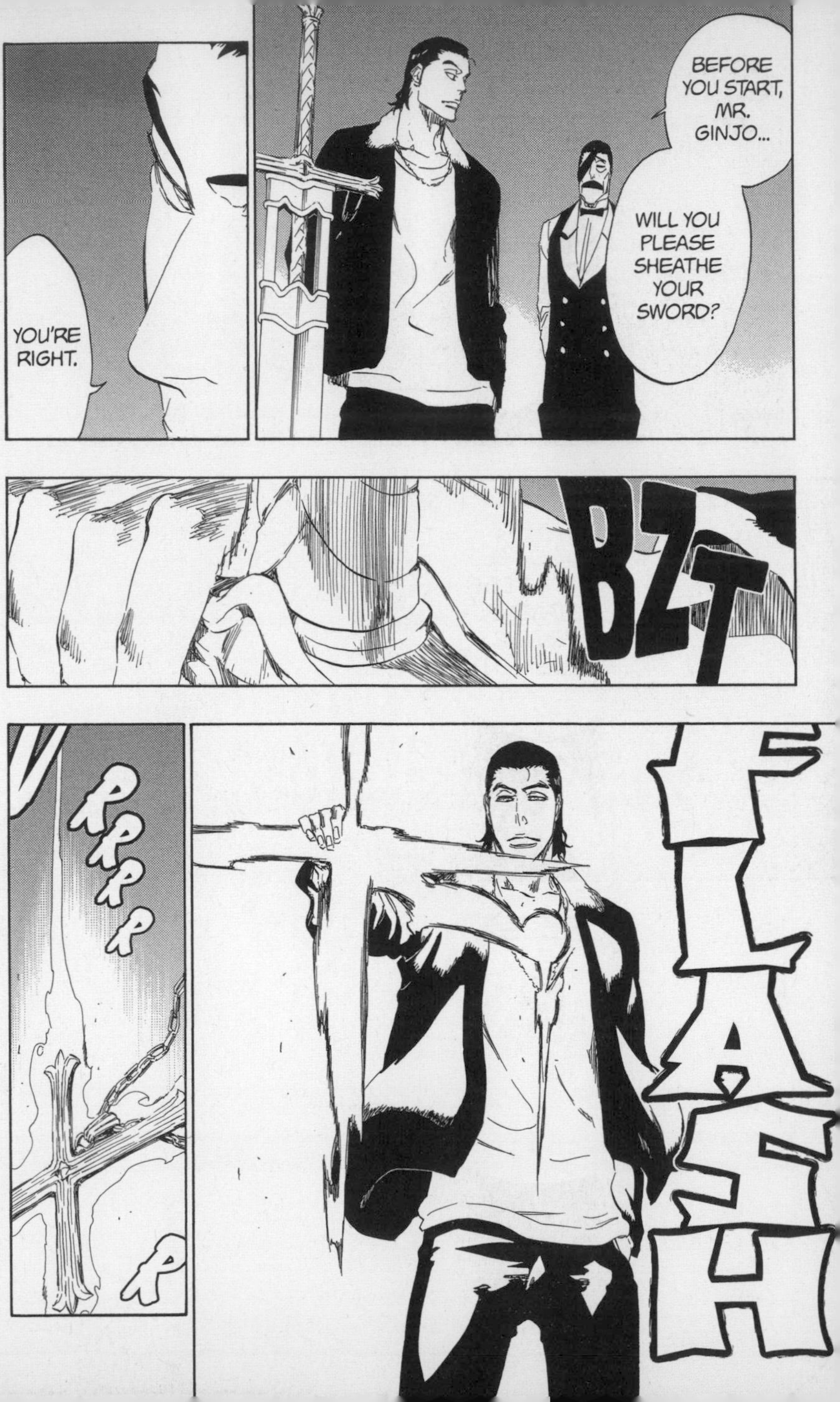
BEFORE YOU START, MR. GINJO...
WILL YOU PLEASE SHEATHE YOUR SWORD?
YOU'RE RIGHT.
BZT
FLASH
RRRR
R

READ THIS WAY

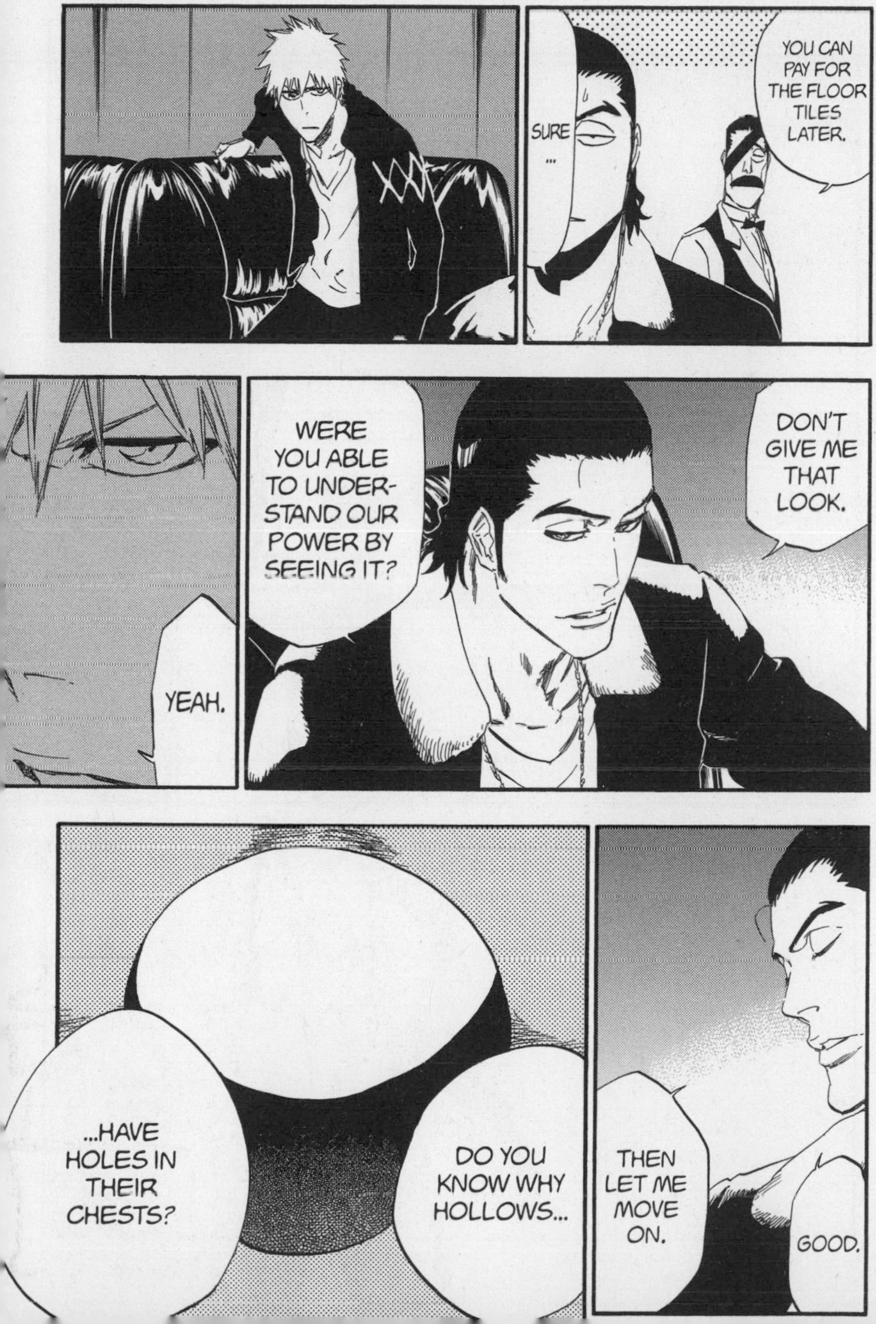
YOU CAN PAY FOR THE FLOOR TILES LATER.
SURE...
DON'T GIVE ME THAT LOOK.
WERE YOU ABLE TO UNDER-STAND OUR POWER BY SEEING IT?
YEAH.
GOOD.
THEN LET ME MOVE ON.
DO YOU KNOW WHY HOLLOWS...
...HAVE HOLES IN THEIR CHESTS?

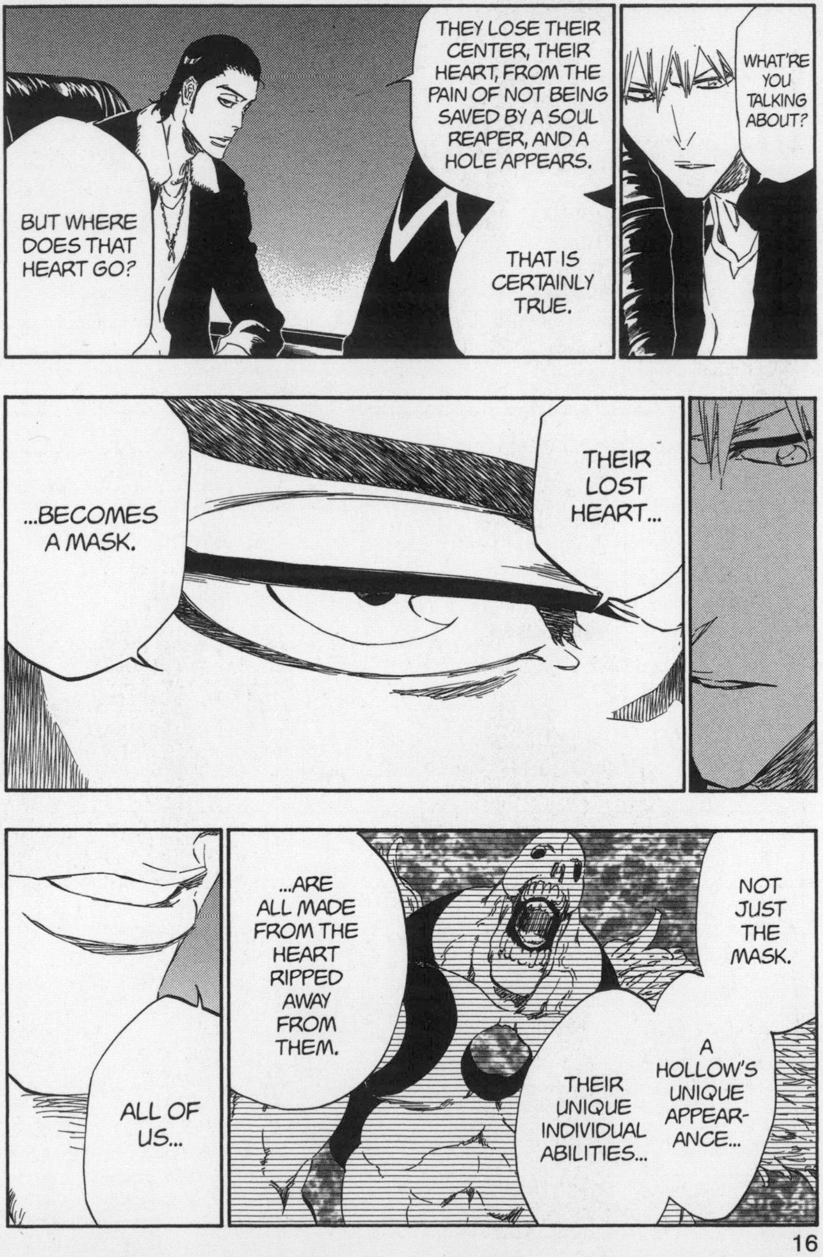
WHAT'RE YOU TALKING ABOUT?
THEY LOSE THEIR CENTER, THEIR HEART, FROM THE PAIN OF NOT BEING SAVED BY A SOUL REAPER, AND A HOLE APPEARS.
THAT IS CERTAINLY TRUE.
BUT WHERE DOES THAT HEART GO?
THEIR LOST HEART...
...BECOMES A MASK.
NOT JUST THE MASK.
A HOLLOW'S UNIQUE APPEAR-ANCE...
THEIR UNIQUE INDIVIDUAL ABILITIES...
...ARE ALL MADE FROM THE HEART RIPPED AWAY FROM THEM.
ALL OF US...

READ THIS WAY

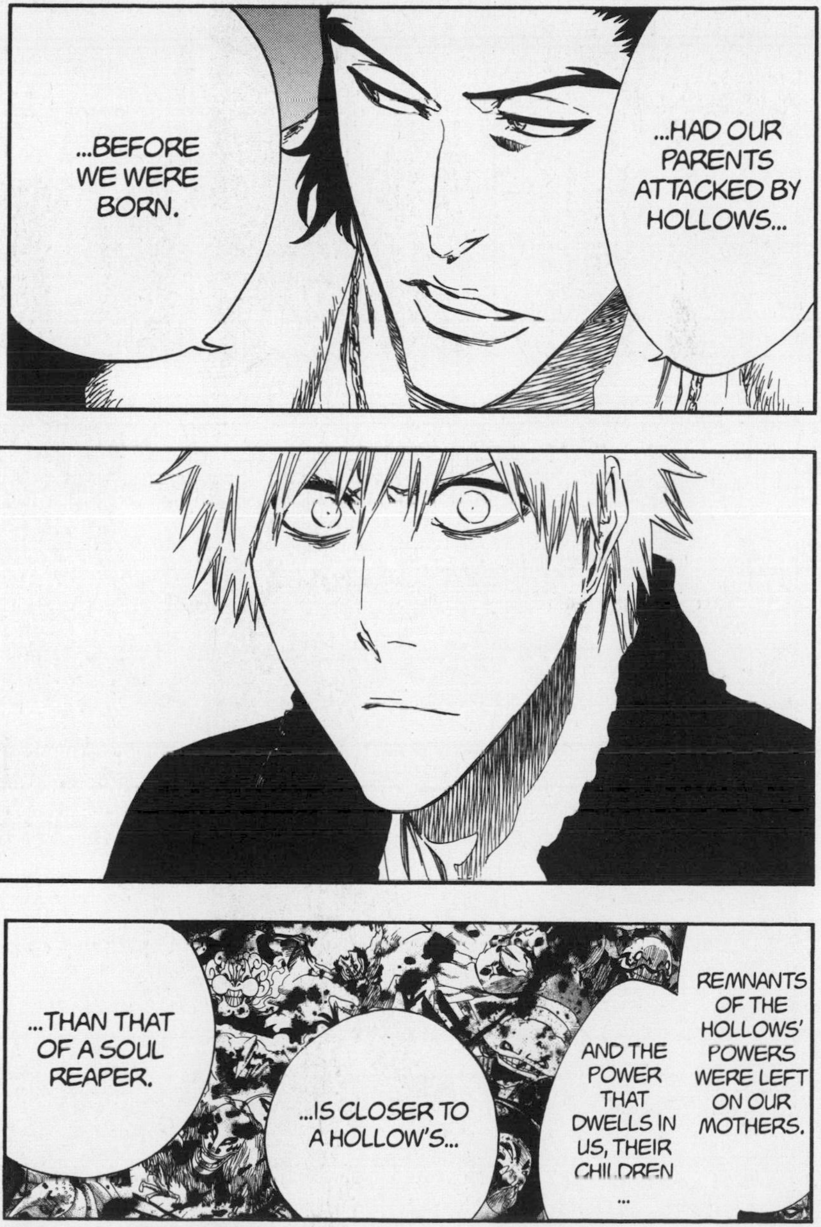
...HAD OUR PARENTS ATTACKED BY HOLLOWS...
...BEFORE WE WERE BORN.
REMNANTS OF THE HOLLOWS' POWERS WERE LEFT ON OUR MOTHERS.
AND THE POWER THAT DWELLS IN US, THEIR CHILDREN ...
...IS CLOSER TO A HOLLOW'S...
...THAN THAT OF A SOUL REAPER.

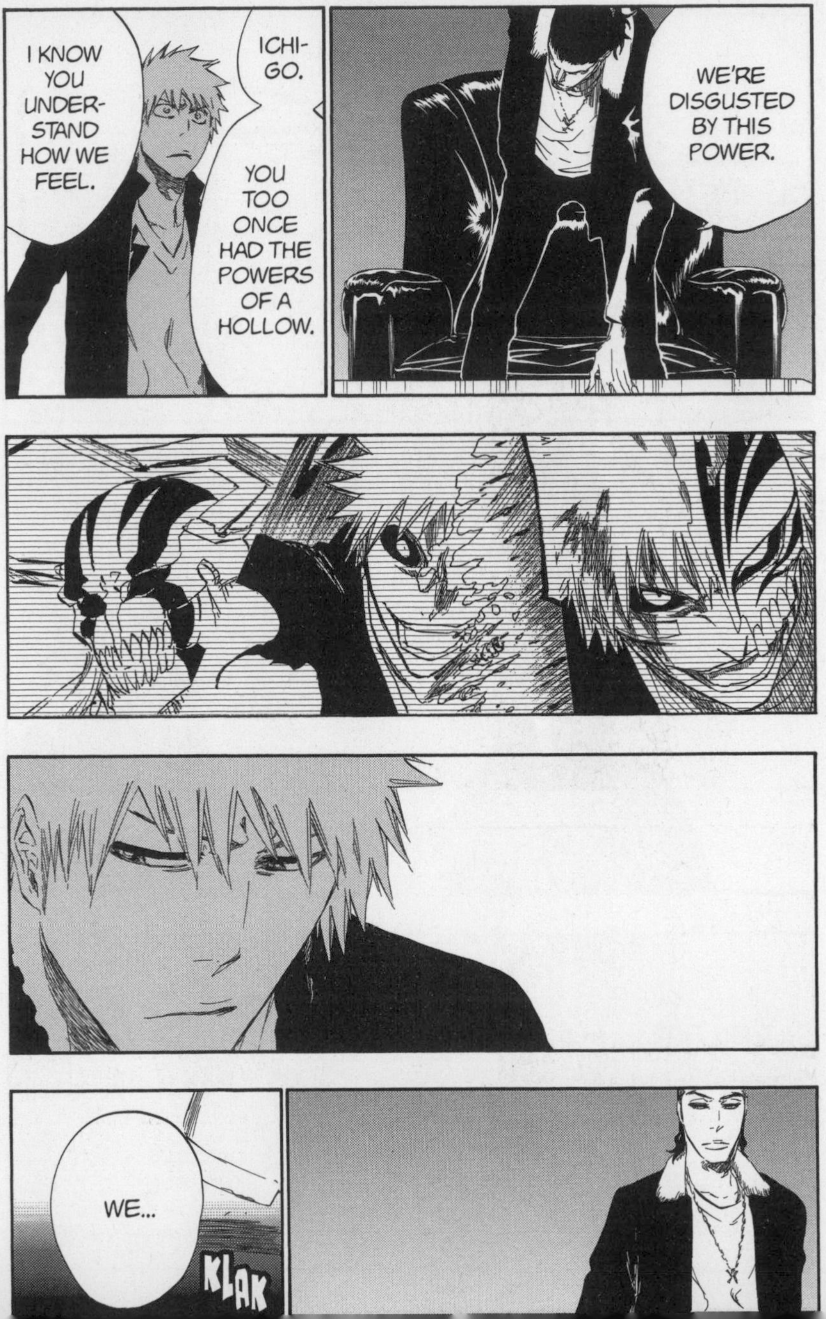
WE'RE DISGUSTED BY THIS POWER.
ICHI-GO.
YOU TOO ONCE HAD THE POWERS OF A HOLLOW.
I KNOW YOU UNDERSTAND HOW WE FEEL.
WE...
KLAK

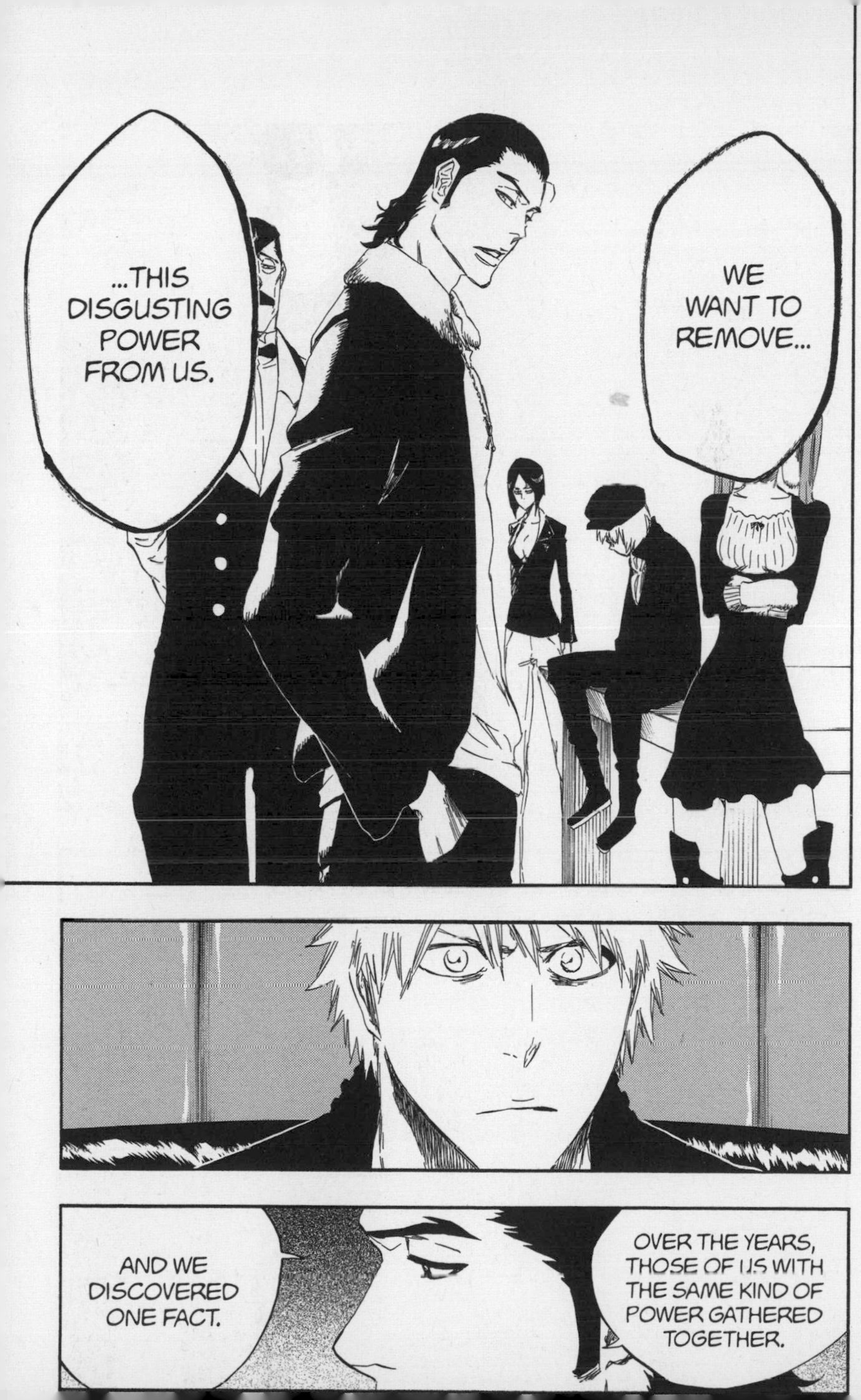
WE WANT TO REMOVE...
...THIS DISGUSTING POWER FROM US.
OVER THE YEARS, THOSE OF US WITH THE SAME KIND OF POWER GATHERED TOGETHER.
AND WE DISCOVERED ONE FACT.

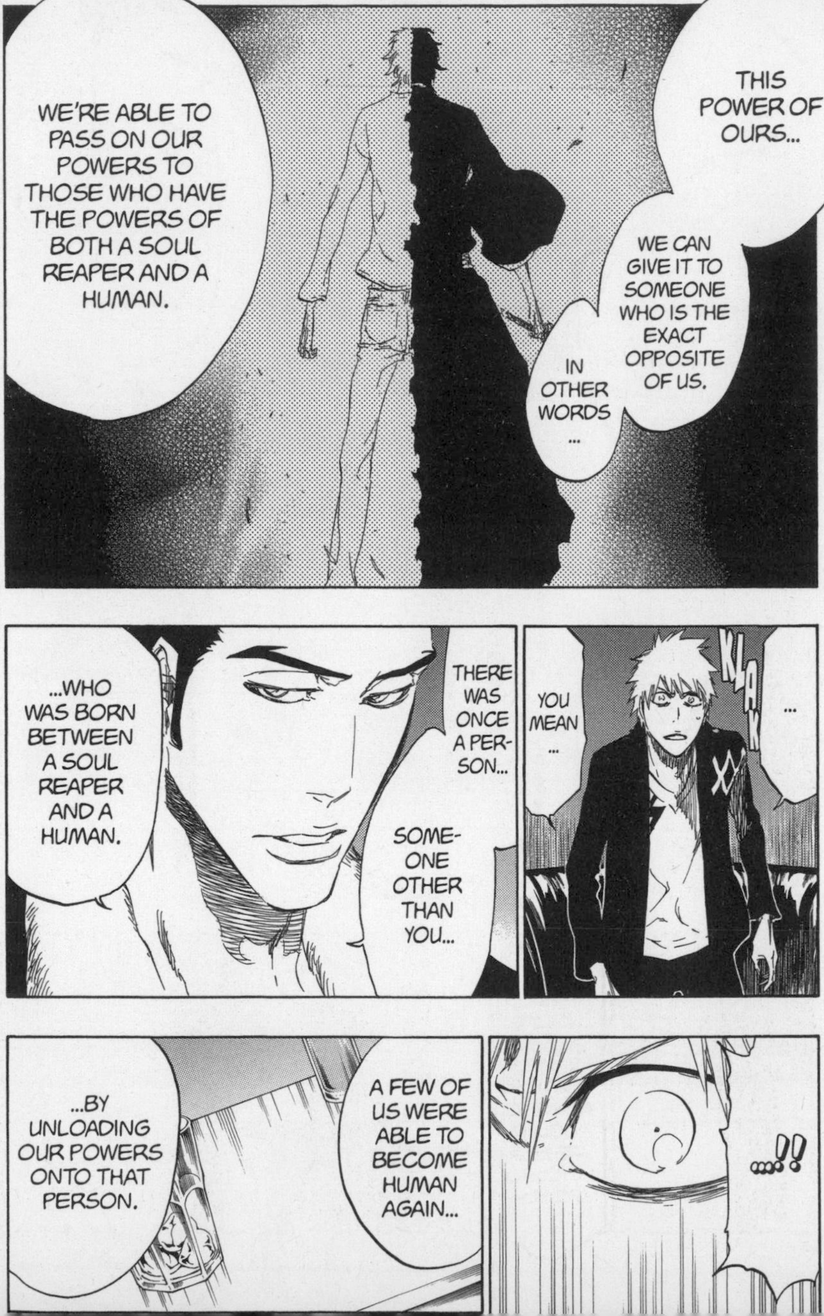
THIS POWER OF OURS...
WE CAN GIVE IT TO SOMEONE WHO IS THE EXACT OPPOSITE OF US.
IN OTHER WORDS...
WE'RE ABLE TO PASS ON OUR POWERS TO THOSE WHO HAVE THE POWERS OF BOTH A SOUL REAPER AND A HUMAN.
...
KLAK
YOU MEAN...
THERE WAS ONCE A PERSON...
SOMEONE OTHER THAN YOU...
...WHO WAS BORN BETWEEN A SOUL REAPER AND A HUMAN.
...!!
A FEW OF US WERE ABLE TO BECOME HUMAN AGAIN...
...BY UNLOADING OUR POWERS ONTO THAT PERSON.

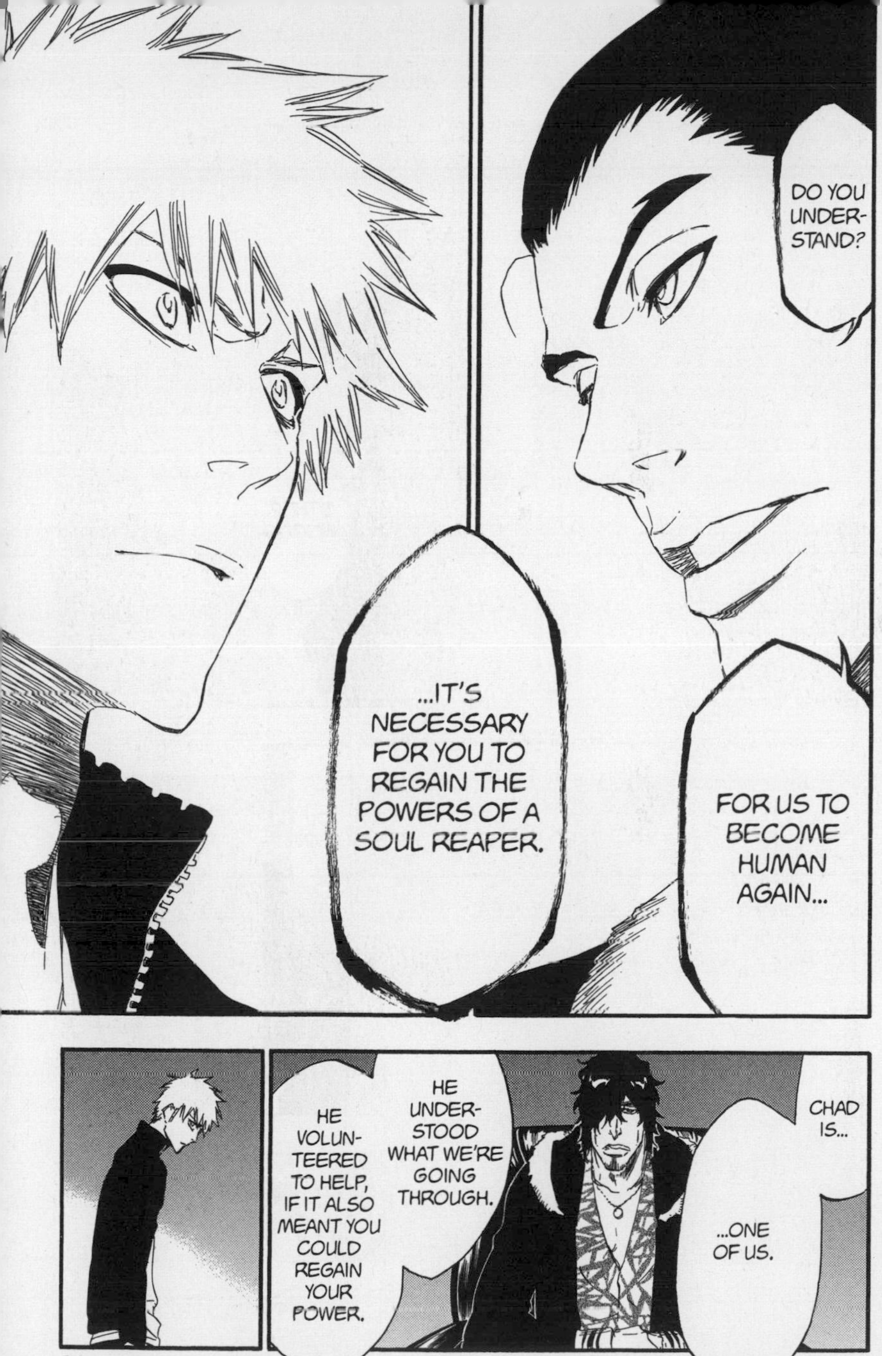
DO YOU UNDER-STAND?
FOR US TO BECOME HUMAN AGAIN...
...IT'S NECESSARY FOR YOU TO REGAIN THE POWERS OF A SOUL REAPER.
CHAD IS...
...ONE OF US.
HE UNDER-STOOD WHAT WE'RE GOING THROUGH.
HE VOLUN-TEERED TO HELP, IF IT ALSO MEANT YOU COULD REGAIN YOUR POWER.

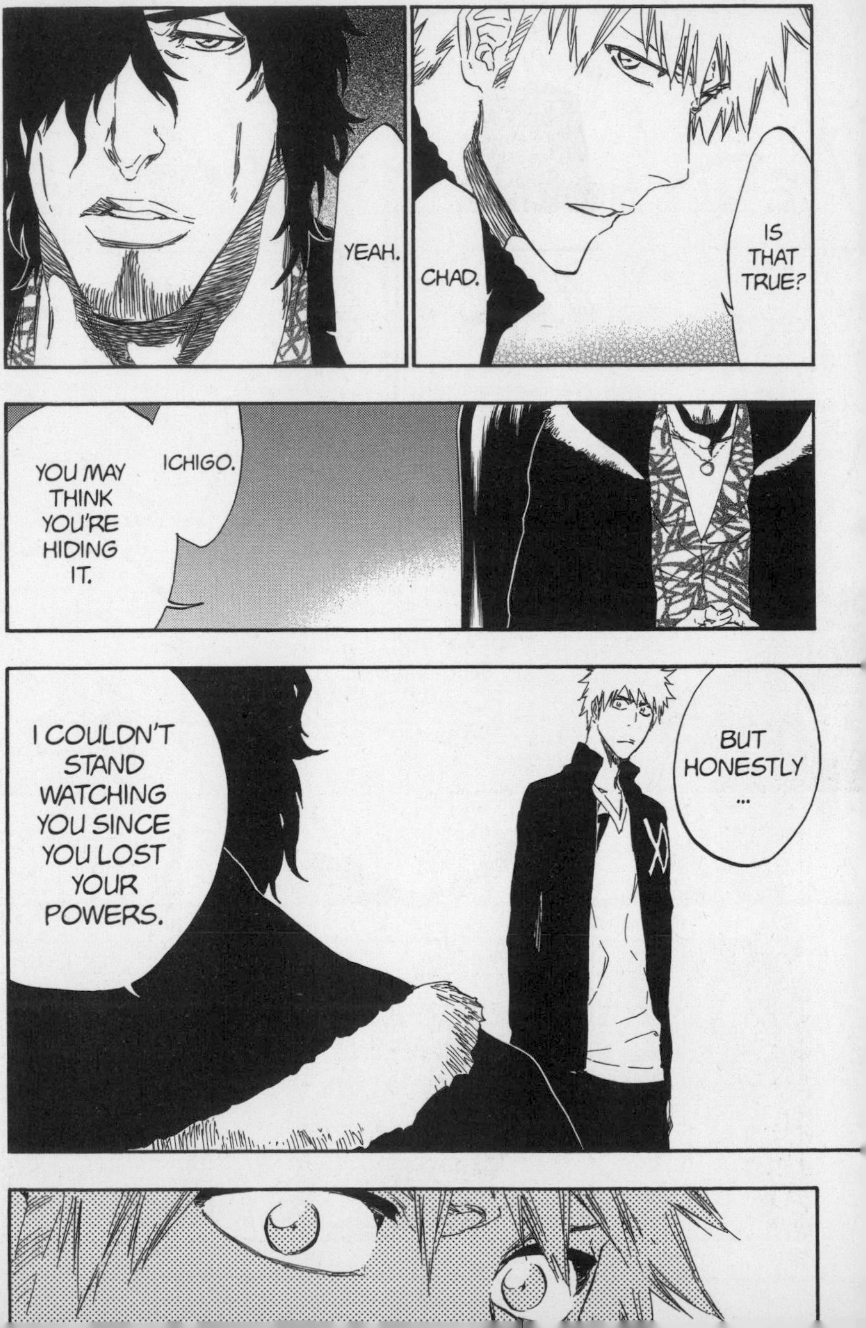
IS THAT TRUE?
CHAD.
YEAH.
ICHIGO.
YOU MAY THINK YOU'RE HIDING IT.
BUT HONESTLY ...
I COULDN'T STAND WATCHING YOU SINCE YOU LOST YOUR POWERS.

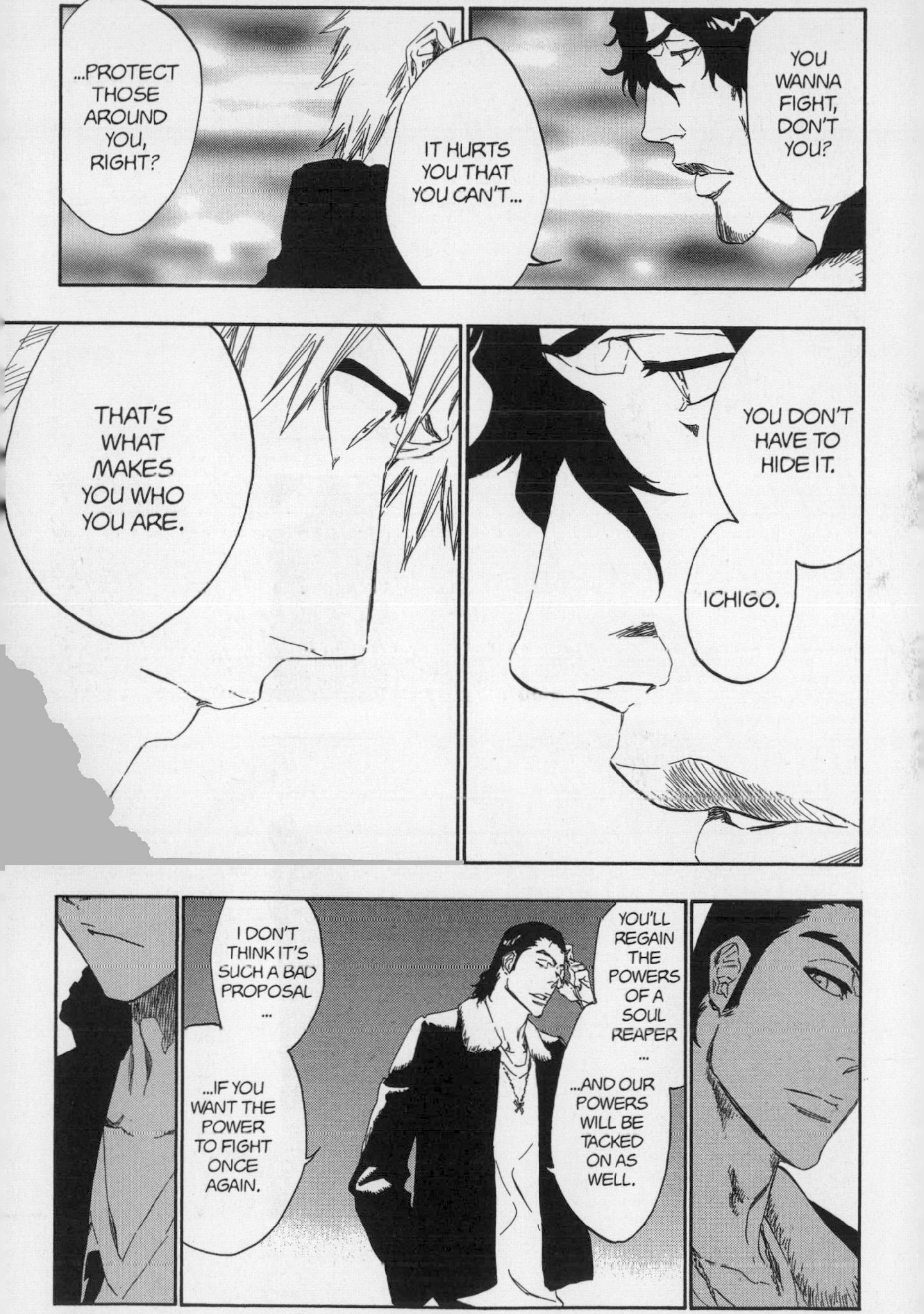
YOU WANNA FIGHT, DON'T YOU?
IT HURTS YOU THAT YOU CAN'T...
...PROTECT THOSE AROUND YOU, RIGHT?
YOU DON'T HAVE TO HIDE IT.
ICHIGO.
THAT'S WHAT MAKES YOU WHO YOU ARE.
YOU'LL REGAIN THE POWERS OF A SOUL REAPER ...
...AND OUR POWERS WILL BE TACKED ON AS WELL.
I DON'T THINK IT'S SUCH A BAD PROPOSAL ...
...IF YOU WANT THE POWER TO FIGHT ONCE AGAIN.

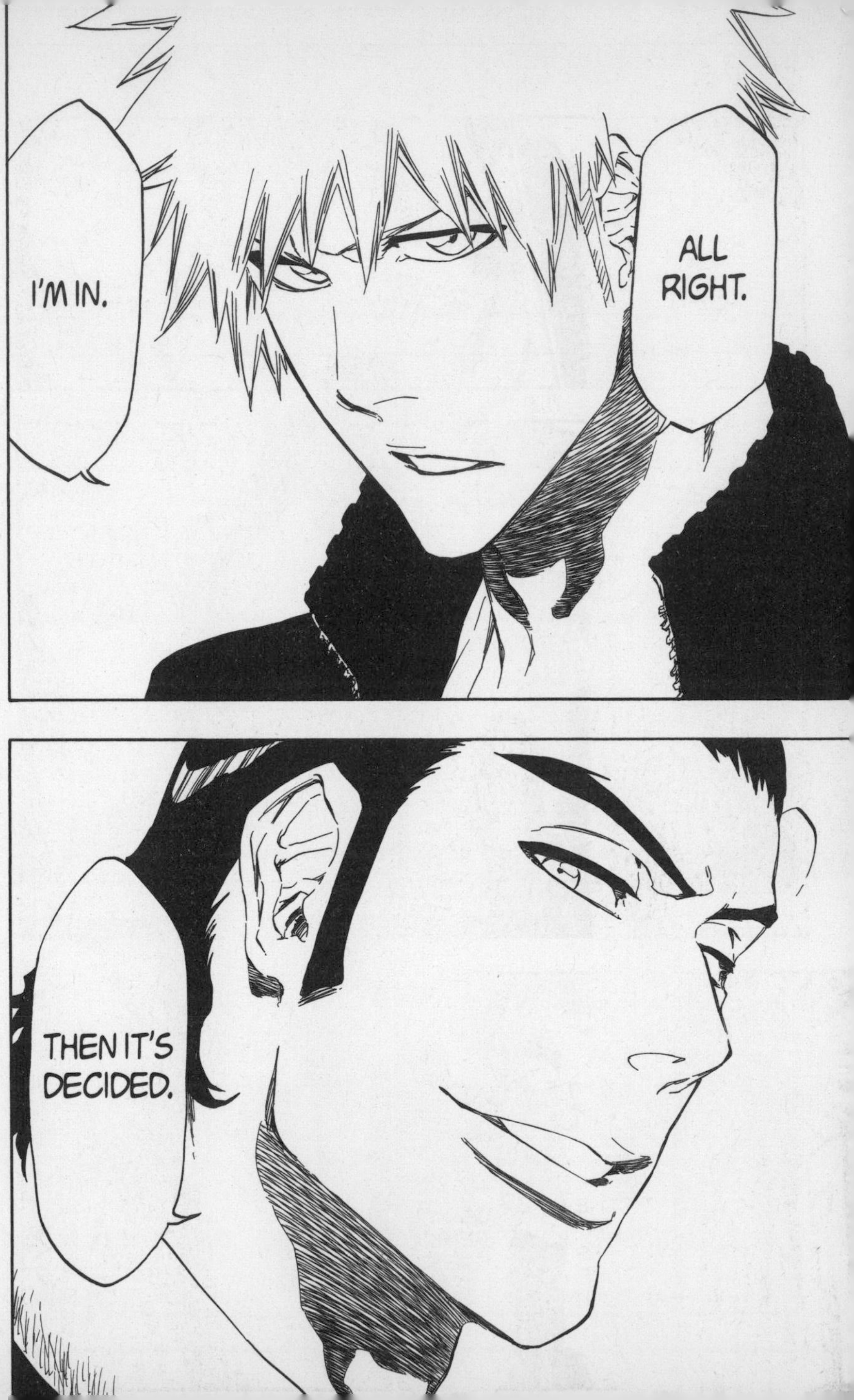
ALL RIGHT.
I'M IN.
THEN IT'S DECIDED.

READ THIS WAY

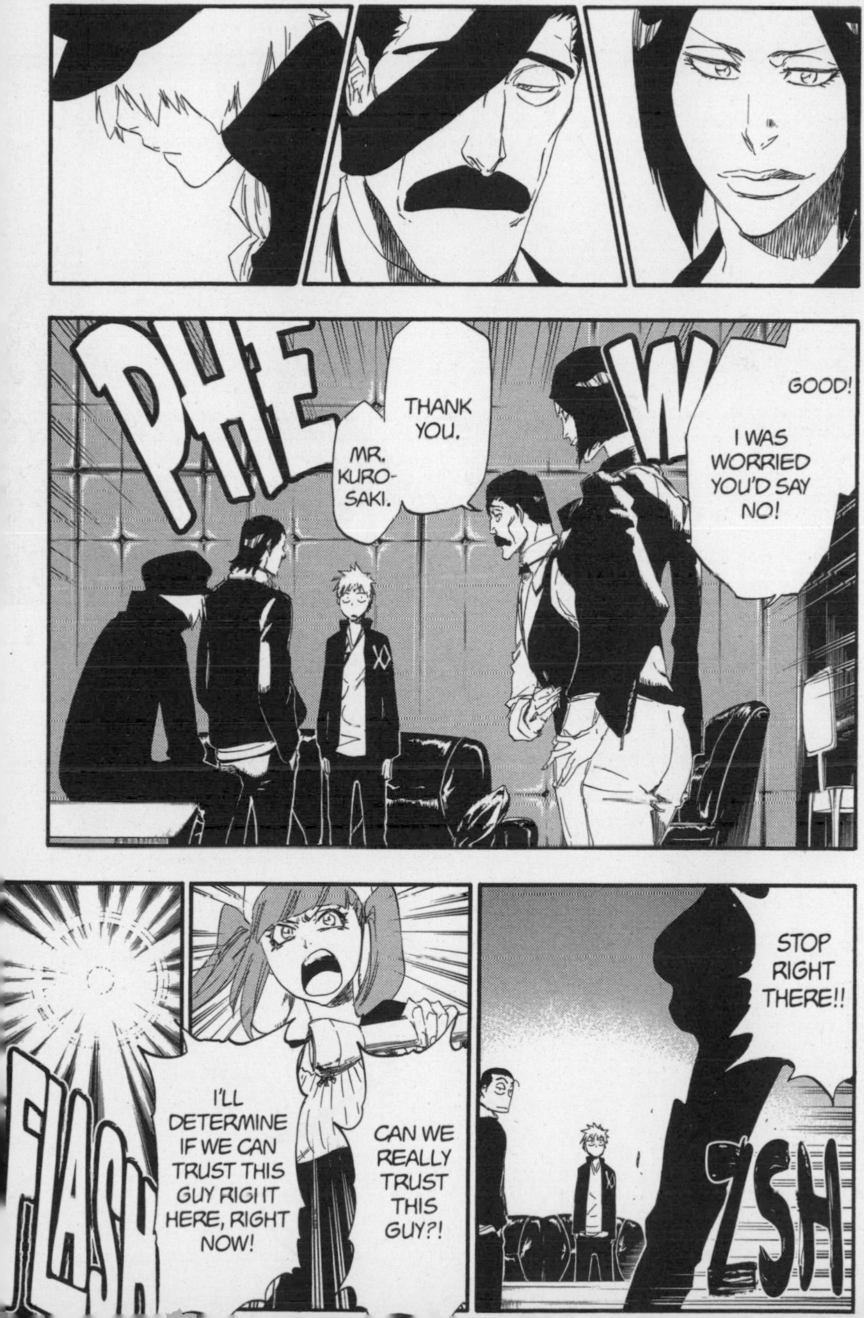
GOOD!
I WAS WORRIED YOU'D SAY NO!
THANK YOU.
MR. KURO-SAKI.
PHEW
STOP RIGHT THERE!!
ZSH
CAN WE REALLY TRUST THIS GUY?!
I'LL DETERMINE IF WE CAN TRUST THIS GUY RIGHT HERE, RIGHT NOW!
FLASH

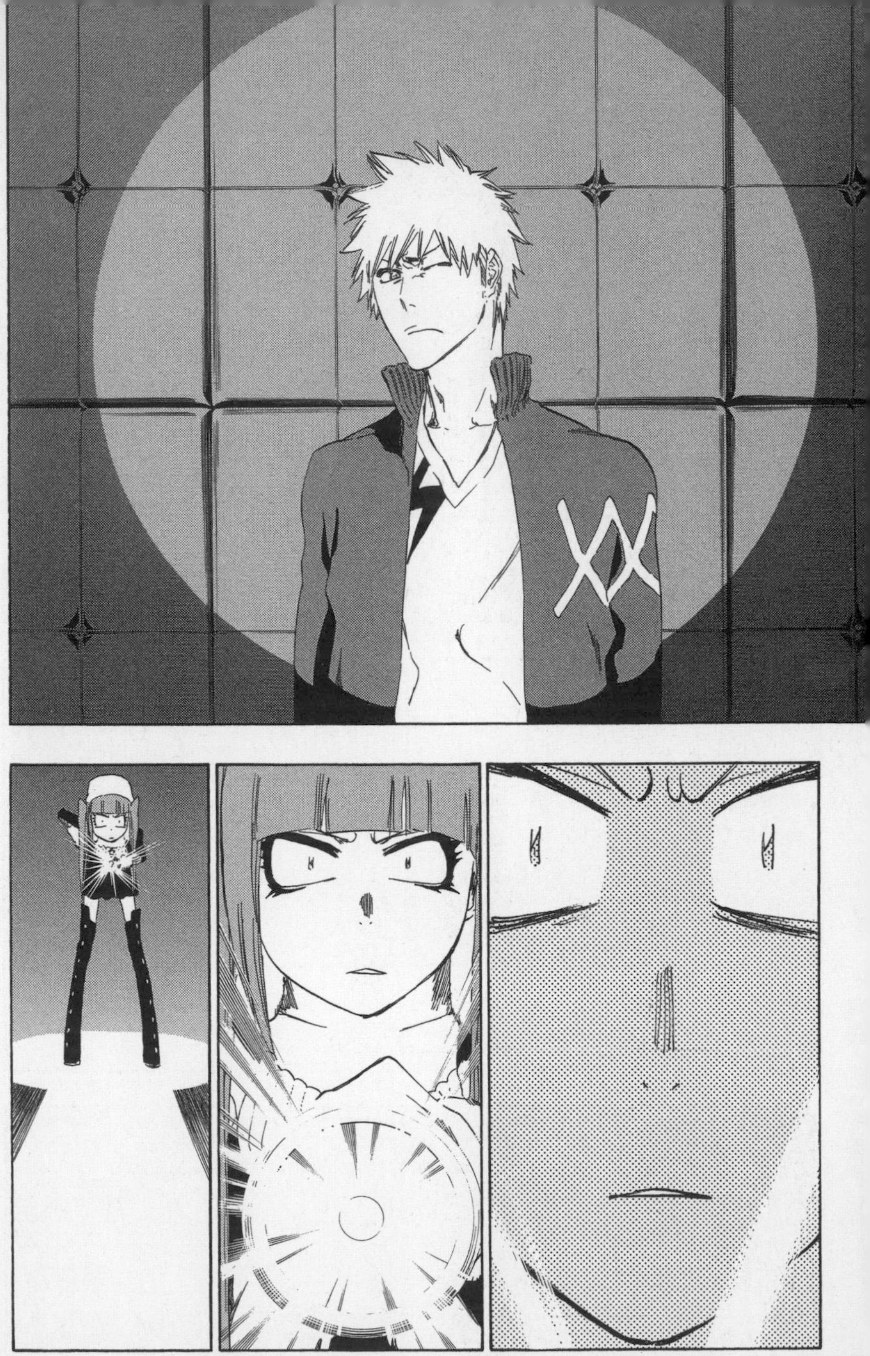

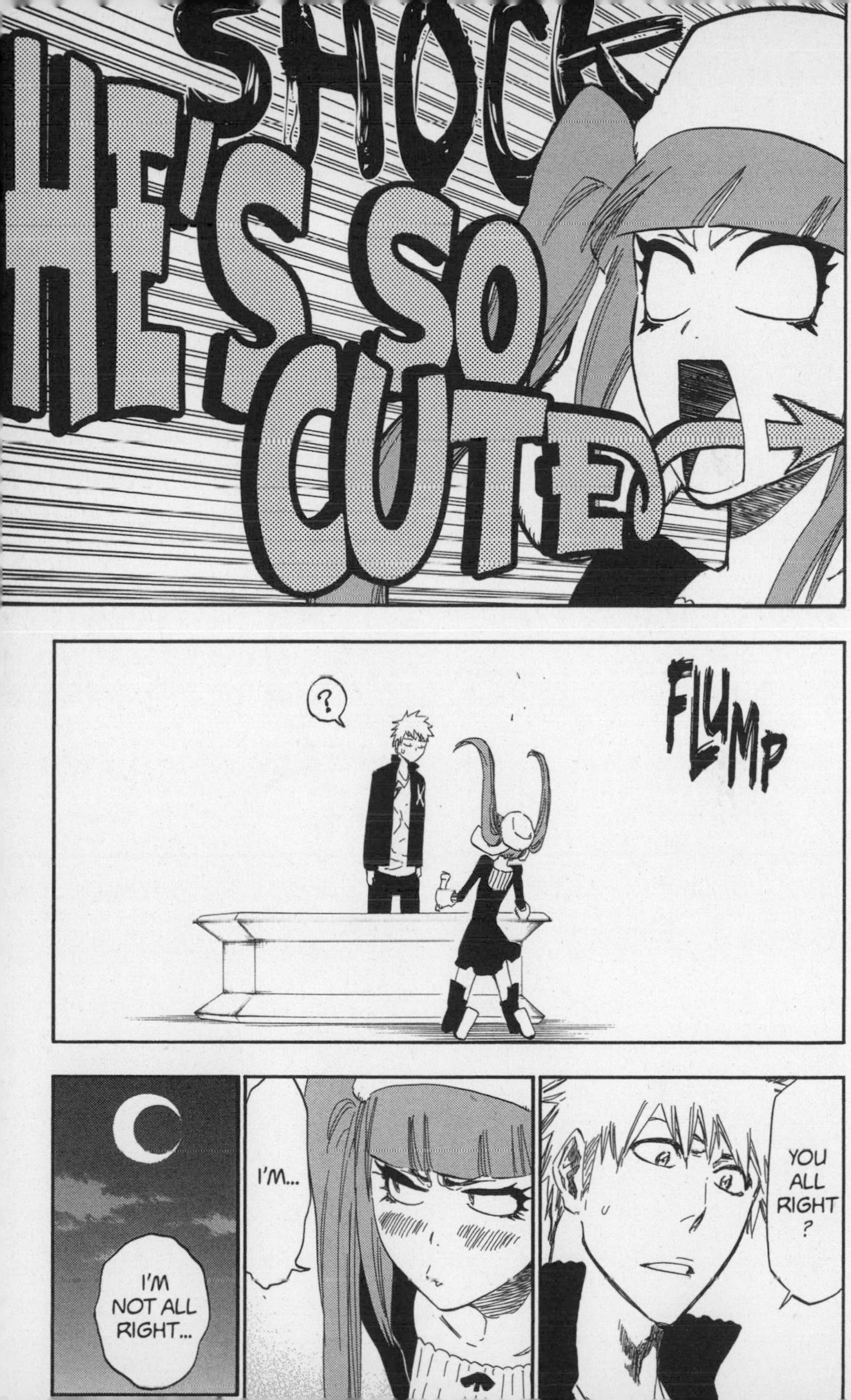
SHOCK
HE'S SO CUTE
?
FLUMP
YOU ALL RIGHT?
I'M...
I'M NOT ALL RIGHT...

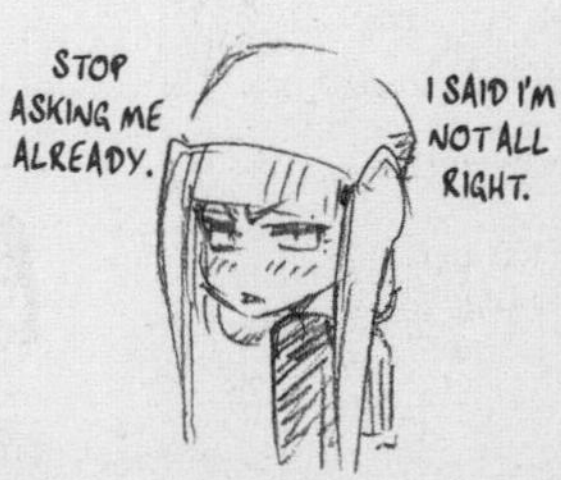
I SAID I'M NOT ALL RIGHT.
STOP ASKING ME ALREADY.

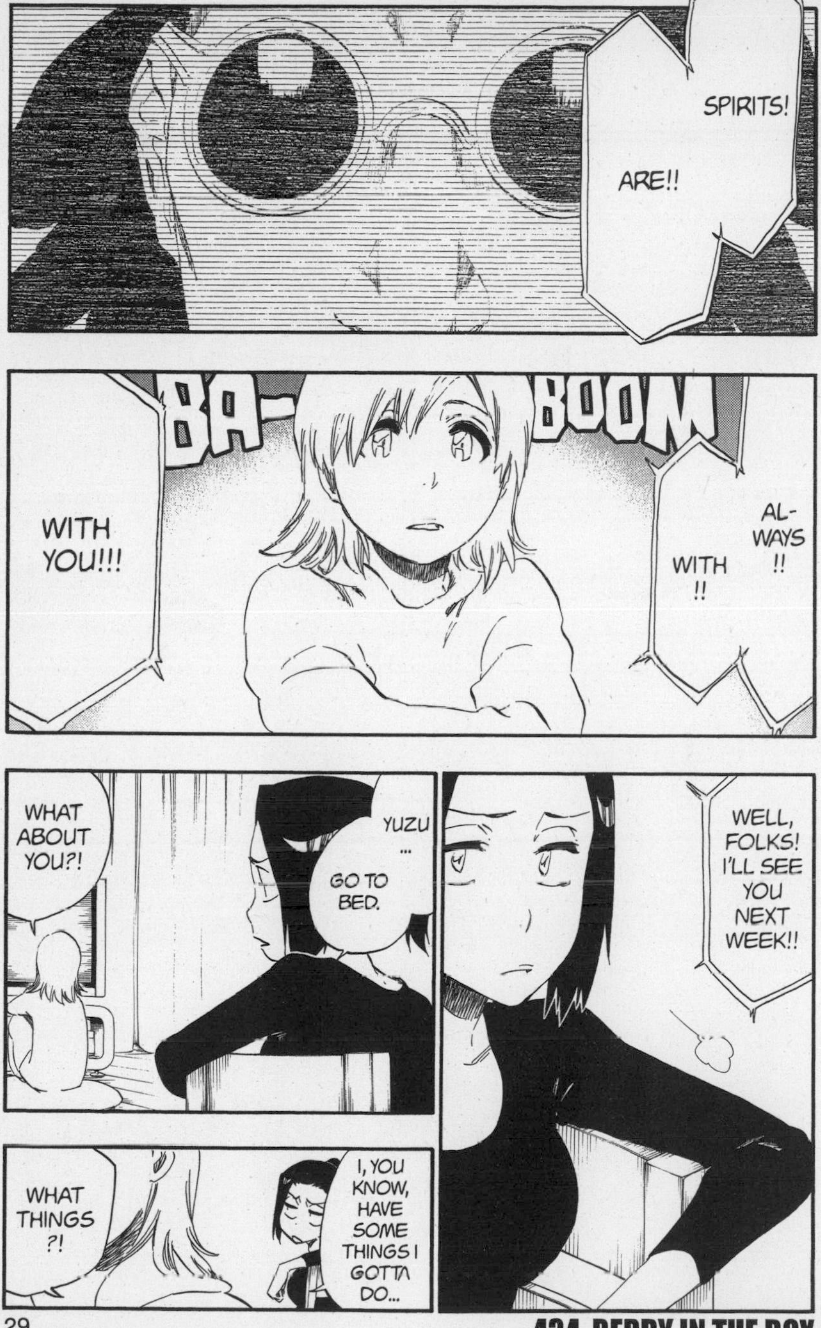
SPIRITS!
ARE!!
BA-BOOM
AL-WAYS !!
WITH !!
WITH YOU!!!
WELL, FOLKS! I'LL SEE YOU NEXT WEEK!!
YUZU ...
GO TO BED.
WHAT ABOUT YOU?!
I, YOU KNOW, HAVE SOME THINGS I GOTTA DO...
WHAT THINGS ?!

434. BERRY IN THE BOX

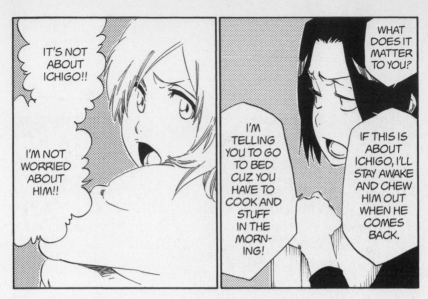

WHAT DOES IT MATTER TO YOU?
IF THIS IS ABOUT ICHIGO, I'LL STAY AWAKE AND CHEW HIM OUT WHEN HE COMES BACK.
I'M TELLING YOU TO GO TO BED CUZ YOU HAVE TO COOK AND STUFF IN THE MORN- ING!
IT'S NOT ABOUT ICHIGO!!
I'M NOT WORRIED ABOUT HIM!!
IT'S OKAY TO BE WORRIED ABOUT HIM!
HE HAS BEEN ACTING STRANGE LATELY.
HE'S BEEN COMING HOME LATE AT NIGHT THE PAST TWO DAYS, SO I UNDERSTAND IF YOU'RE WORRIED!
I'M NOT WORRIED!!
YOU ARE!
I'M NOT! LEAVE ME ALONE!!
WHAT ?!
KLATCH

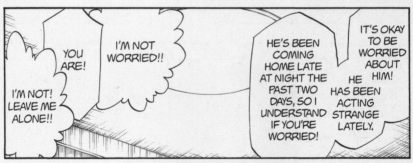

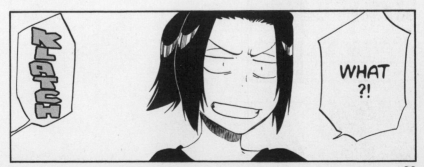

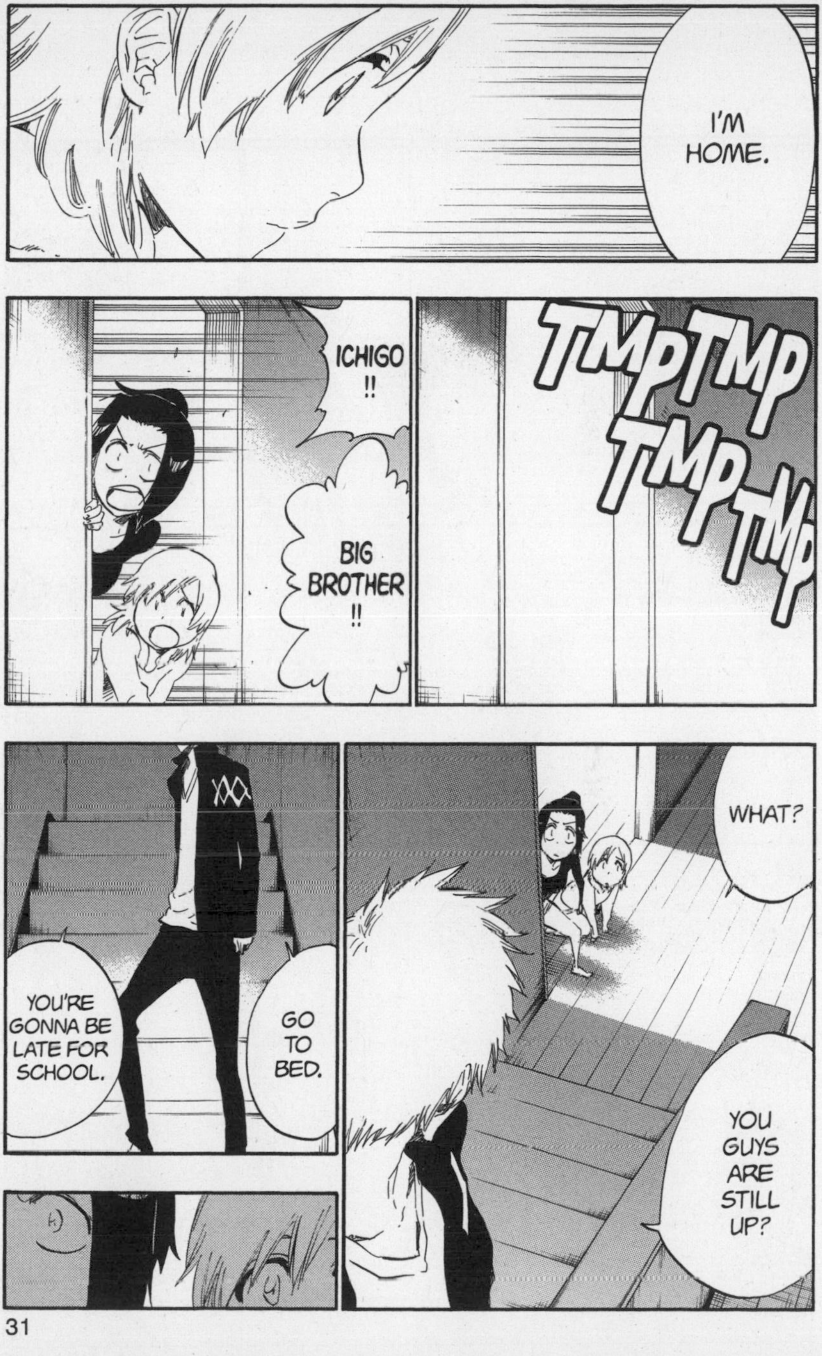
I'M HOME.
TMPTMP TMPTMP
ICHIGO!!
BIG BROTHER!!
WHAT?
YOU GUYS ARE STILL UP?
GO TO BED.
YOU'RE GONNA BE LATE FOR SCHOOL.

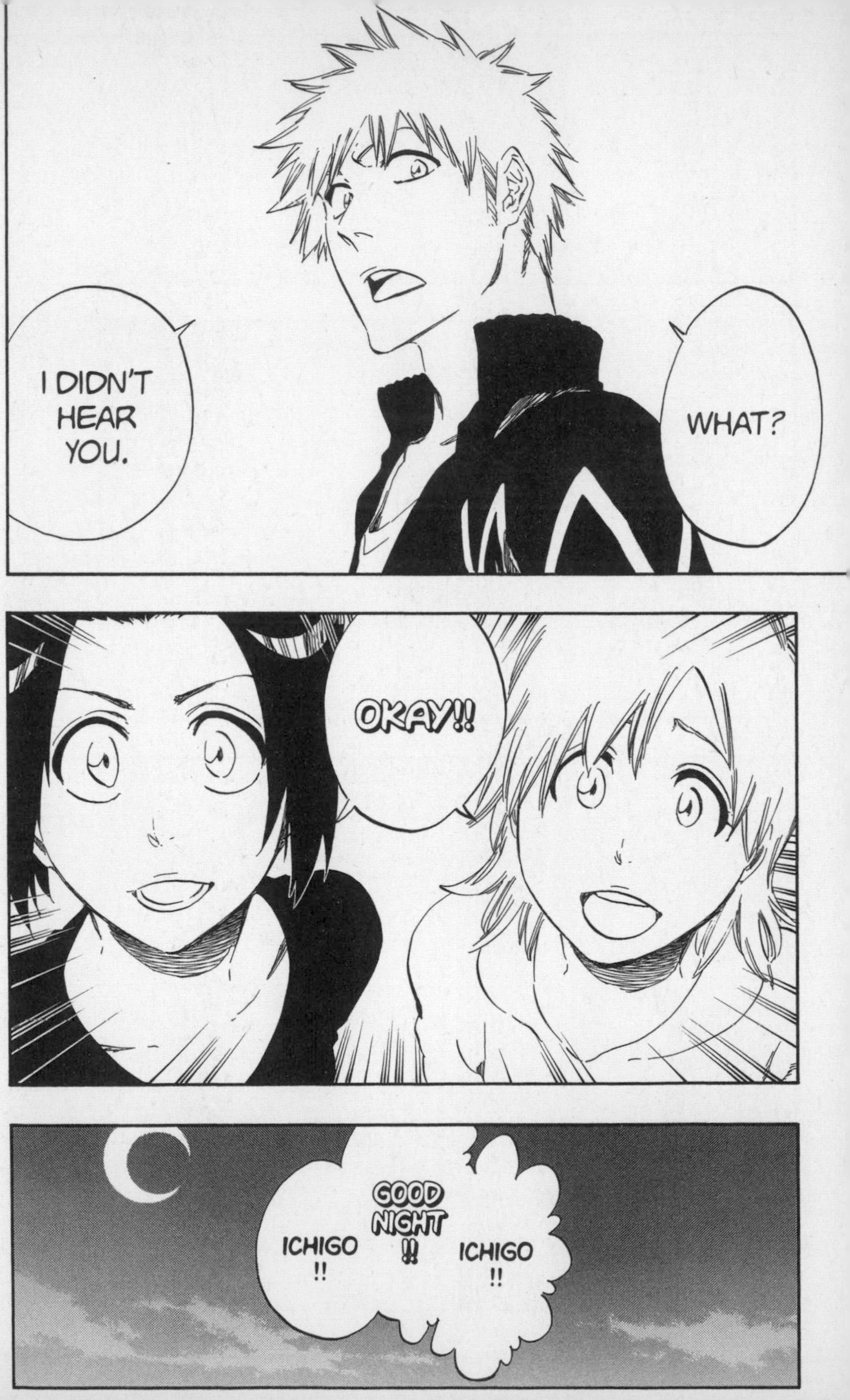
WHAT?
I DIDN'T HEAR YOU.
OKAY!!
ICHIGO !!
GOOD NIGHT !!
ICHIGO !!

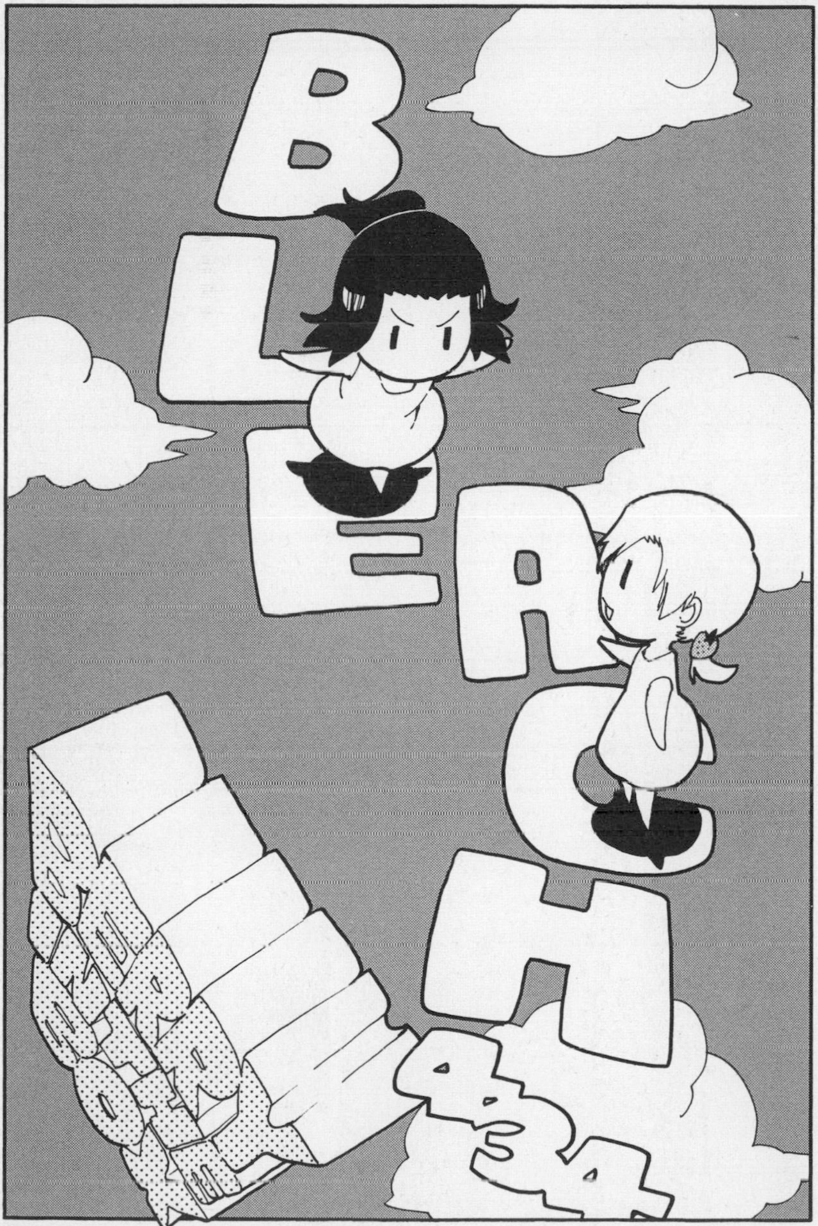
BLEACH
434

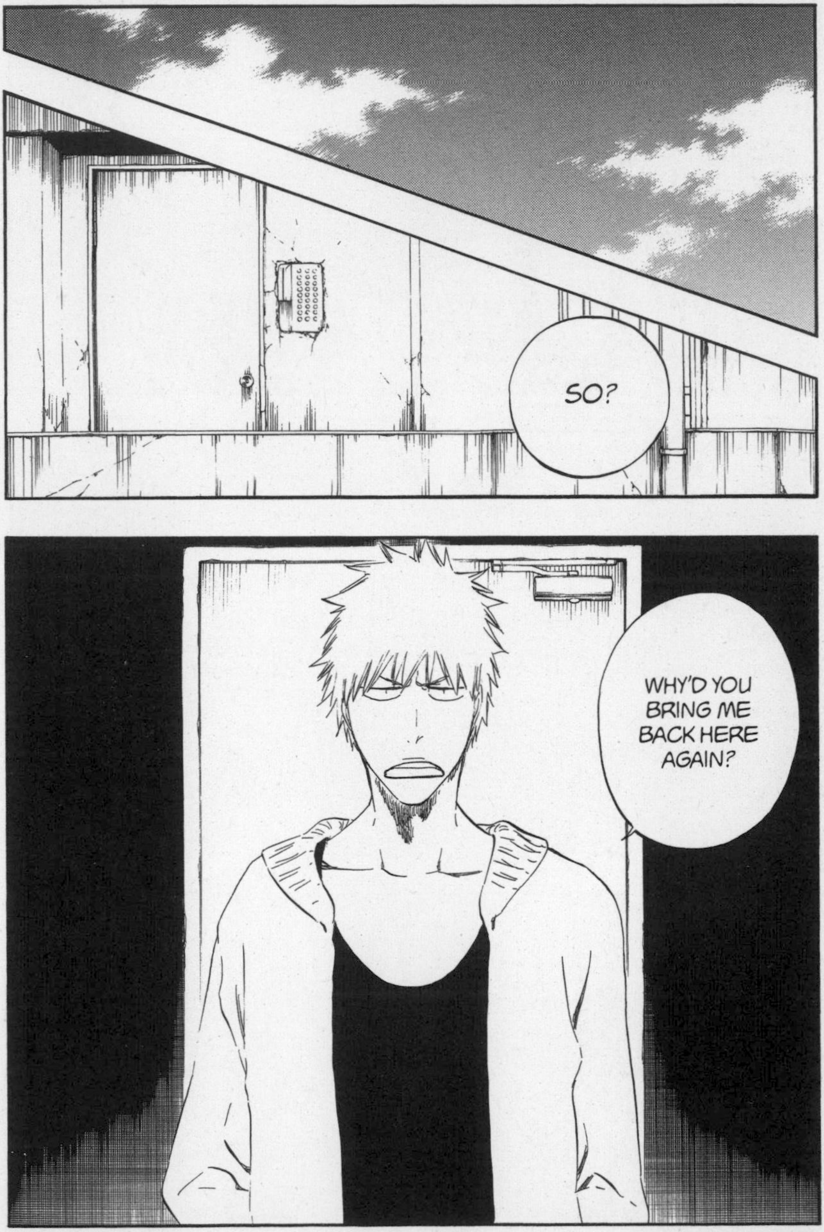
SO?
WHY'D YOU BRING ME BACK HERE AGAIN?

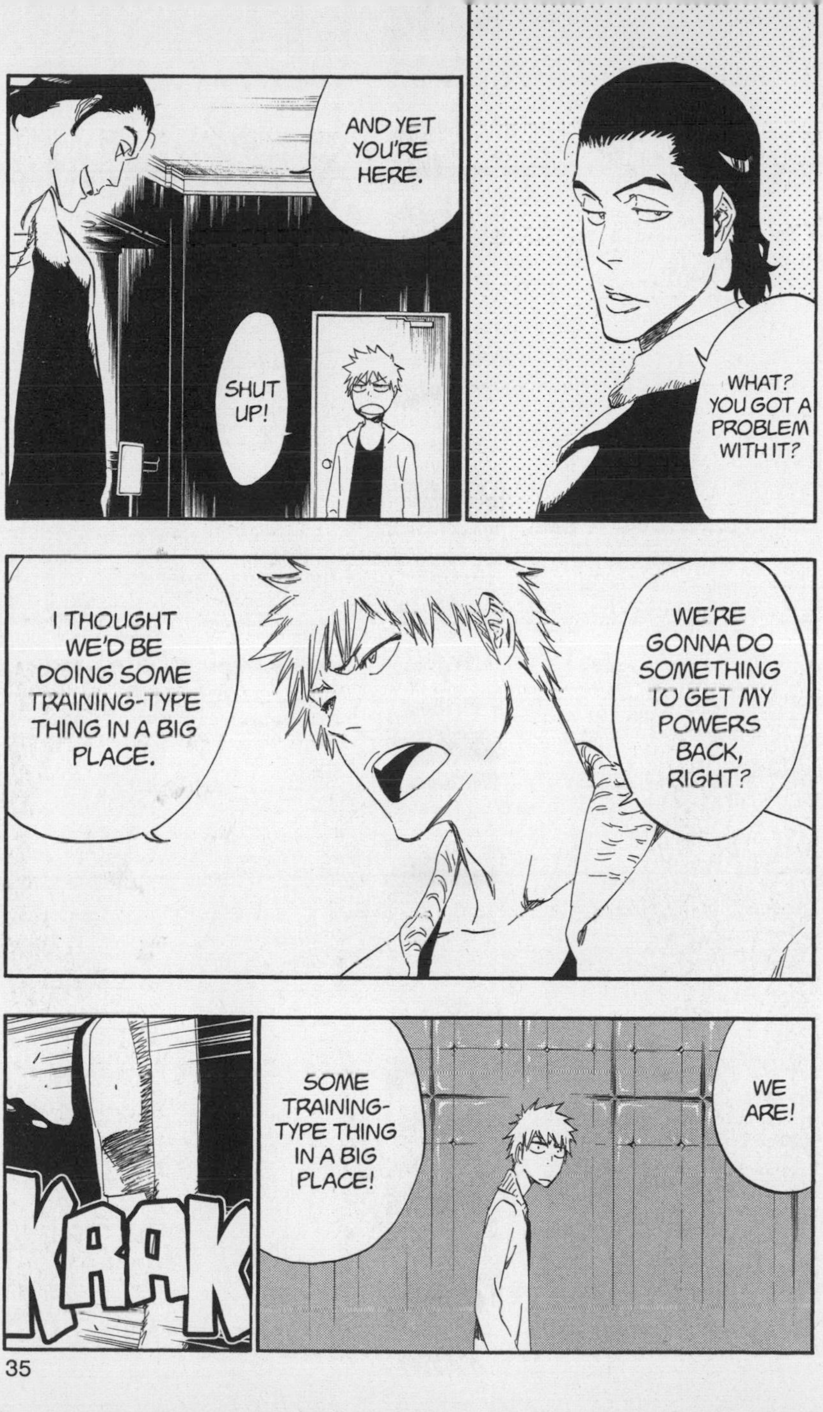
WHAT? YOU GOT A PROBLEM WITH IT?
AND YET YOU'RE HERE.
SHUT UP!
WE'RE GONNA DO SOMETHING TO GET MY POWERS BACK, RIGHT?
I THOUGHT WE'D BE DOING SOME TRAINING-TYPE THING IN A BIG PLACE.
WE ARE!
SOME TRAINING-TYPE THING IN A BIG PLACE!
KRAAK

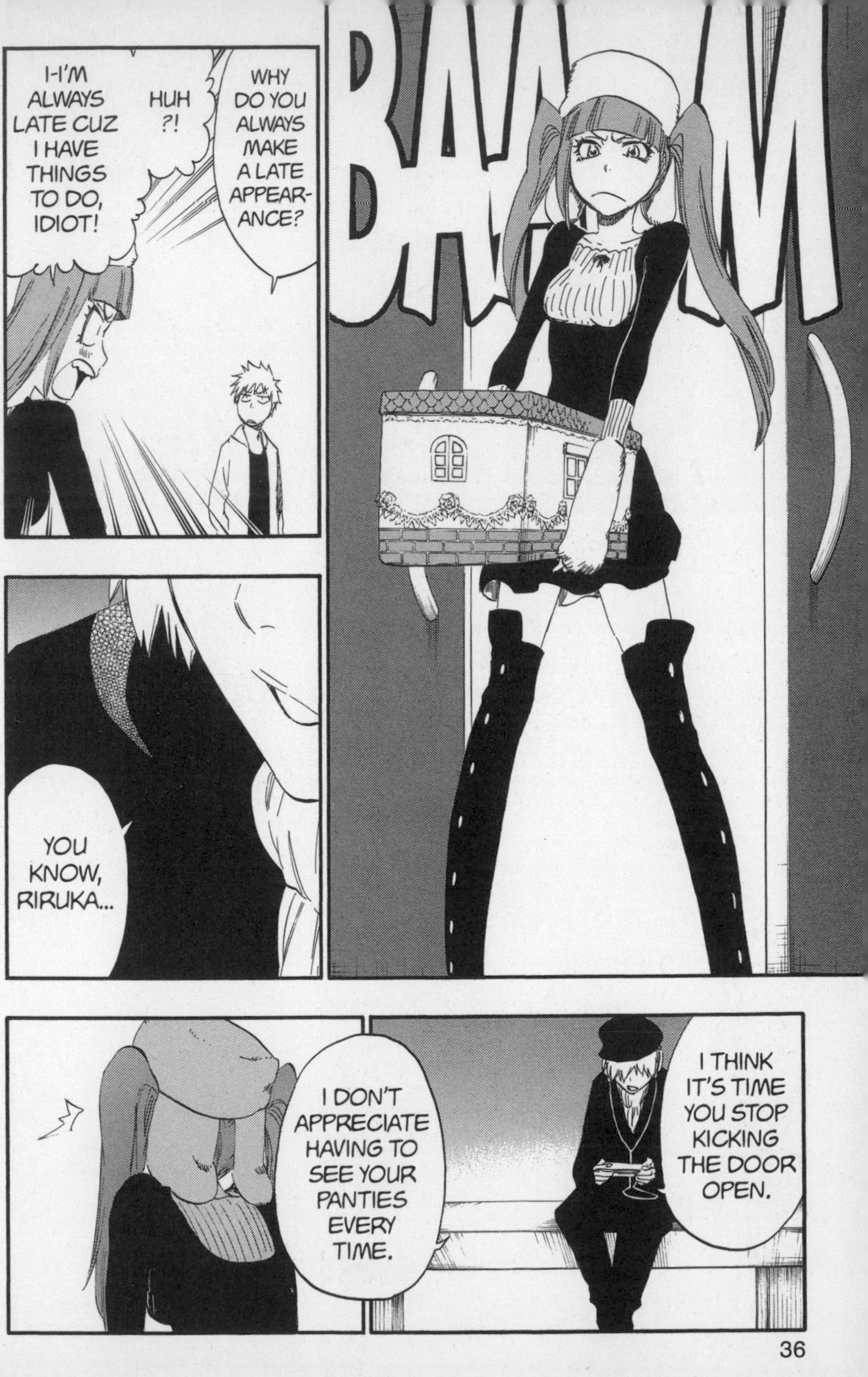
BAM
WHY DO YOU ALWAYS MAKE A LATE APPEARANCE?
HUH?!
I-I'M ALWAYS LATE CUZ I HAVE THINGS TO DO, IDIOT!
YOU KNOW, RIRUKA...
I THINK IT'S TIME YOU STOP KICKING THE DOOR OPEN.
I DON'T APPRECIATE HAVING TO SEE YOUR PANTIES EVERY TIME.

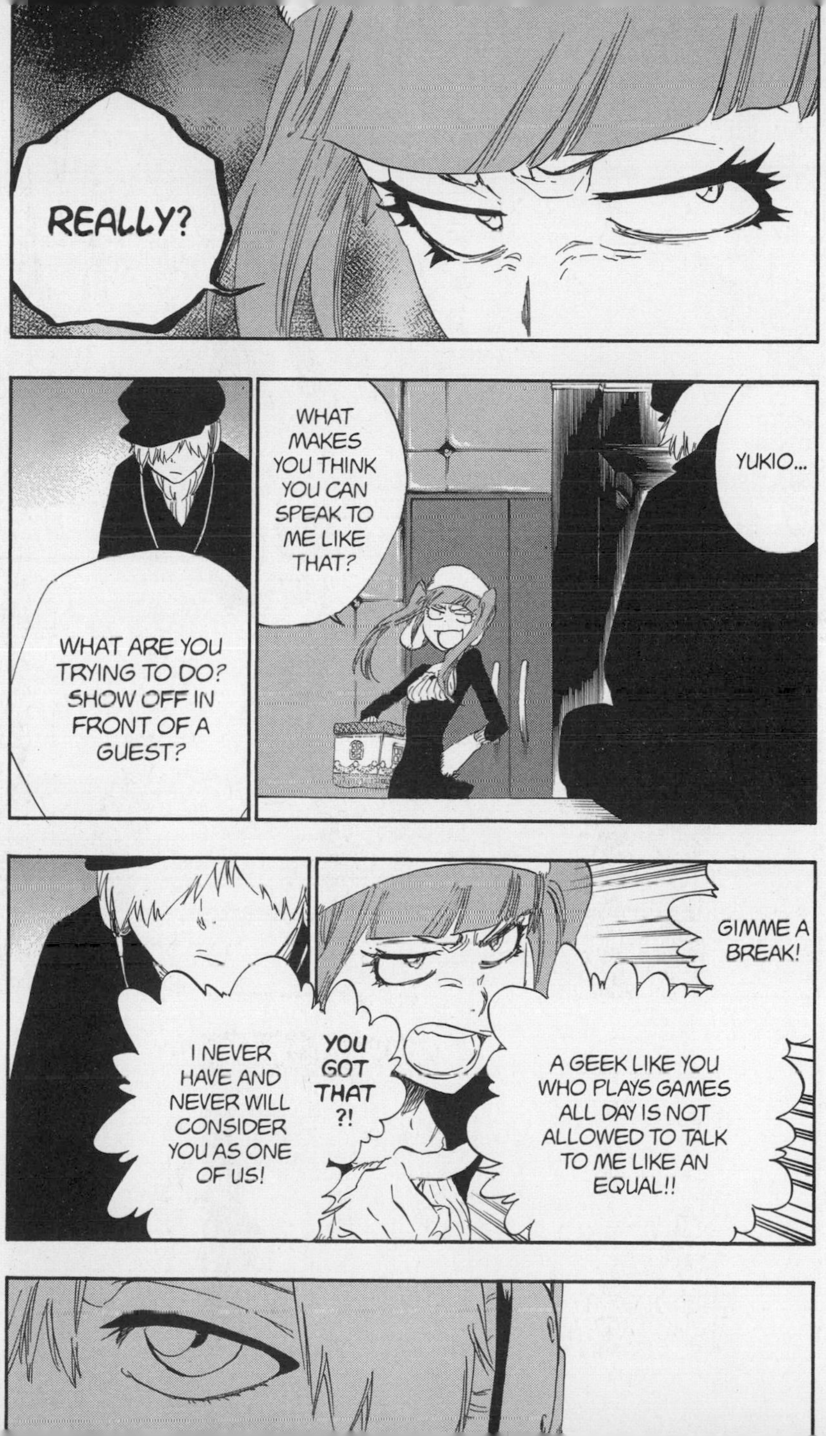
REALLY?
YUKIO...
WHAT MAKES YOU THINK YOU CAN SPEAK TO ME LIKE THAT?
WHAT ARE YOU TRYING TO DO? SHOW OFF IN FRONT OF A GUEST?
GIMME A BREAK!
A GEEK LIKE YOU WHO PLAYS GAMES ALL DAY IS NOT ALLOWED TO TALK TO ME LIKE AN EQUAL!!
YOU GOT THAT?!
I NEVER HAVE AND NEVER WILL CONSIDER YOU AS ONE OF US!

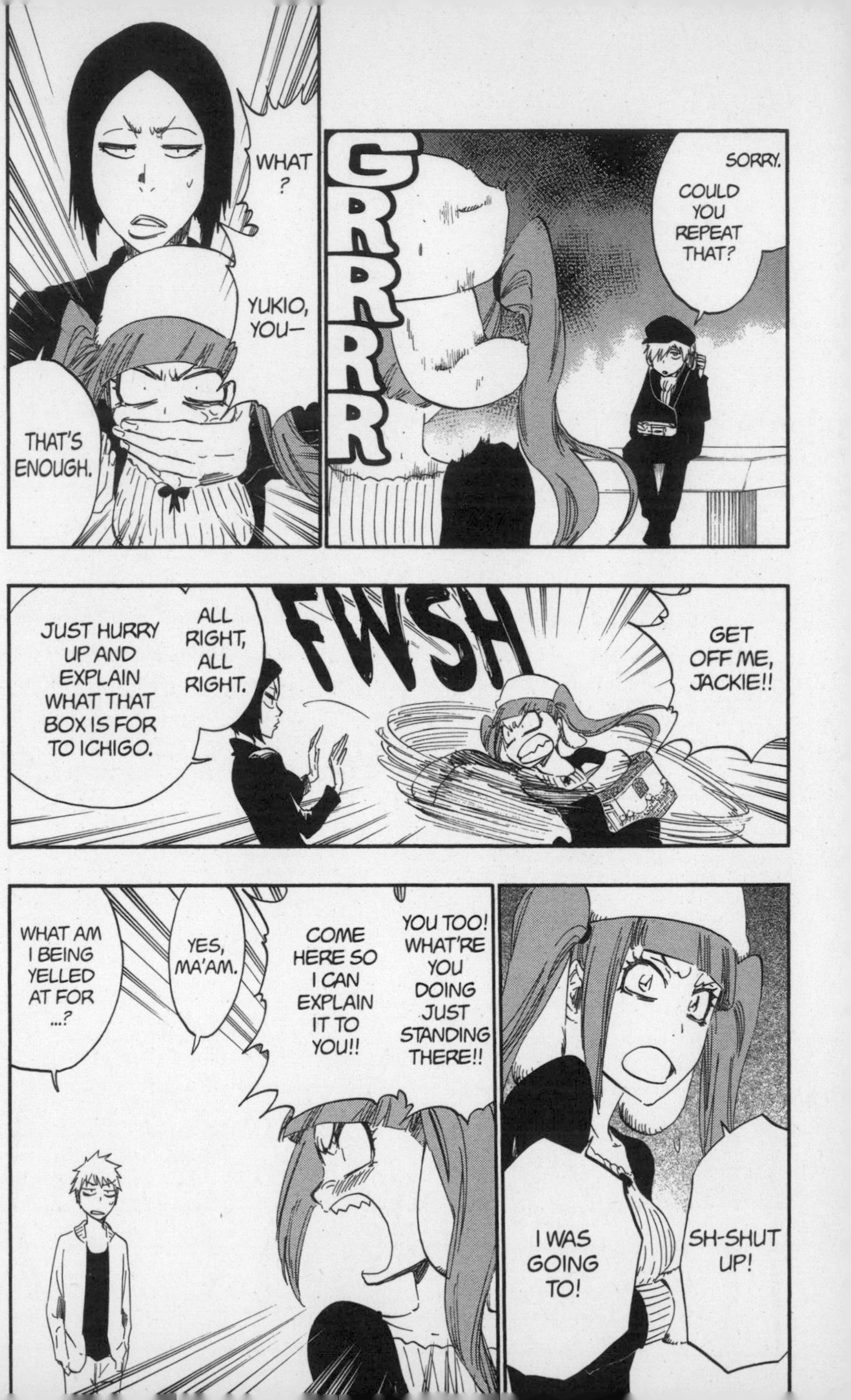
SORRY.
COULD YOU REPEAT THAT?
GRRRR
WHAT?
YUKIO, YOU—
THAT'S ENOUGH.
GET OFF ME, JACKIE!!
FWSH
ALL RIGHT, ALL RIGHT.
JUST HURRY UP AND EXPLAIN WHAT THAT BOX IS FOR TO ICHIGO.
SH-SHUT UP!
I WAS GOING TO!
YOU TOO! WHAT'RE YOU DOING JUST STANDING THERE!!
COME HERE SO I CAN EXPLAIN IT TO YOU!!
YES, MA'AM.
WHAT AM I BEING YELLED AT FOR ...?

READ THIS WAY

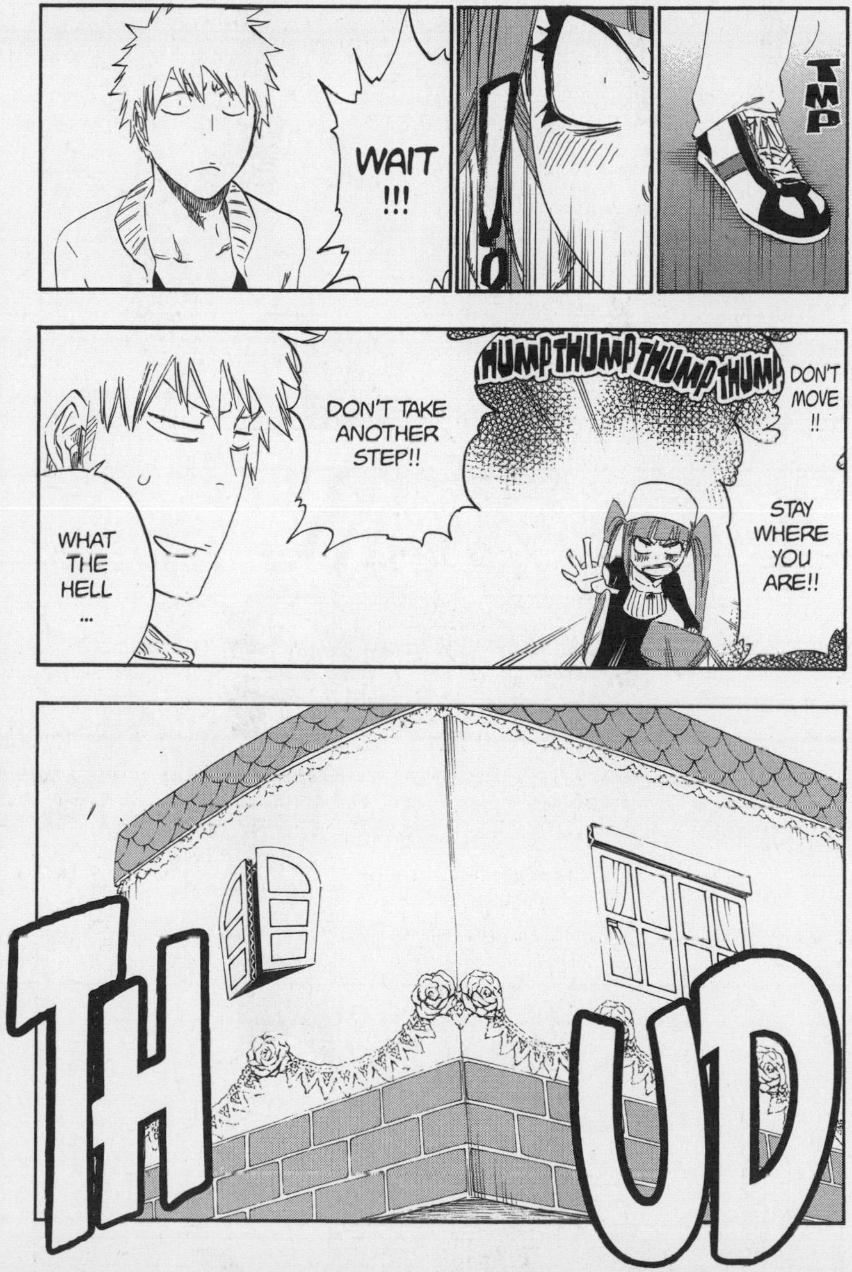
TMP
WAIT!!!
DON'T MOVE!!
THUMP THUMP THUMP THUMP
STAY WHERE YOU ARE!!
DON'T TAKE ANOTHER STEP!!
WHAT THE HELL...
THUD

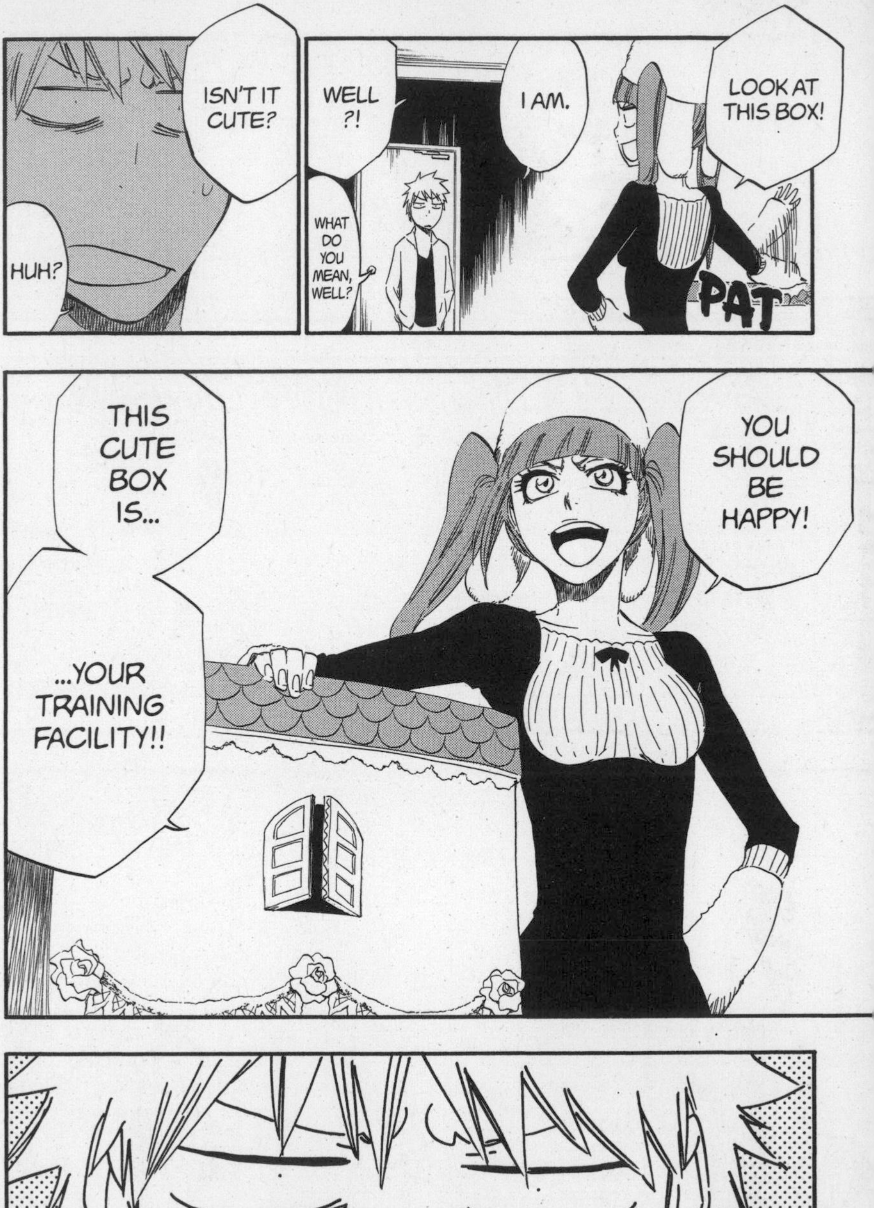
LOOK AT THIS BOX!
PAT
I AM.
WELL ?!
WHAT DO YOU MEAN, WELL?
ISN'T IT CUTE?
HUH?
YOU SHOULD BE HAPPY!
THIS CUTE BOX IS...
...YOUR TRAINING FACILITY!!

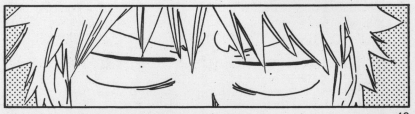

READ THIS WAY

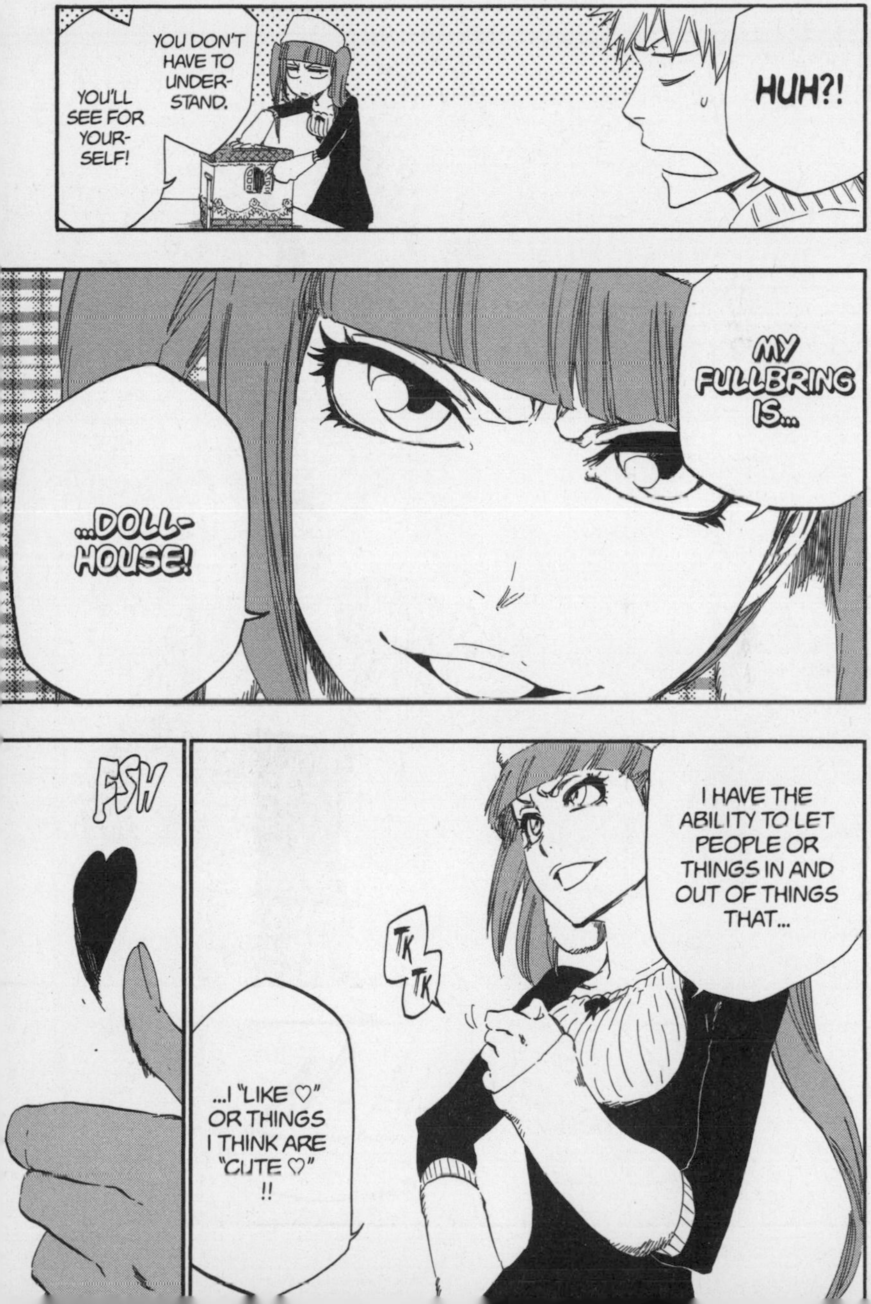
HUH?!
YOU DON'T HAVE TO UNDER-STAND.
YOU'LL SEE FOR YOUR-SELF!
MY FULLBRING IS...
...DOLL-HOUSE!
I HAVE THE ABILITY TO LET PEOPLE OR THINGS IN AND OUT OF THINGS THAT...
TK TK
...I "LIKE ♡" OR THINGS I THINK ARE "CUTE ♡" !!
FSH

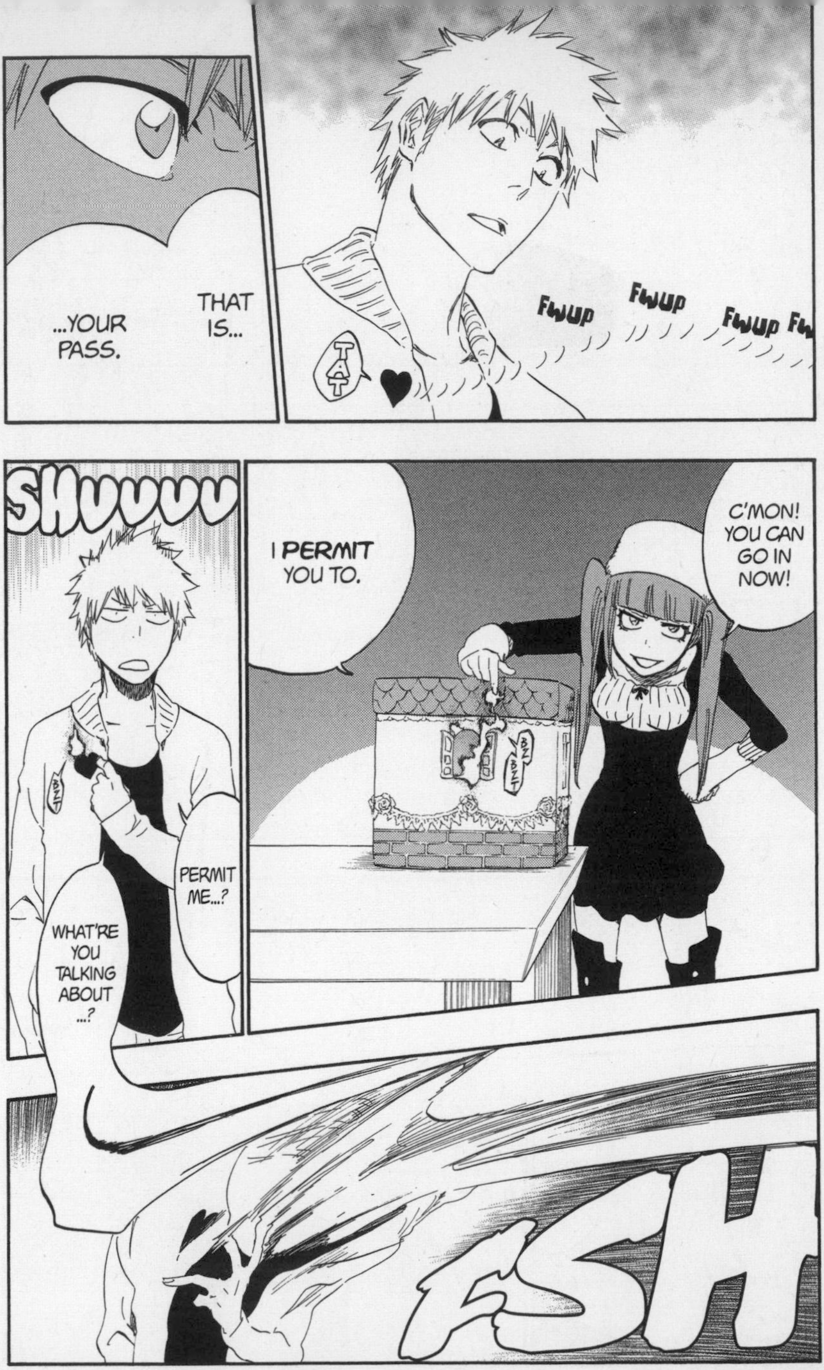
FWUP FWUP FWUP FW
TAT
THAT IS...
...YOUR PASS.
C'MON! YOU CAN GO IN NOW!
I PERMIT YOU TO.
SHUUUU
PERMIT ME...?
WHAT'RE YOU TALKING ABOUT ...?
FSH

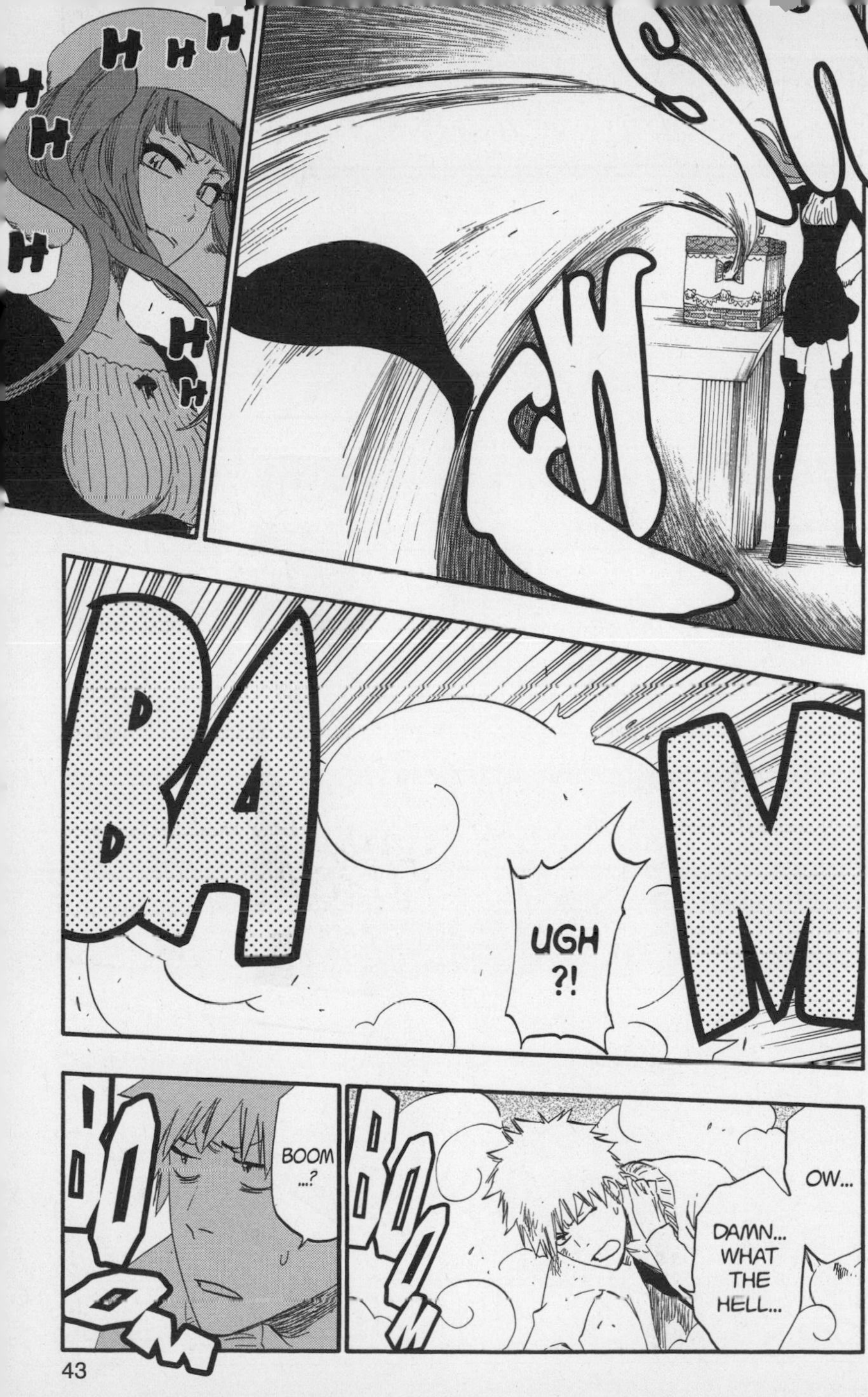
BAM
UGH ?!
OW...
DAMN... WHAT THE HELL...
BOOM ...?

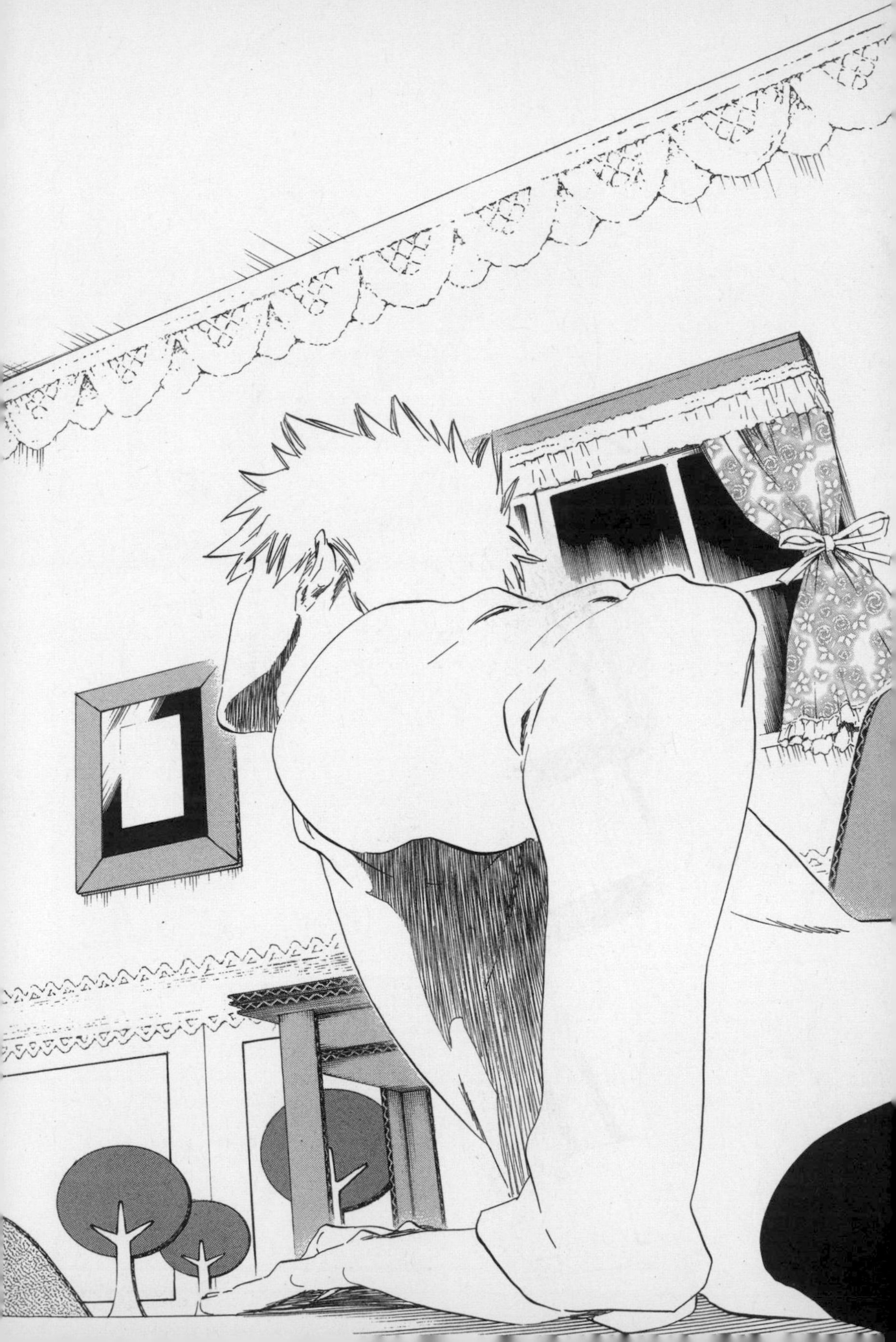

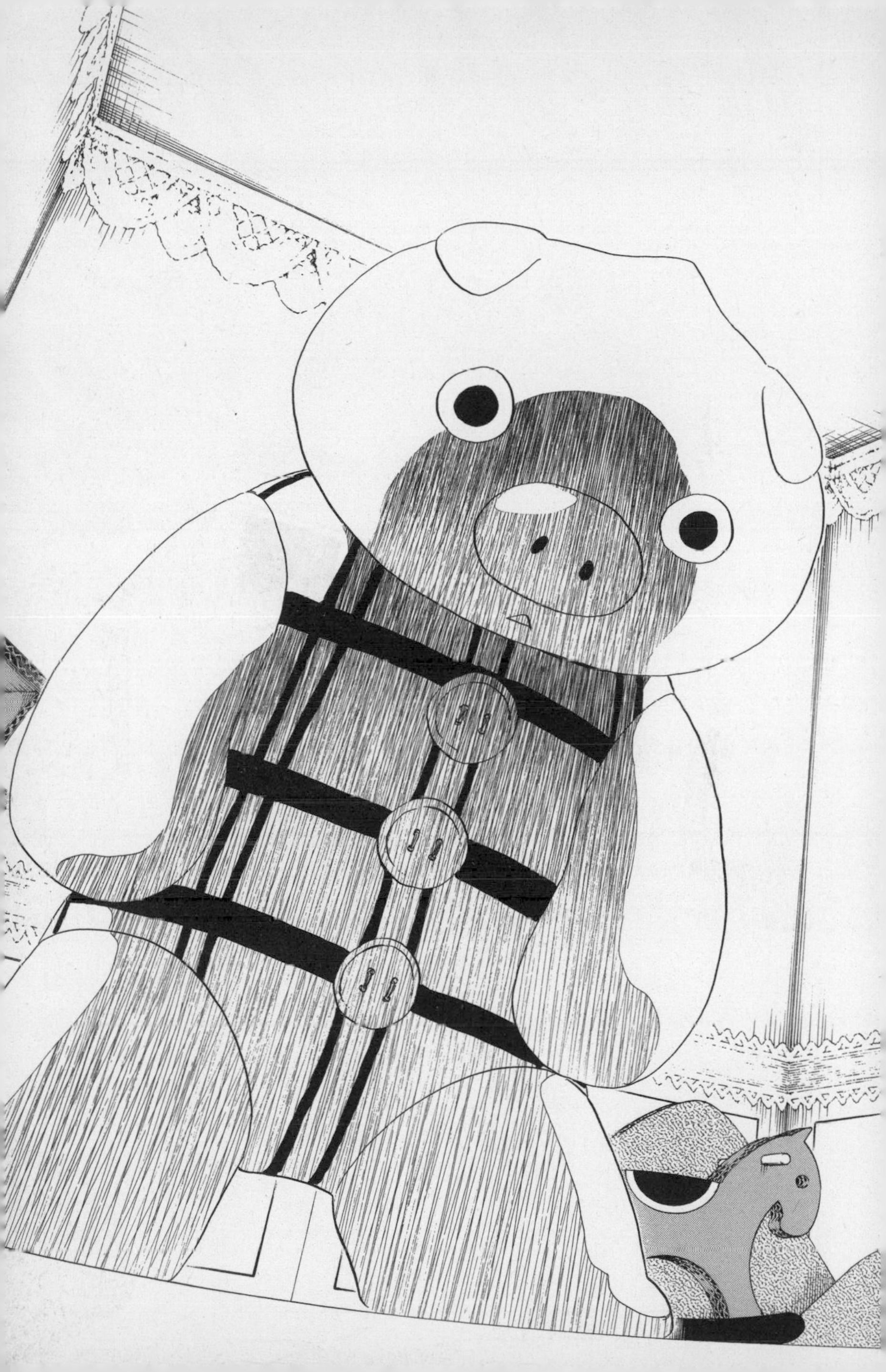

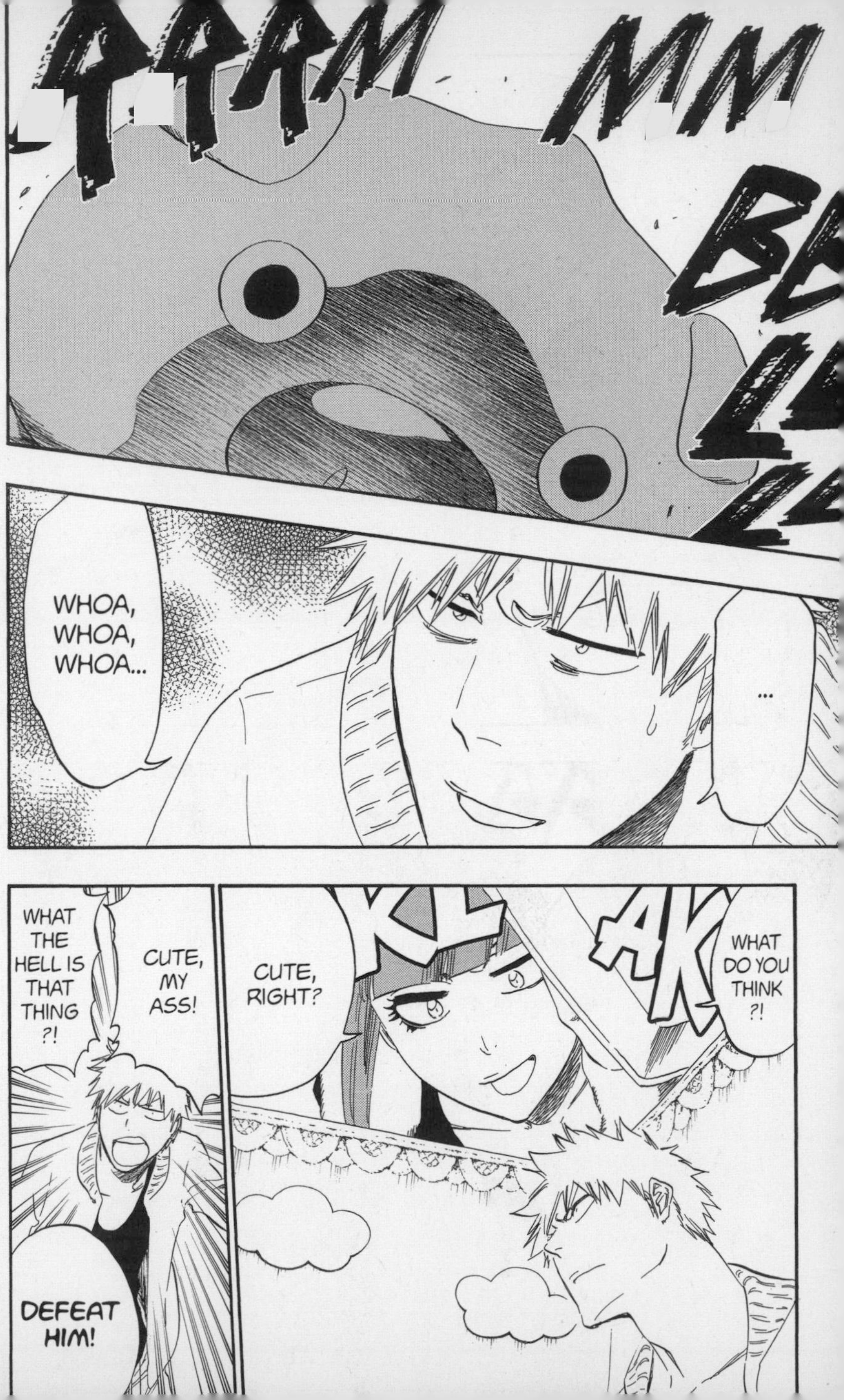
...
WHOA, WHOA, WHOA...
WHAT DO YOU THINK ?!
CUTE, RIGHT?
CUTE, MY ASS!
WHAT THE HELL IS THAT THING ?!
DEFEAT HIM!

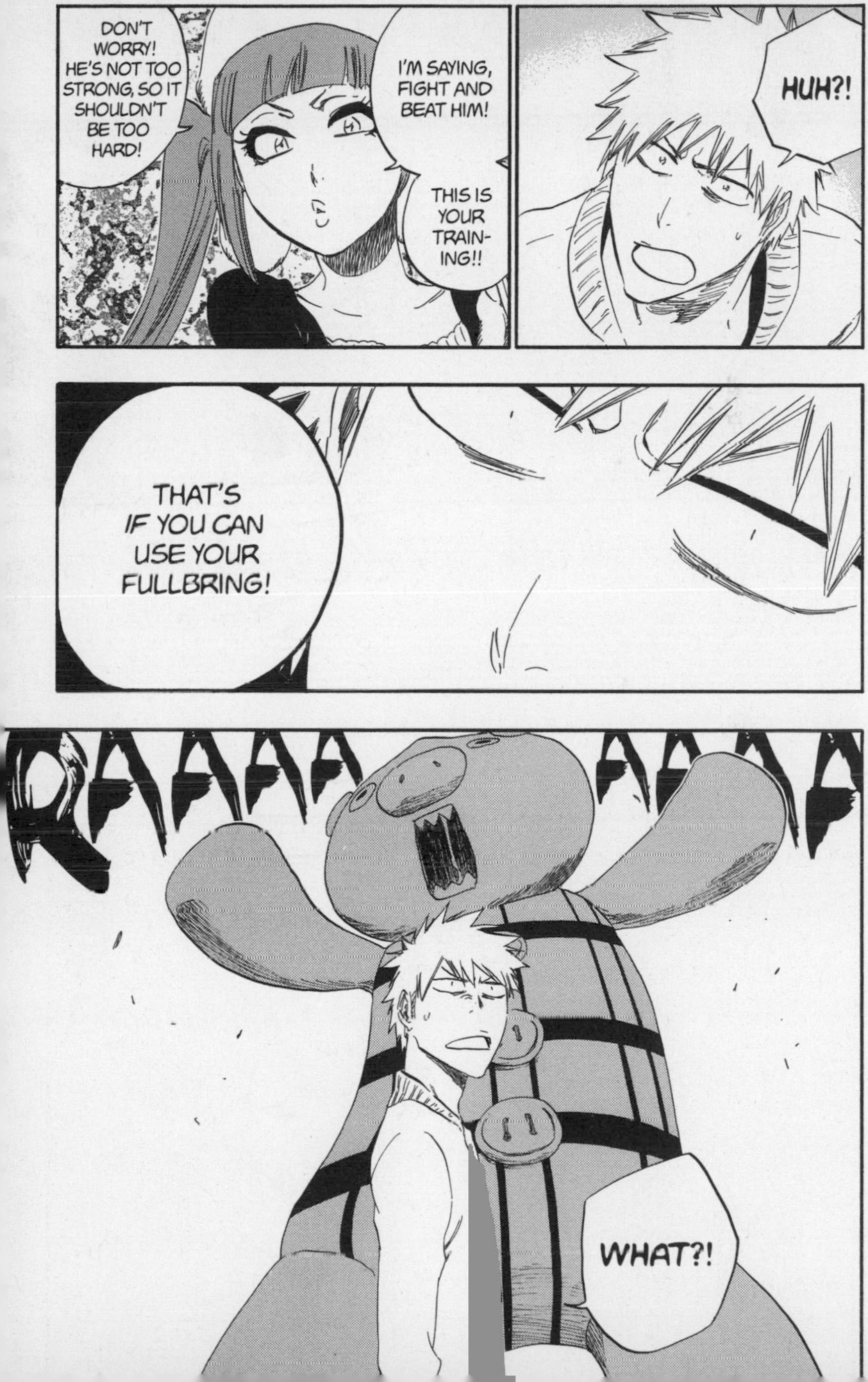
HUH?!
I'M SAYING, FIGHT AND BEAT HIM!
THIS IS YOUR TRAIN-ING!!
DON'T WORRY! HE'S NOT TOO STRONG, SO IT SHOULDN'T BE TOO HARD!
THAT'S IF YOU CAN USE YOUR FULLBRING!
RAAAAAAAA
WHAT?!

I HAVE A LATE-NIGHT SHOW NOW!
PROOF THAT I'M GAINING POPULARITY!

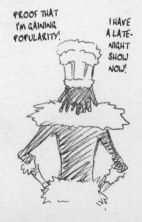

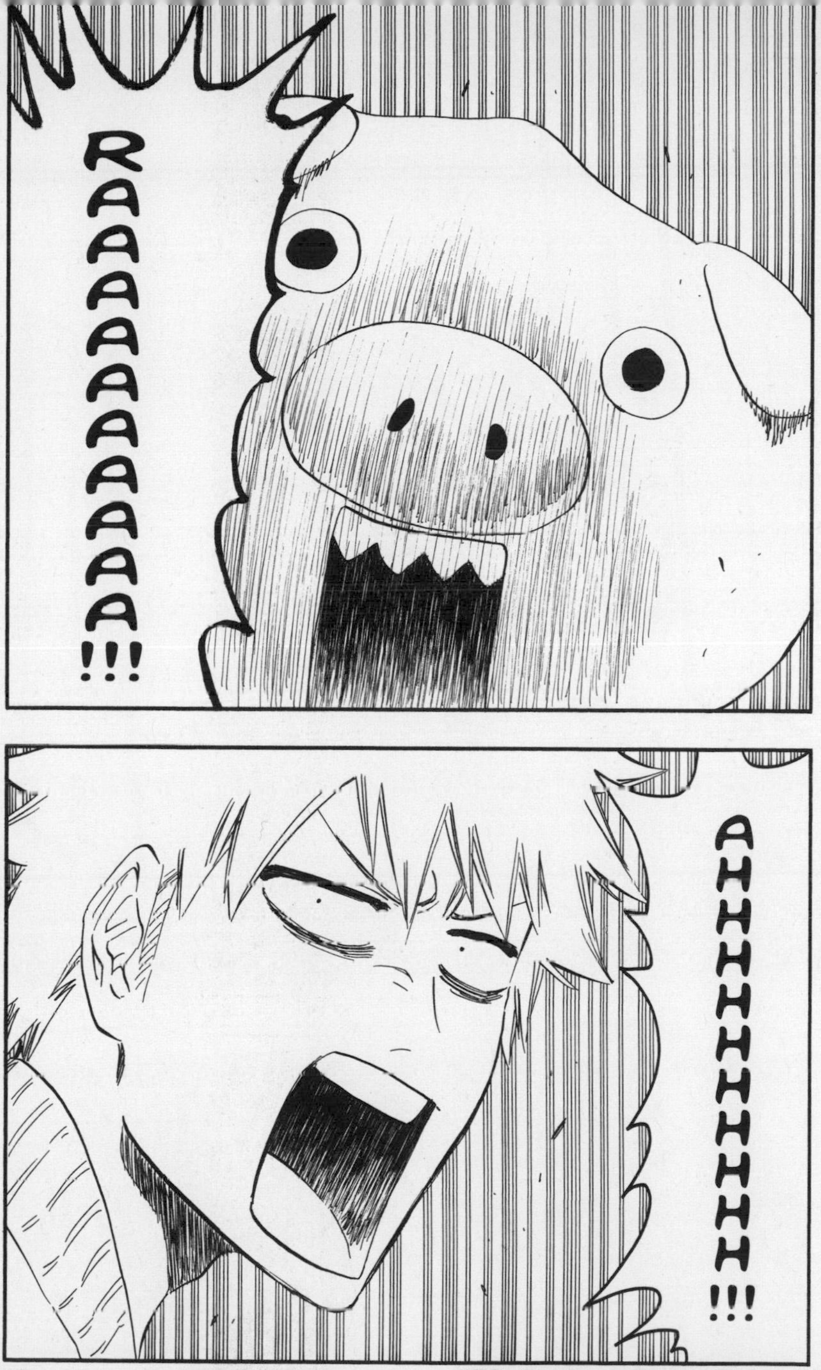
RAAAAAAAAAA!!!
AHHHHHHHHHH!!!

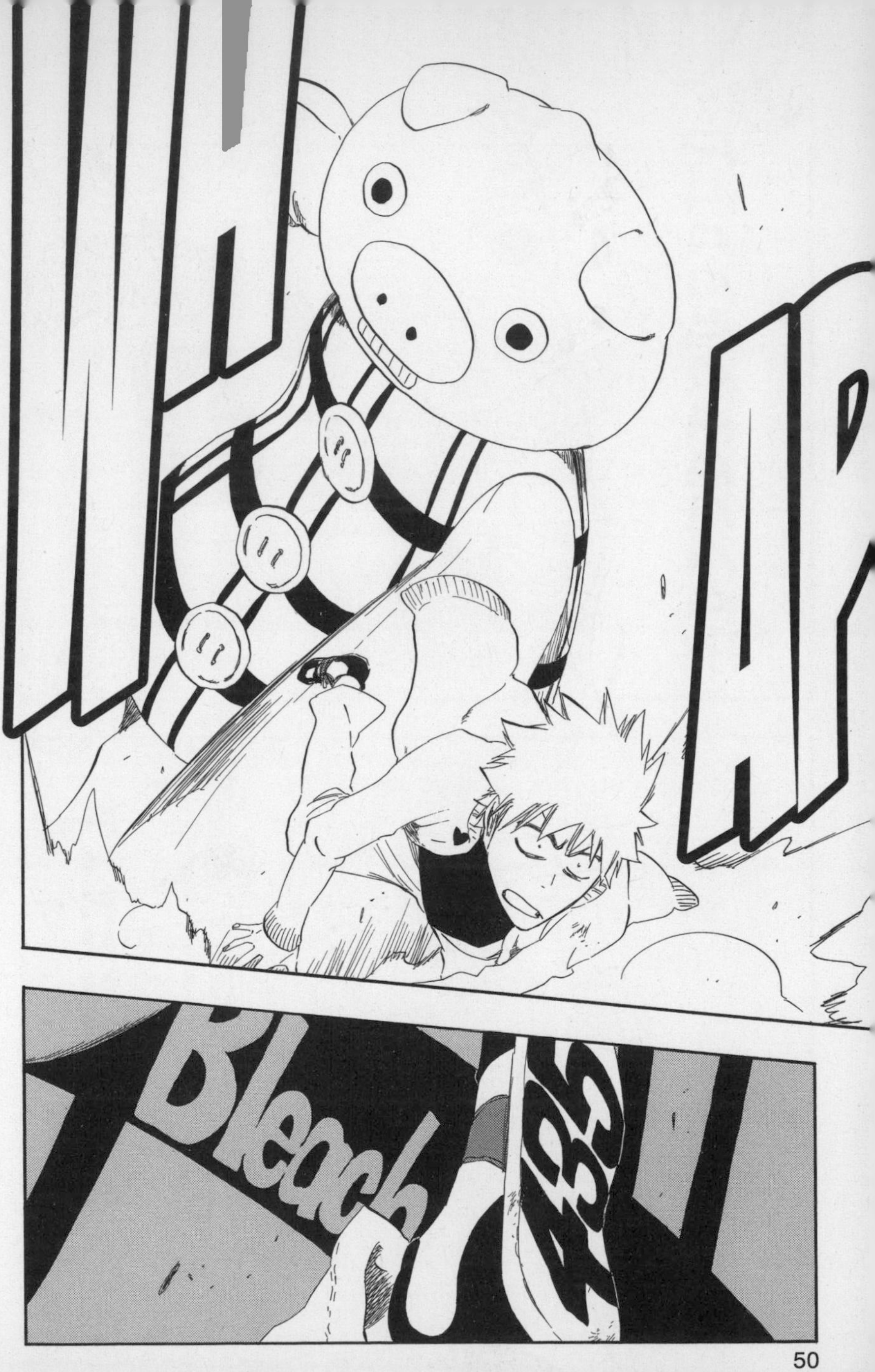
WHAP
Bleach

READ THIS WAY

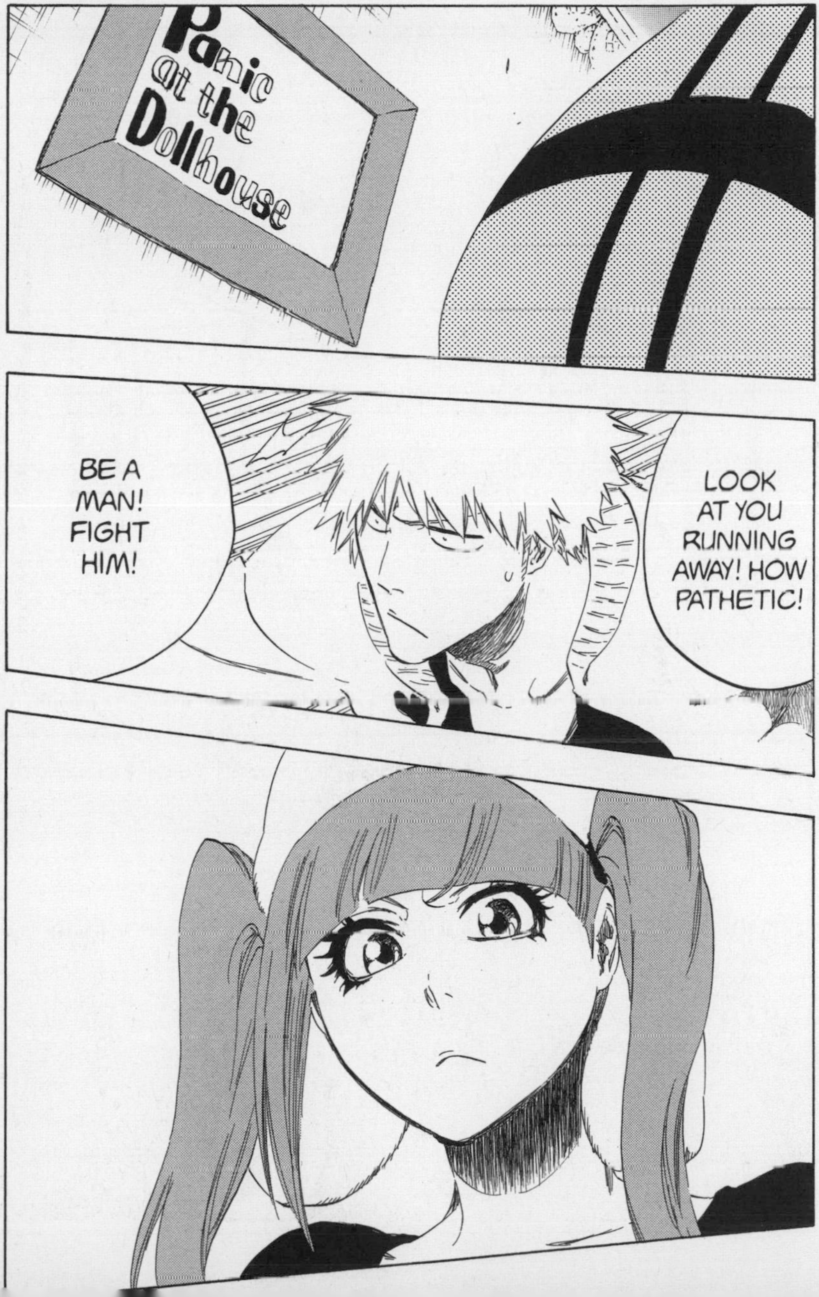
Panic at the Dollhouse
LOOK AT YOU RUNNING AWAY! HOW PATHETIC!
BE A MAN! FIGHT HIM!

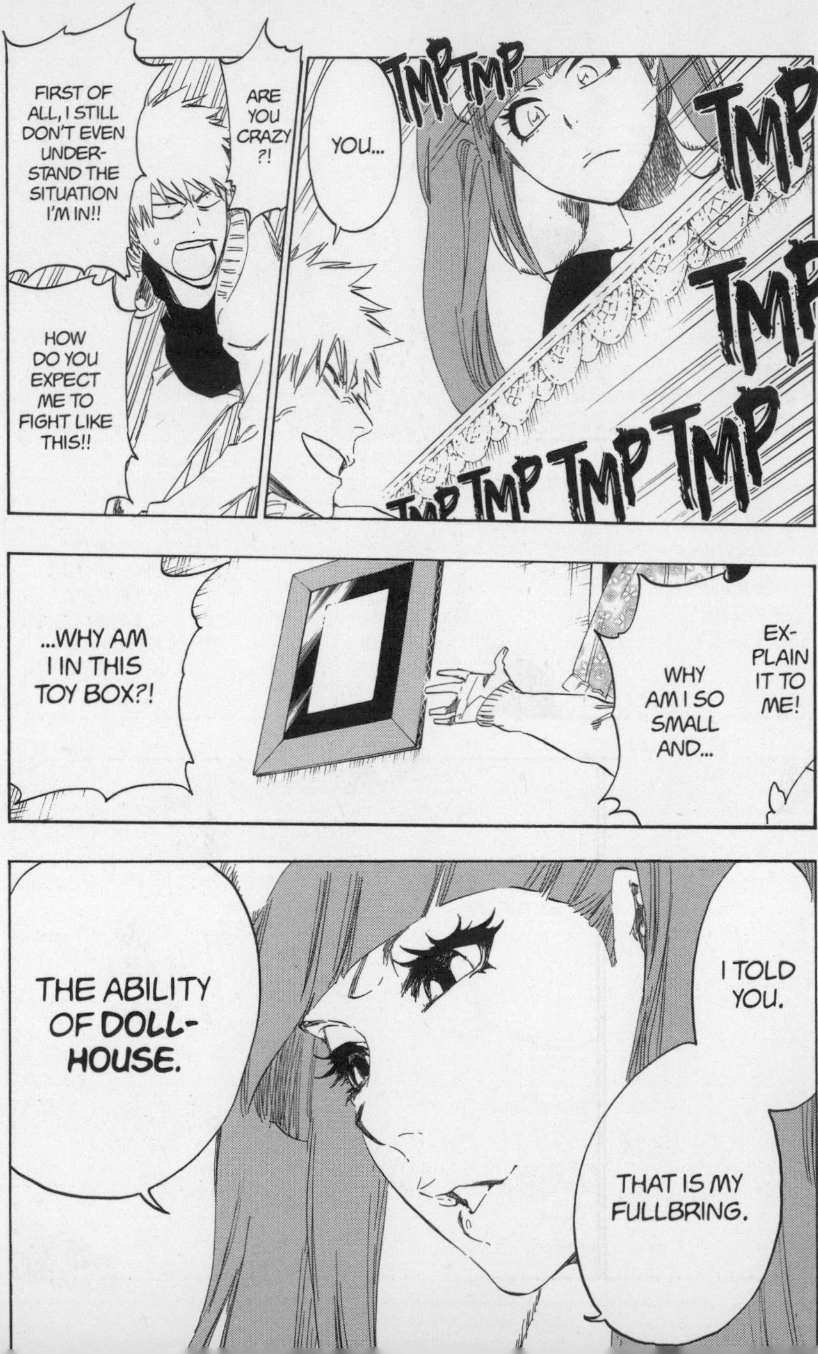
TMPTMP
YOU...
TMP TMP
TMPTMPTMPTMP
ARE YOU CRAZY?!
FIRST OF ALL, I STILL DON'T EVEN UNDER-STAND THE SITUATION I'M IN!!
HOW DO YOU EXPECT ME TO FIGHT LIKE THIS!!
EX-PLAIN IT TO ME!
WHY AM I SO SMALL AND...
...WHY AM I IN THIS TOY BOX?!
I TOLD YOU.
THAT IS MY FULLBRING.
THE ABILITY OF DOLL-HOUSE.

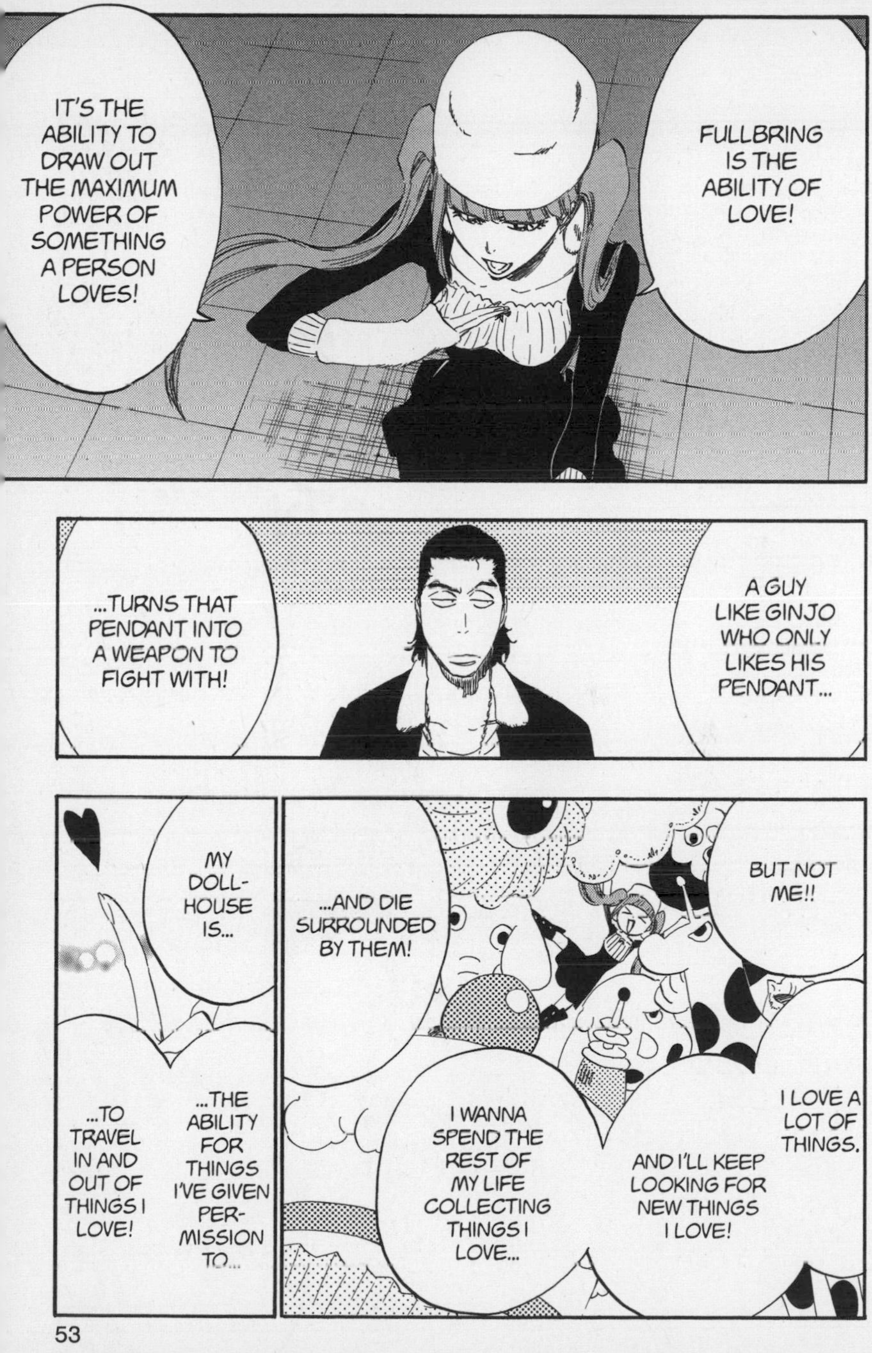
FULLBRING IS THE ABILITY OF LOVE!
IT'S THE ABILITY TO DRAW OUT THE MAXIMUM POWER OF SOMETHING A PERSON LOVES!
A GUY LIKE GINJO WHO ONLY LIKES HIS PENDANT...
...TURNS THAT PENDANT INTO A WEAPON TO FIGHT WITH!
BUT NOT ME!!
I LOVE A LOT OF THINGS.
AND I'LL KEEP LOOKING FOR NEW THINGS I LOVE!
I WANNA SPEND THE REST OF MY LIFE COLLECTING THINGS I LOVE...
...AND DIE SURROUNDED BY THEM!
MY DOLLHOUSE IS...
...THE ABILITY FOR THINGS I'VE GIVEN PERMISSION TO...
...TO TRAVEL IN AND OUT OF THINGS I LOVE!

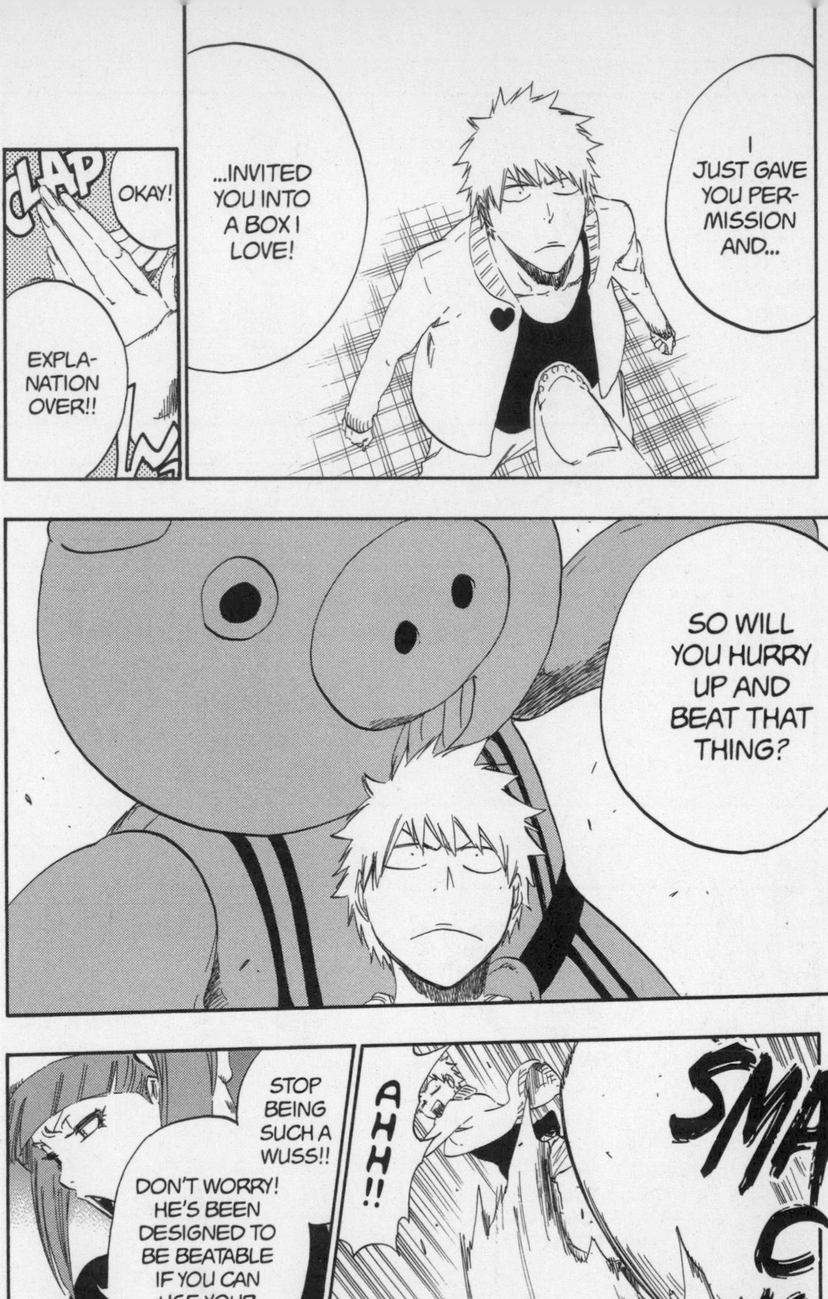
I JUST GAVE YOU PERMISSION AND...
...INVITED YOU INTO A BOX I LOVE!
CLAP
OKAY!
EXPLANATION OVER!!
SO WILL YOU HURRY UP AND BEAT THAT THING?
SMACK
AHHH!!
STOP BEING SUCH A WUSS!!
DON'T WORRY! HE'S BEEN DESIGNED TO BE BEATABLE IF YOU CAN USE YOUR FULLBRING!

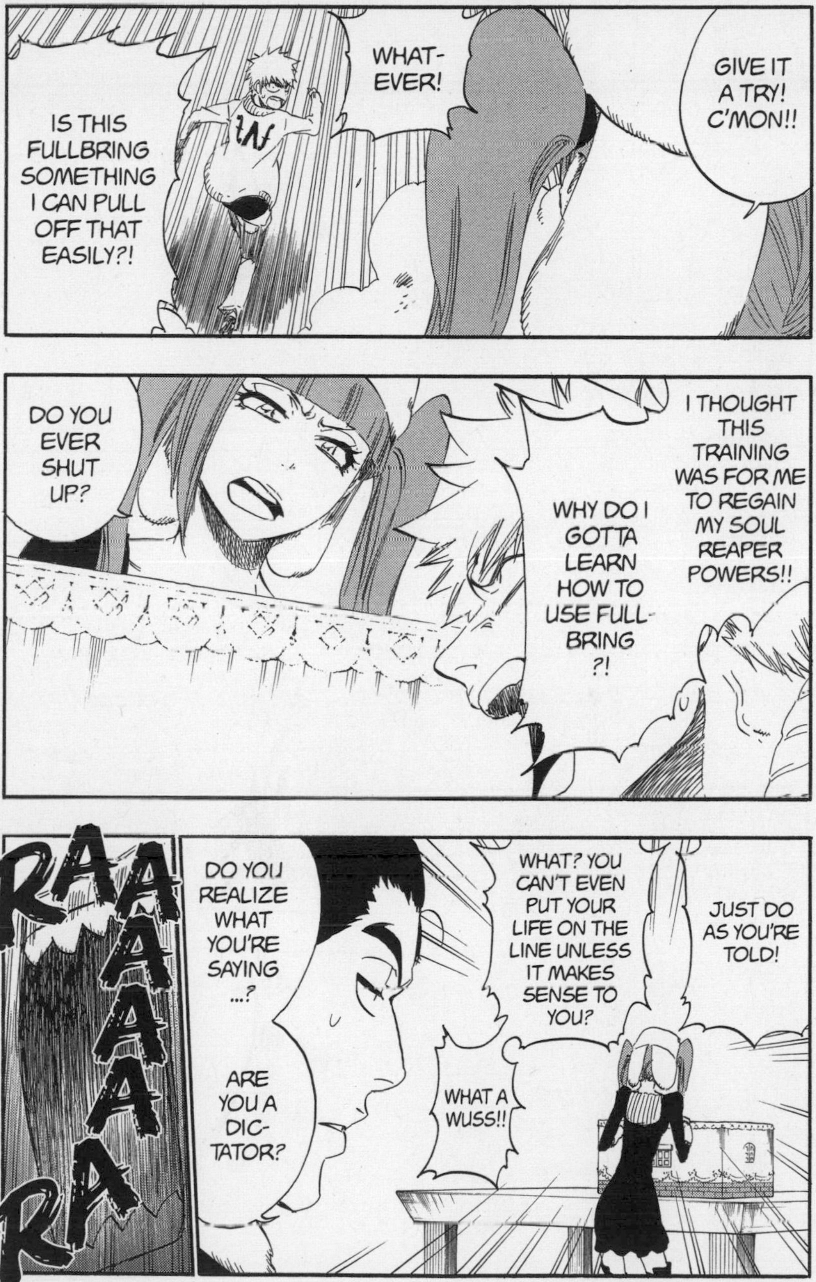
GIVE IT A TRY! C'MON!!
WHAT-EVER!
IS THIS FULLBRING SOMETHING I CAN PULL OFF THAT EASILY?!
I THOUGHT THIS TRAINING WAS FOR ME TO REGAIN MY SOUL REAPER POWERS!!
WHY DO I GOTTA LEARN HOW TO USE FULL-BRING ?!
DO YOU EVER SHUT UP?
JUST DO AS YOU'RE TOLD!
WHAT? YOU CAN'T EVEN PUT YOUR LIFE ON THE LINE UNLESS IT MAKES SENSE TO YOU?
DO YOU REALIZE WHAT YOU'RE SAYING ...?
WHAT A WUSS!!
ARE YOU A DIC-TATOR?
RAAAAAARA

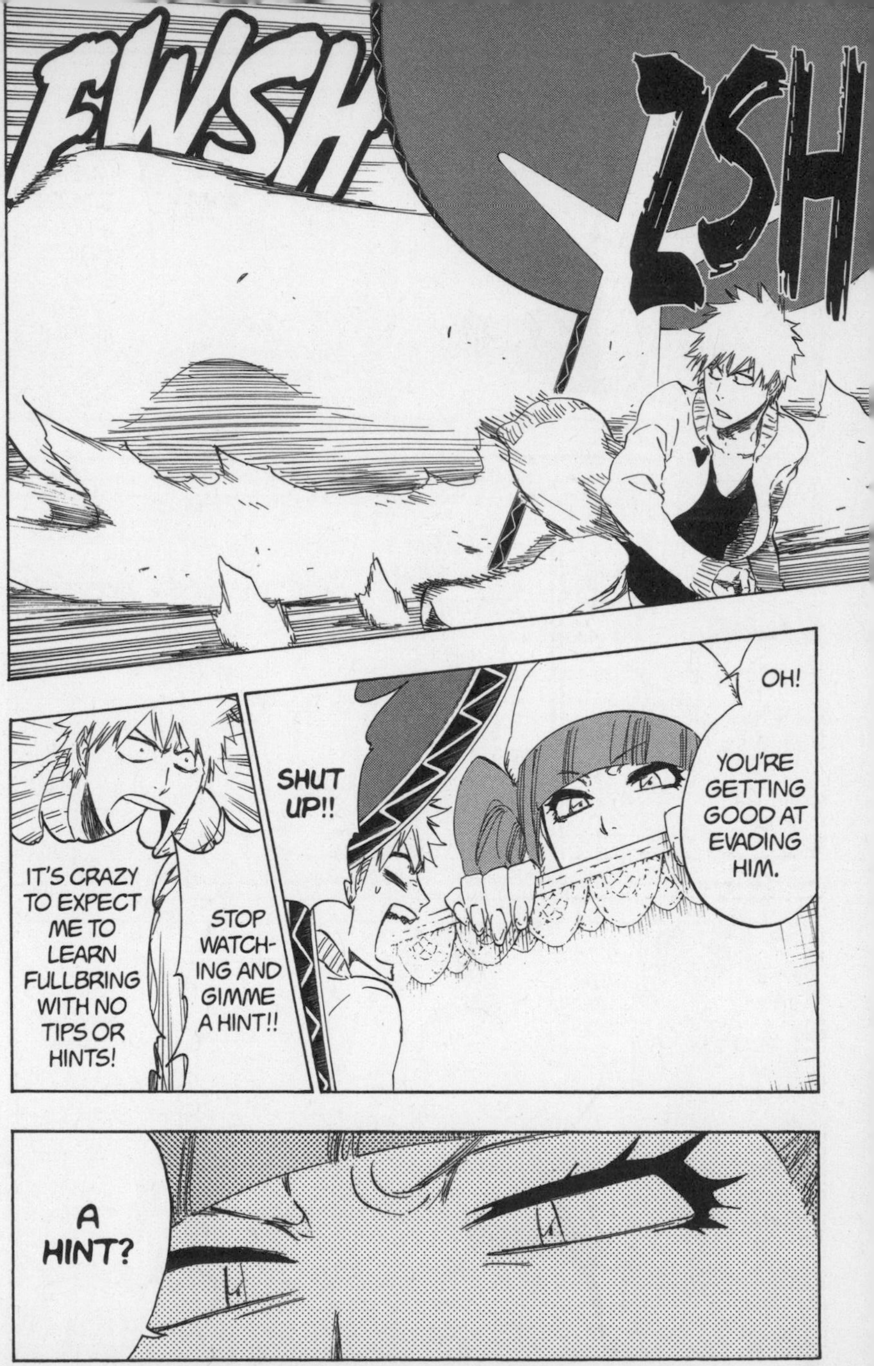
ZSH
FWSH
OH!
YOU'RE GETTING GOOD AT EVADING HIM.
SHUT UP!!
STOP WATCH-ING AND GIMME A HINT!!
IT'S CRAZY TO EXPECT ME TO LEARN FULLBRING WITH NO TIPS OR HINTS!
A HINT?

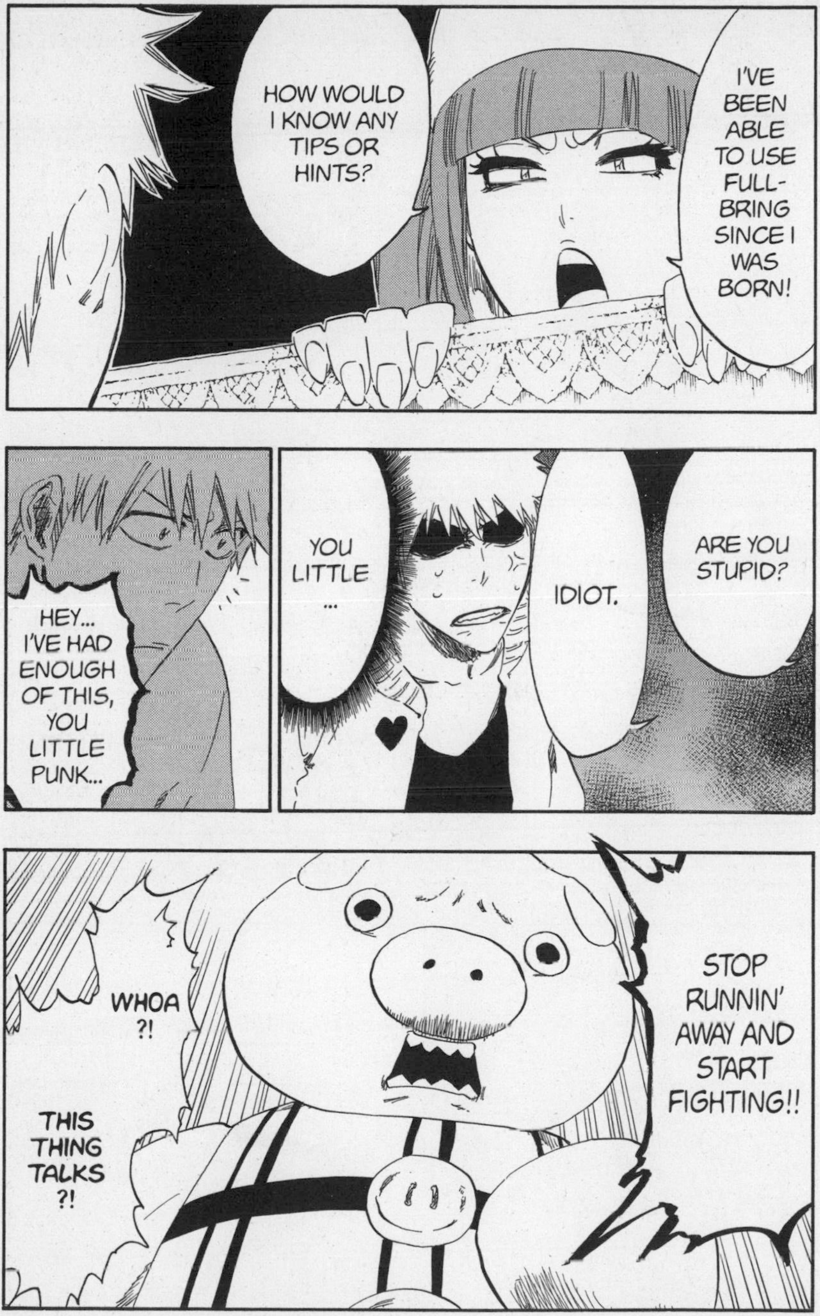
I'VE BEEN ABLE TO USE FULL-BRING SINCE I WAS BORN!
HOW WOULD I KNOW ANY TIPS OR HINTS?
ARE YOU STUPID?
IDIOT.
YOU LITTLE ...
HEY... I'VE HAD ENOUGH OF THIS, YOU LITTLE PUNK...
STOP RUNNIN' AWAY AND START FIGHTING!!
WHOA?!
THIS THING TALKS?!

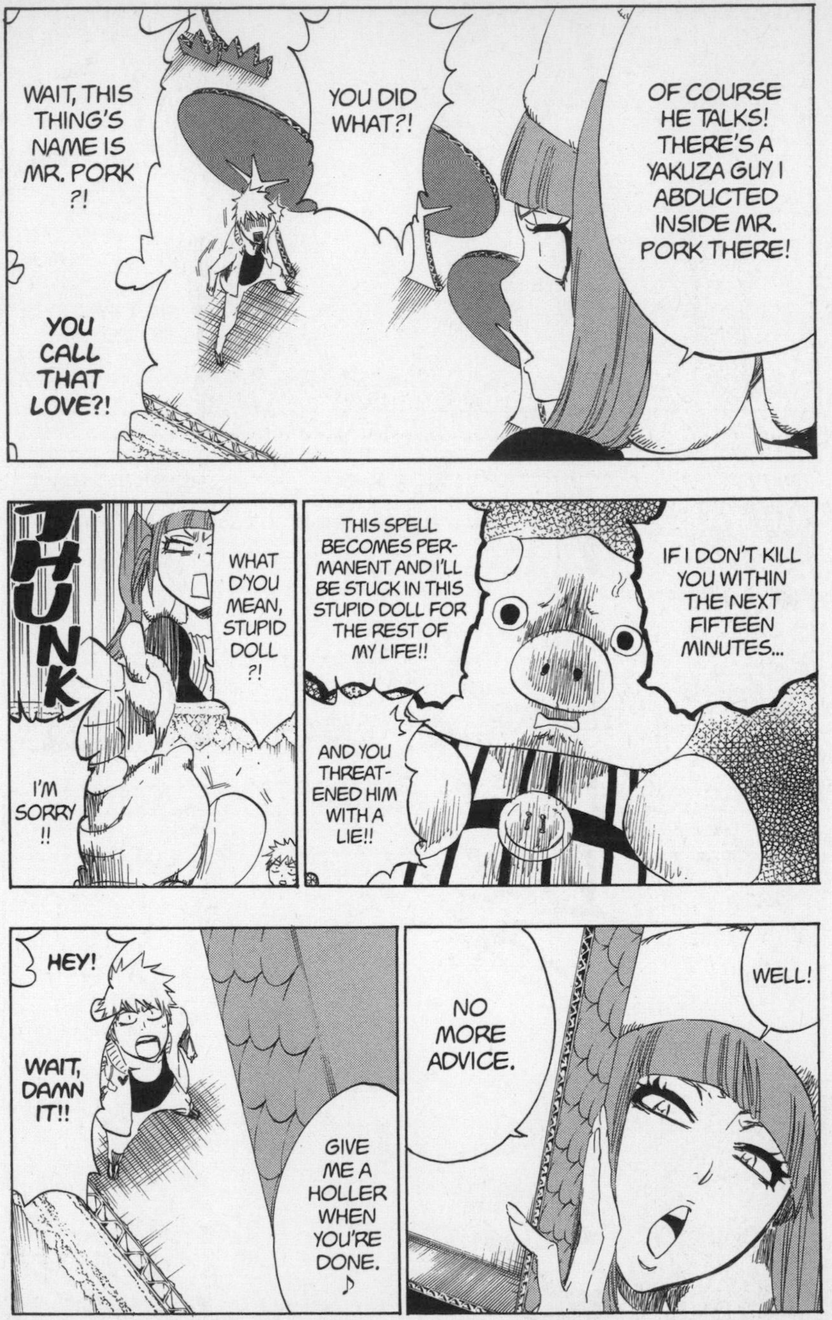
OF COURSE HE TALKS! THERE'S A YAKUZA GUY I ABDUCTED INSIDE MR. PORK THERE!
YOU DID WHAT?!
WAIT, THIS THING'S NAME IS MR. PORK ?!
YOU CALL THAT LOVE?!
IF I DON'T KILL YOU WITHIN THE NEXT FIFTEEN MINUTES...
THIS SPELL BECOMES PER-MANENT AND I'LL BE STUCK IN THIS STUPID DOLL FOR THE REST OF MY LIFE!!
AND YOU THREAT-ENED HIM WITH A LIE!!
WHAT D'YOU MEAN, STUPID DOLL ?!
THUNK
I'M SORRY !!
WELL!
NO MORE ADVICE.
GIVE ME A HOLLER WHEN YOU'RE DONE. ♪
HEY!
WAIT, DAMN IT!!

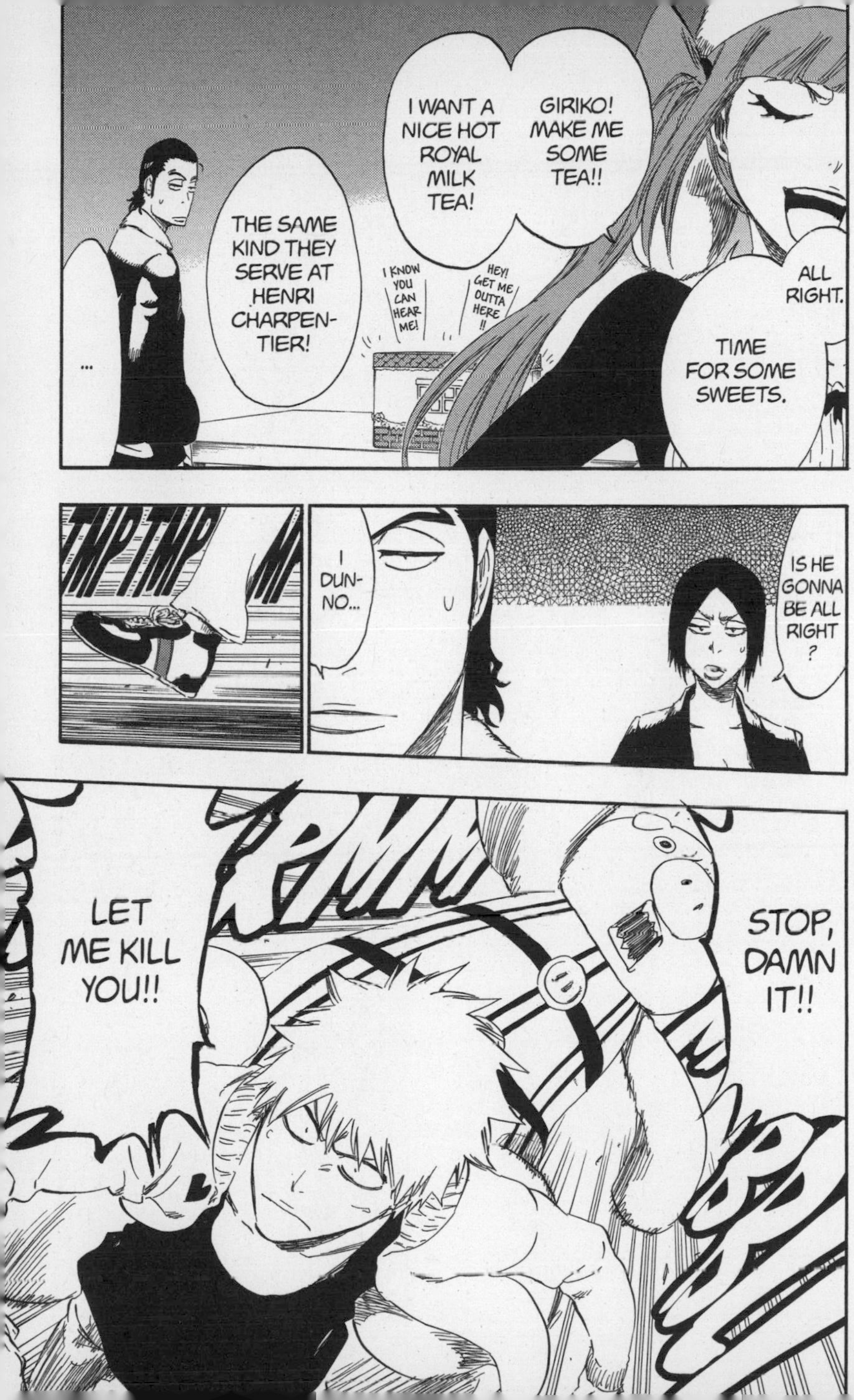
ALL RIGHT.
TIME FOR SOME SWEETS.
GIRIKO! MAKE ME SOME TEA!!
I WANT A NICE HOT ROYAL MILK TEA!
HEY! GET ME OUTTA HERE!!
I KNOW YOU CAN HEAR ME!
THE SAME KIND THEY SERVE AT HENRI CHARPEN-TIER!
...
IS HE GONNA BE ALL RIGHT?
I DUN-NO...
TMP TMP
STOP, DAMN IT!!
LET ME KILL YOU!!

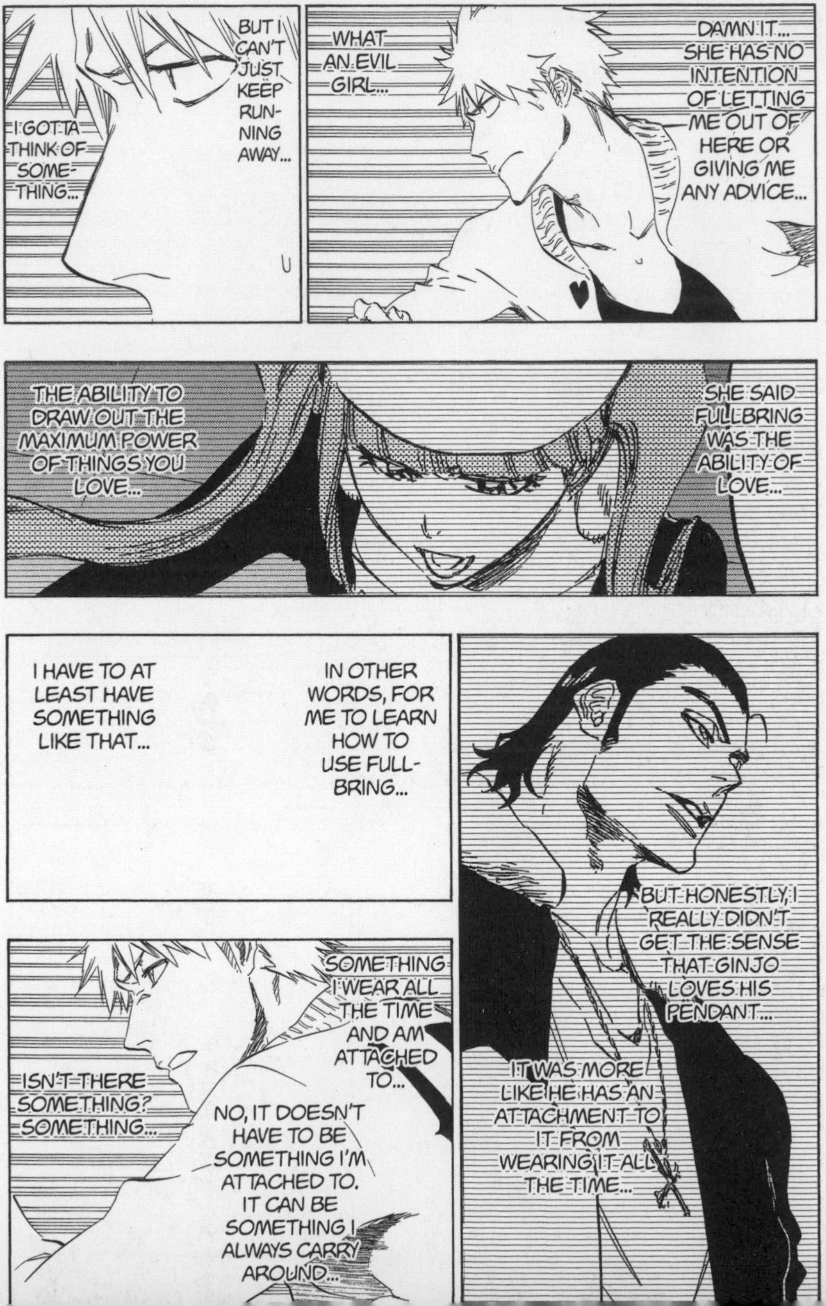
DAMN IT... SHE HAS NO INTENTION OF LETTING ME OUT OF HERE OR GIVING ME ANY ADVICE...
WHAT AN EVIL GIRL...
BUT I CAN'T JUST KEEP RUN-NING AWAY...
I GOTTA THINK OF SOME-THING...
SHE SAID FULLBRING WAS THE ABILITY OF LOVE...
THE ABILITY TO DRAW OUT THE MAXIMUM POWER OF THINGS YOU LOVE...
BUT HONESTLY, I REALLY DIDN'T GET THE SENSE THAT GINJO LOVES HIS PENDANT...
IT WAS MORE LIKE HE HAS AN ATTACHMENT TO IT FROM WEARING IT ALL THE TIME...
IN OTHER WORDS, FOR ME TO LEARN HOW TO USE FULL-BRING...
I HAVE TO AT LEAST HAVE SOMETHING LIKE THAT...
SOMETHING I WEAR ALL THE TIME AND AM ATTACHED TO...
ISN'T THERE SOMETHING? SOMETHING...
NO, IT DOESN'T HAVE TO BE SOMETHING I'M ATTACHED TO. IT CAN BE SOMETHING I ALWAYS CARRY AROUND...

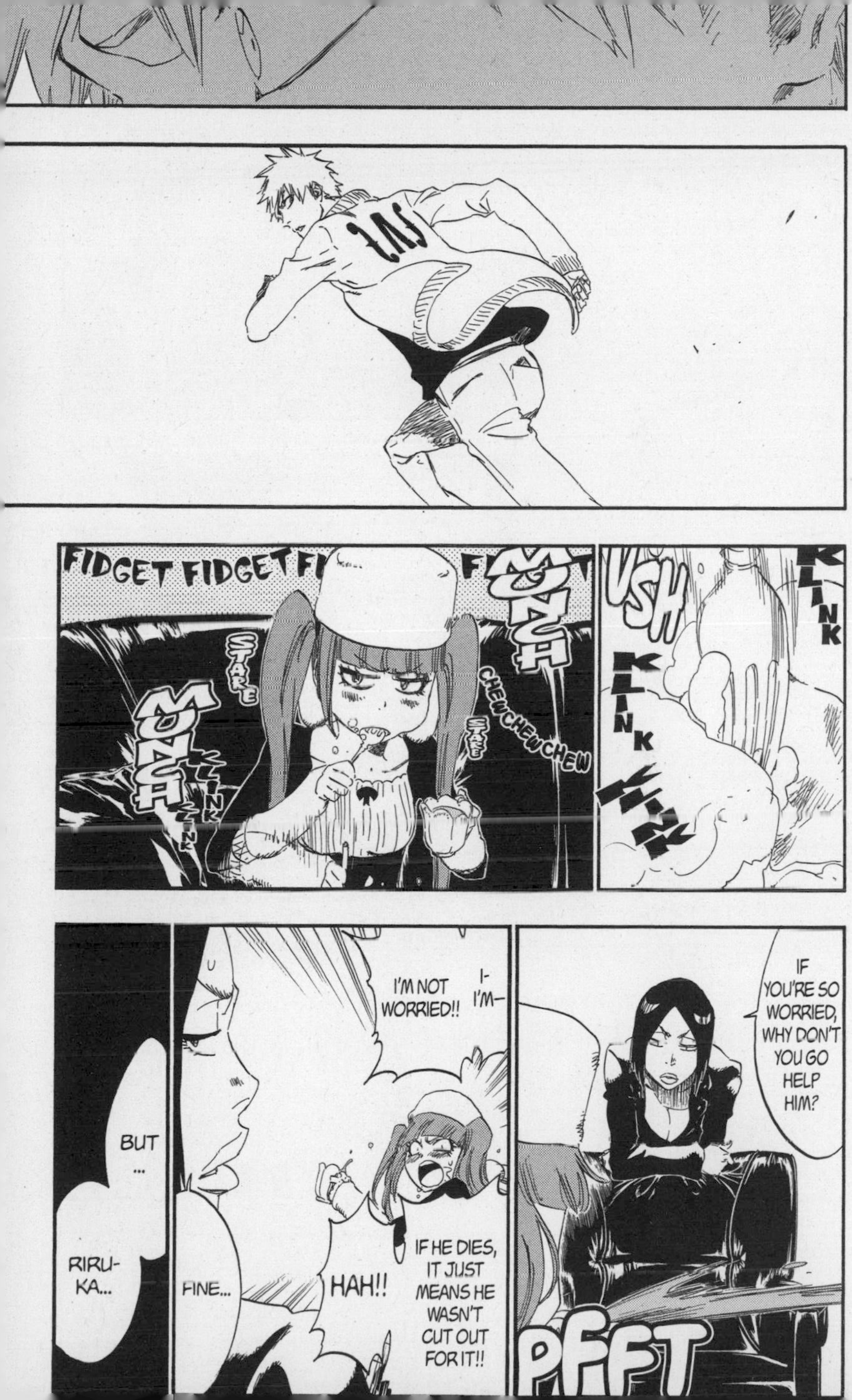
USH
KLINK
KLINK
KLINK
FIDGET FIDGET FI
MUNCH
CHEWCHEWCHEW
STARE
STARE
MUNCH
KLINK
IF YOU'RE SO WORRIED, WHY DON'T YOU GO HELP HIM?
PFFT
I- I'M-
I'M NOT WORRIED!!
IF HE DIES, IT JUST MEANS HE WASN'T CUT OUT FOR IT!!
HAH!!
FINE...
BUT ...
RIRU-KA...

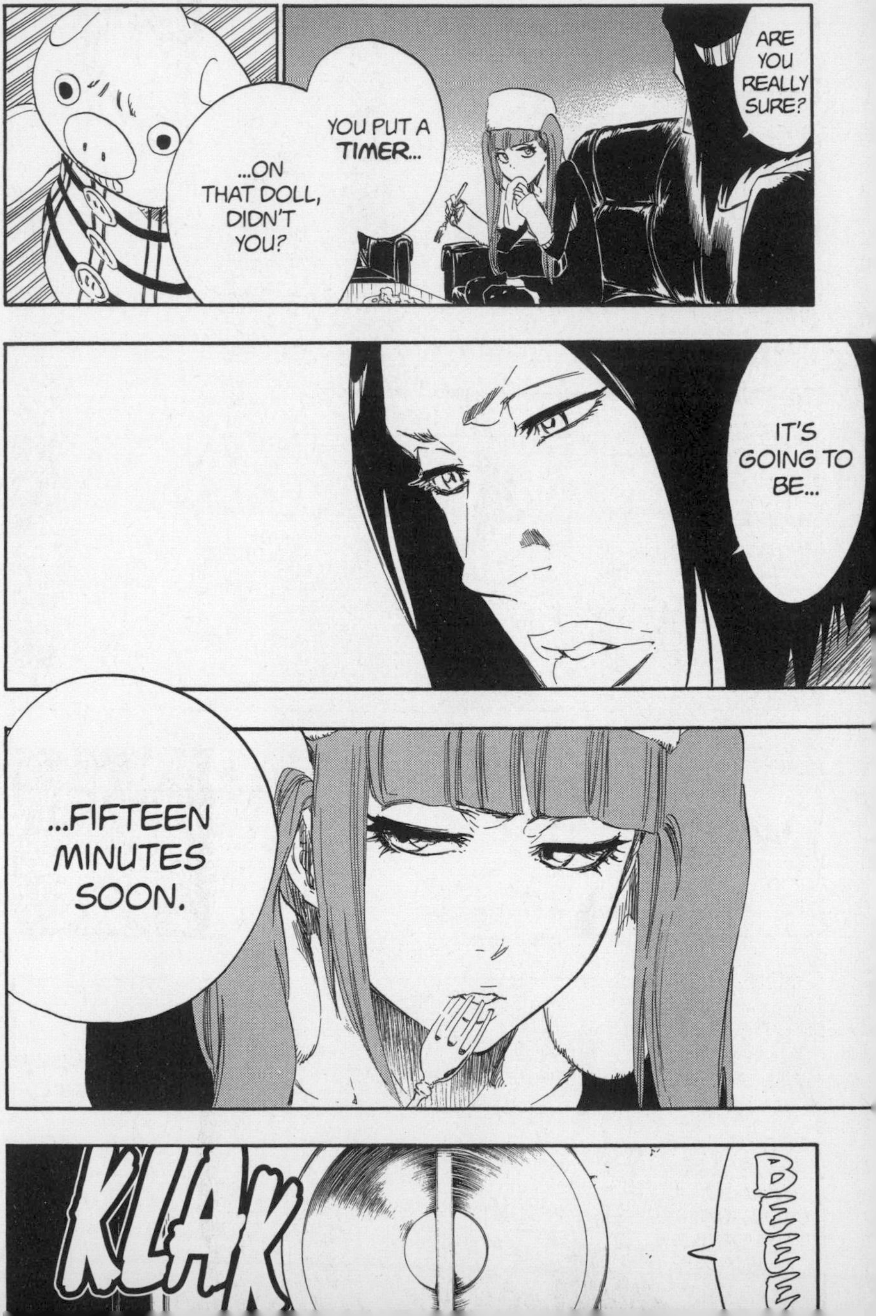
ARE YOU REALLY SURE?
YOU PUT A TIMER...
...ON THAT DOLL, DIDN'T YOU?
IT'S GOING TO BE...
...FIFTEEN MINUTES SOON.
BEEEE
KLAK

READ THIS WAY

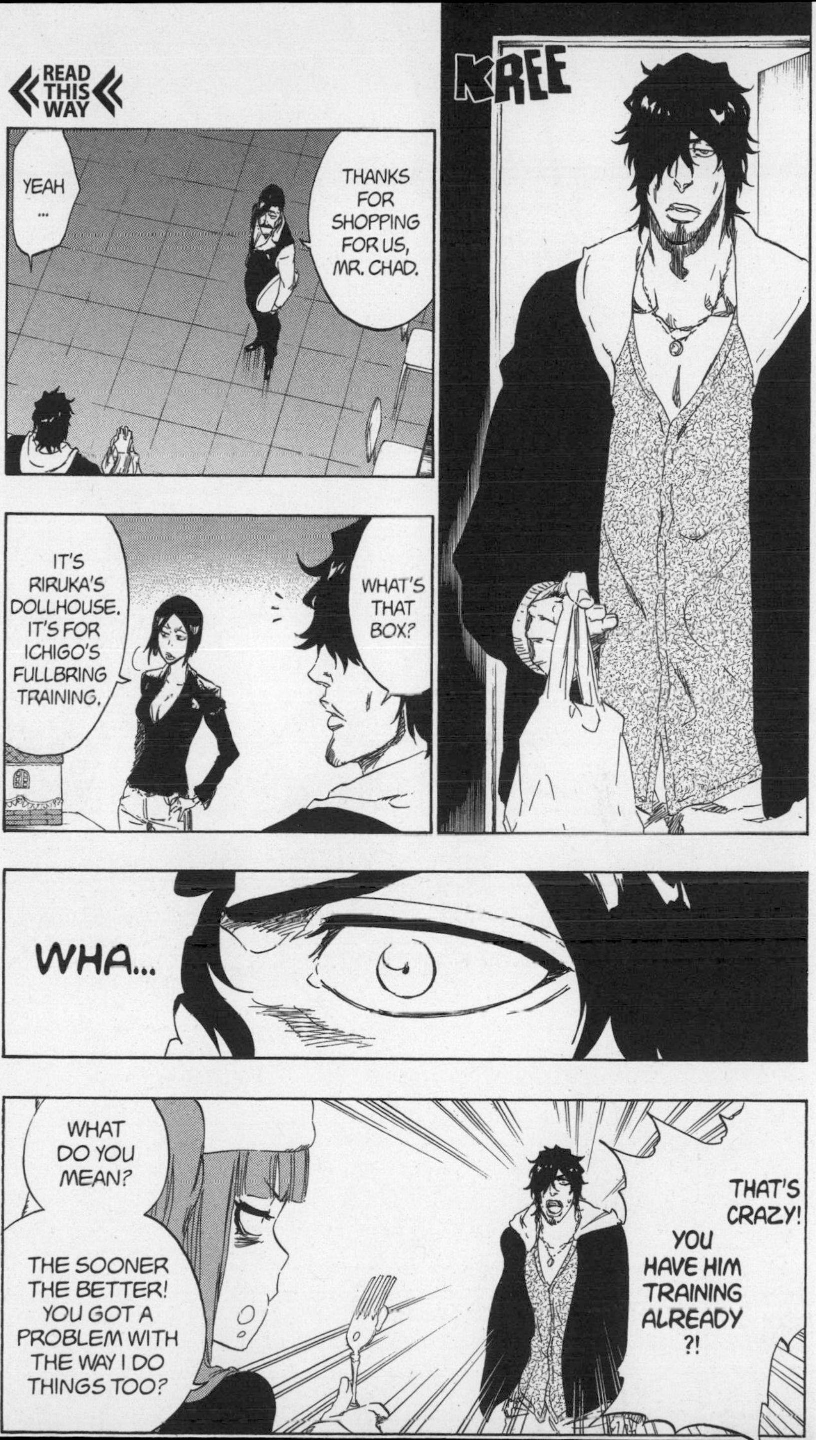
KREE
THANKS FOR SHOPPING FOR US, MR. CHAD.
YEAH ...
WHAT'S THAT BOX?
IT'S RIRUKA'S DOLLHOUSE. IT'S FOR ICHIGO'S FULLBRING TRAINING.
WHA...
THAT'S CRAZY!
YOU HAVE HIM TRAINING ALREADY?!
WHAT DO YOU MEAN?
THE SOONER THE BETTER! YOU GOT A PROBLEM WITH THE WAY I DO THINGS TOO?

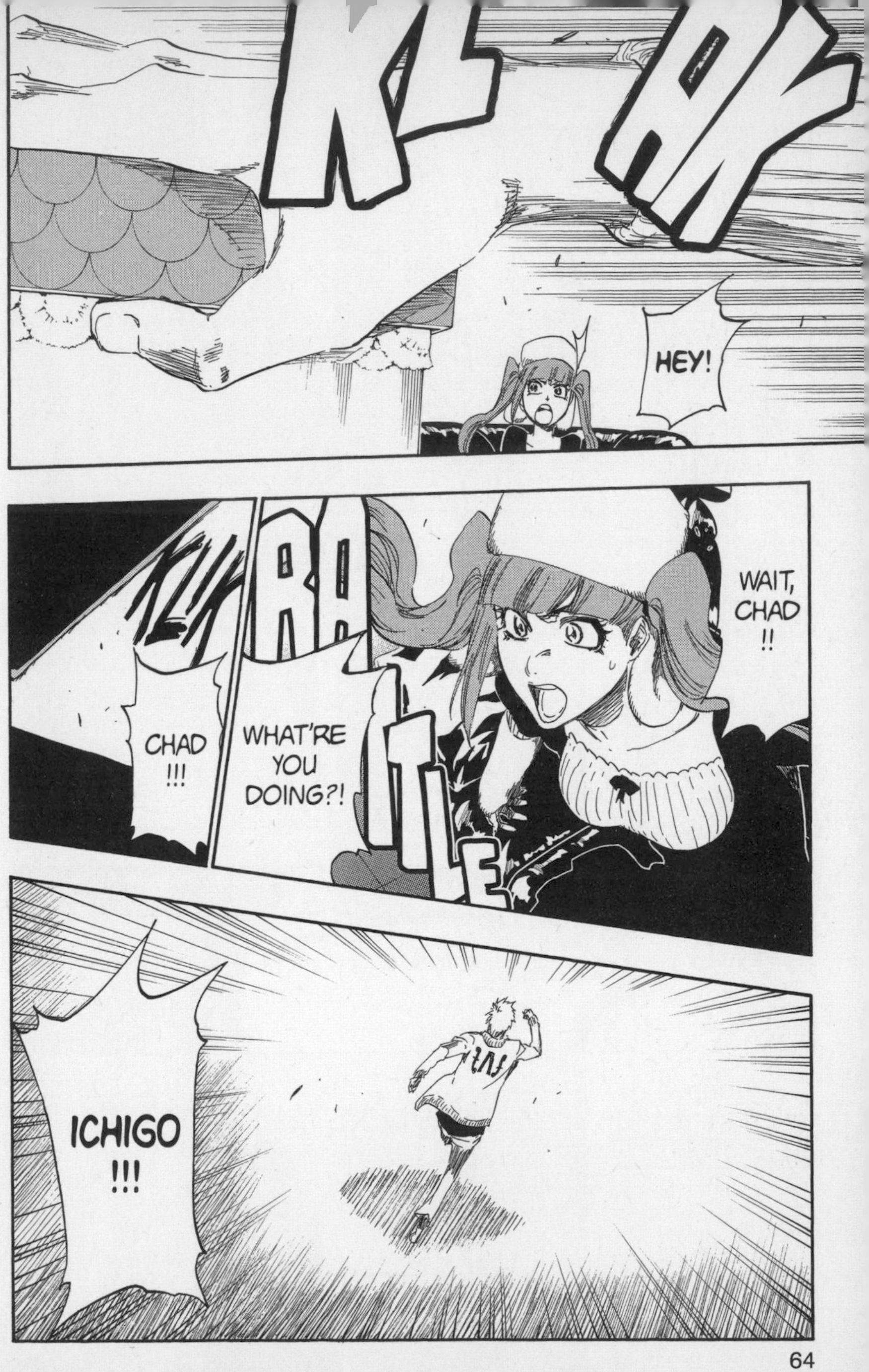
HEY!
WAIT, CHAD !!
WHAT'RE YOU DOING?!
CHAD !!!
ICHIGO !!!

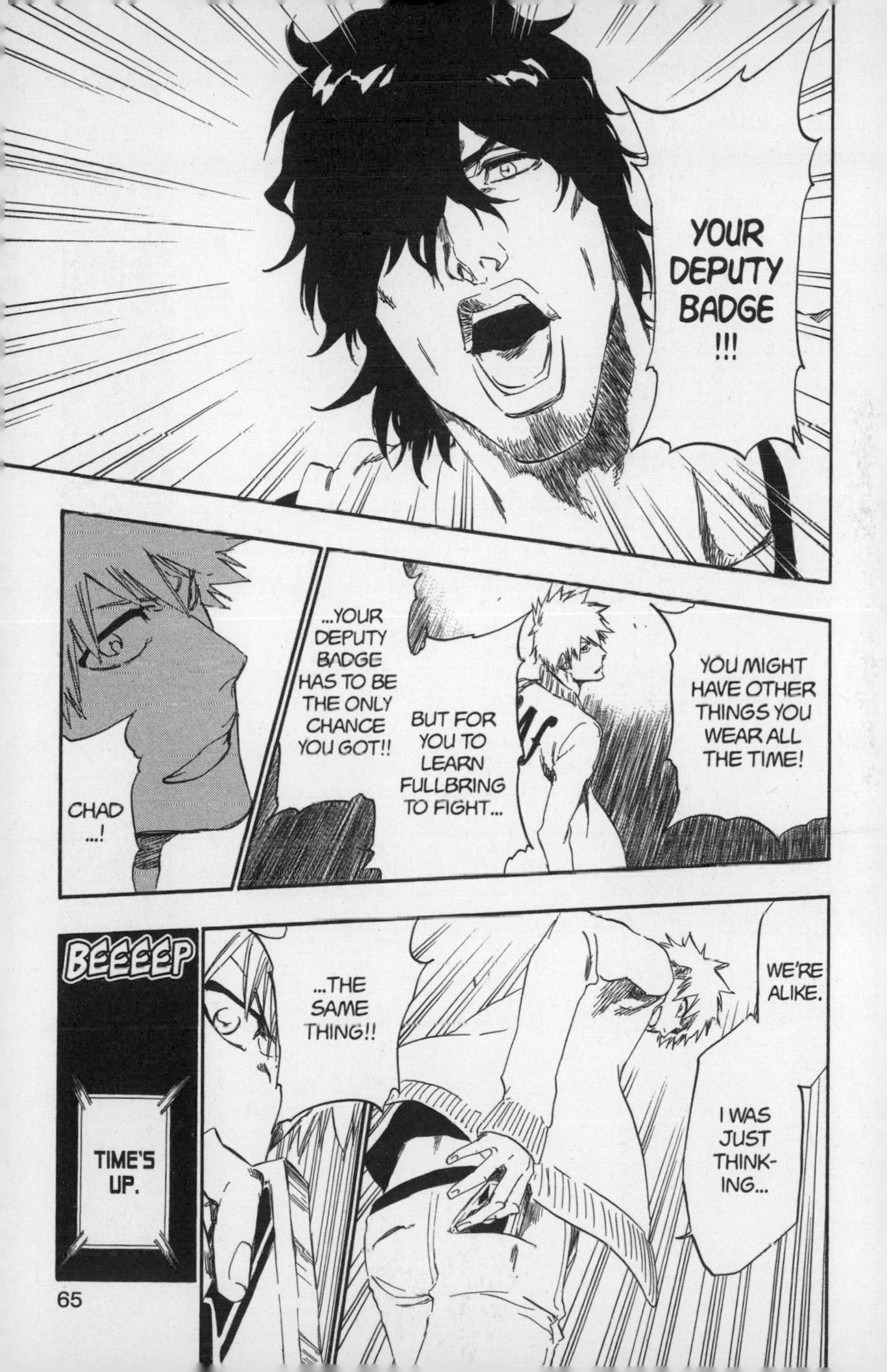
YOUR DEPUTY BADGE!!!
YOU MIGHT HAVE OTHER THINGS YOU WEAR ALL THE TIME!
BUT FOR YOU TO LEARN FULLBRING TO FIGHT...
...YOUR DEPUTY BADGE HAS TO BE THE ONLY CHANCE YOU GOT!!
CHAD ...!
WE'RE ALIKE.
I WAS JUST THINK-ING...
...THE SAME THING!!
BEEEEEP
TIME'S UP.

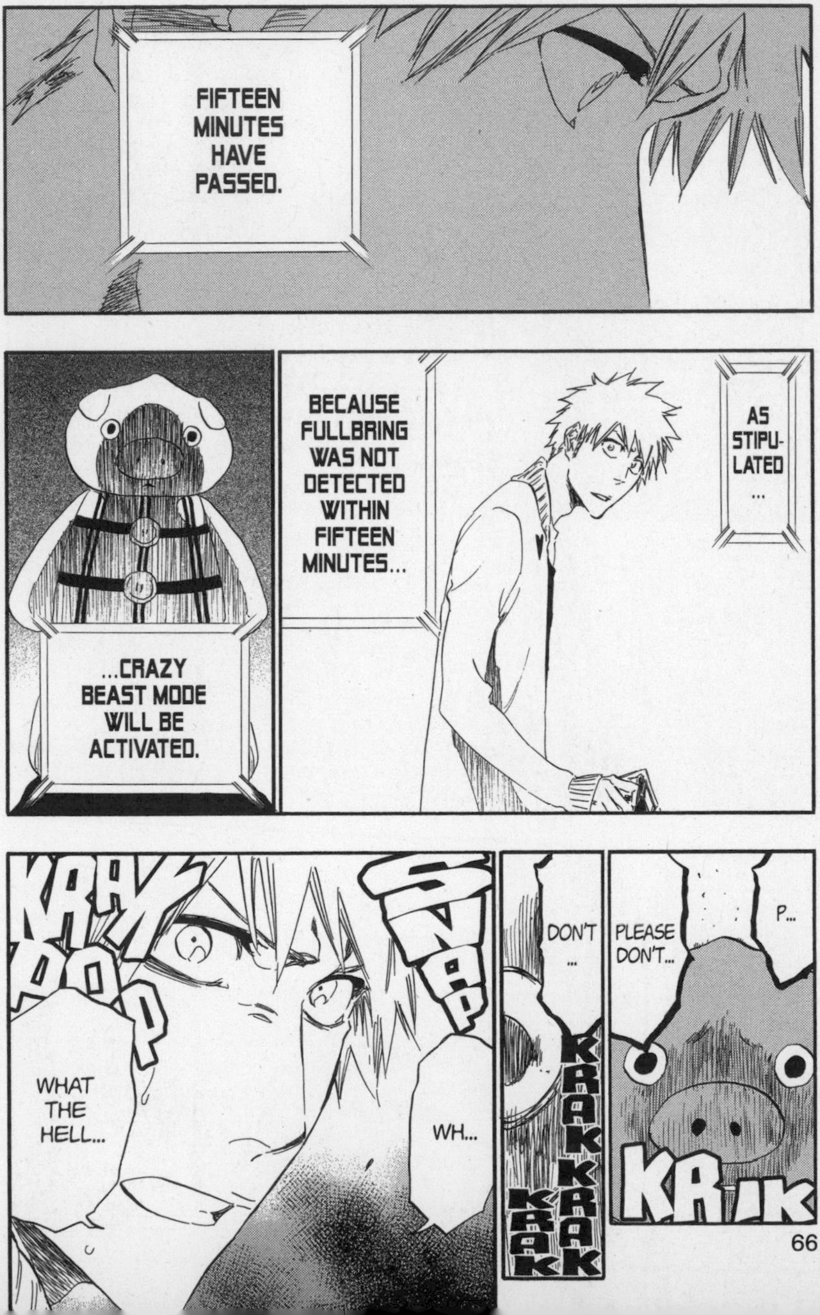
FIFTEEN MINUTES HAVE PASSED.
AS STIPULATED...
BECAUSE FULLBRING WAS NOT DETECTED WITHIN FIFTEEN MINUTES...
...CRAZY BEAST MODE WILL BE ACTIVATED.
P...
PLEASE DON'T...
KRIK
DON'T...
KRAK KRAK KRAK
SNAP
KRAK
POP
WH...
WHAT THE HELL...

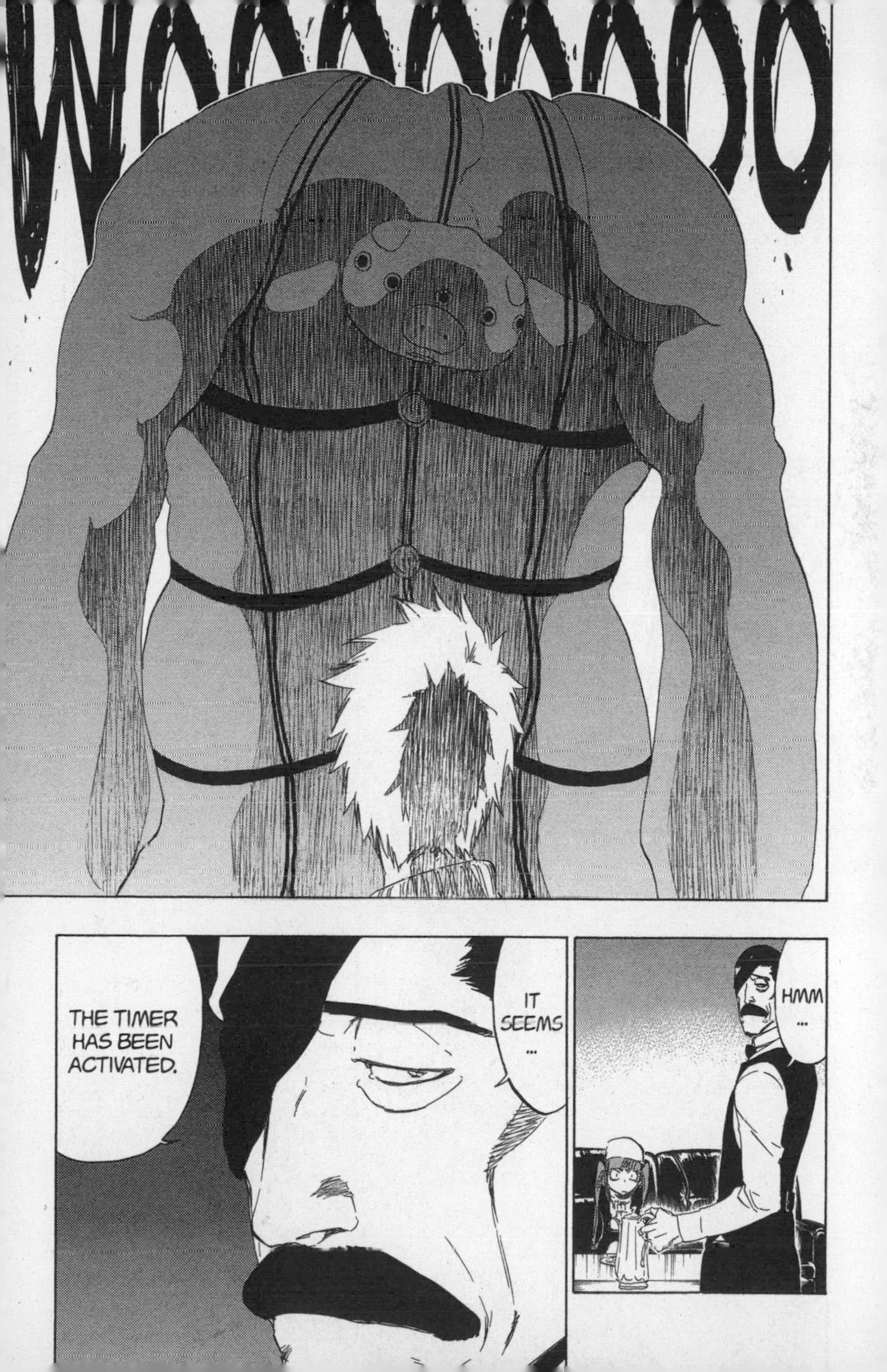
HMM ...
IT SEEMS ...
THE TIMER HAS BEEN ACTIVATED.

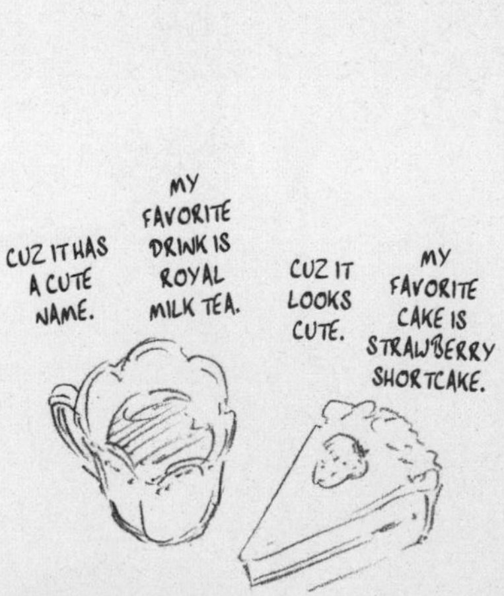
MY FAVORITE CAKE IS STRAWBERRY SHORTCAKE.
CUZ IT LOOKS CUTE.
MY FAVORITE DRINK IS ROYAL MILK TEA.
CUZ IT HAS A CUTE NAME.

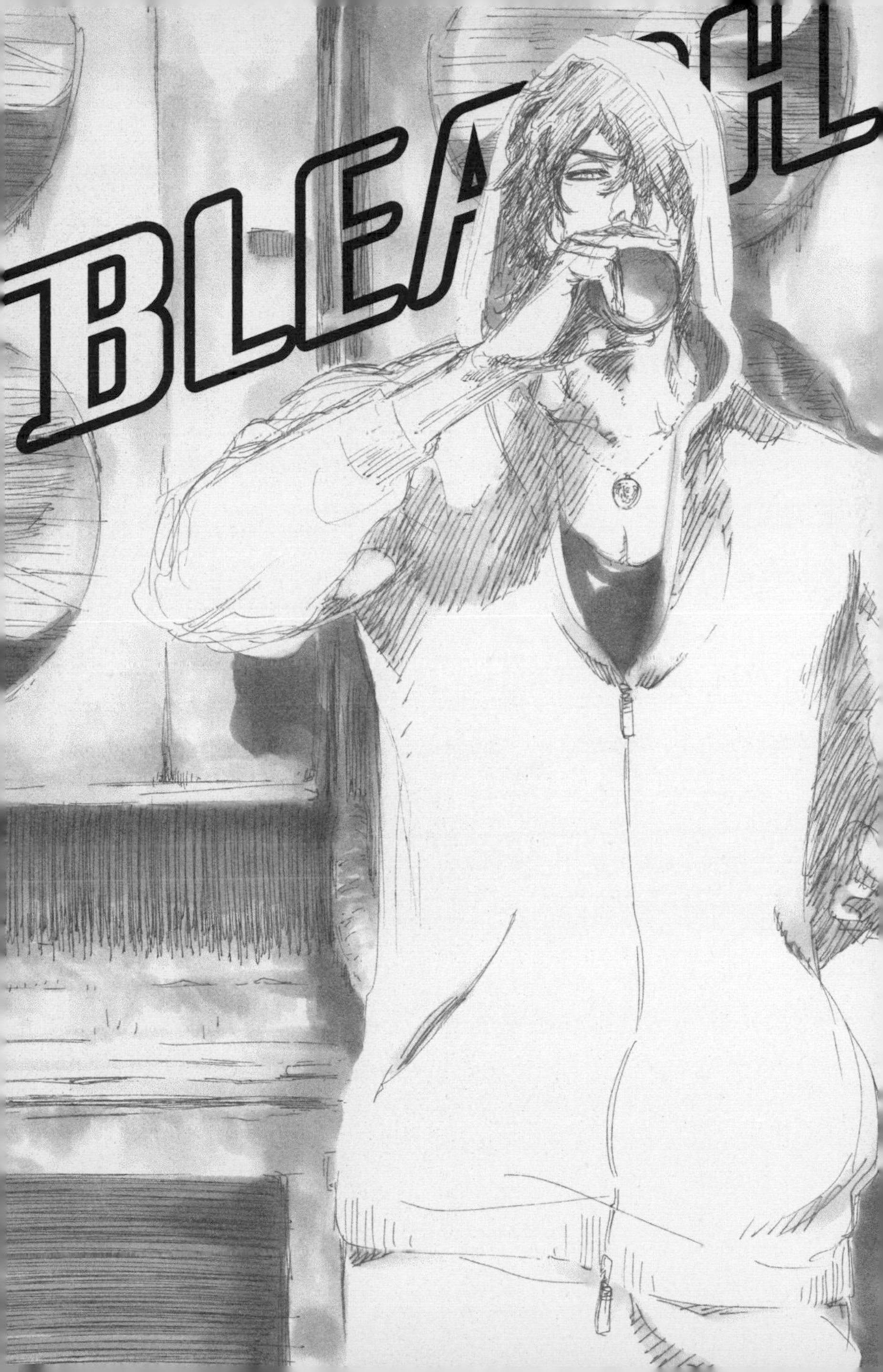

BLEACH
ブリーチ

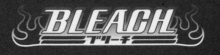

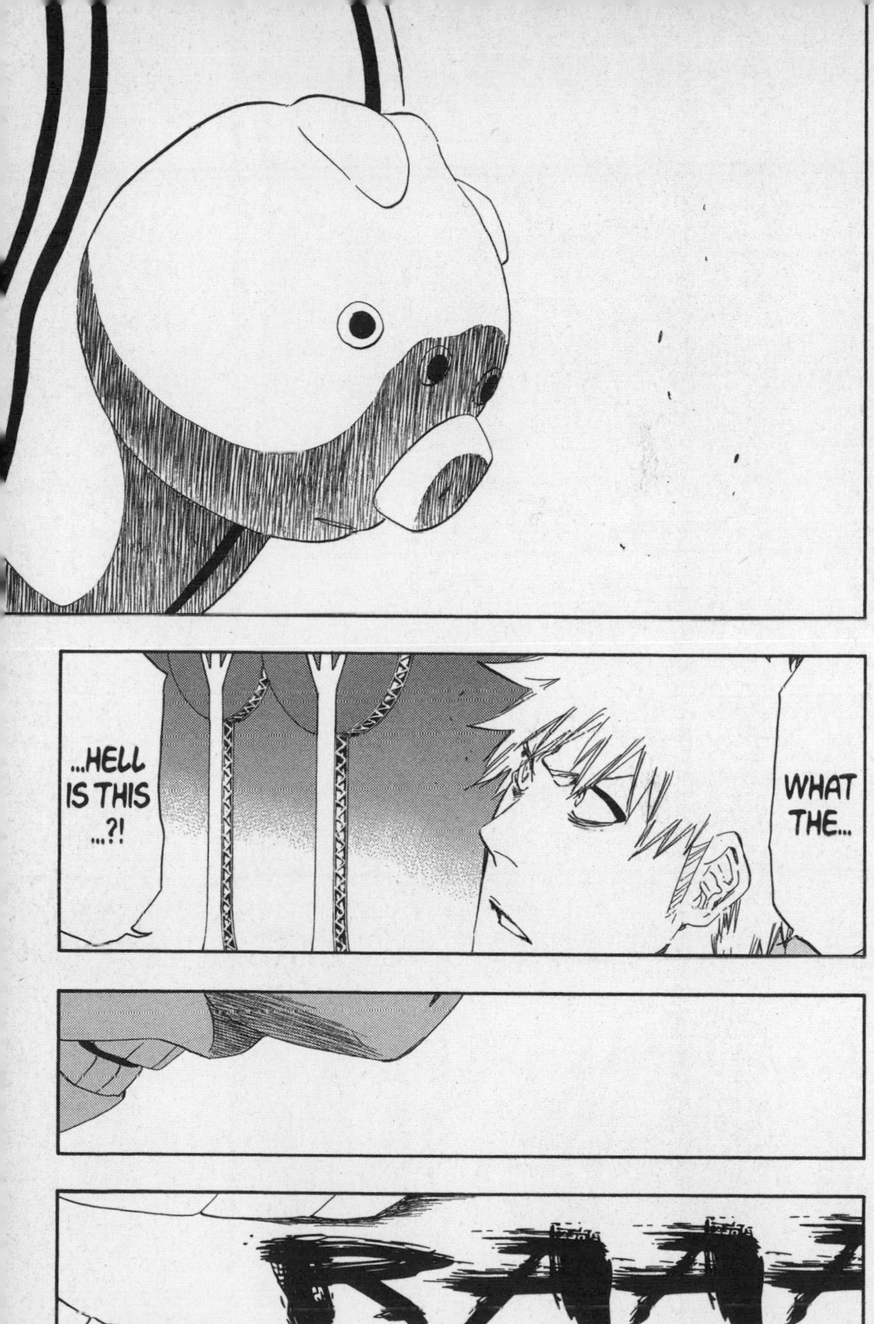
WHAT THE...
...HELL IS THIS ...?!

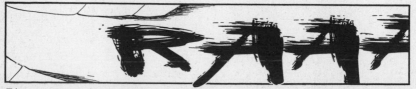

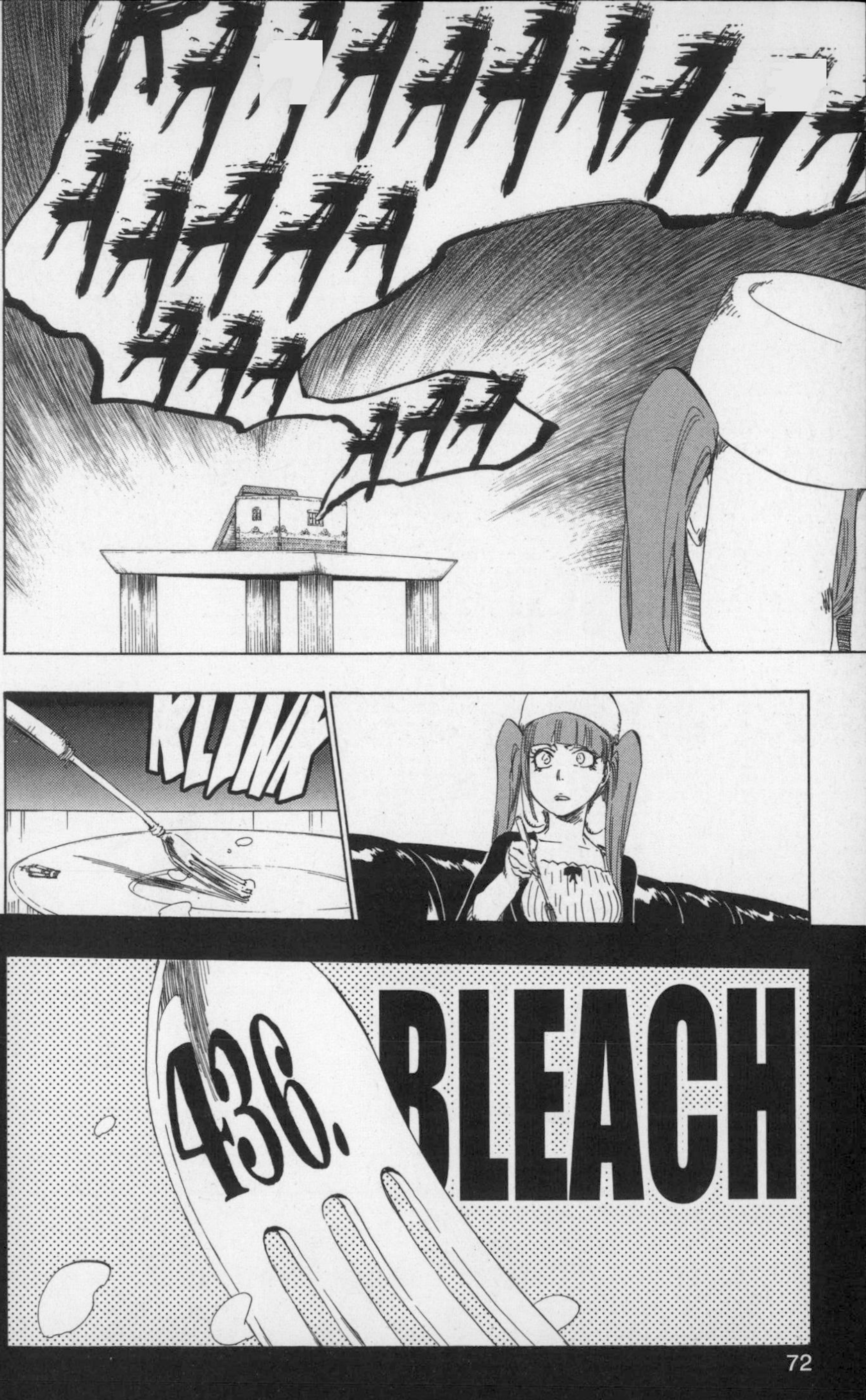
KRAAAAAAAAAAAAAAAAAAAAAAA
KLINK
436.
BLEACH

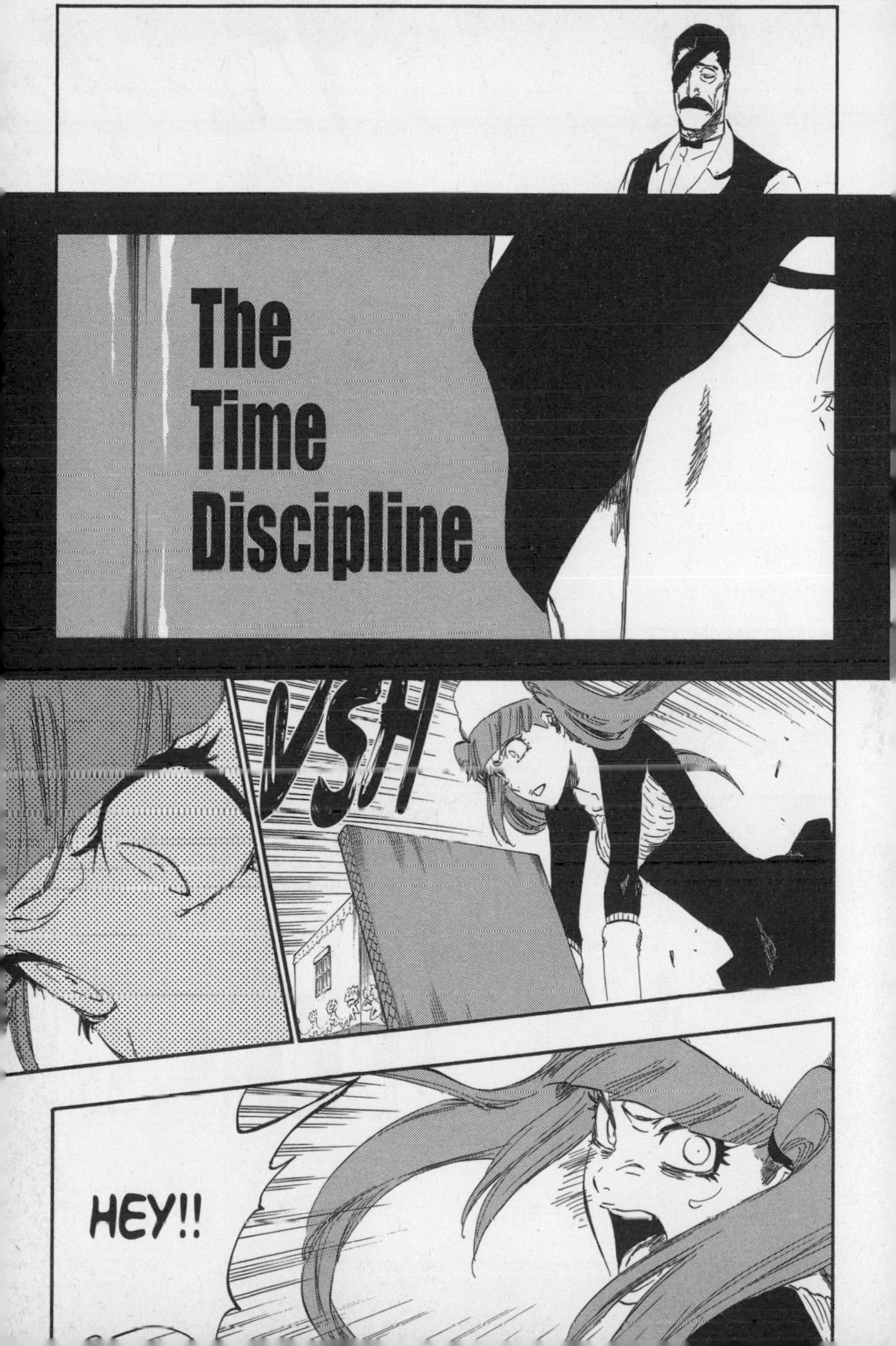

The Time Discipline
VSH
HEY!!

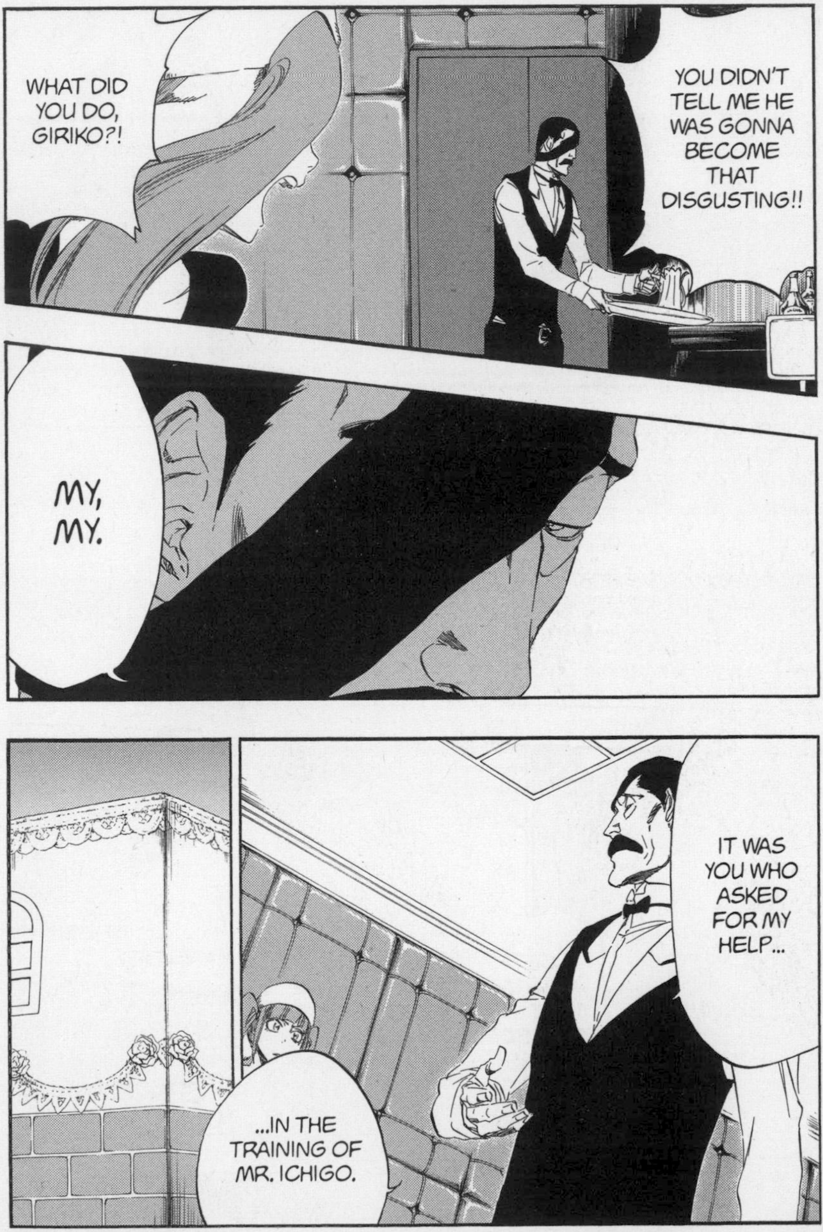
YOU DIDN'T TELL ME HE WAS GONNA BECOME THAT DISGUSTING!!
WHAT DID YOU DO, GIRIKO?!
MY, MY.
IT WAS YOU WHO ASKED FOR MY HELP...
...IN THE TRAINING OF MR. ICHIGO.

READ THIS WAY

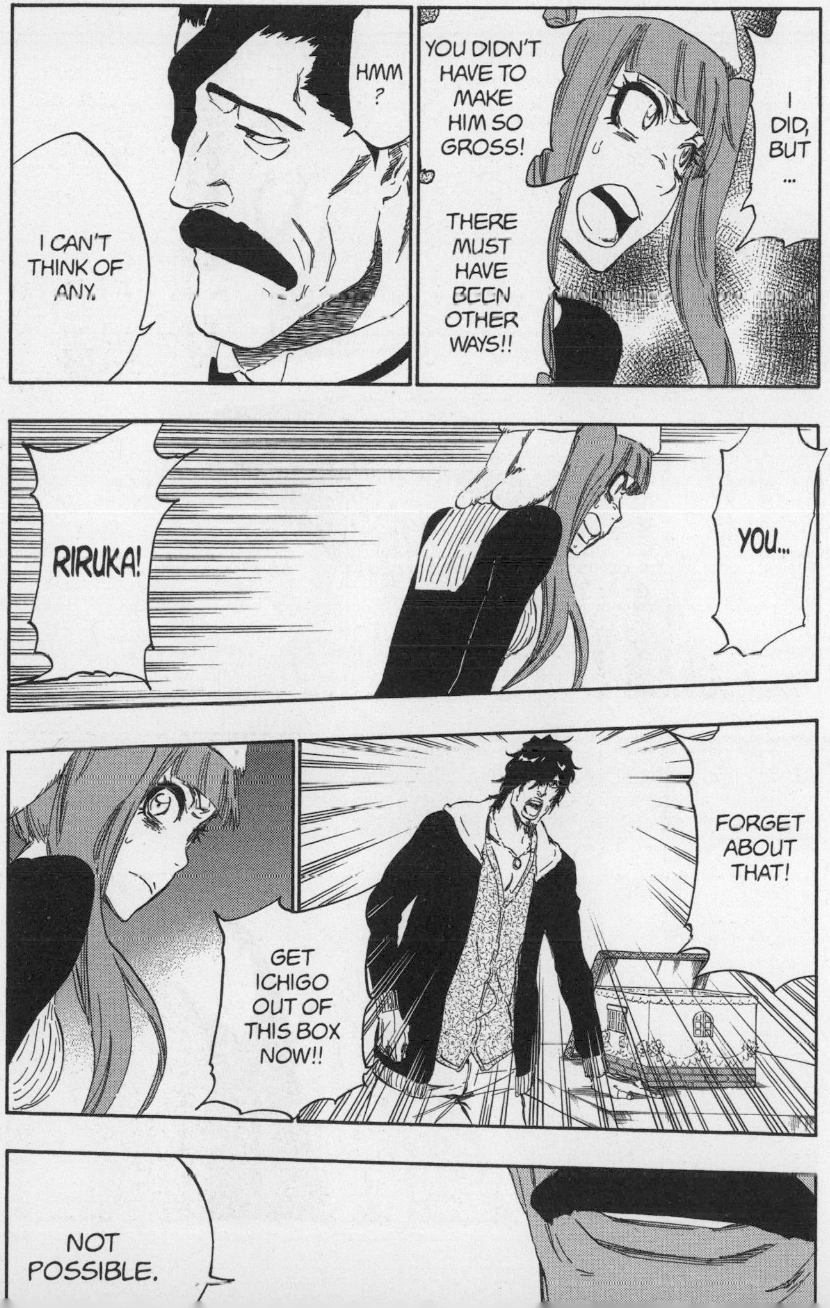
I DID, BUT ...
YOU DIDN'T HAVE TO MAKE HIM SO GROSS!
THERE MUST HAVE BEEN OTHER WAYS!!
HMM?
I CAN'T THINK OF ANY.
YOU...
RIRUKA!
FORGET ABOUT THAT!
GET ICHIGO OUT OF THIS BOX NOW!!
NOT POSSIBLE.

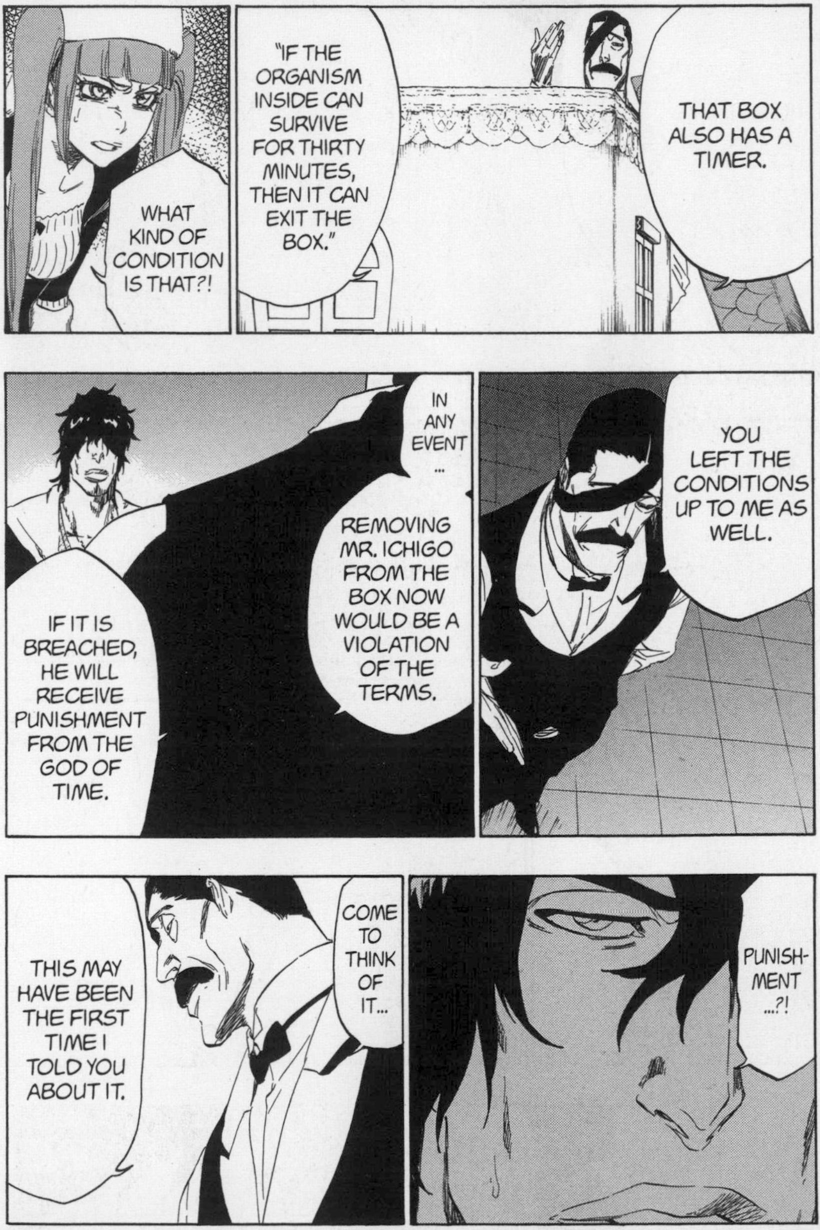
THAT BOX ALSO HAS A TIMER.
"IF THE ORGANISM INSIDE CAN SURVIVE FOR THIRTY MINUTES, THEN IT CAN EXIT THE BOX."
WHAT KIND OF CONDITION IS THAT?!
YOU LEFT THE CONDITIONS UP TO ME AS WELL.
IN ANY EVENT ...
REMOVING MR. ICHIGO FROM THE BOX NOW WOULD BE A VIOLATION OF THE TERMS.
IF IT IS BREACHED, HE WILL RECEIVE PUNISHMENT FROM THE GOD OF TIME.
PUNISH-MENT ...?!
COME TO THINK OF IT...
THIS MAY HAVE BEEN THE FIRST TIME I TOLD YOU ABOUT IT.

READ THIS WAY

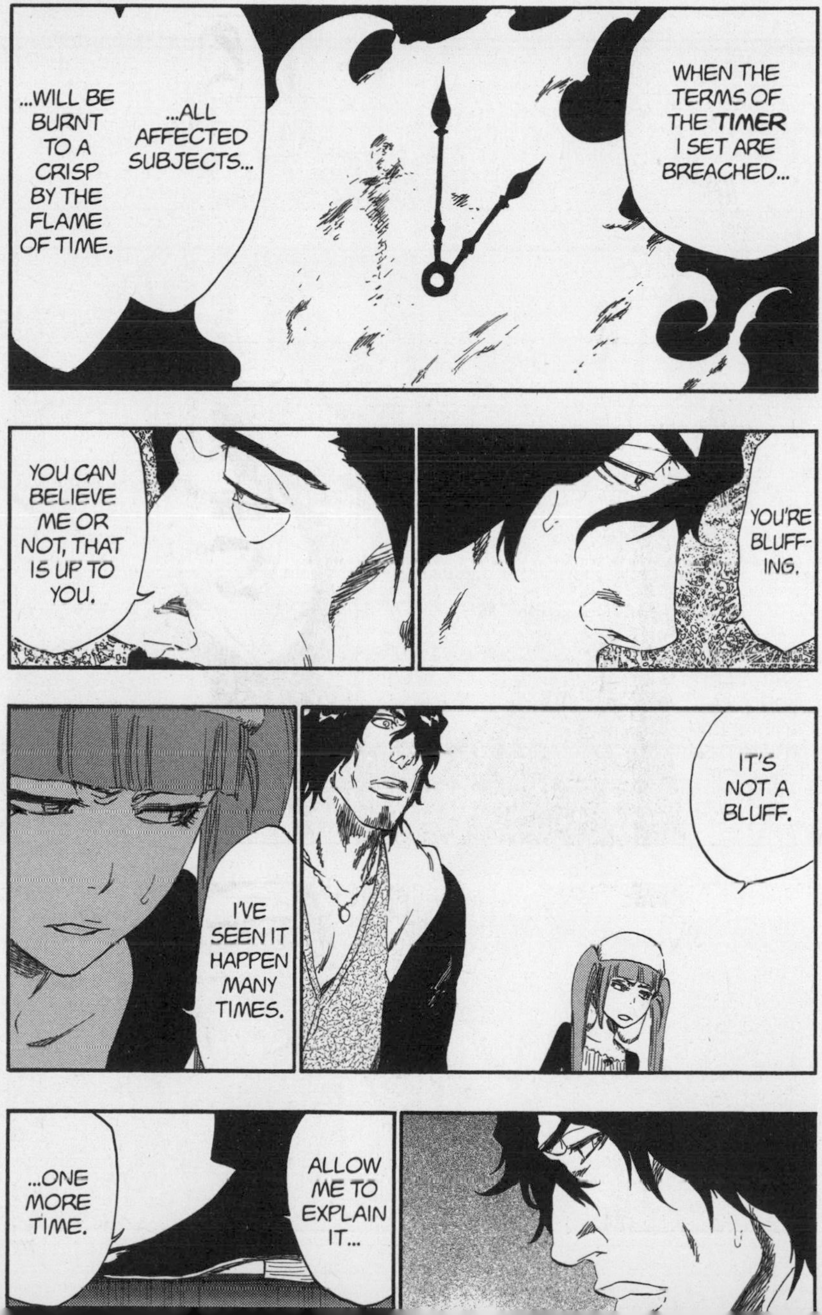
WHEN THE TERMS OF THE **TIMER** I SET ARE BREACHED...
...ALL AFFECTED SUBJECTS...
...WILL BE BURNT TO A CRISP BY THE FLAME OF TIME.
YOU'RE BLUFF-ING.
YOU CAN BELIEVE ME OR NOT, THAT IS UP TO YOU.
IT'S NOT A BLUFF.
I'VE SEEN IT HAPPEN MANY TIMES.
ALLOW ME TO EXPLAIN IT...
...ONE MORE TIME.

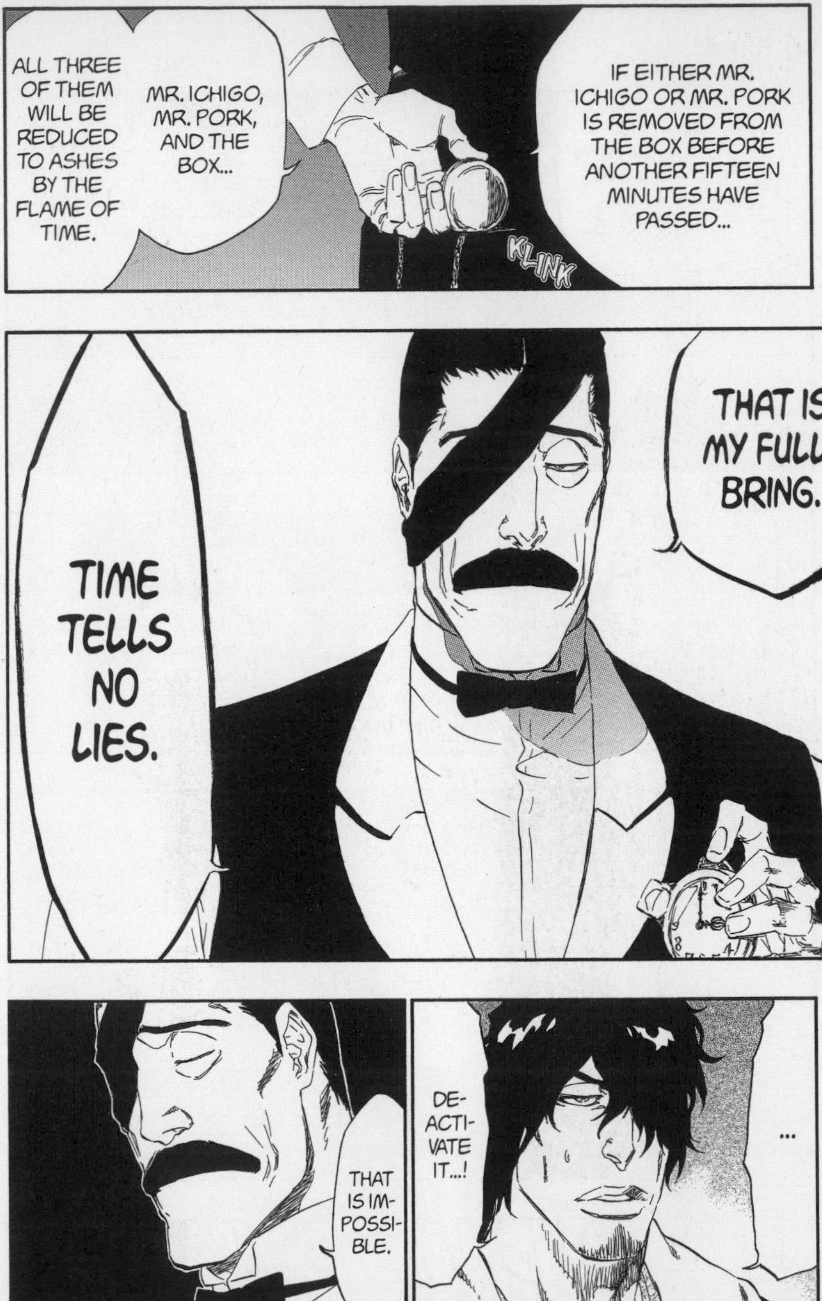
IF EITHER MR. ICHIGO OR MR. PORK IS REMOVED FROM THE BOX BEFORE ANOTHER FIFTEEN MINUTES HAVE PASSED...
KLINK
MR. ICHIGO, MR. PORK, AND THE BOX...
ALL THREE OF THEM WILL BE REDUCED TO ASHES BY THE FLAME OF TIME.
THAT IS MY FULL-BRING.
TIME TELLS NO LIES.
...
DE-ACTI-VATE IT...!
THAT IS IM-POSSI-BLE.

READ THIS WAY

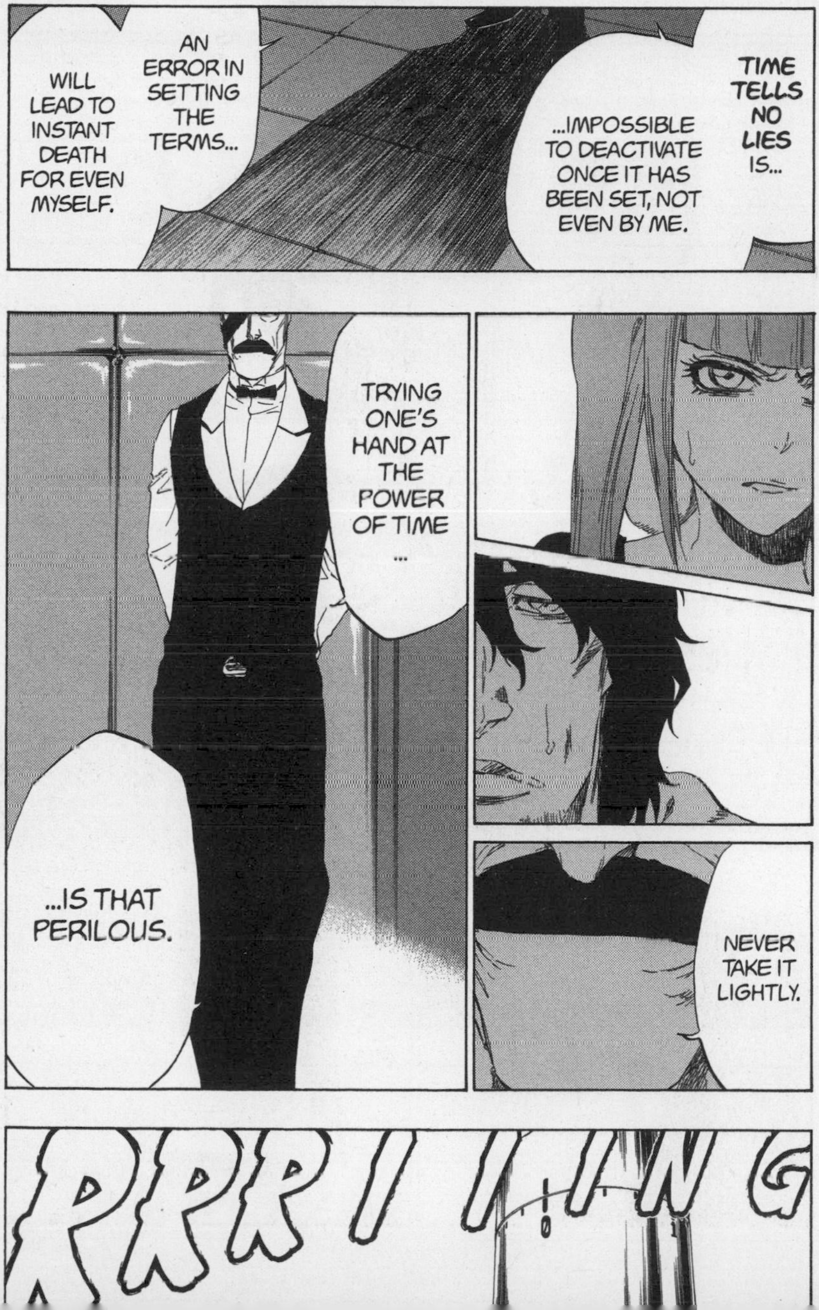
TIME TELLS NO LIES IS...
...IMPOSSIBLE TO DEACTIVATE ONCE IT HAS BEEN SET, NOT EVEN BY ME.
AN ERROR IN SETTING THE TERMS...
WILL LEAD TO INSTANT DEATH FOR EVEN MYSELF.
NEVER TAKE IT LIGHTLY.
TRYING ONE'S HAND AT THE POWER OF TIME ...
...IS THAT PERILOUS.
RRRIIING

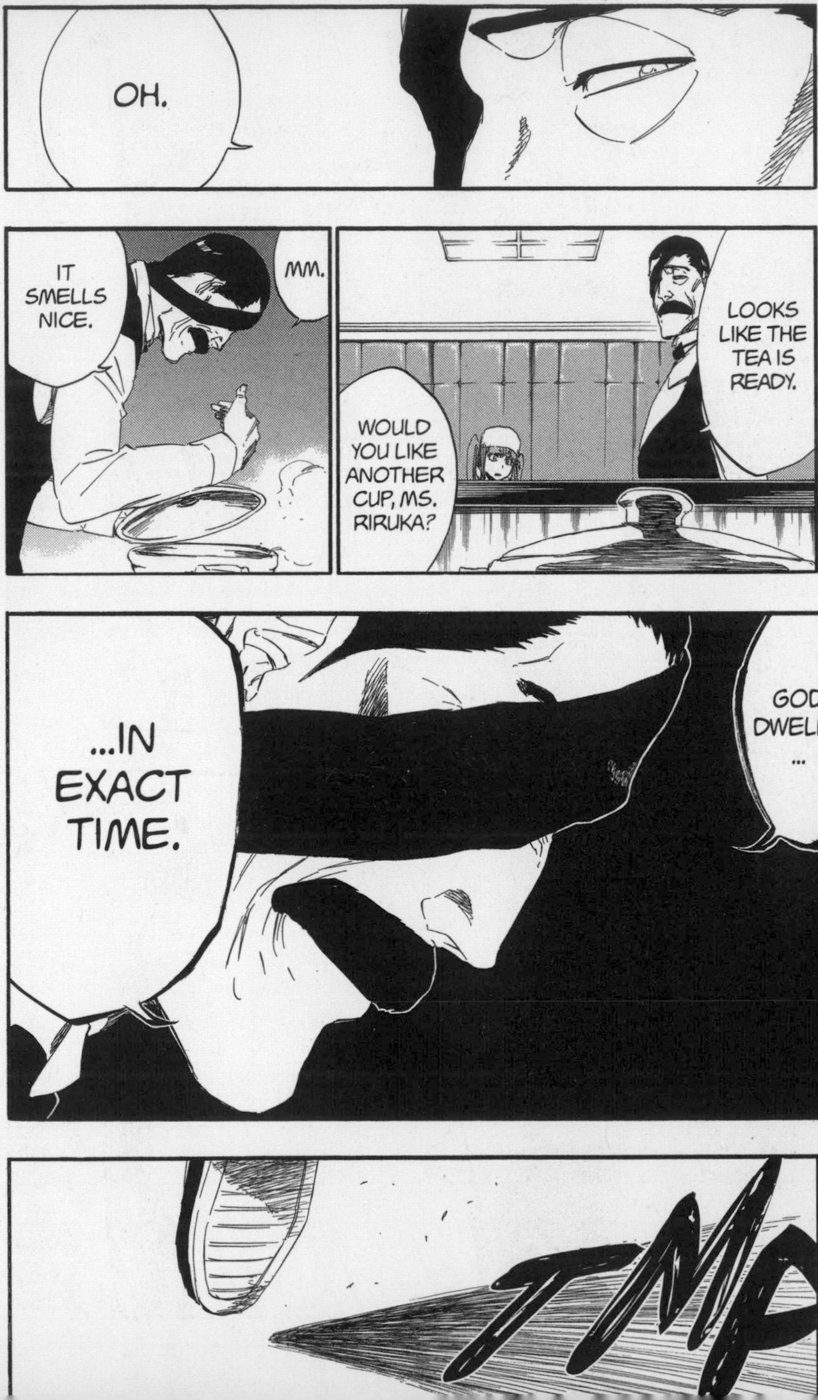
OH.
LOOKS LIKE THE TEA IS READY.
WOULD YOU LIKE ANOTHER CUP, MS. RIRUKA?
MM.
IT SMELLS NICE.
GOD DWELLS ...
...IN EXACT TIME.
TMP

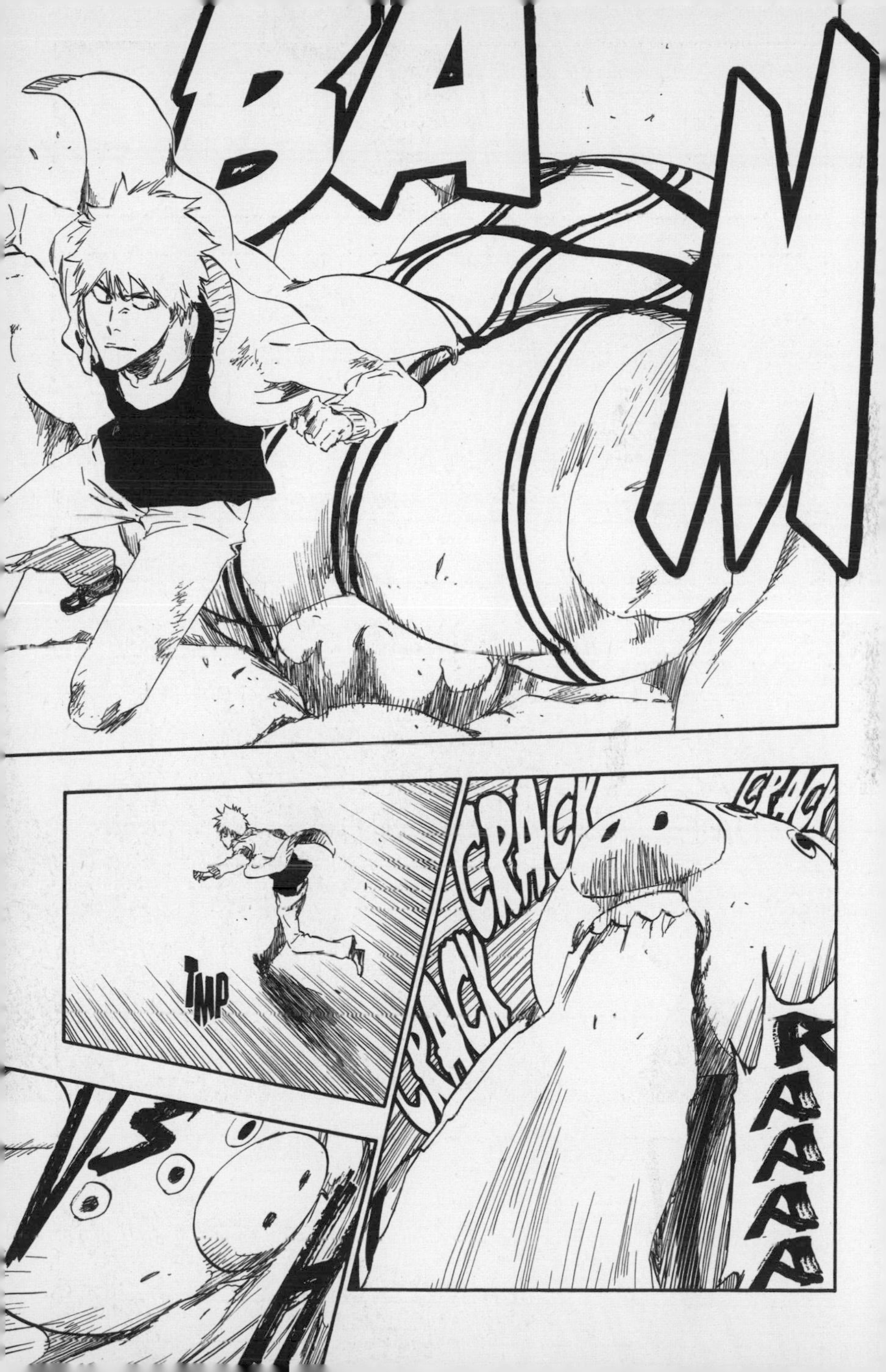
BAM
CRACK
CRACK
CRACK
CRACK
RAAAAA
TMP

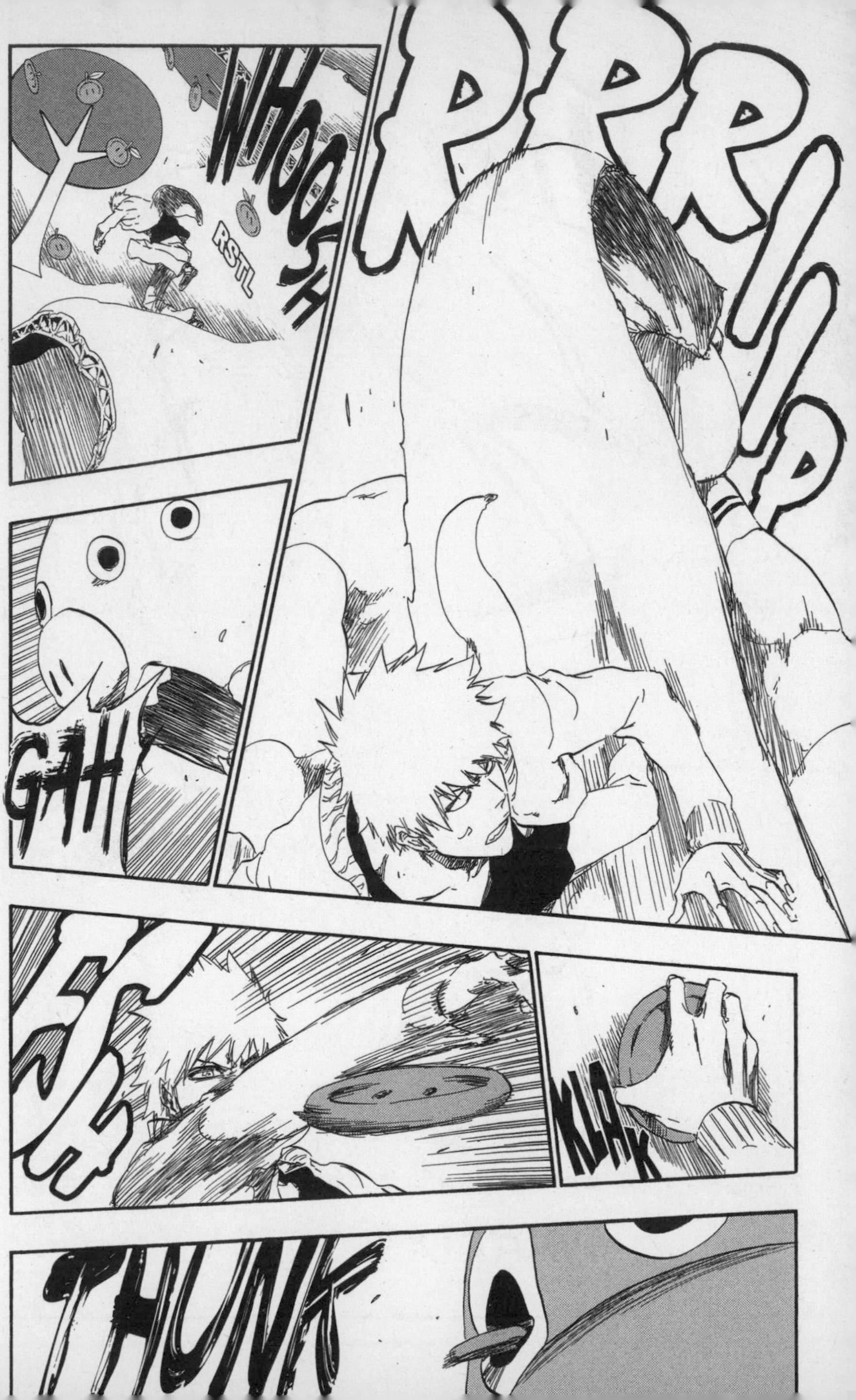
RRRIIP
WHOOSH
RSTL
GAH
KLAK
THUNK

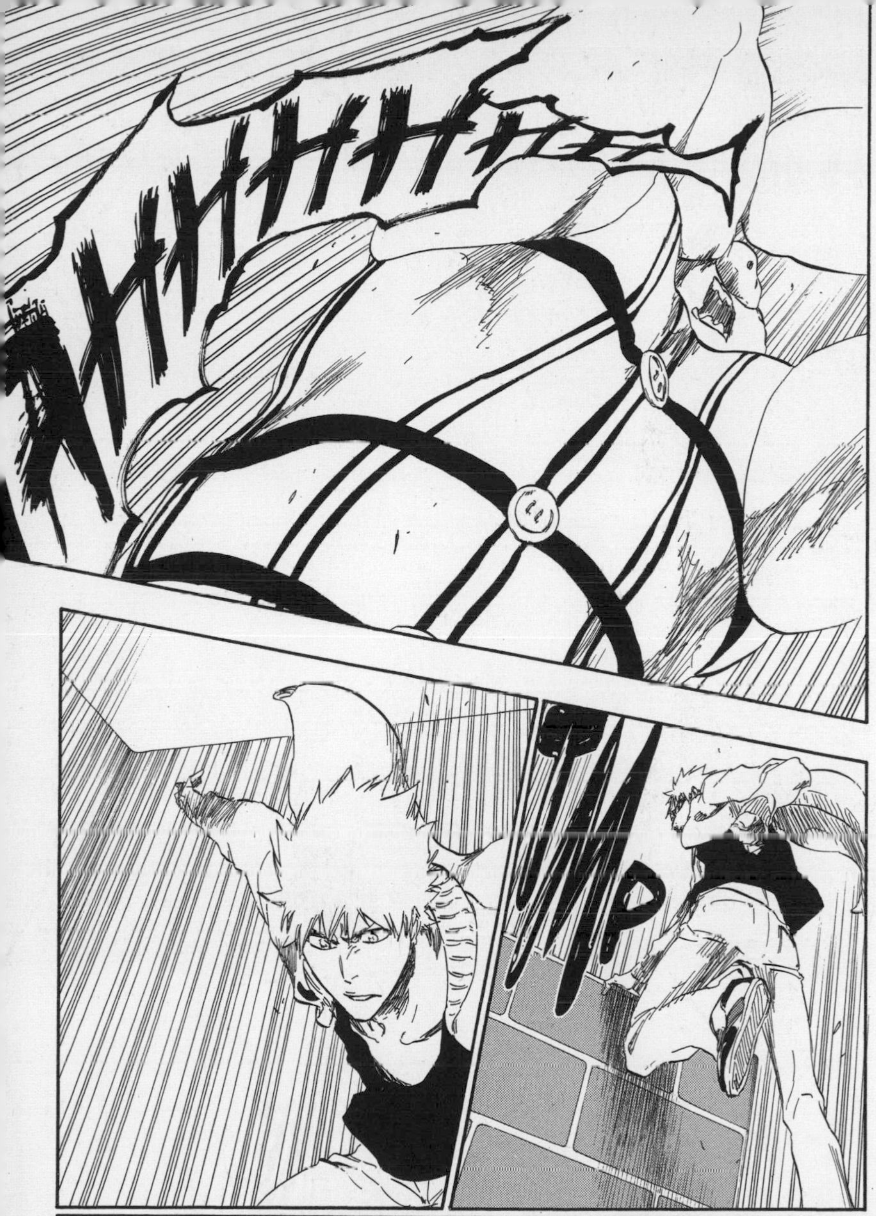
WHAT DO I DO...?

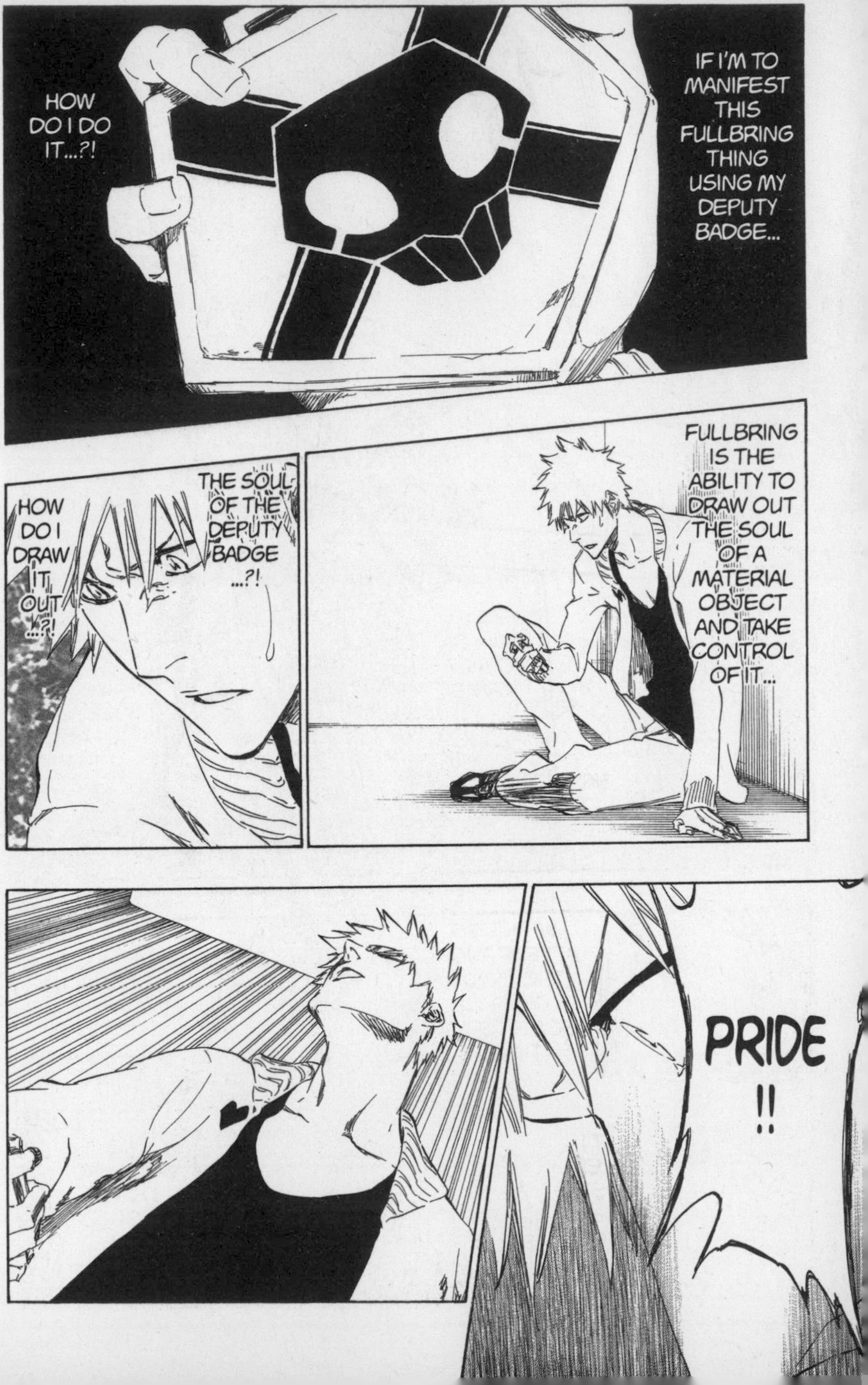
IF I'M TO MANIFEST THIS FULLBRING THING USING MY DEPUTY BADGE...
HOW DO I DO IT...?!
FULLBRING IS THE ABILITY TO DRAW OUT THE SOUL OF A MATERIAL OBJECT AND TAKE CONTROL OF IT...
THE SOUL OF THE DEPUTY BADGE ...?!
HOW DO I DRAW IT OUT ...?!
PRIDE !!

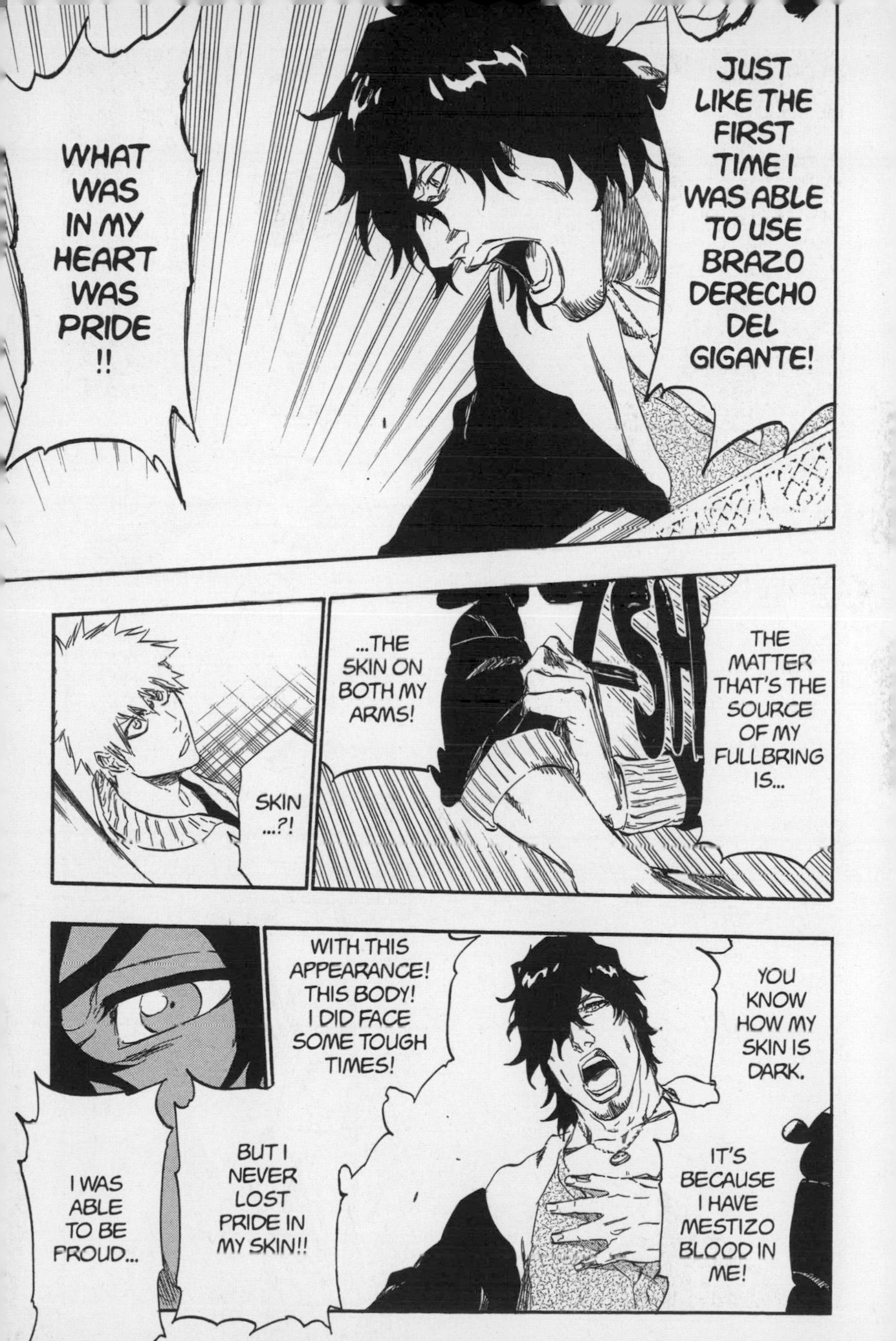
JUST LIKE THE FIRST TIME I WAS ABLE TO USE BRAZO DERECHO DEL GIGANTE!
WHAT WAS IN MY HEART WAS PRIDE !!
THE MATTER THAT'S THE SOURCE OF MY FULLBRING IS...
...THE SKIN ON BOTH MY ARMS!
SKIN ...?!
YOU KNOW HOW MY SKIN IS DARK.
WITH THIS APPEARANCE! THIS BODY! I DID FACE SOME TOUGH TIMES!
IT'S BECAUSE I HAVE MESTIZO BLOOD IN ME!
BUT I NEVER LOST PRIDE IN MY SKIN!!
I WAS ABLE TO BE PROUD...

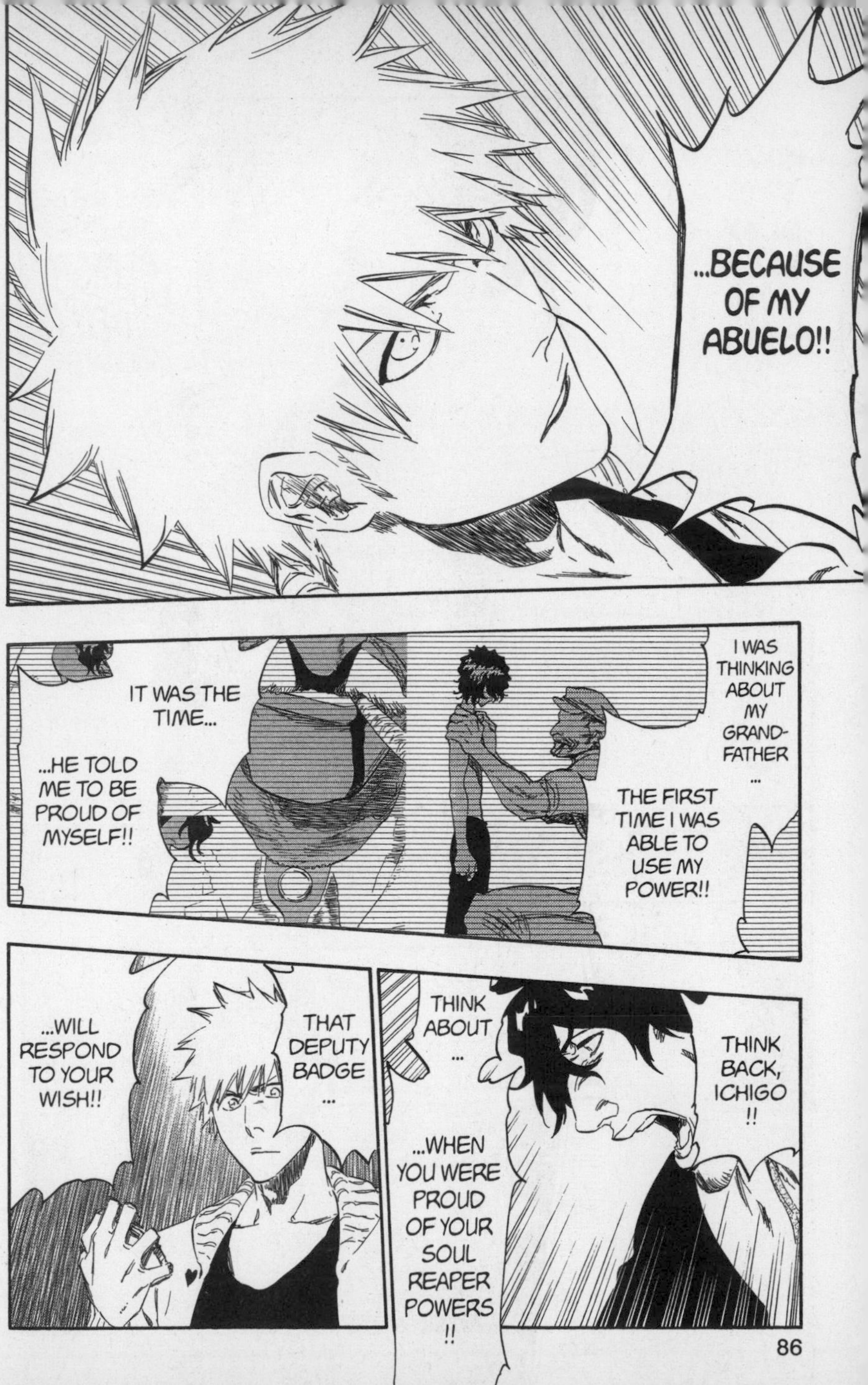
...BECAUSE OF MY ABUELO!!
I WAS THINKING ABOUT MY GRAND-FATHER...
THE FIRST TIME I WAS ABLE TO USE MY POWER!!
IT WAS THE TIME...
...HE TOLD ME TO BE PROUD OF MYSELF!!
THINK BACK, ICHIGO!!
THINK ABOUT...
...WHEN YOU WERE PROUD OF YOUR SOUL REAPER POWERS!!
THAT DEPUTY BADGE...
...WILL RESPOND TO YOUR WISH!!

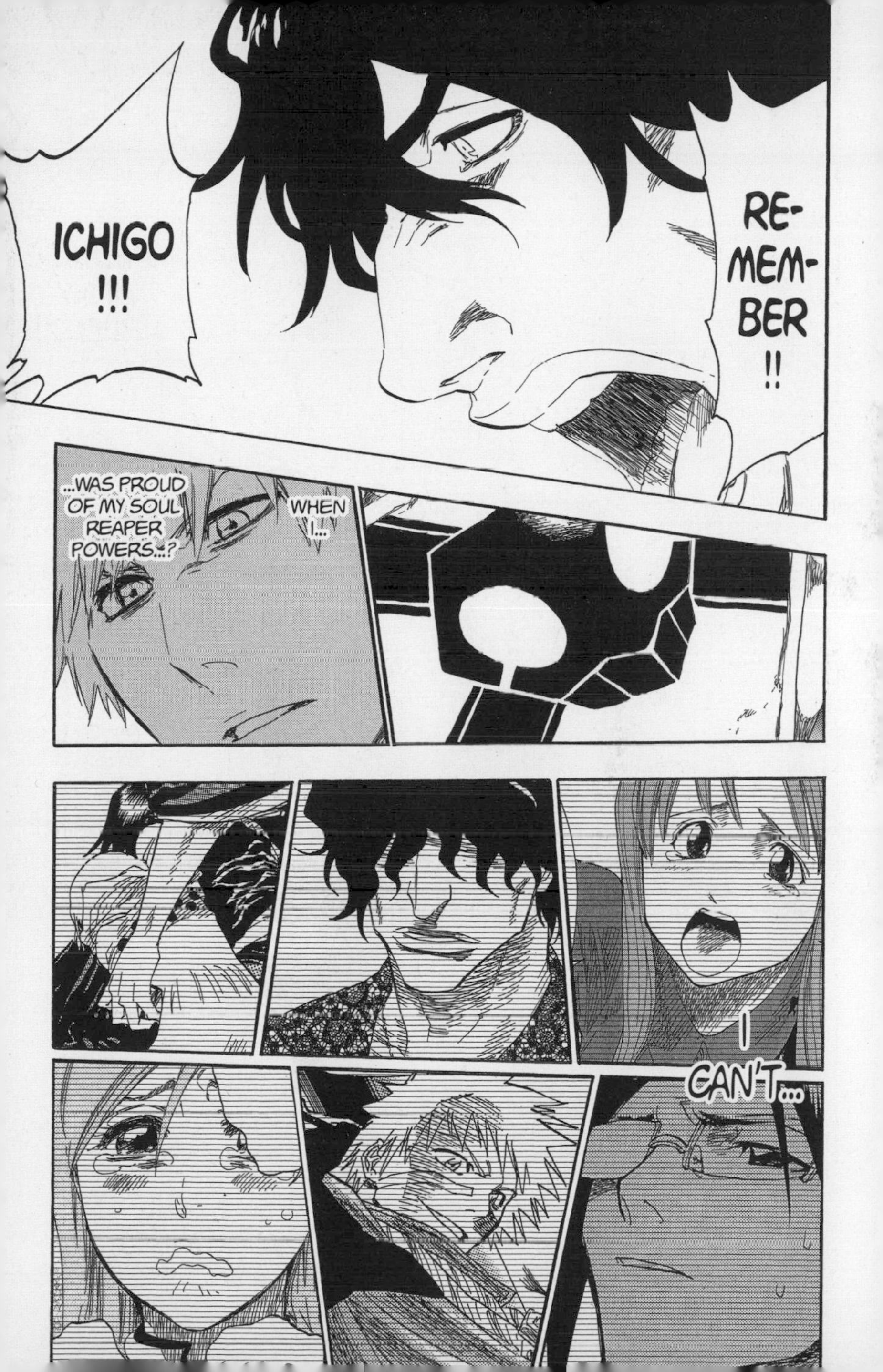
RE-MEM-BER!!
ICHIGO!!!
WHEN I...
...WAS PROUD OF MY SOUL REAPER POWERS...?
I CAN'T...

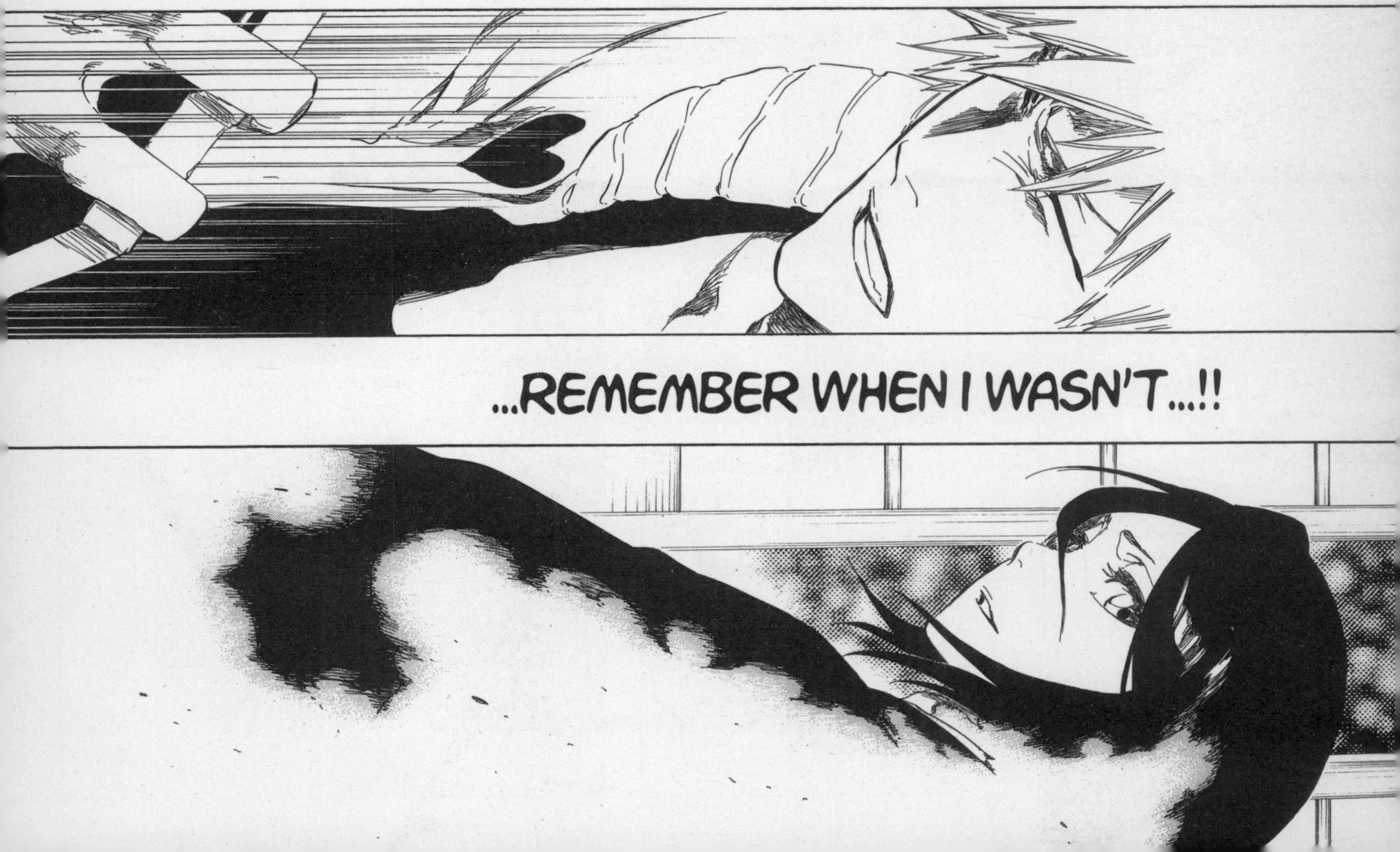
...REMEMBER WHEN I WASN'T...!!

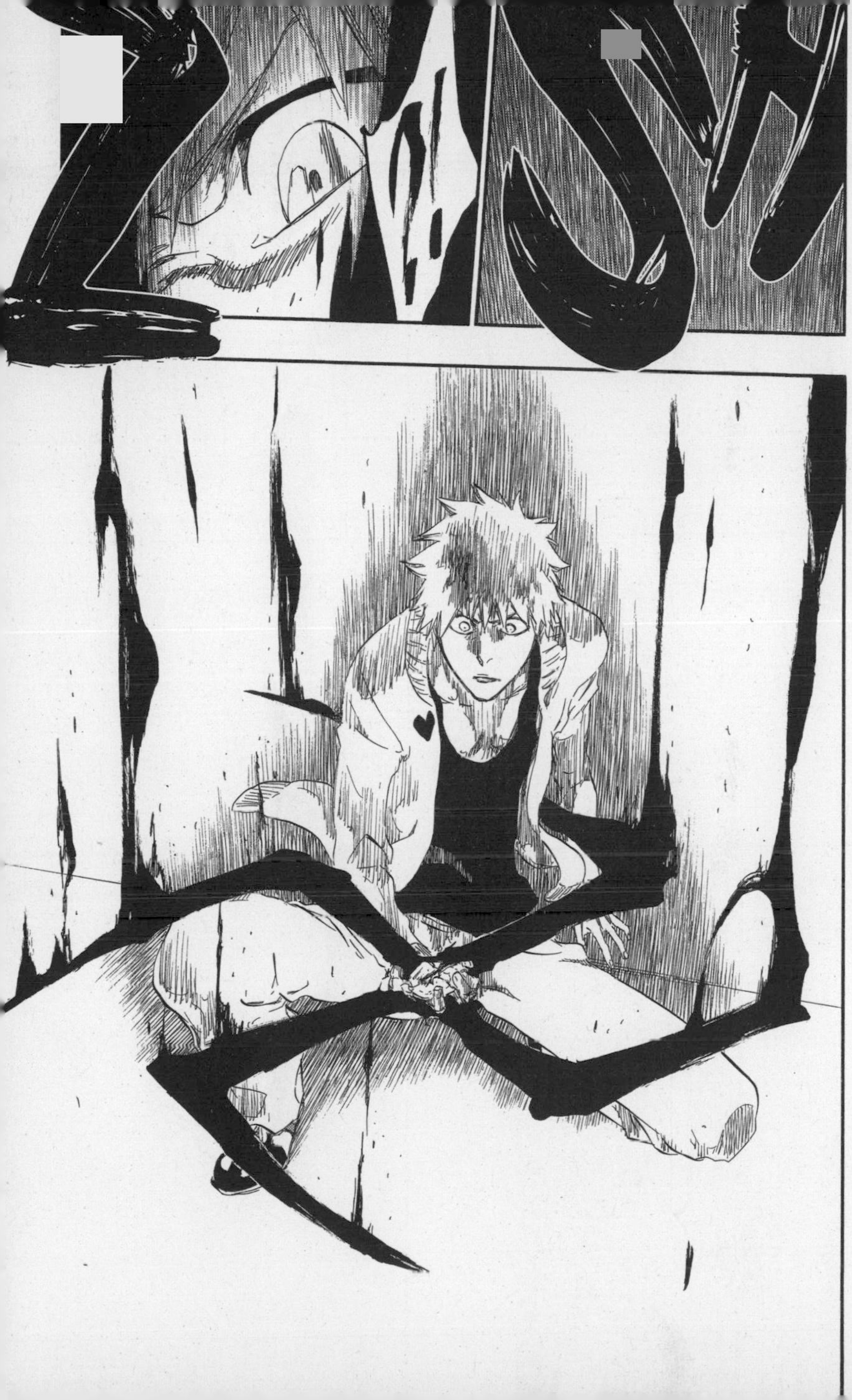

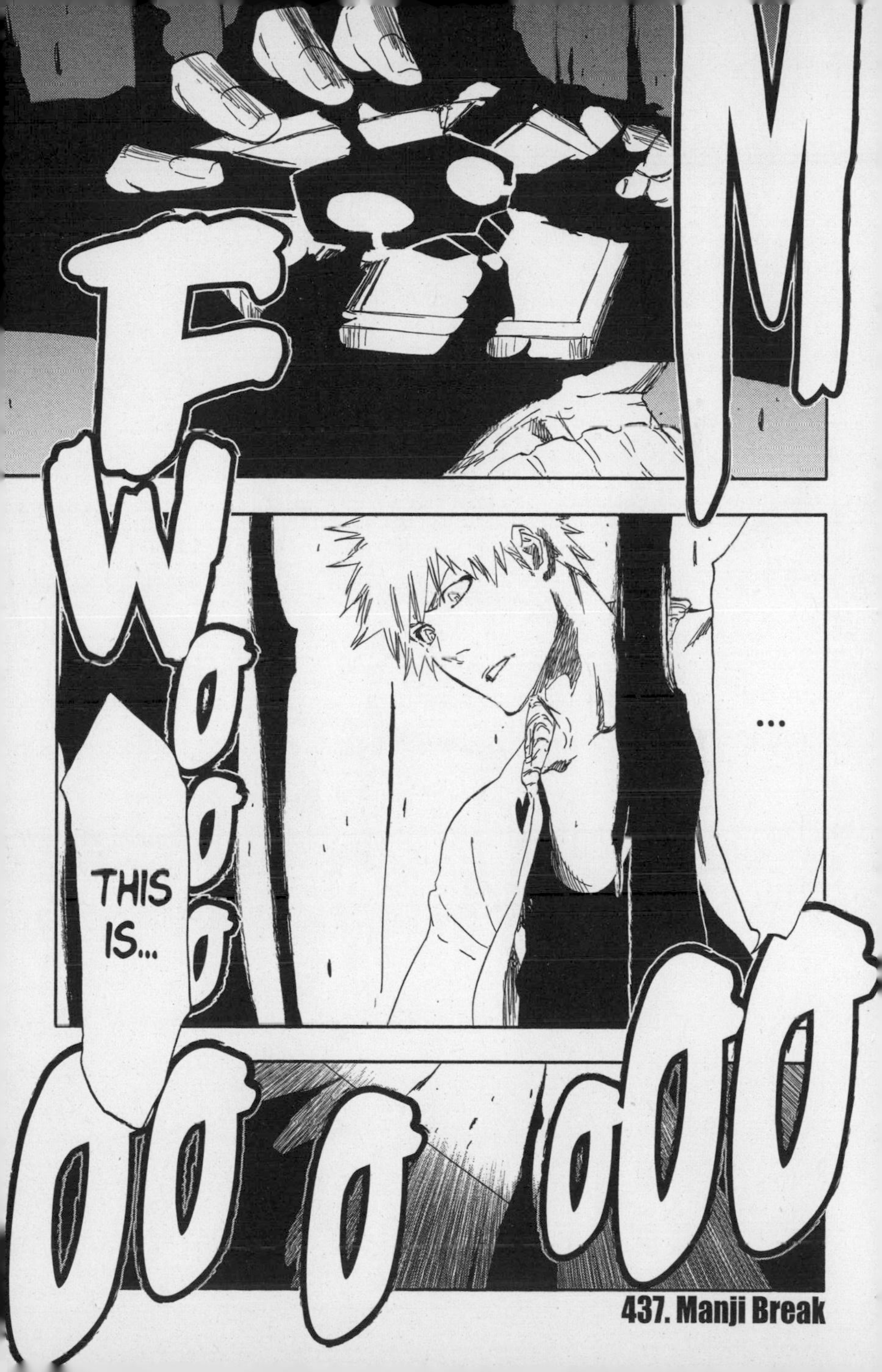
FWOOOOOOOOOOM
...
THIS IS...

437. Manji Break

Manji Break

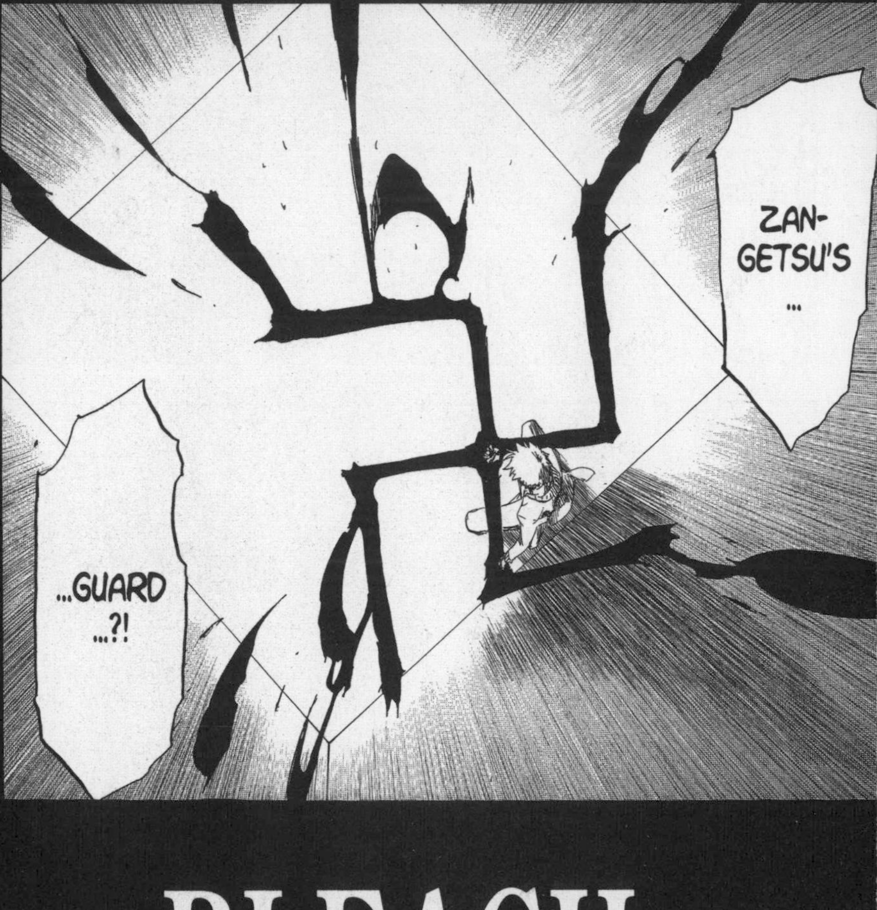
ZAN-
GETSU'S
...
...GUARD
...?!

BLEACH 437.

THIS IS ICHI-GO'S...

...FULL-BRING...?!

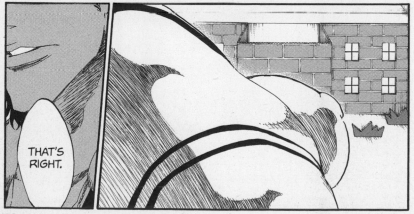

THAT'S RIGHT.

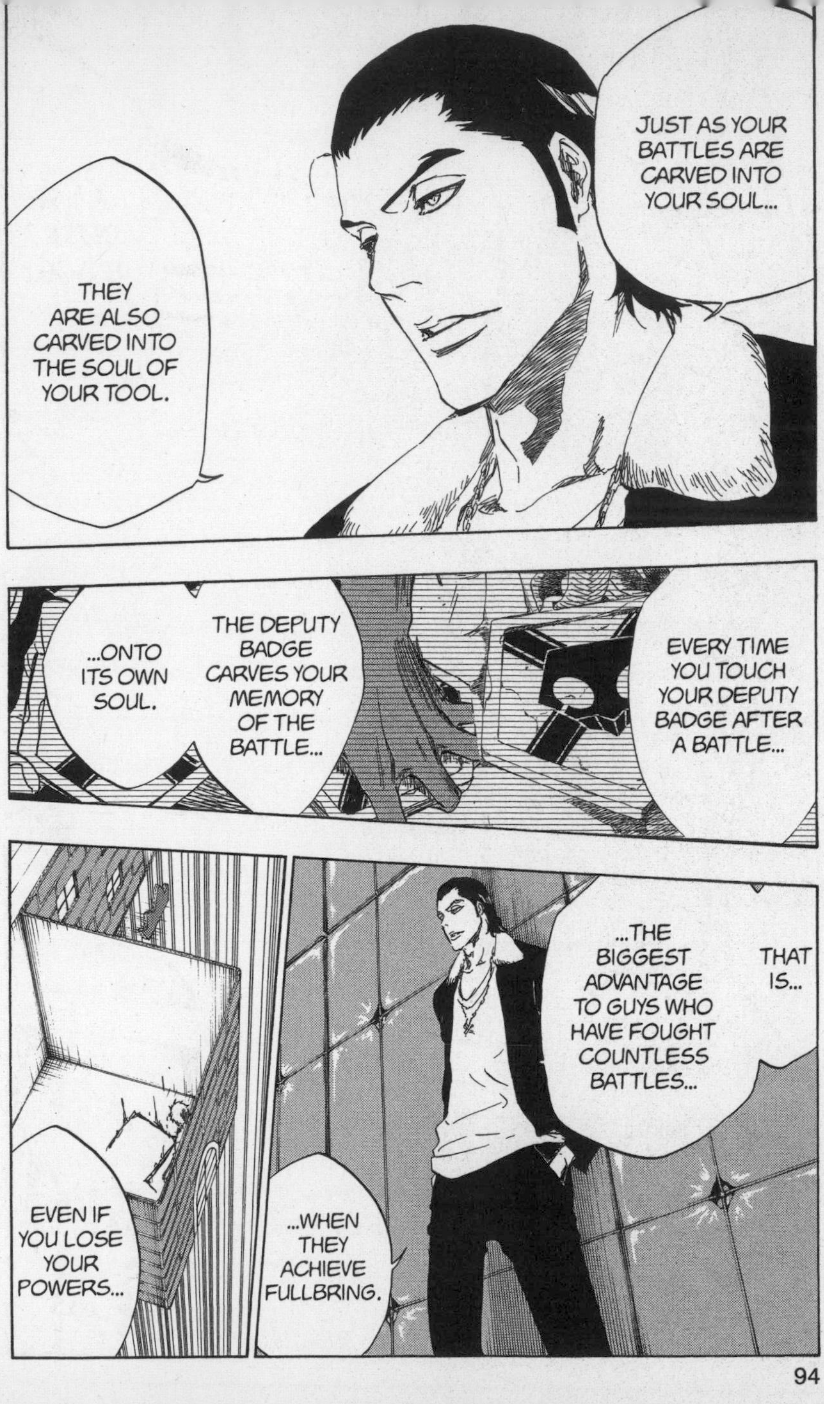
JUST AS YOUR BATTLES ARE CARVED INTO YOUR SOUL...
THEY ARE ALSO CARVED INTO THE SOUL OF YOUR TOOL.
EVERY TIME YOU TOUCH YOUR DEPUTY BADGE AFTER A BATTLE...
THE DEPUTY BADGE CARVES YOUR MEMORY OF THE BATTLE...
...ONTO ITS OWN SOUL.
THAT IS...
...THE BIGGEST ADVANTAGE TO GUYS WHO HAVE FOUGHT COUNTLESS BATTLES...
...WHEN THEY ACHIEVE FULLBRING.
EVEN IF YOU LOSE YOUR POWERS...

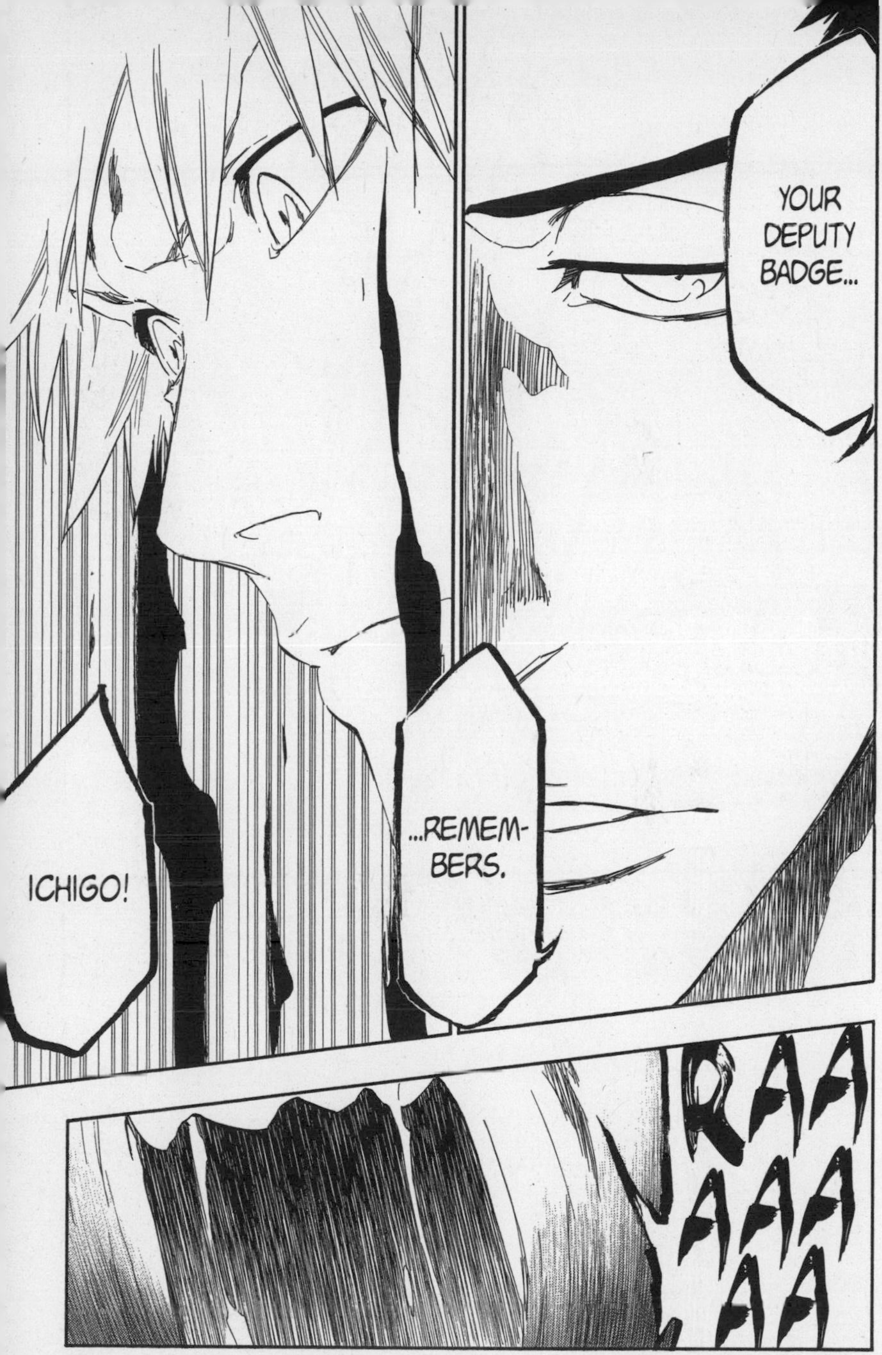
YOUR DEPUTY BADGE...
...REMEM-BERS.
ICHIGO!
RAAAAAAAAA

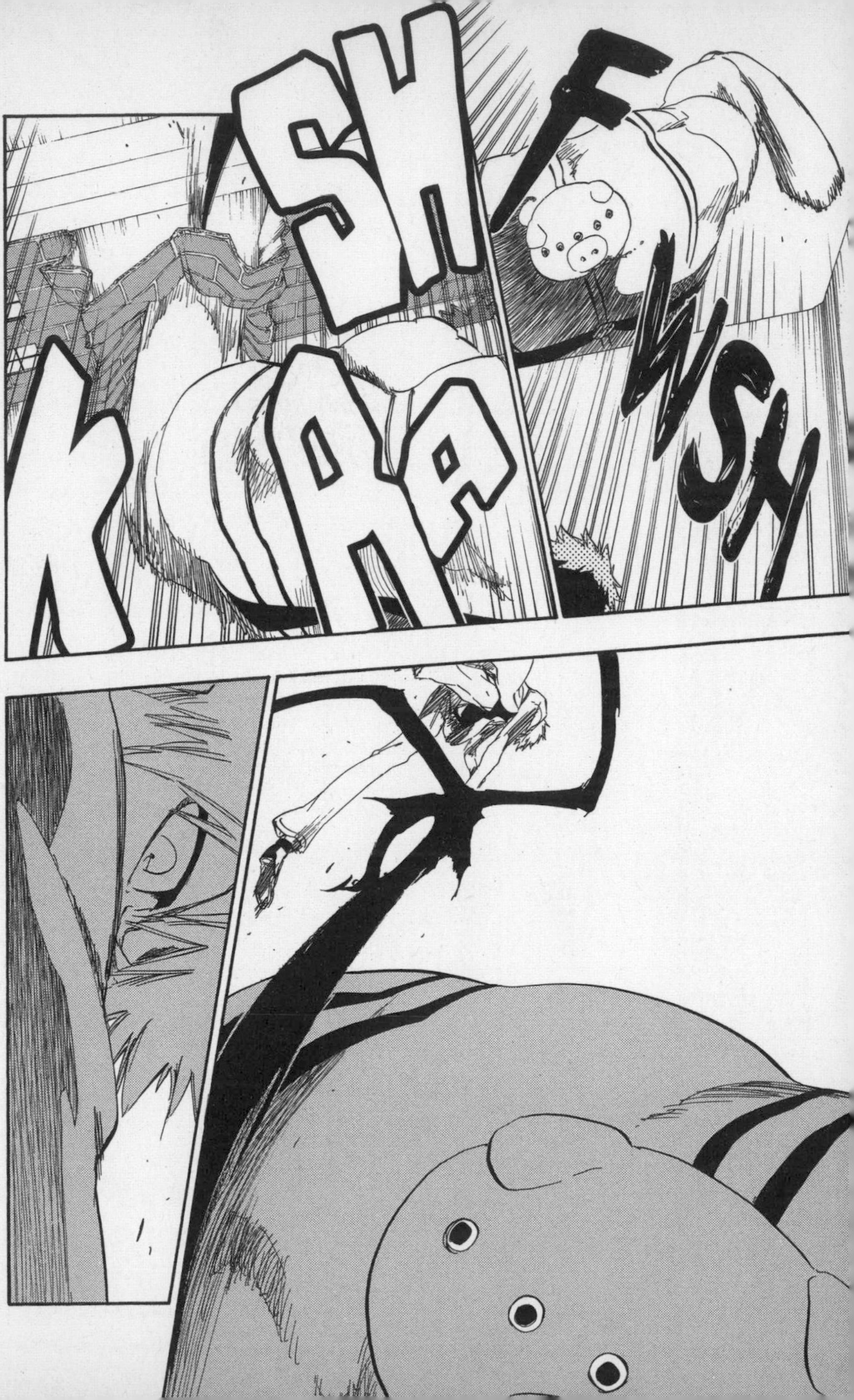
WSH
KRASH

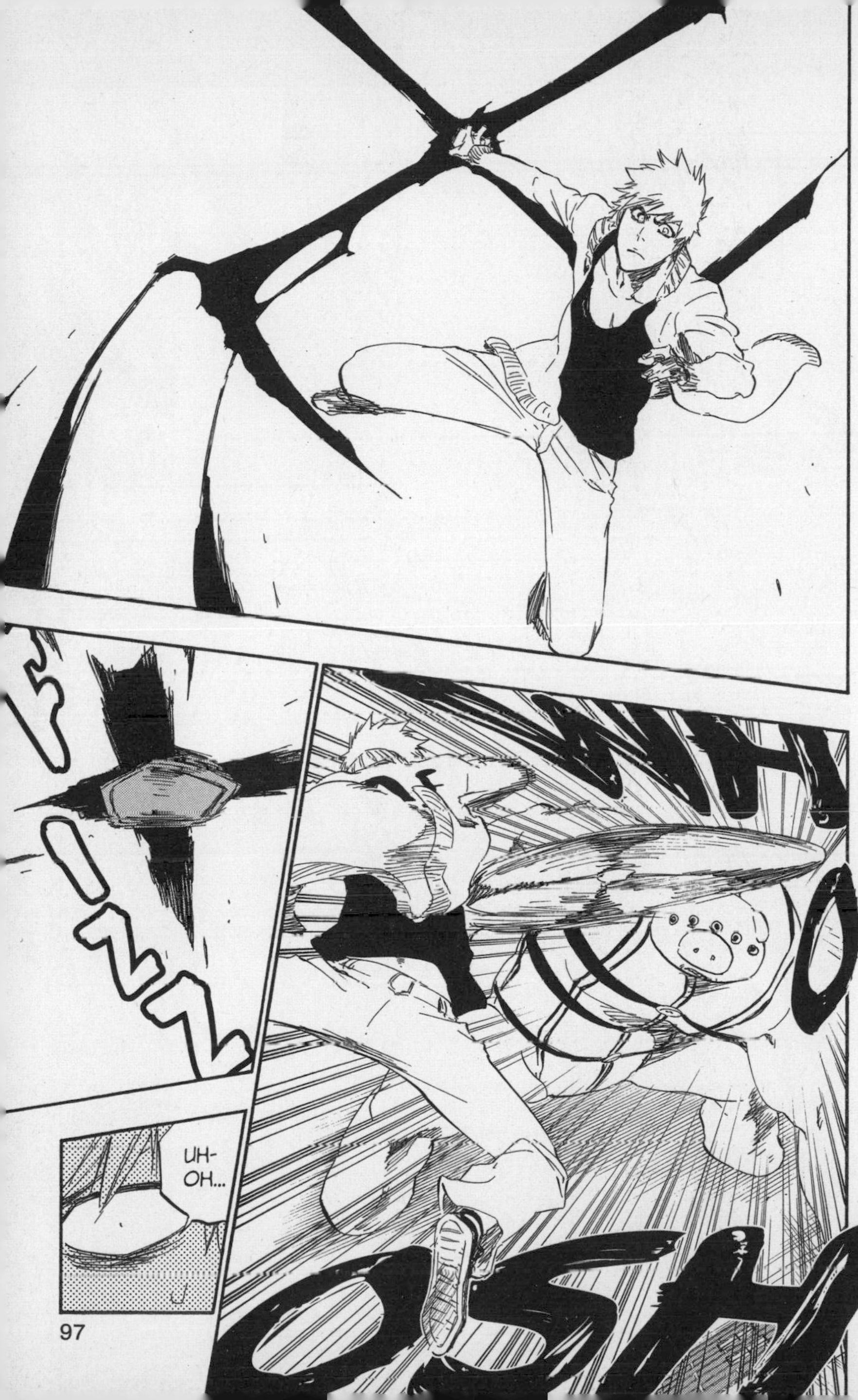
UH-
OH...

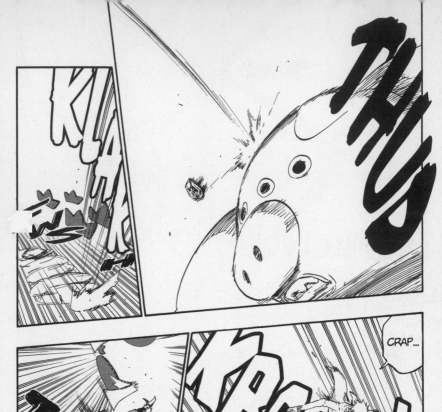

CRAP...

GUESS
THAT
WASN'T
THE WAY
TO USE
IT...

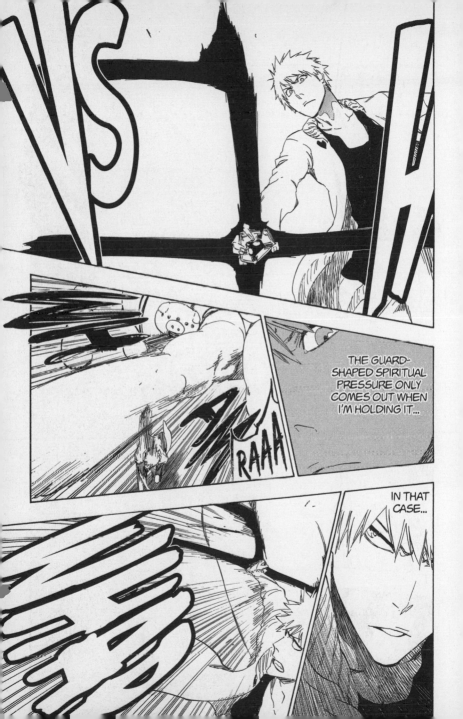

THE GUARD-SHAPED SPIRITUAL PRESSURE ONLY COMES OUT WHEN I'M HOLDING IT...

IN THAT CASE...

RAAA

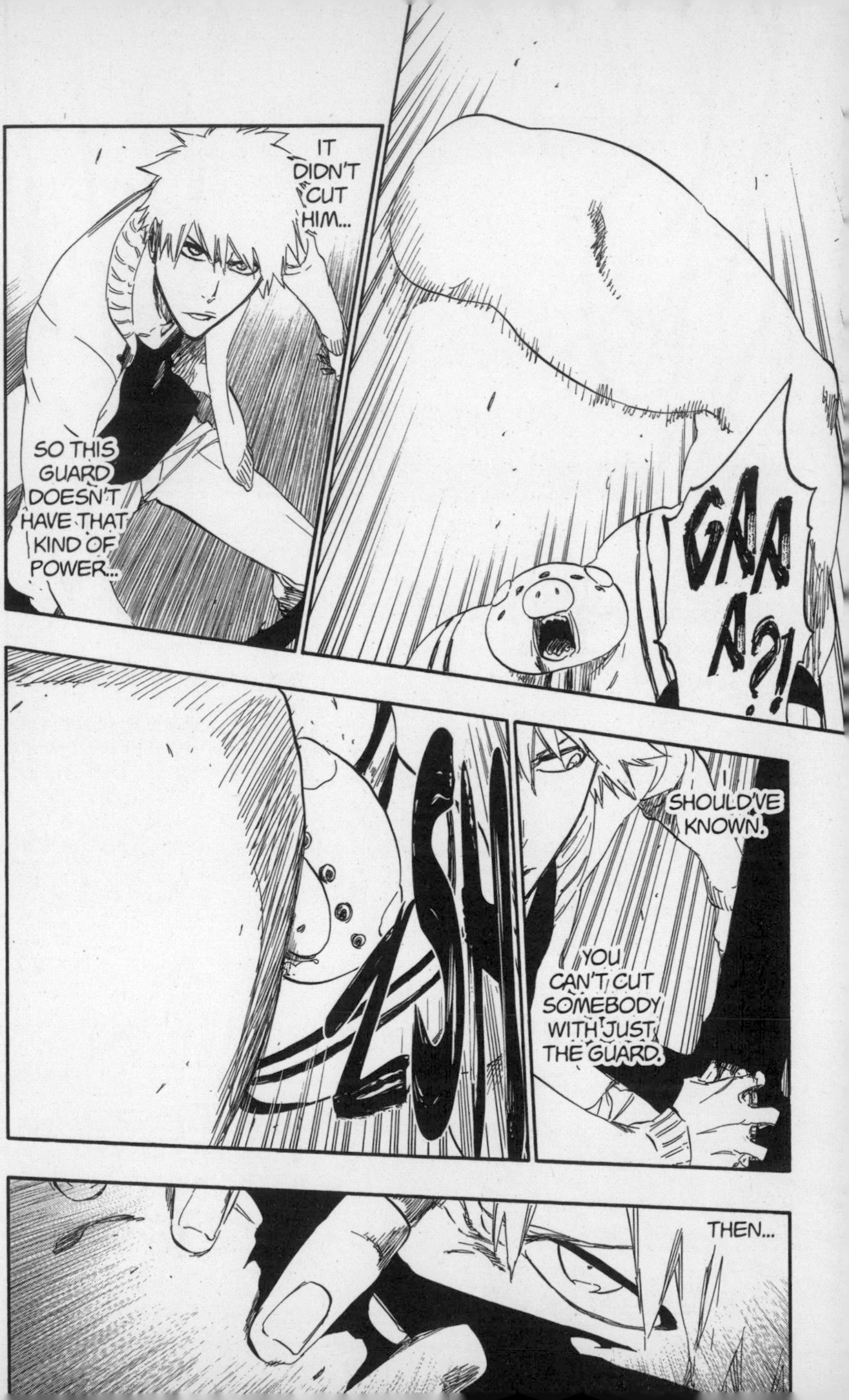
GAAA?!
IT DIDN'T CUT HIM...
SO THIS GUARD DOESN'T HAVE THAT KIND OF POWER...
SHOULD'VE KNOWN.
YOU CAN'T CUT SOMEBODY WITH JUST THE GUARD.
ZSH
THEN...

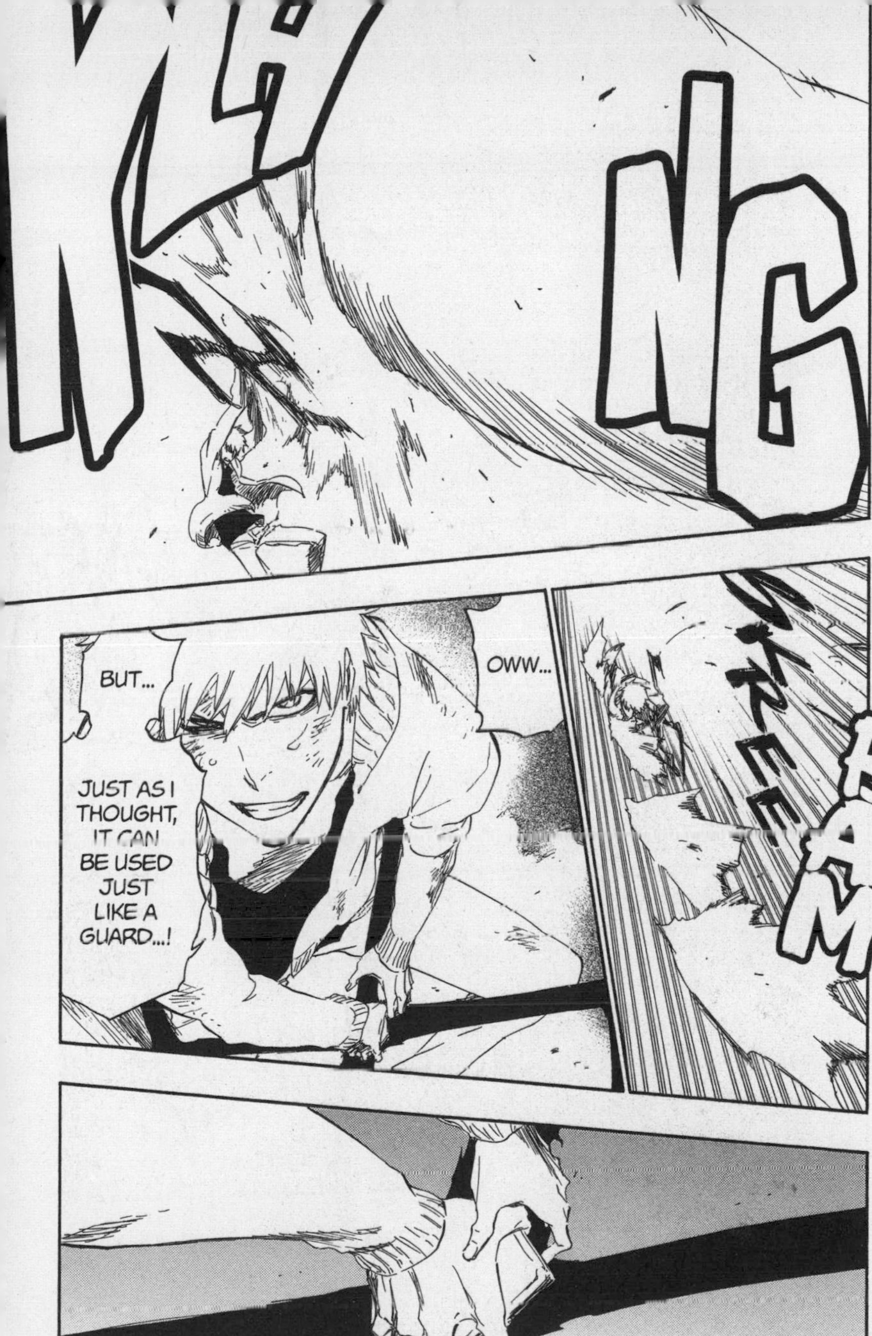
NG
SKREE
BAM
OWW...
BUT...
JUST AS I THOUGHT, IT CAN BE USED JUST LIKE A GUARD...!

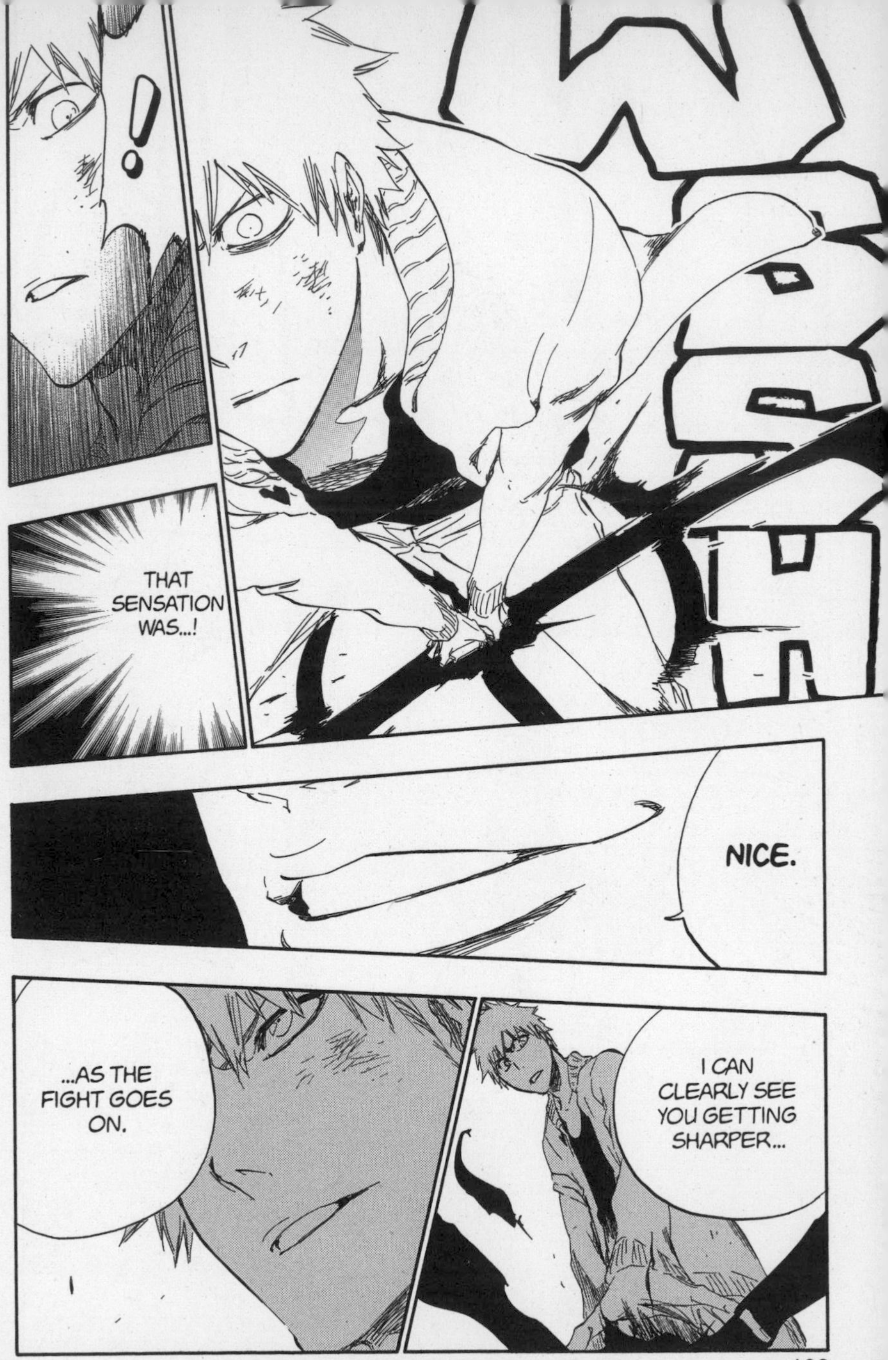
!
THAT SENSATION WAS...!
NICE.
I CAN CLEARLY SEE YOU GETTING SHARPER...
...AS THE FIGHT GOES ON.

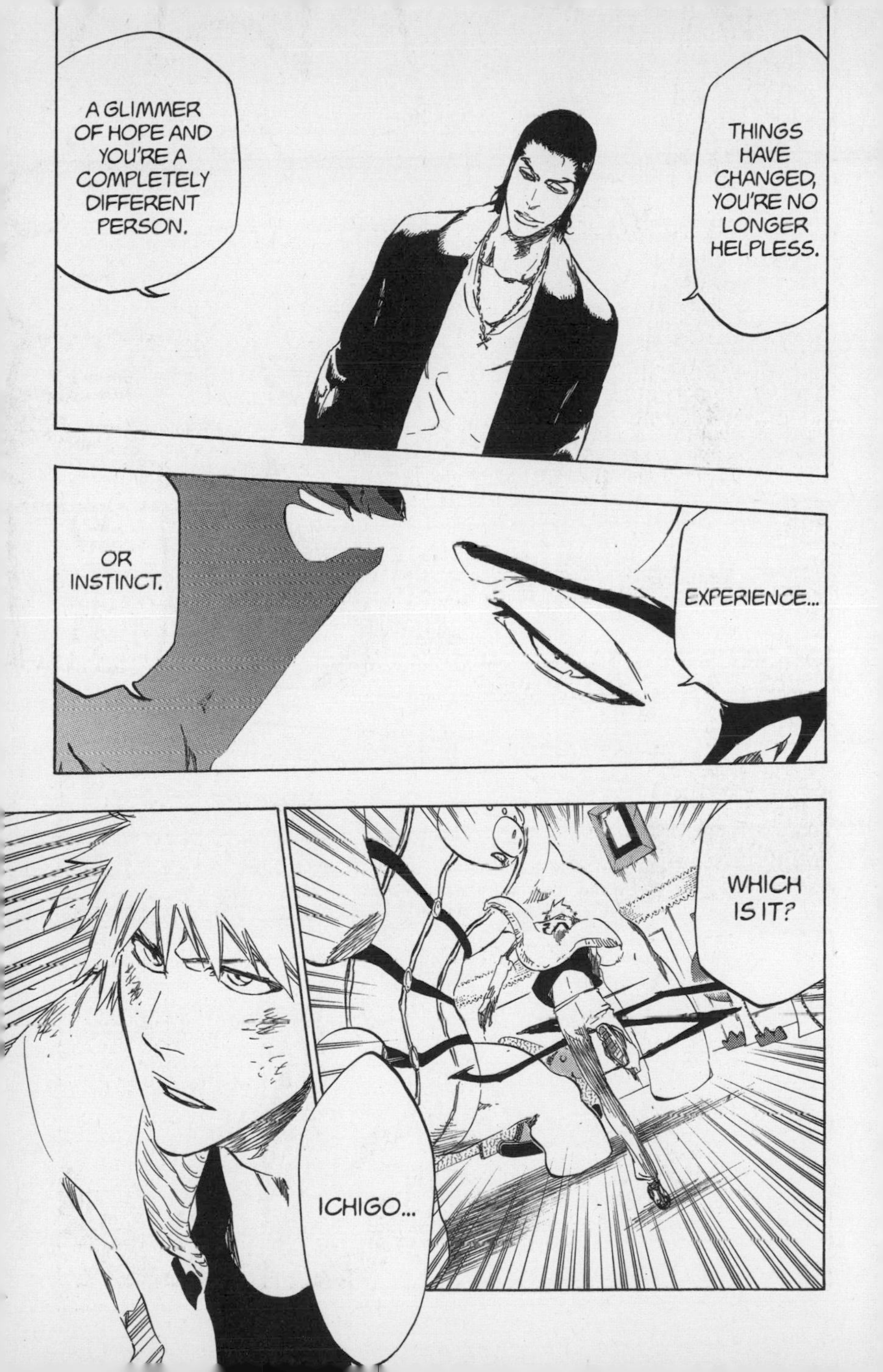
THINGS HAVE CHANGED, YOU'RE NO LONGER HELPLESS.
A GLIMMER OF HOPE AND YOU'RE A COMPLETELY DIFFERENT PERSON.
EXPERIENCE...
OR INSTINCT.
WHICH IS IT?
ICHIGO...

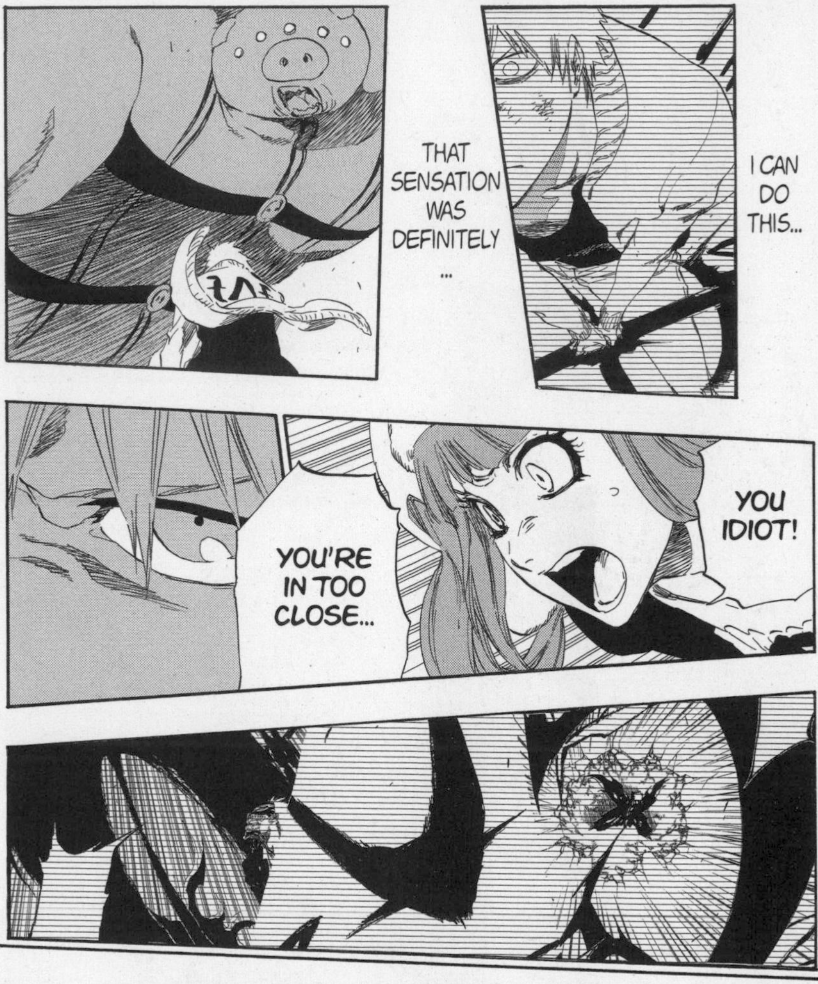
THAT SENSATION WAS DEFINITELY ...
I CAN DO THIS...
YOU IDIOT!
YOU'RE IN TOO CLOSE...

THE SENSATION OF GETSUGA TENSHO!!

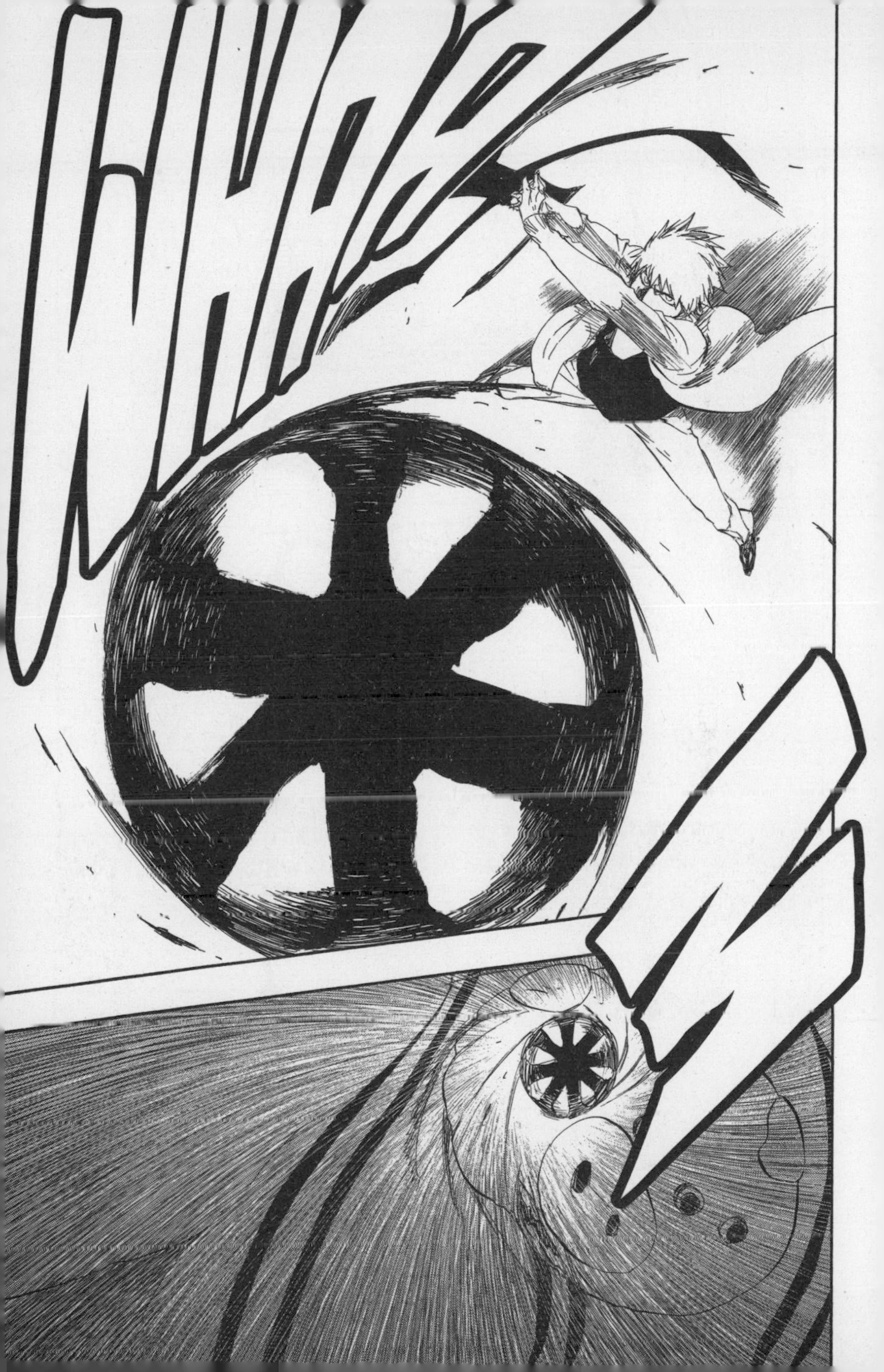

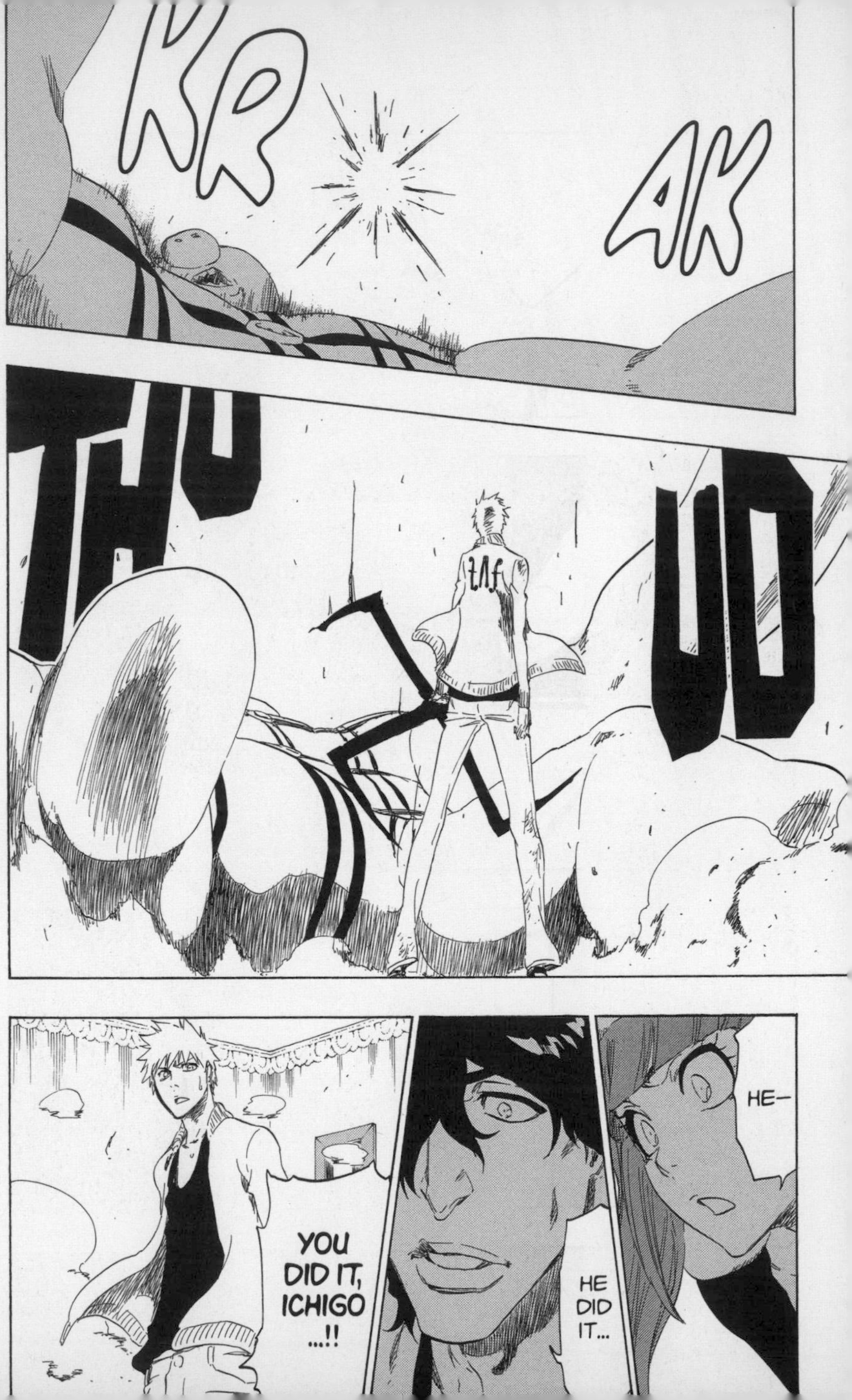
KR
AK
THU
UD
HE—
HE DID IT...
YOU DID IT, ICHIGO ...!!

READ THIS WAY

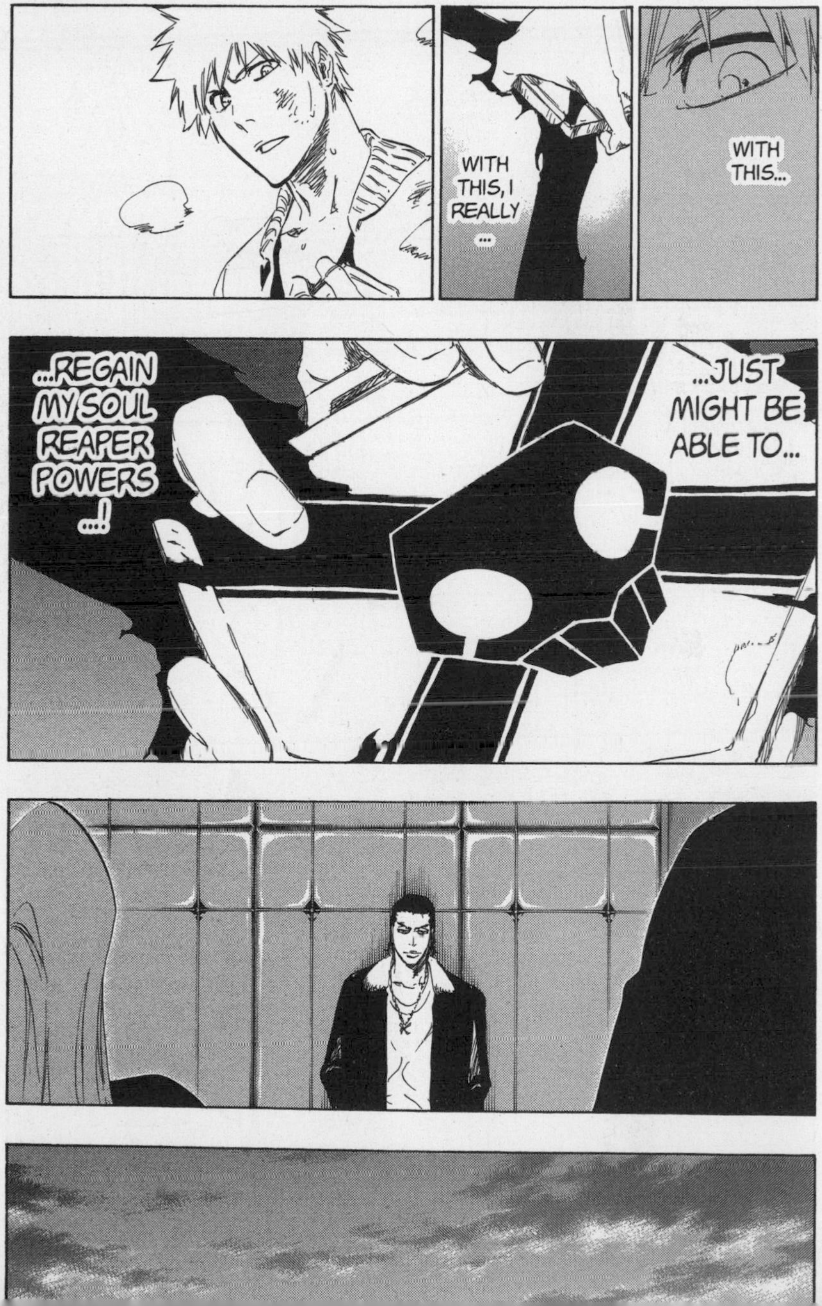
WITH THIS...
WITH THIS, I REALLY ...
...JUST MIGHT BE ABLE TO...
...REGAIN MY SOUL REAPER POWERS ...!

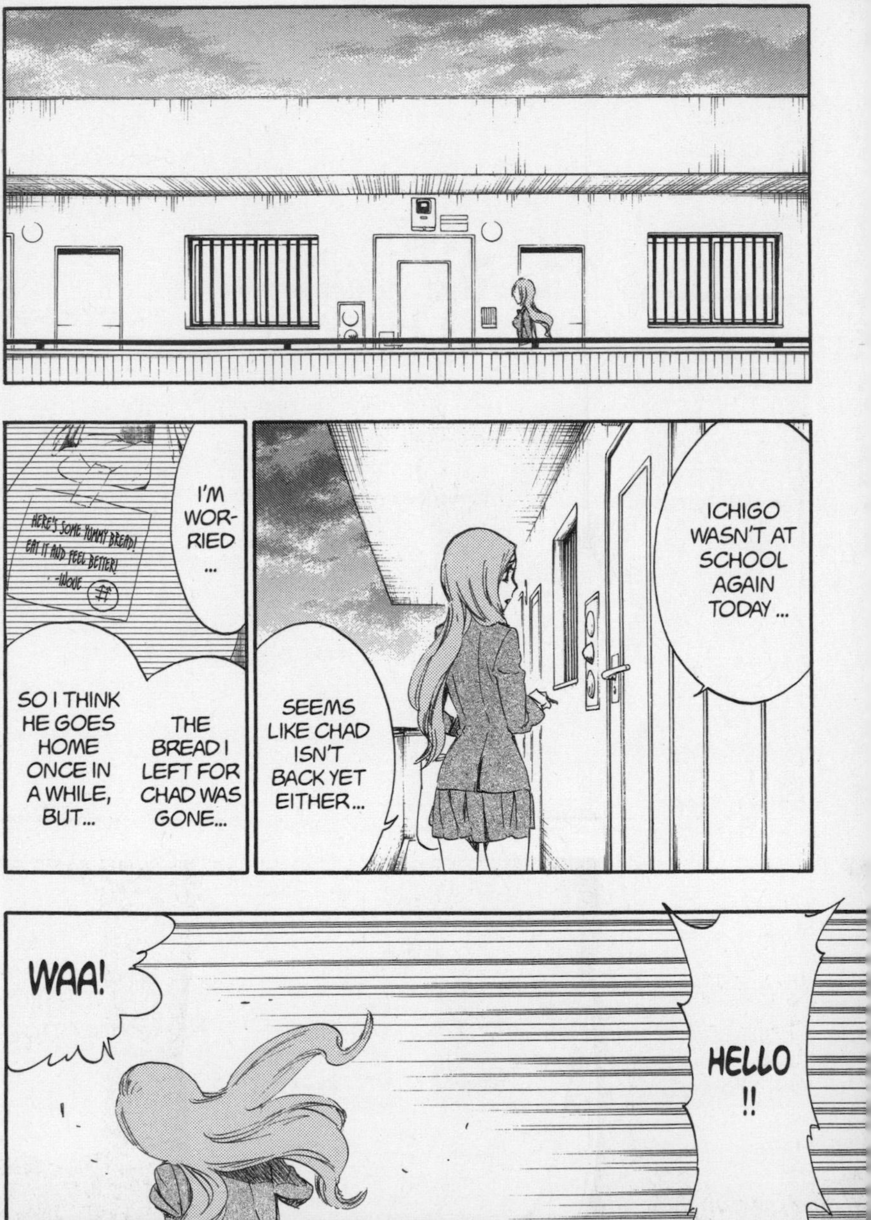
ICHIGO WASN'T AT SCHOOL AGAIN TODAY...
SEEMS LIKE CHAD ISN'T BACK YET EITHER...
I'M WOR-RIED...
HERE'S SOME YUMMY BREAD! EAT IT AND FEEL BETTER! -INOUE
THE BREAD I LEFT FOR CHAD WAS GONE...
SO I THINK HE GOES HOME ONCE IN A WHILE, BUT...
HELLO!!
WAA!

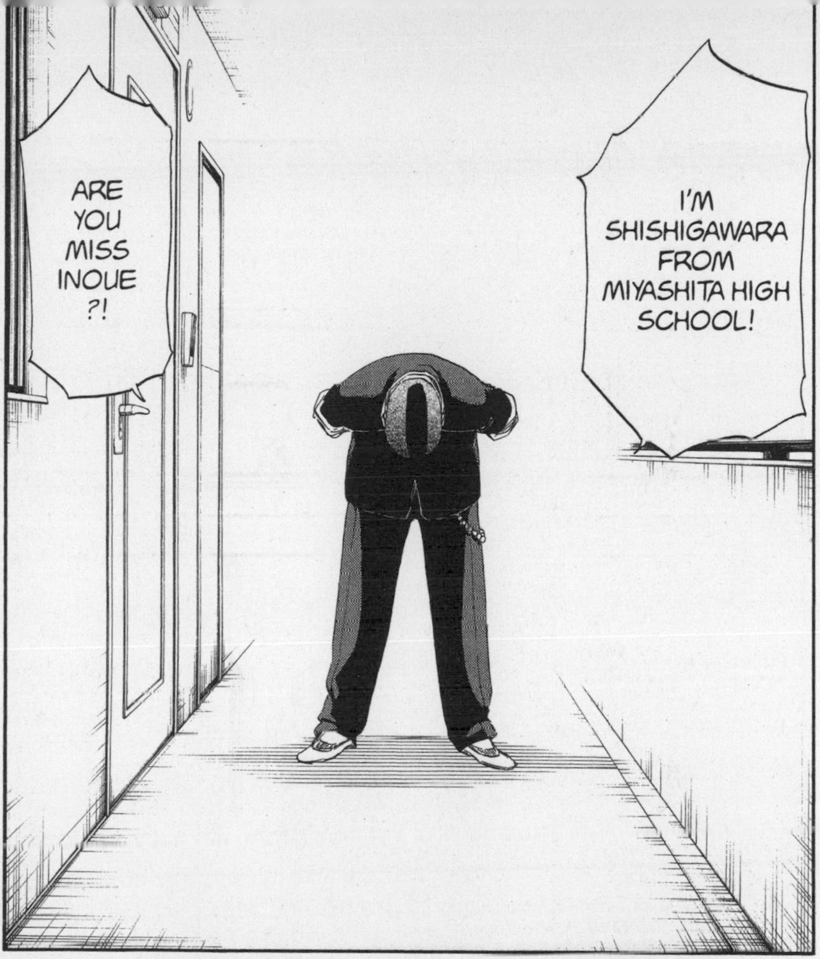
I'M SHISHIGAWARA FROM MIYASHITA HIGH SCHOOL!
ARE YOU MISS INOUE ?!

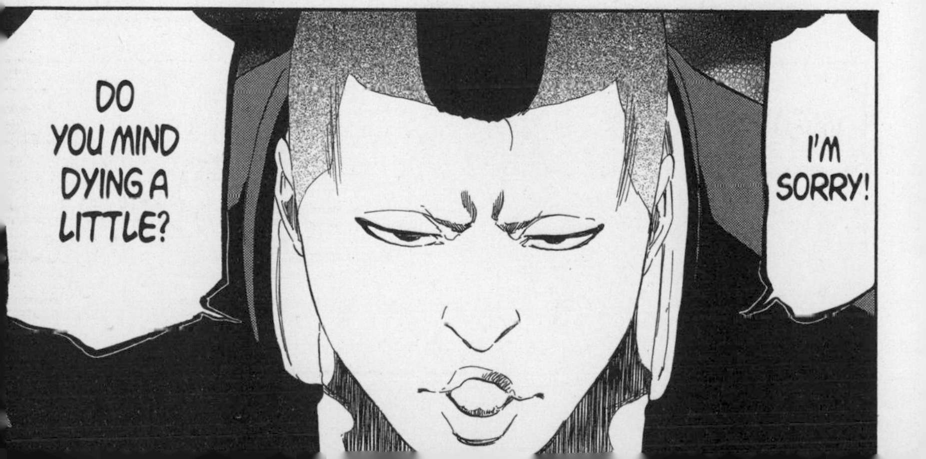
I'M SORRY!
DO YOU MIND DYING A LITTLE?

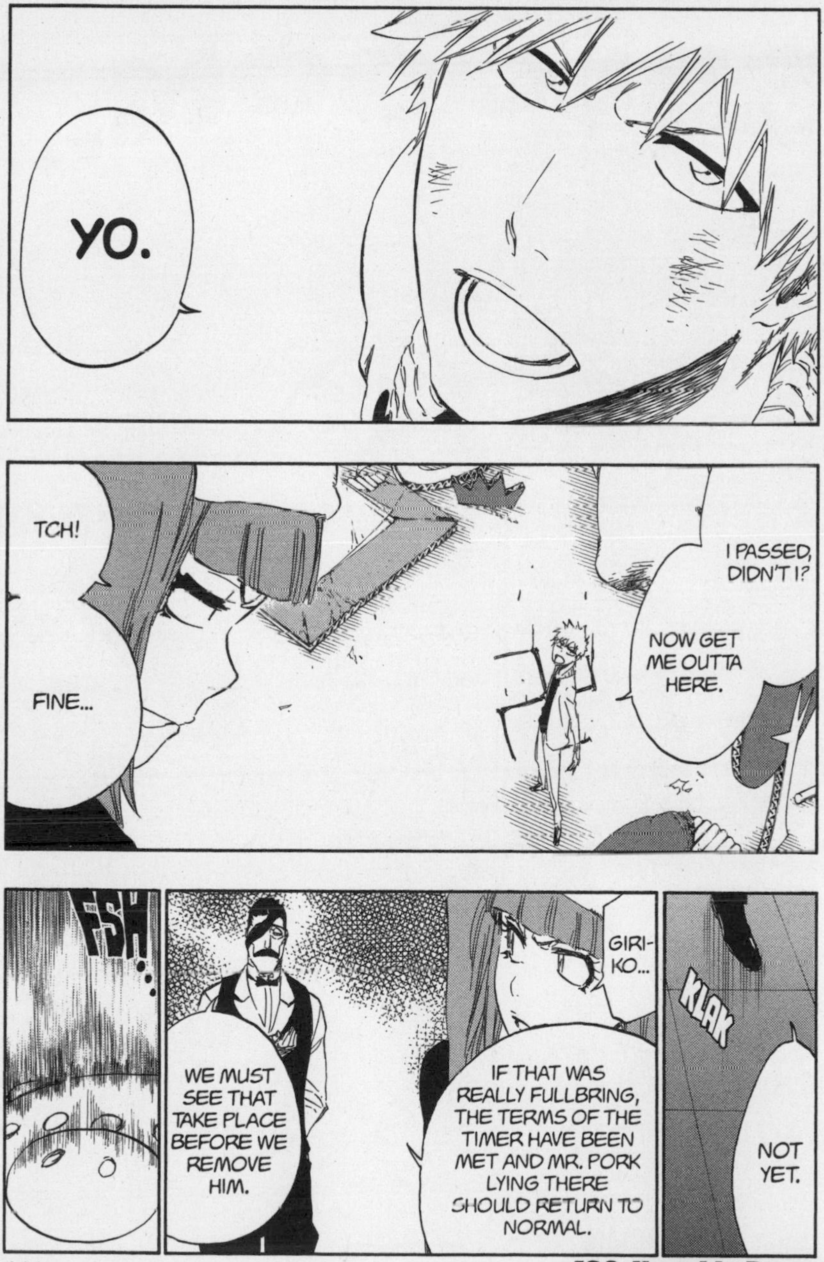
YO.
I PASSED, DIDN'T I?
NOW GET ME OUTTA HERE.
TCH!
FINE...
KLAK
NOT YET.
GIRI-KO...
IF THAT WAS REALLY FULLBRING, THE TERMS OF THE TIMER HAVE BEEN MET AND MR. PORK LYING THERE SHOULD RETURN TO NORMAL.
WE MUST SEE THAT TAKE PLACE BEFORE WE REMOVE HIM.
FSH

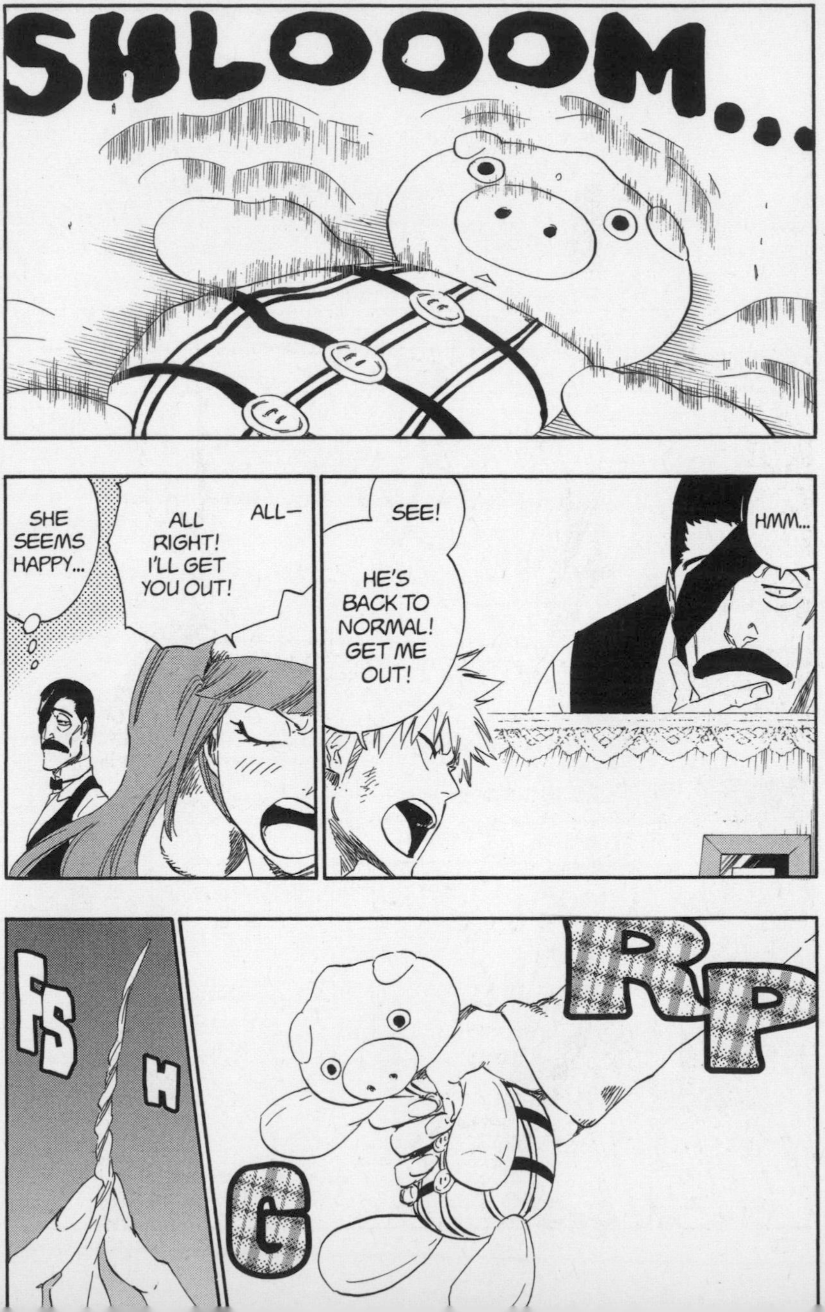
SHLOOOM...
HMM...
SEE!
HE'S BACK TO NORMAL! GET ME OUT!
ALL—
ALL RIGHT! I'LL GET YOU OUT!
SHE SEEMS HAPPY...
RP
C
FS
H

READ THIS WAY

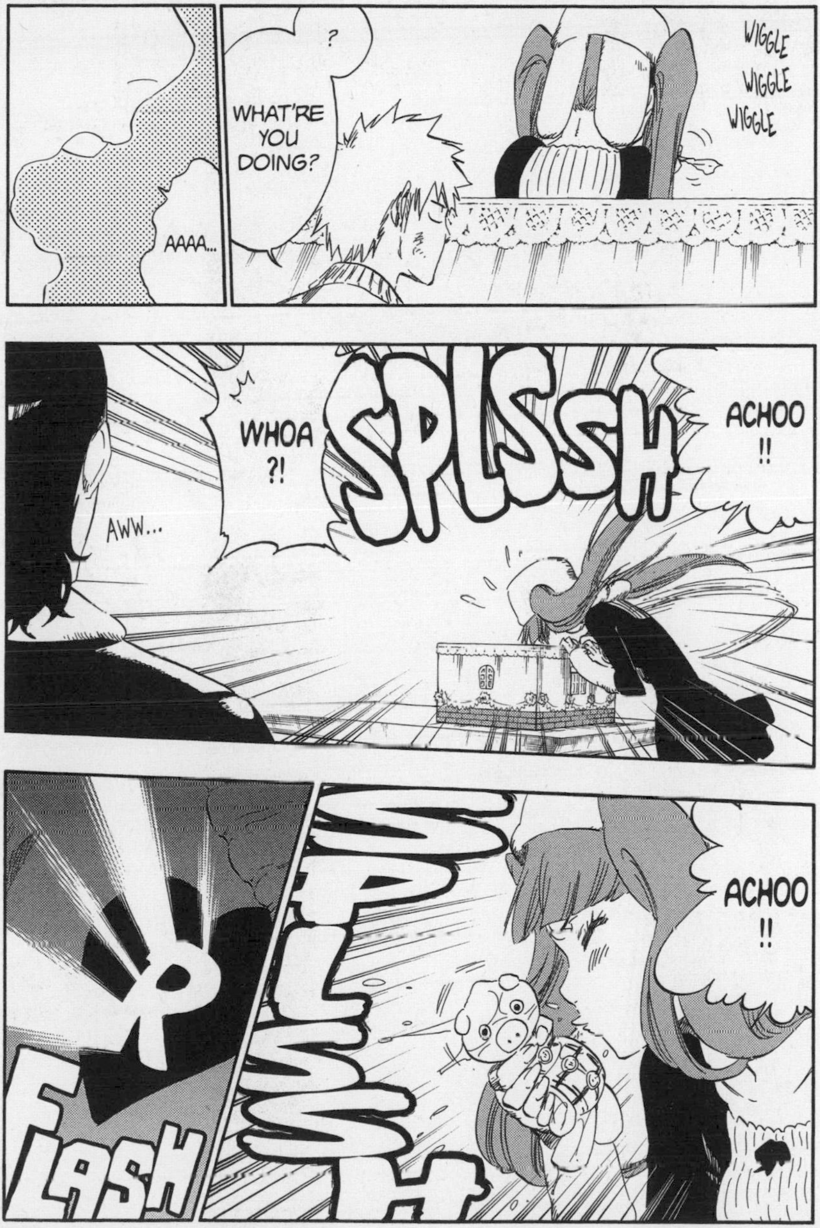

WIGGLE WIGGLE WIGGLE
?
WHAT'RE YOU DOING?
AAAA...
ACHOO !!
SPLSSH
WHOA ?!
AWW...
ACHOO !!
SPLSSH
FLASH

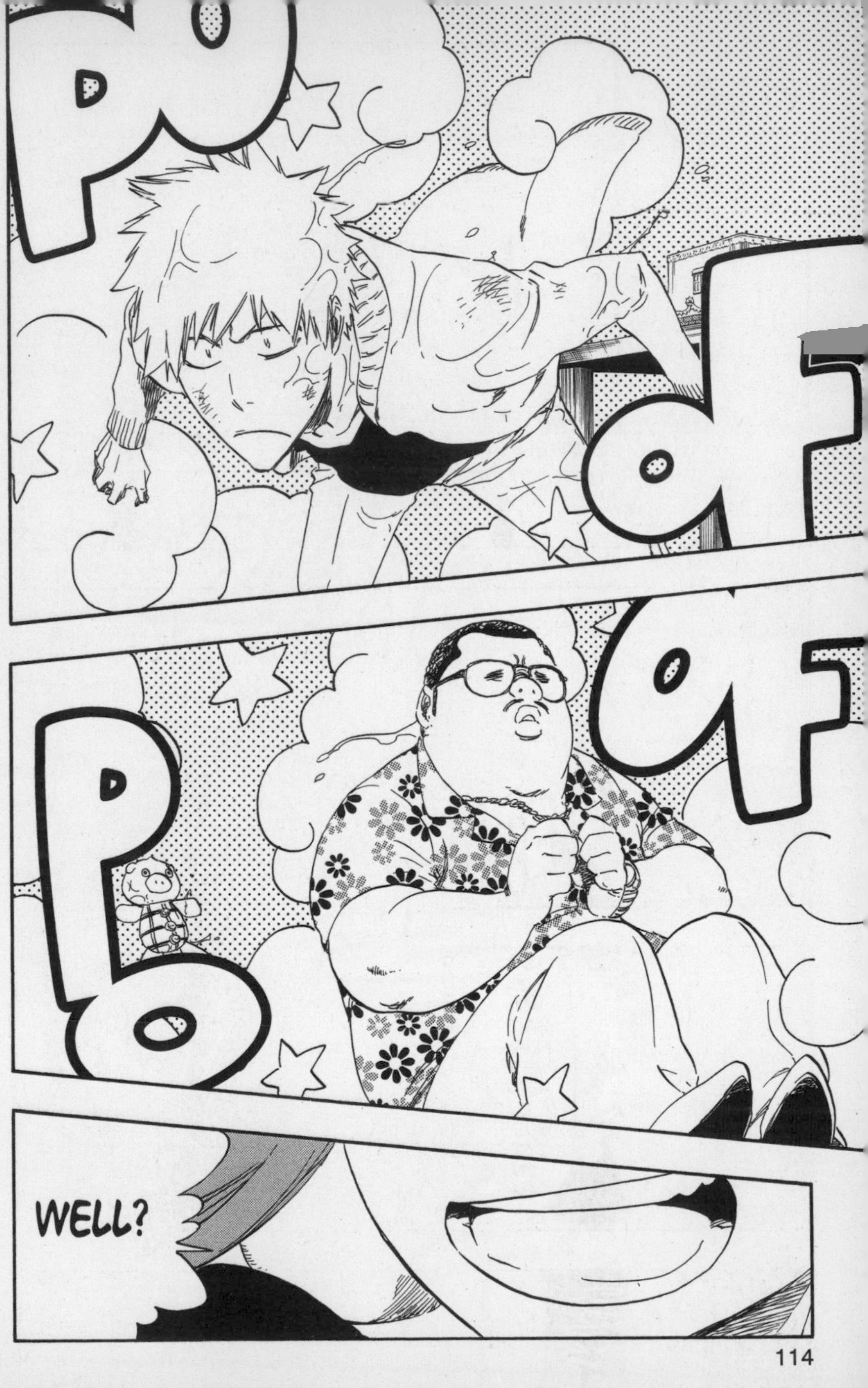
POOF
POOF
WELL?

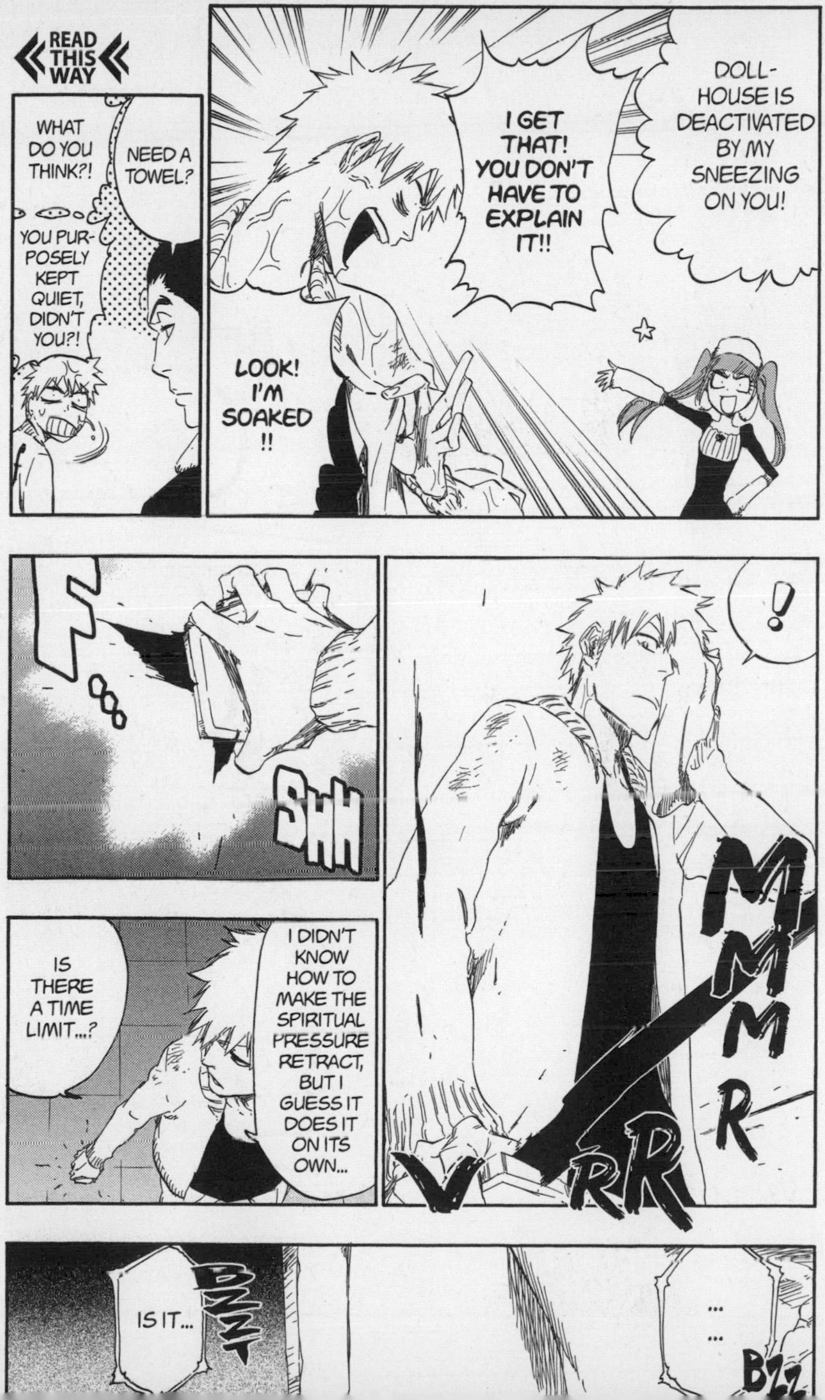
READ THIS WAY
DOLL-HOUSE IS DEACTIVATED BY MY SNEEZING ON YOU!
I GET THAT! YOU DON'T HAVE TO EXPLAIN IT!!
LOOK! I'M SOAKED!!
NEED A TOWEL?
WHAT DO YOU THINK?!
YOU PURPOSELY KEPT QUIET, DIDN'T YOU?!
!
MMMR
VRR
SHH
I DIDN'T KNOW HOW TO MAKE THE SPIRITUAL PRESSURE RETRACT, BUT I GUESS IT DOES IT ON ITS OWN...
IS THERE A TIME LIMIT...?
... ...
BZZ
BZZT
IS IT...

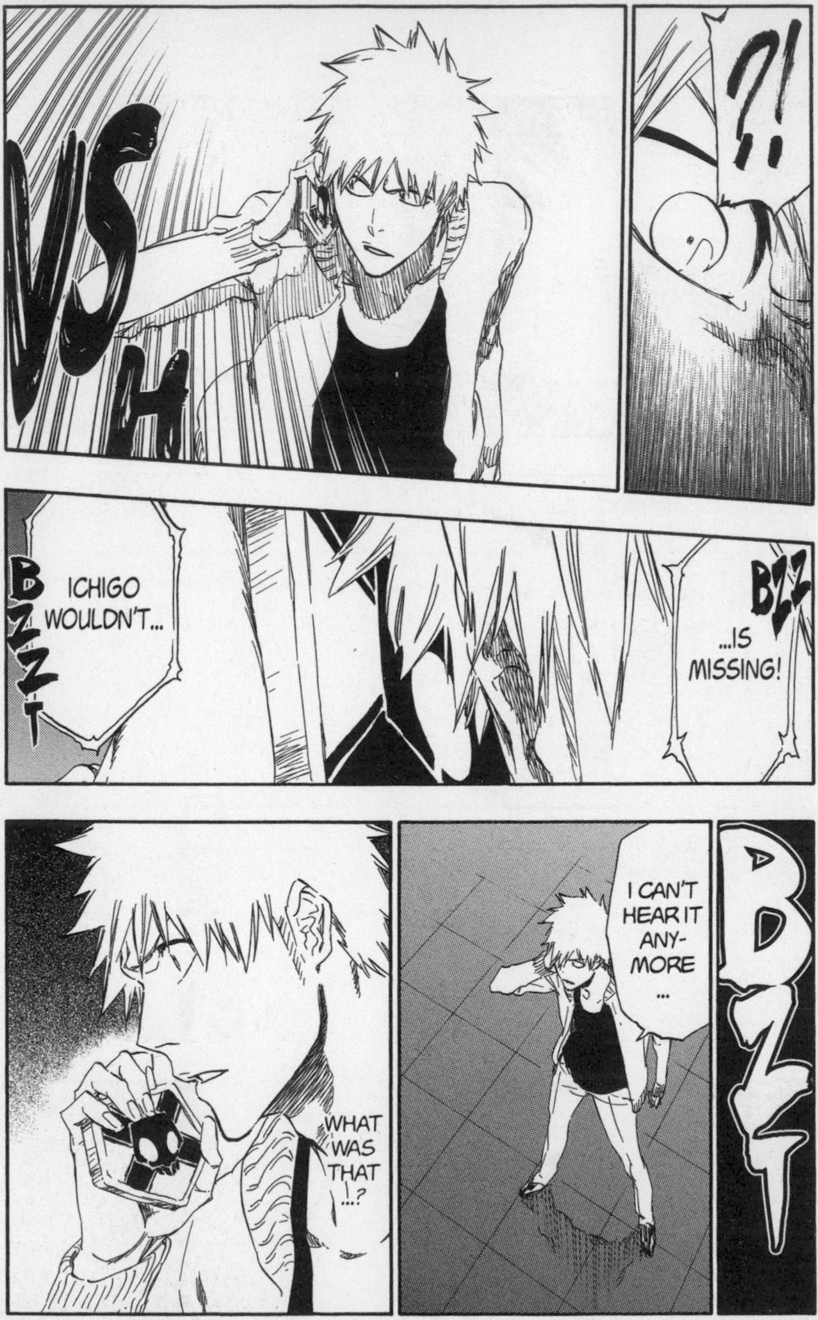
?!
VVSH
BZZ
...IS MISSING!
BZZZT
ICHIGO WOULDN'T...
BZZ
I CAN'T HEAR IT ANY-MORE ...
WHAT WAS THAT !...?

...RUKIA'S VOICE!

THAT WAS...

WHAT'S GOING ON...?

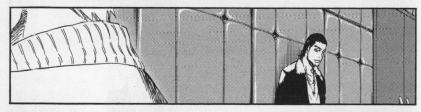

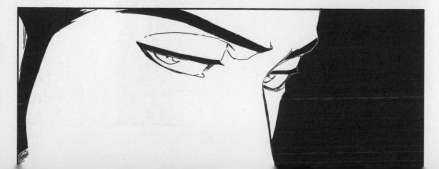

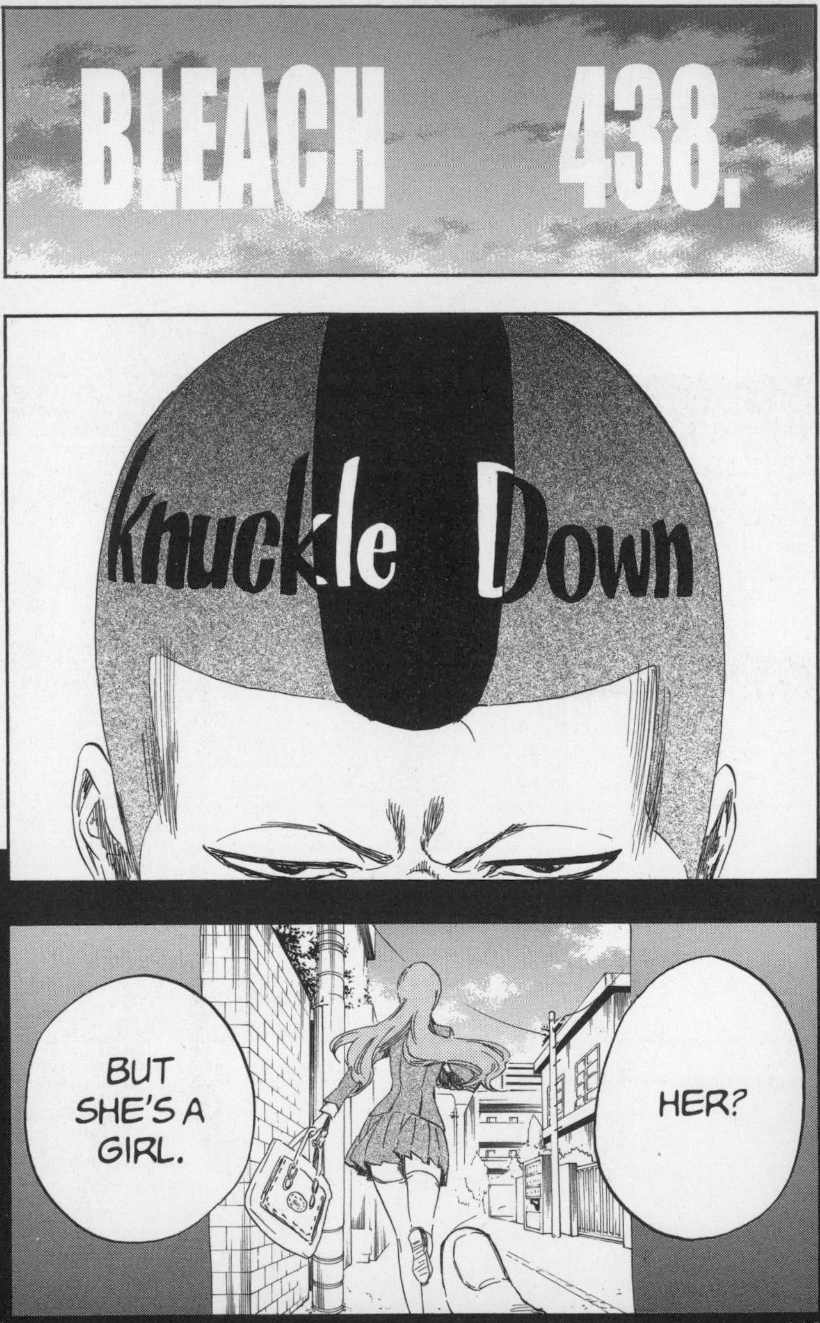
BLEACH 438.
Knuckle Down
HER?
BUT SHE'S A GIRL.

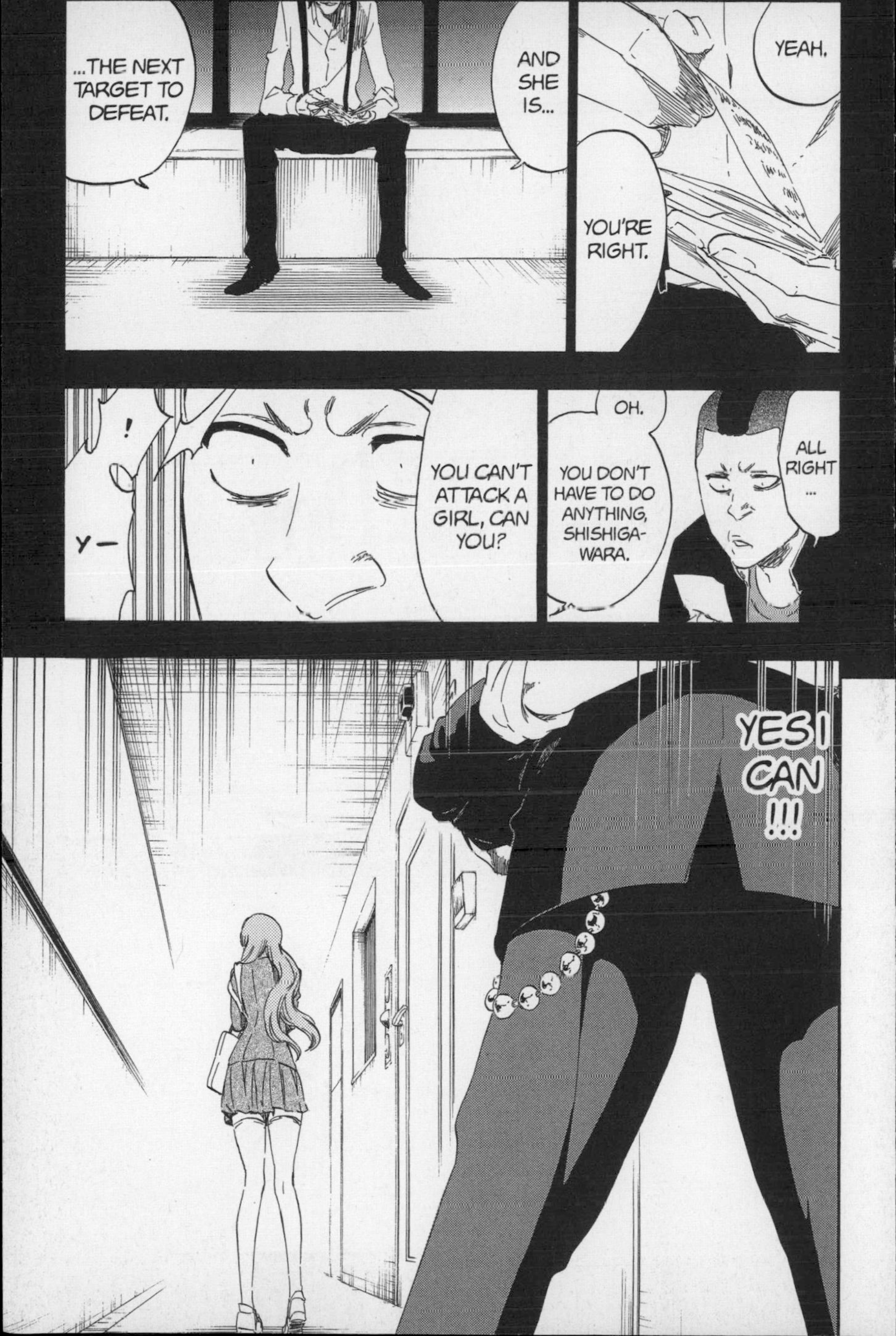
YEAH.
YOU'RE RIGHT.
AND SHE IS...
...THE NEXT TARGET TO DEFEAT.
OH.
YOU DON'T HAVE TO DO ANYTHING, SHISHIGA-WARA.
ALL RIGHT ...
YOU CAN'T ATTACK A GIRL, CAN YOU?
!
Y—
YES I CAN !!!

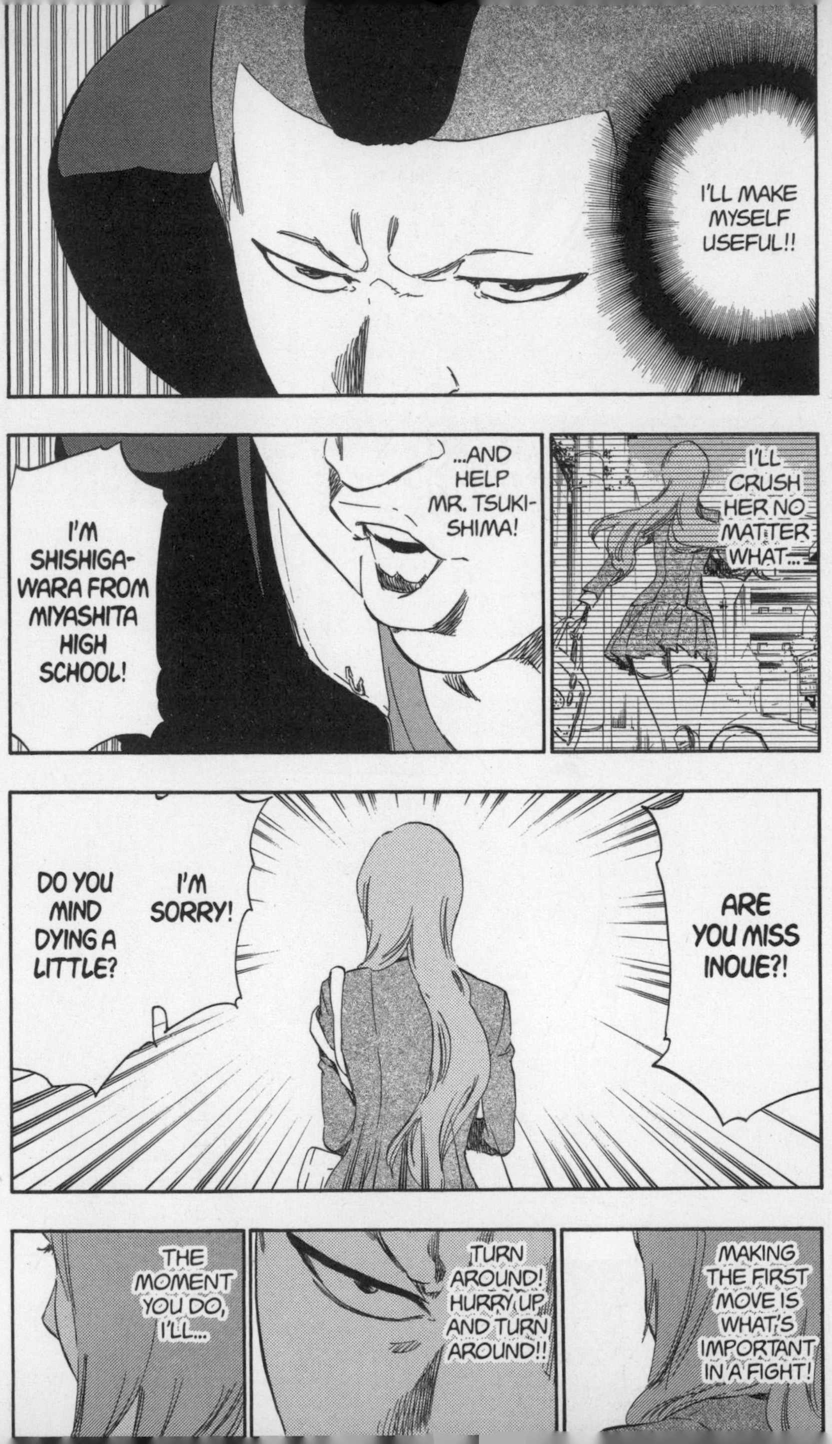
I'LL MAKE MYSELF USEFUL!!
I'LL CRUSH HER NO MATTER WHAT...
...AND HELP MR. TSUKISHIMA!
I'M SHISHIGAWARA FROM MIYASHITA HIGH SCHOOL!
ARE YOU MISS INOUE?!
I'M SORRY!
DO YOU MIND DYING A LITTLE?
MAKING THE FIRST MOVE IS WHAT'S IMPORTANT IN A FIGHT!
TURN AROUND! HURRY UP AND TURN AROUND!!
THE MOMENT YOU DO, I'LL...

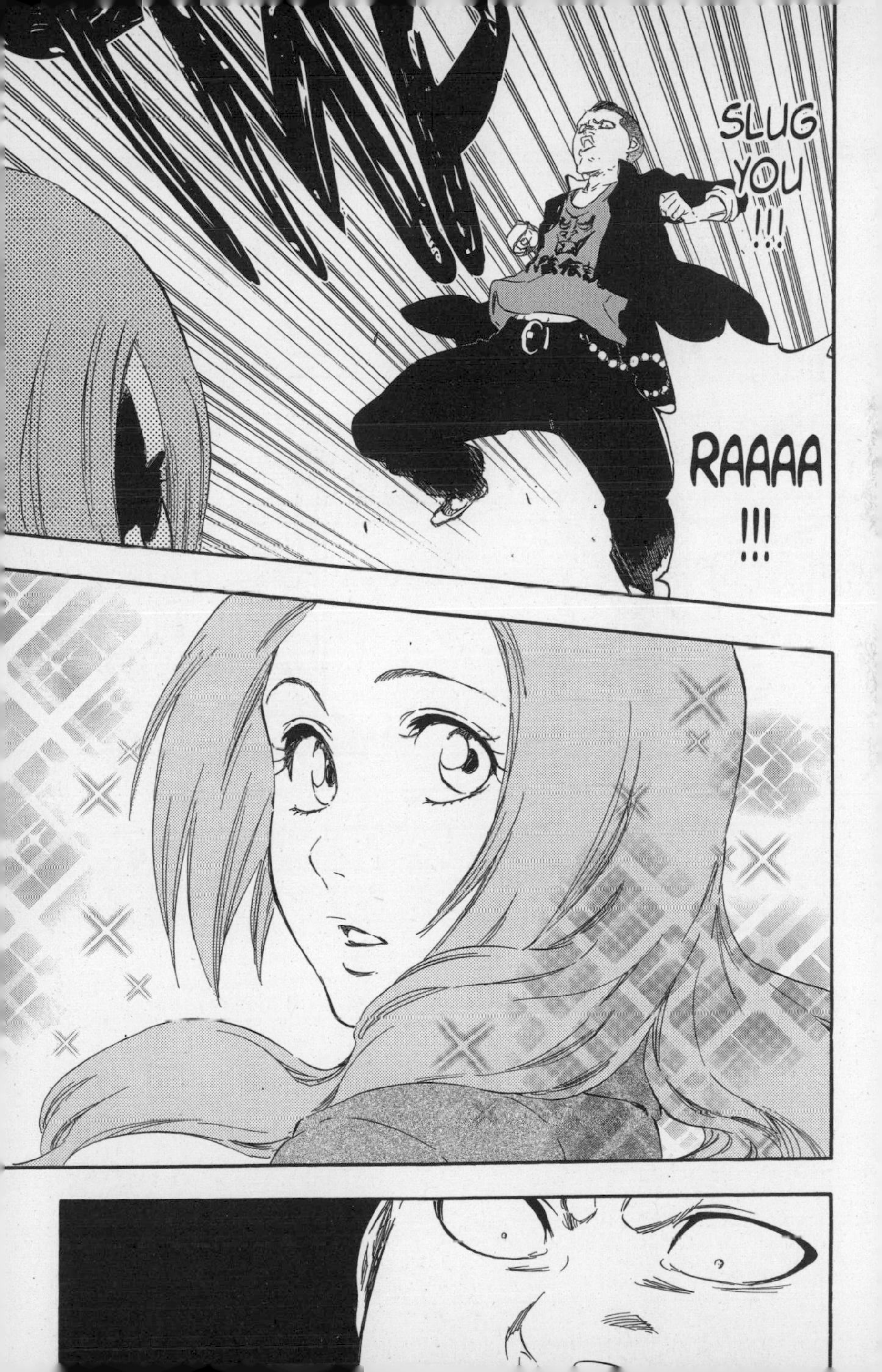
SLUG YOU !!!
RAAAA !!!

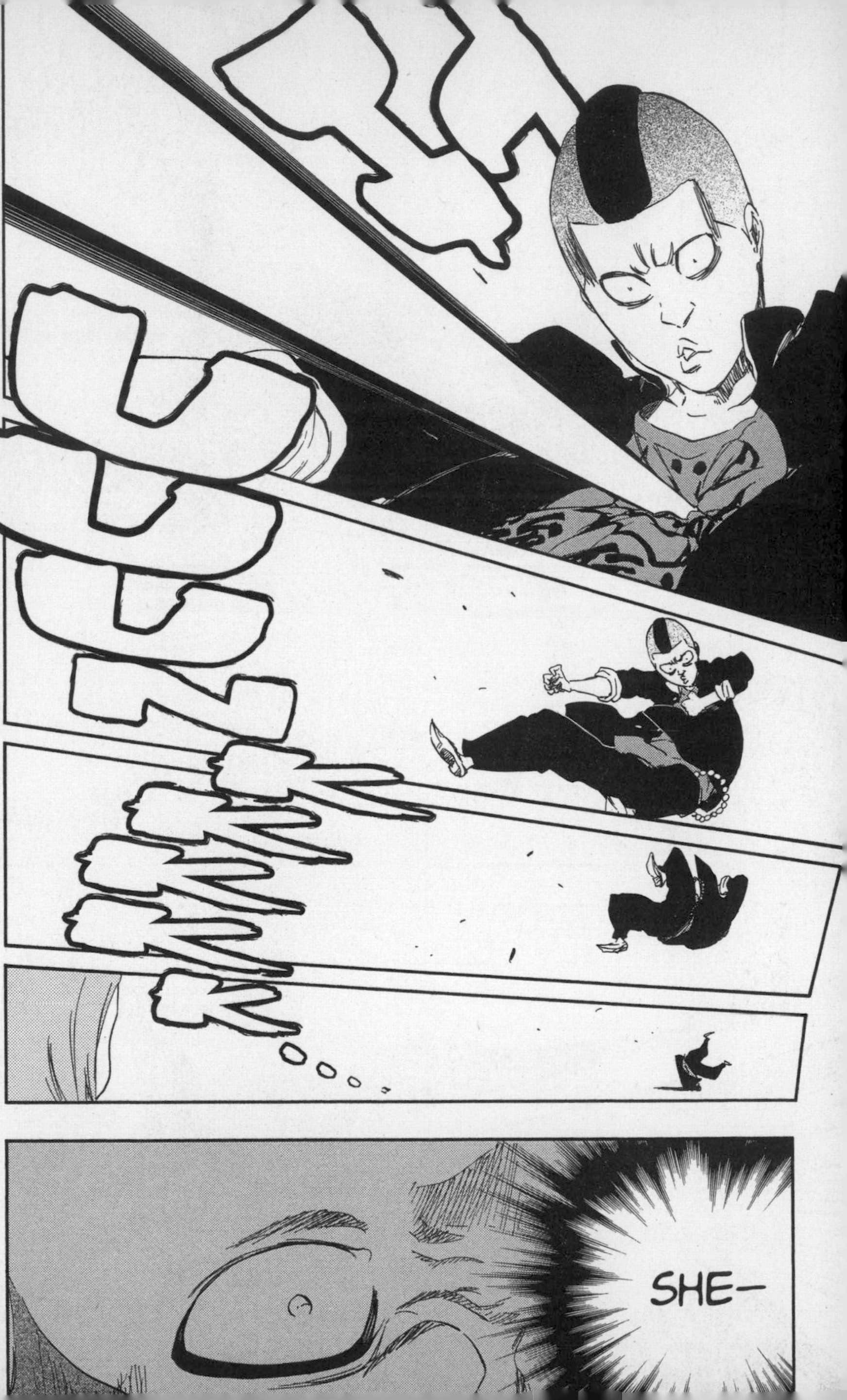
SHE–

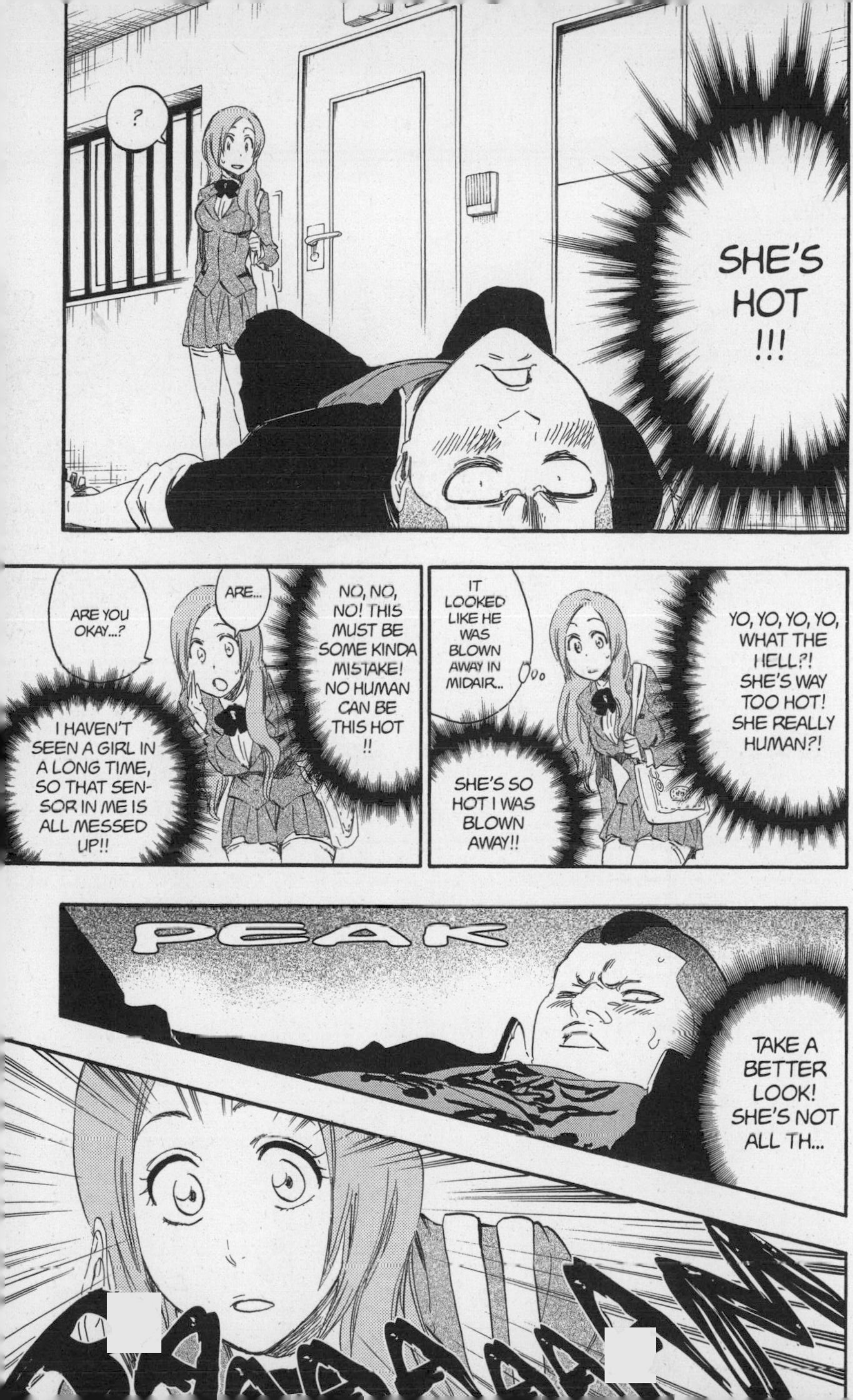
?
SHE'S HOT !!!
YO, YO, YO, YO, WHAT THE HELL?! SHE'S WAY TOO HOT! SHE REALLY HUMAN?!
IT LOOKED LIKE HE WAS BLOWN AWAY IN MIDAIR...
SHE'S SO HOT I WAS BLOWN AWAY!!
NO, NO, NO! THIS MUST BE SOME KINDA MISTAKE! NO HUMAN CAN BE THIS HOT !!
ARE...
ARE YOU OKAY...?
I HAVEN'T SEEN A GIRL IN A LONG TIME, SO THAT SEN-SOR IN ME IS ALL MESSED UP!!
PEAK
TAKE A BETTER LOOK! SHE'S NOT ALL TH...

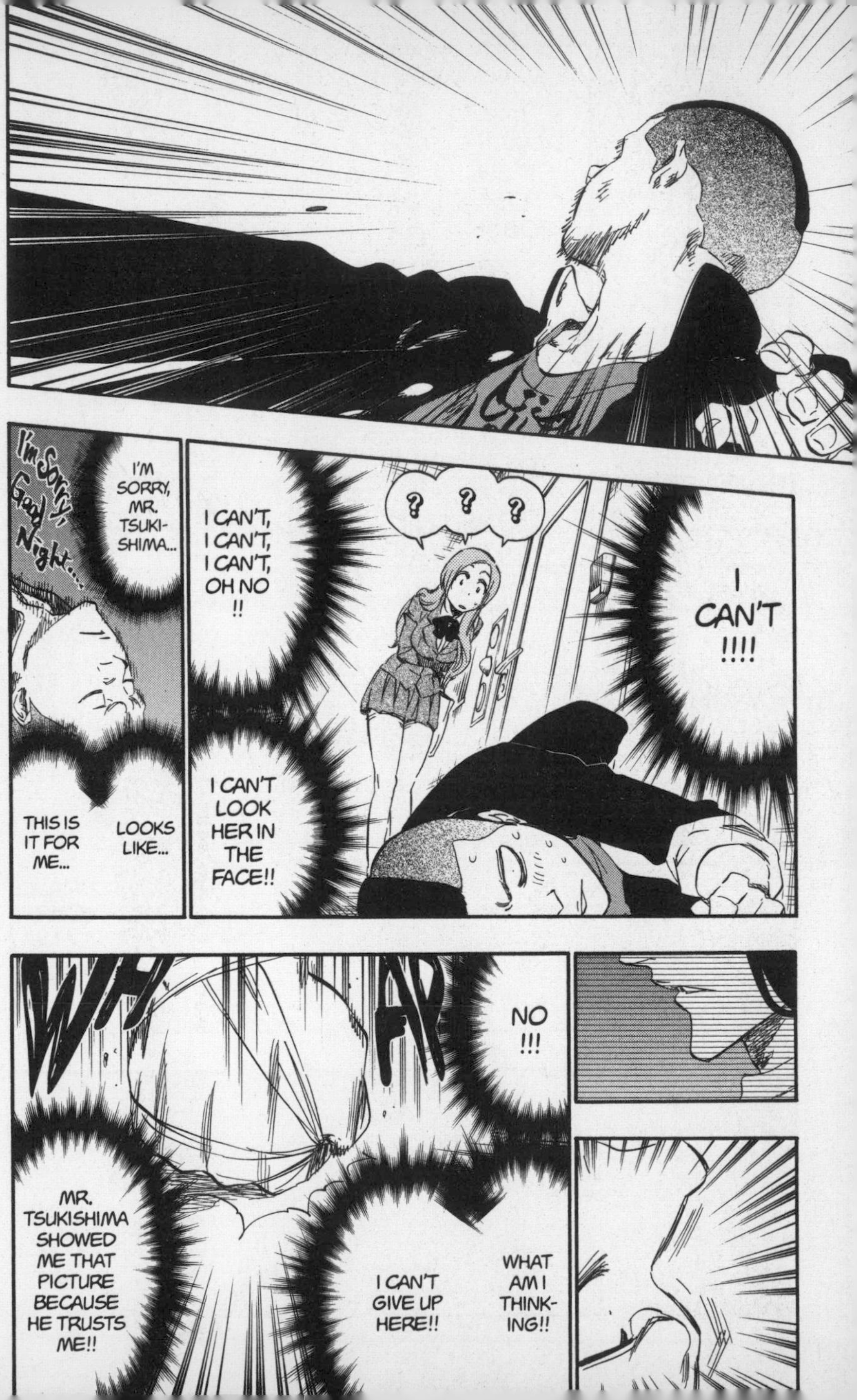

I CAN'T !!!!
???
I CAN'T, I CAN'T, I CAN'T, OH NO !!
I CAN'T LOOK HER IN THE FACE!!
I'M SORRY, MR. TSUKI-SHIMA...
I'm Sorry, Good Night....
LOOKS LIKE...
THIS IS IT FOR ME...
NO !!!
WHAP
WHAT AM I THINK-ING!!
I CAN'T GIVE UP HERE!!
MR. TSUKISHIMA SHOWED ME THAT PICTURE BECAUSE HE TRUSTS ME!!

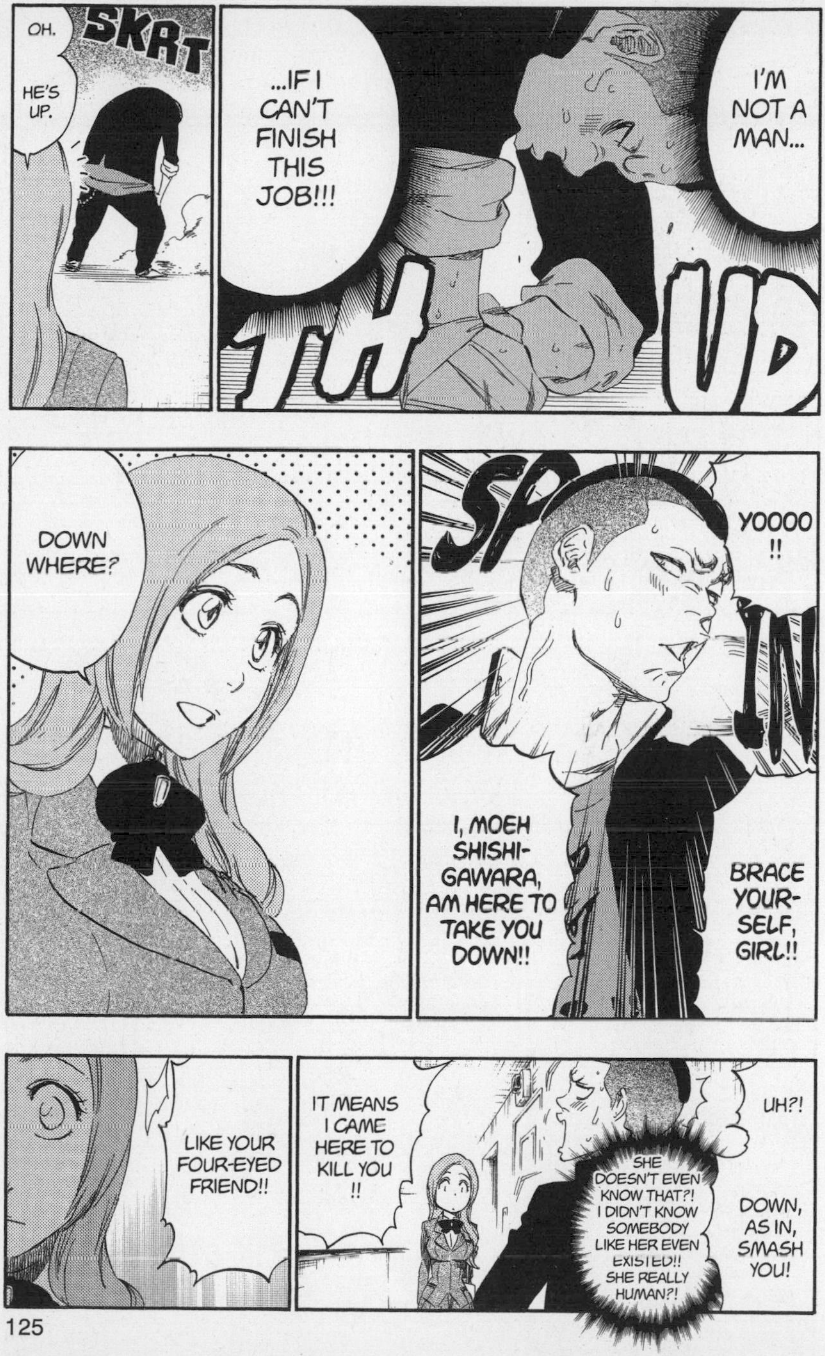
I'M NOT A MAN...
...IF I CAN'T FINISH THIS JOB!!!
TH
UD
SKRT
OH.
HE'S UP.
SP
IN
YOOOO!!
BRACE YOURSELF, GIRL!!
I, MOEH SHISHIGAWARA, AM HERE TO TAKE YOU DOWN!!
DOWN WHERE?
UH?!
DOWN, AS IN, SMASH YOU!
SHE DOESN'T EVEN KNOW THAT?! I DIDN'T KNOW SOMEBODY LIKE HER EVEN EXISTED!! SHE REALLY HUMAN?!
IT MEANS I CAME HERE TO KILL YOU!!
LIKE YOUR FOUR-EYED FRIEND!!

ARE YOU THE ONE...

...WHO ATTACKED URYU?

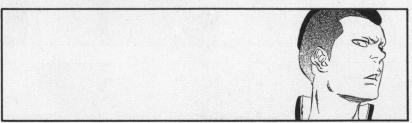

NOT BAD.

HER DEMEANOR'S SUDDENLY...

ANSWER ME.

I CAN FIGHT HER NOW.

'SUPER EVIL

READ THIS WAY

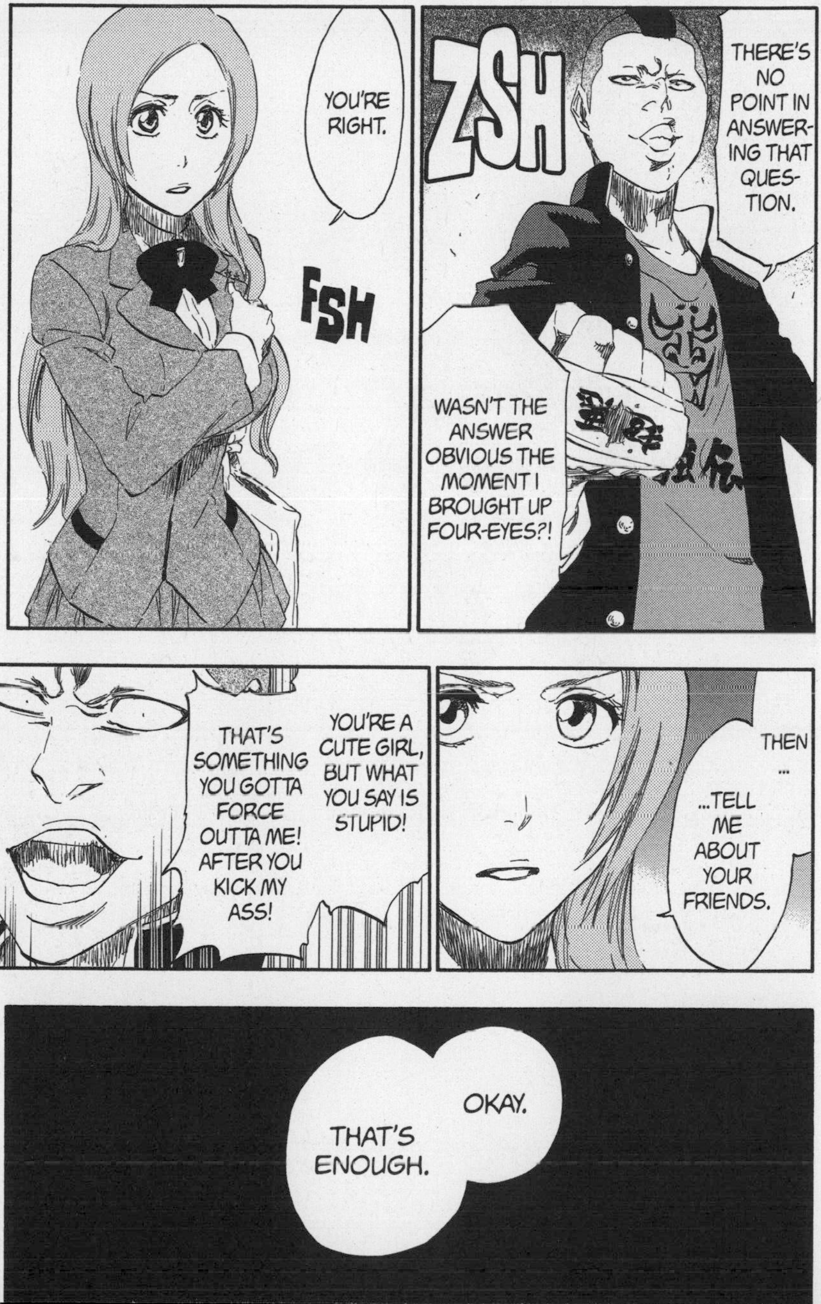
ZSH
THERE'S NO POINT IN ANSWERING THAT QUESTION.
WASN'T THE ANSWER OBVIOUS THE MOMENT I BROUGHT UP FOUR-EYES?!
YOU'RE RIGHT.
FSH
THEN ...
...TELL ME ABOUT YOUR FRIENDS.
YOU'RE A CUTE GIRL, BUT WHAT YOU SAY IS STUPID!
THAT'S SOMETHING YOU GOTTA FORCE OUTTA ME! AFTER YOU KICK MY ASS!
OKAY.
THAT'S ENOUGH.

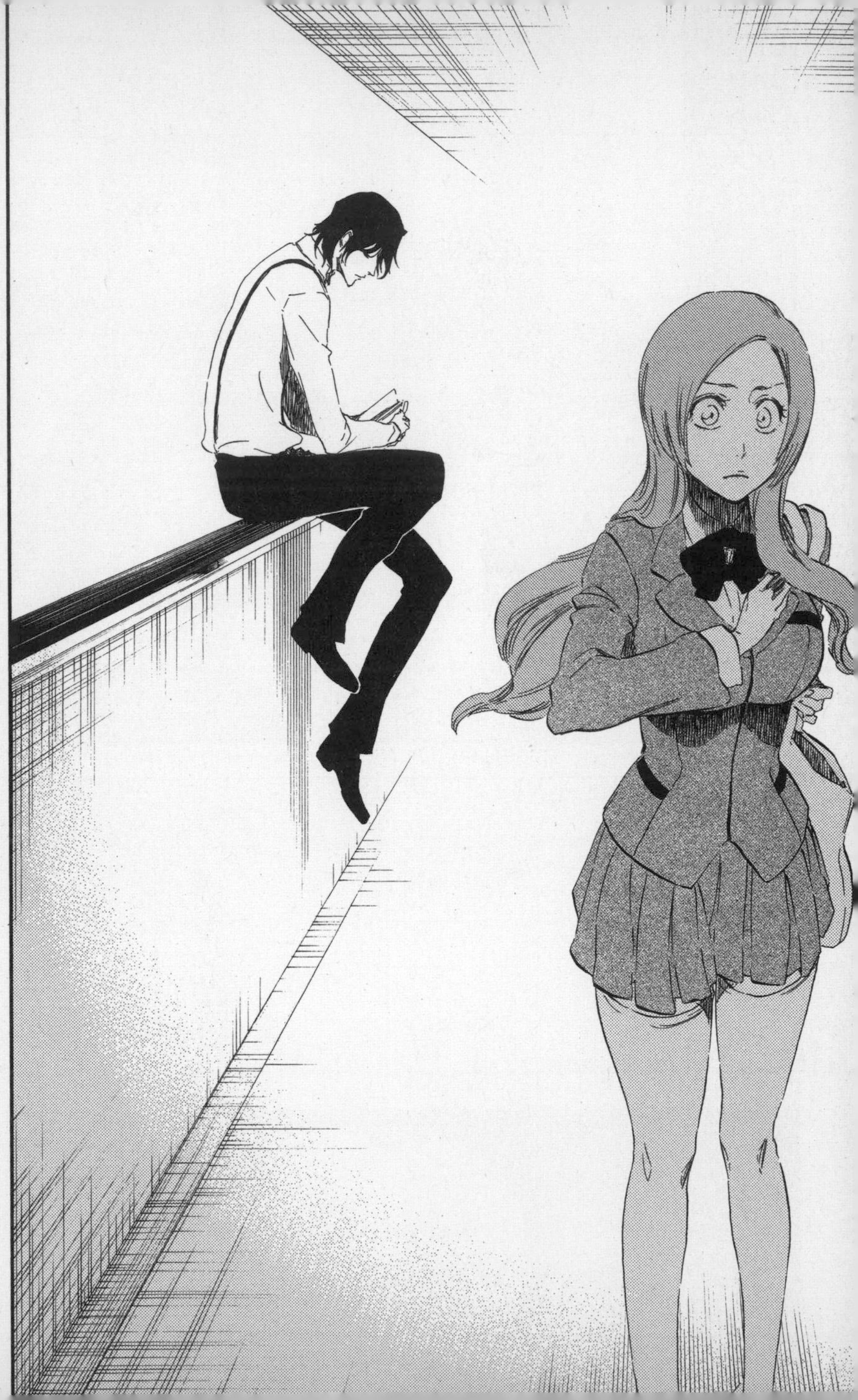

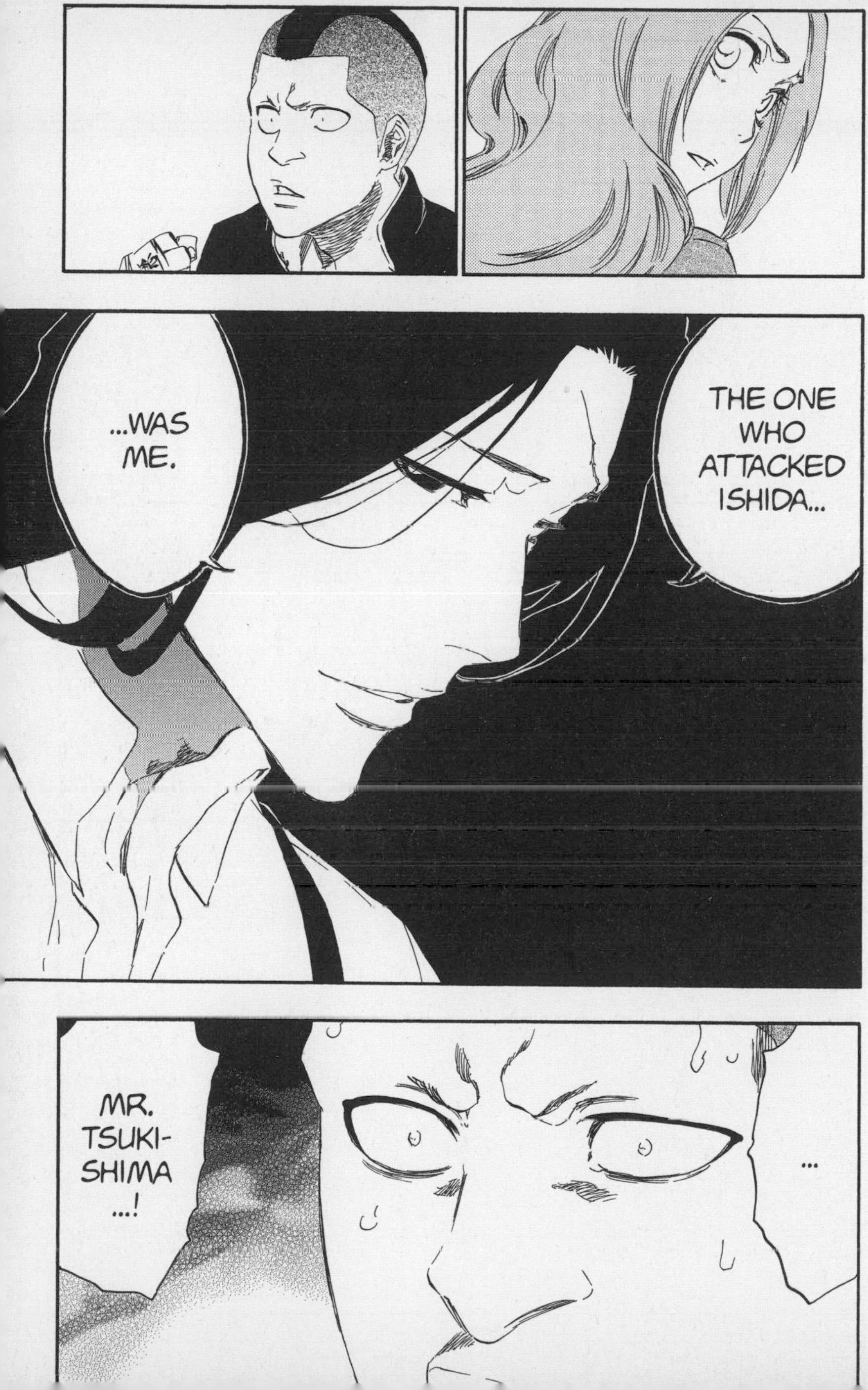
THE ONE WHO ATTACKED ISHIDA...
...WAS ME.
...
MR. TSUKI-SHIMA ...!

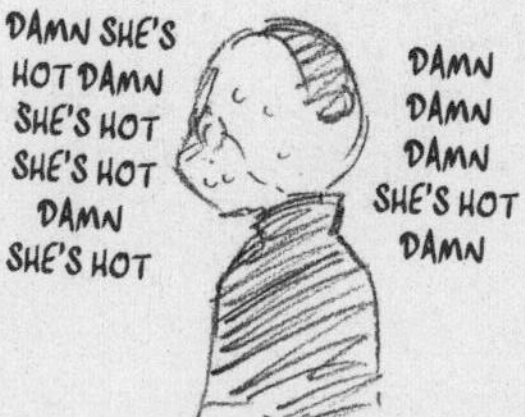
DAMN SHE'S HOT DAMN SHE'S HOT SHE'S HOT DAMN SHE'S HOT
DAMN DAMN DAMN SHE'S HOT DAMN

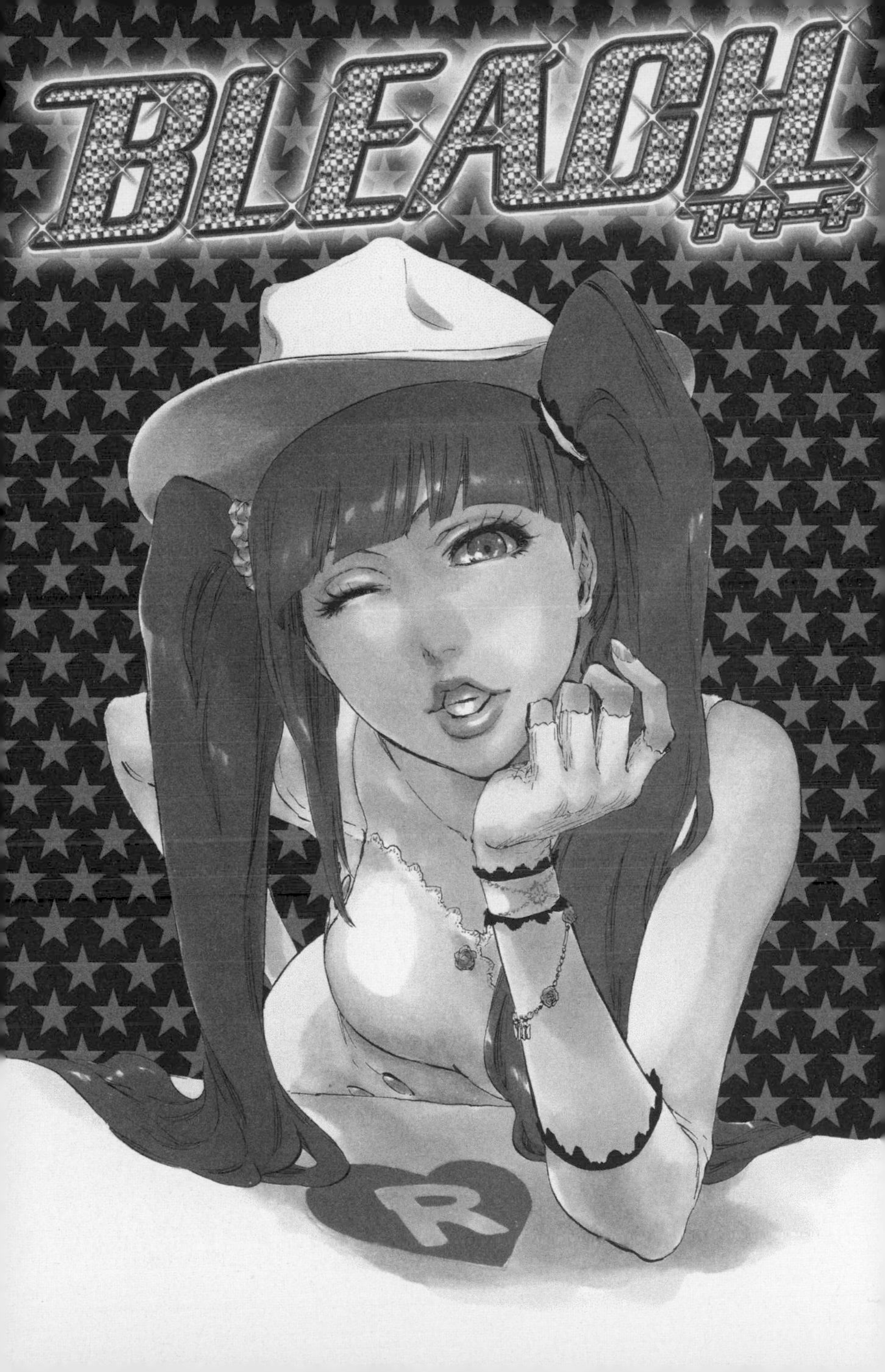
BLEACH

BLEACH
ブリーチ

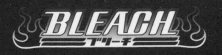

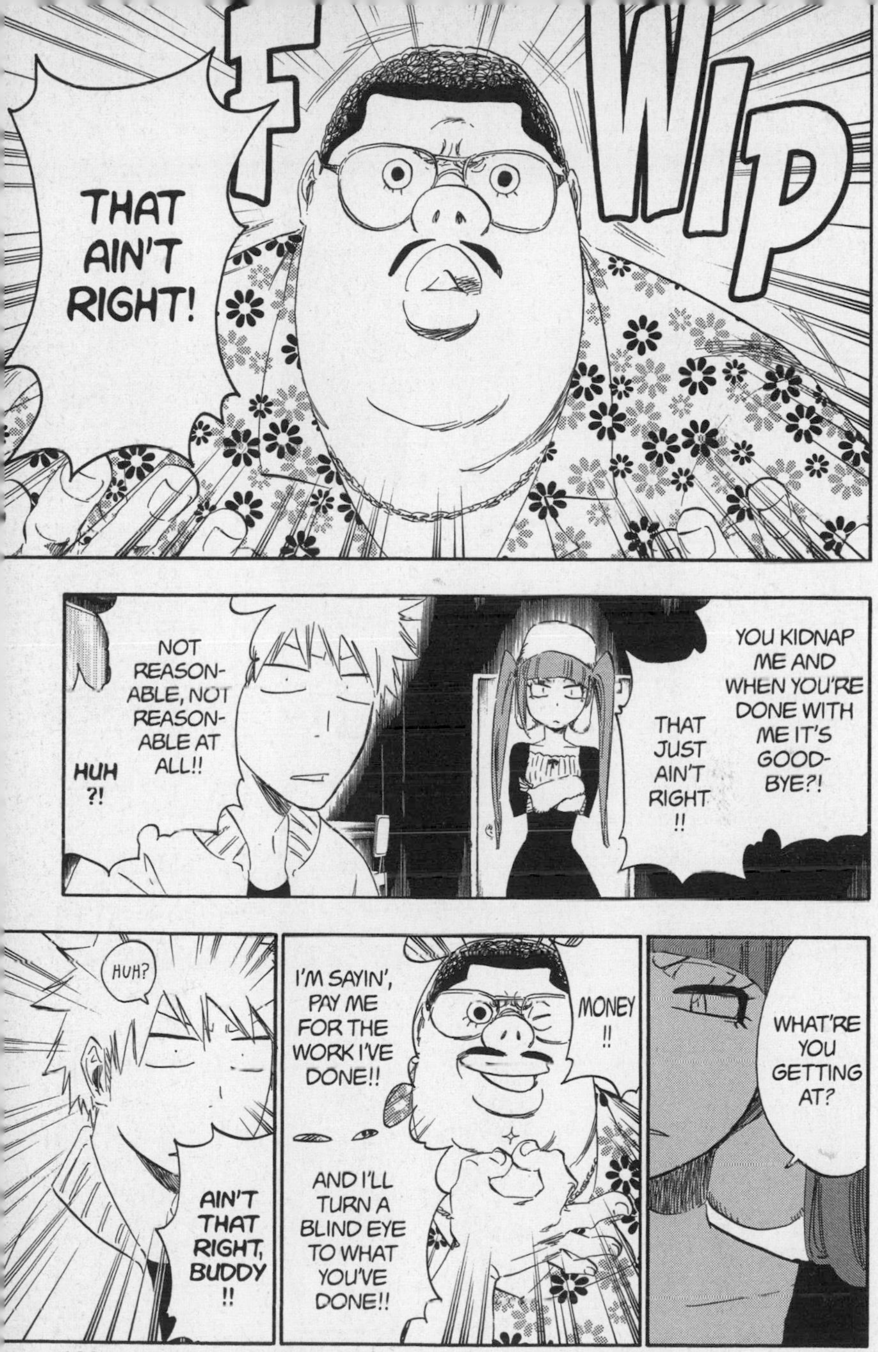
FWIP
THAT AIN'T RIGHT!
YOU KIDNAP ME AND WHEN YOU'RE DONE WITH ME IT'S GOOD-BYE?!
THAT JUST AIN'T RIGHT!!
NOT REASONABLE, NOT REASONABLE AT ALL!!
HUH?!
WHAT'RE YOU GETTING AT?
MONEY!!
I'M SAYIN', PAY ME FOR THE WORK I'VE DONE!!
AND I'LL TURN A BLIND EYE TO WHAT YOU'VE DONE!!
HUH?
AIN'T THAT RIGHT, BUDDY!!

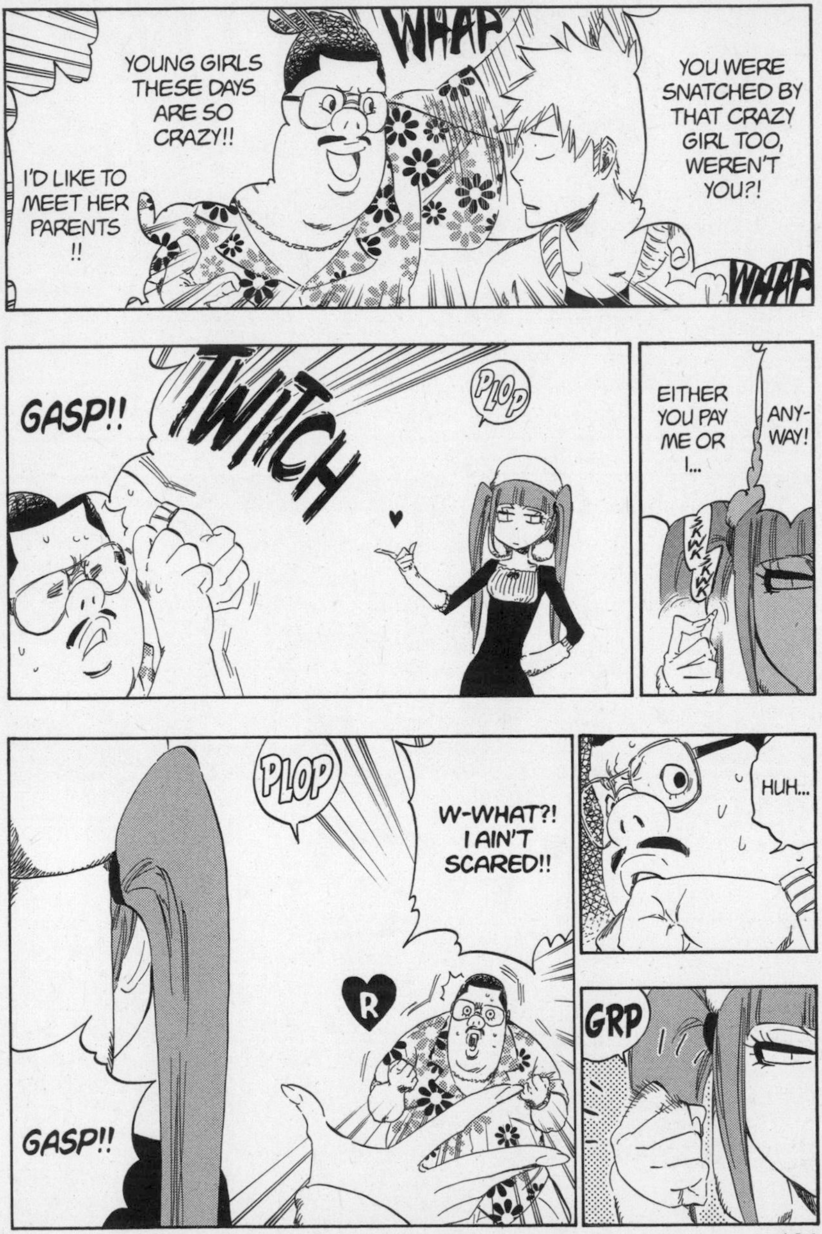
WHAP
YOU WERE SNATCHED BY THAT CRAZY GIRL TOO, WEREN'T YOU?!
YOUNG GIRLS THESE DAYS ARE SO CRAZY!!
I'D LIKE TO MEET HER PARENTS !!
WHAP
ANY-WAY!
EITHER YOU PAY ME OR I...
SKWK SKWK
PLOP
TWITCH
GASP!!
HUH...
GRP
W-WHAT?! I AIN'T SCARED!!
PLOP
R
GASP!!

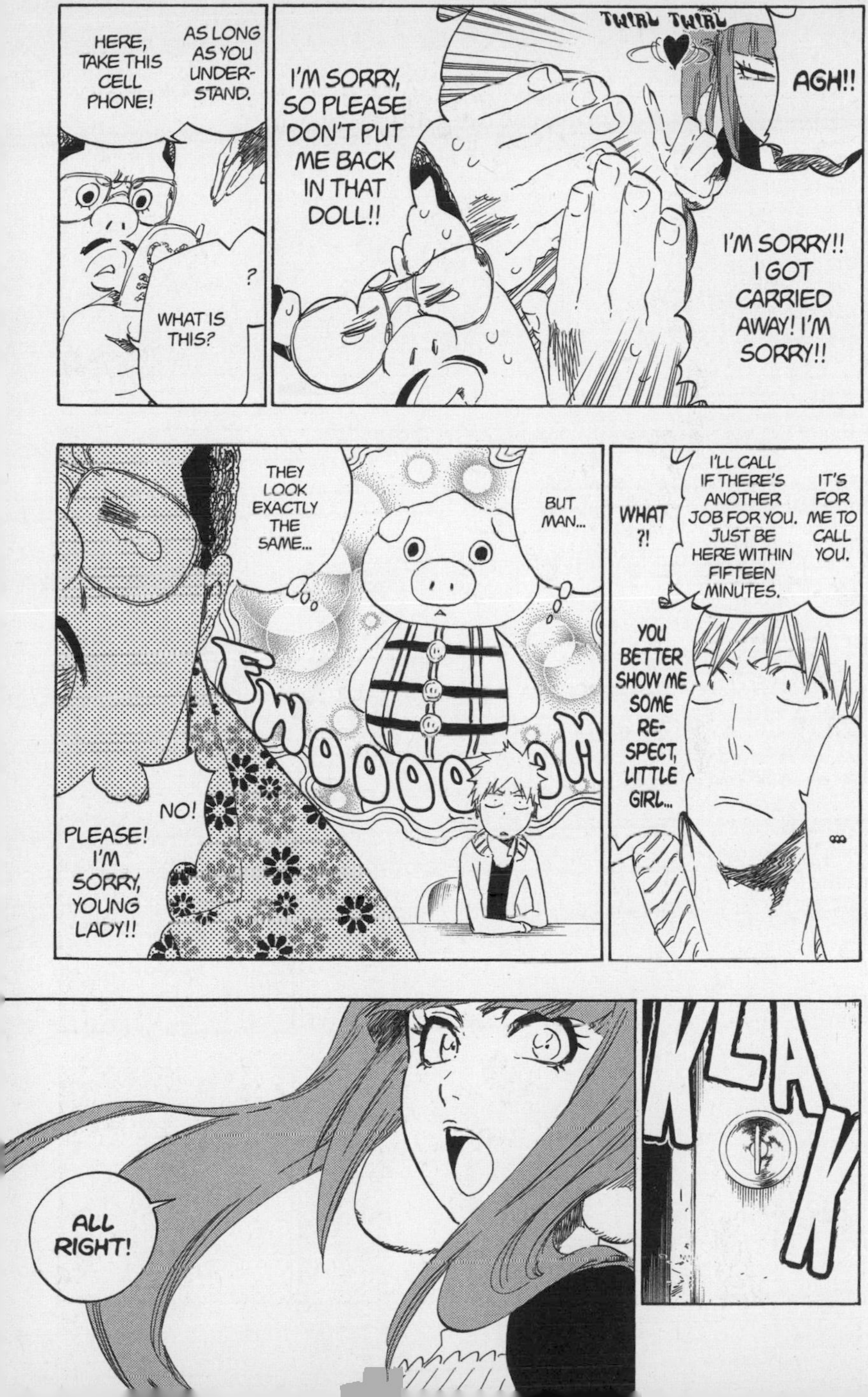
TWIRL TWIRL
AGH!!
I'M SORRY!! I GOT CARRIED AWAY! I'M SORRY!!
I'M SORRY, SO PLEASE DON'T PUT ME BACK IN THAT DOLL!!
AS LONG AS YOU UNDER-STAND.
HERE, TAKE THIS CELL PHONE!
?
WHAT IS THIS?
IT'S FOR ME TO CALL YOU.
I'LL CALL IF THERE'S ANOTHER JOB FOR YOU. JUST BE HERE WITHIN FIFTEEN MINUTES.
WHAT ?!
YOU BETTER SHOW ME SOME RE-SPECT, LITTLE GIRL...
...
BUT MAN...
THEY LOOK EXACTLY THE SAME...
FWOOOOOH
NO!
PLEASE! I'M SORRY, YOUNG LADY!!
KLAK
ALL RIGHT!

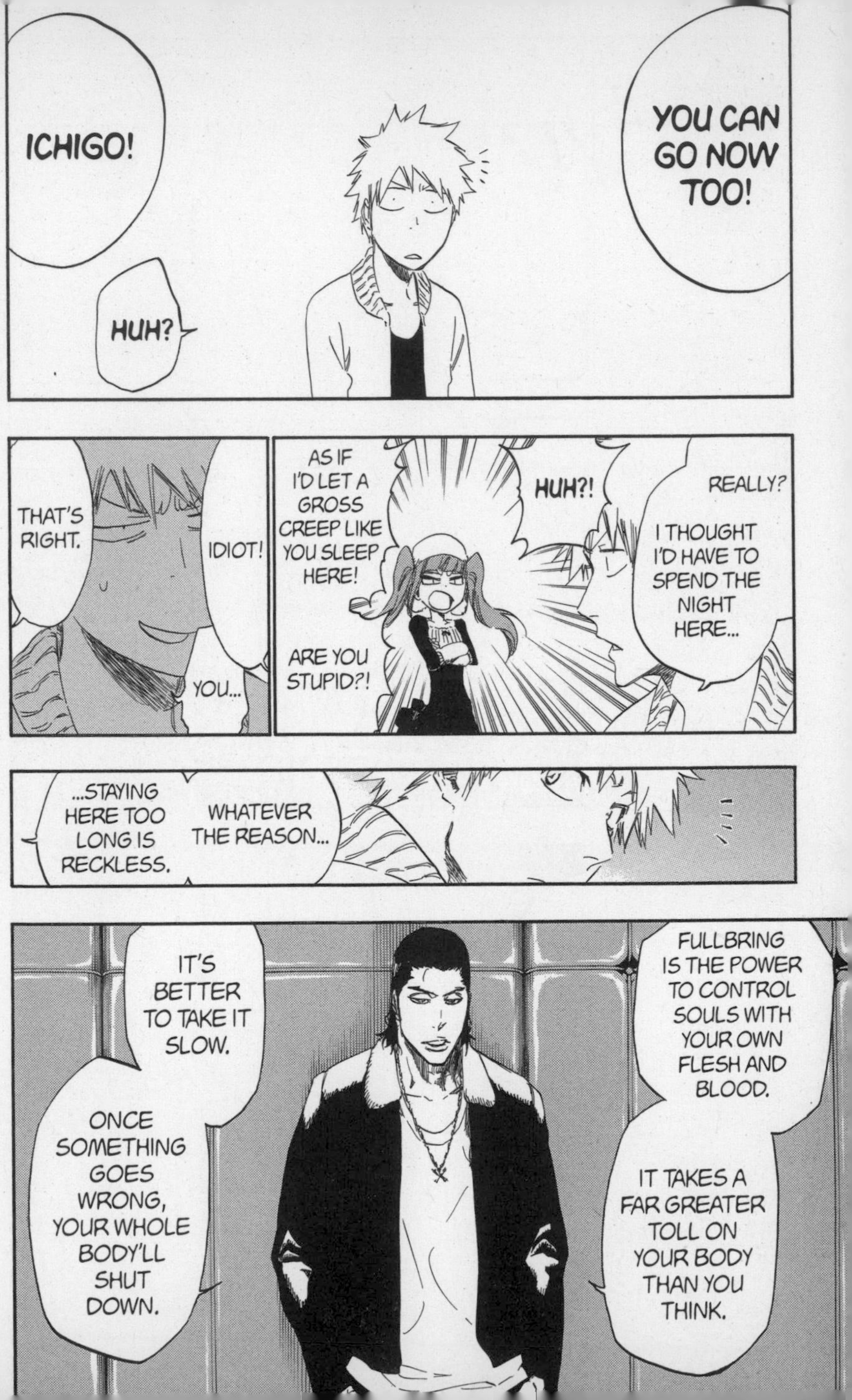
YOU CAN GO NOW TOO!
ICHIGO!
HUH?
REALLY?
I THOUGHT I'D HAVE TO SPEND THE NIGHT HERE...
HUH?!
AS IF I'D LET A GROSS CREEP LIKE YOU SLEEP HERE!
ARE YOU STUPID?!
IDIOT!
YOU...
THAT'S RIGHT.
WHATEVER THE REASON...
...STAYING HERE TOO LONG IS RECKLESS.
FULLBRING IS THE POWER TO CONTROL SOULS WITH YOUR OWN FLESH AND BLOOD.
IT TAKES A FAR GREATER TOLL ON YOUR BODY THAN YOU THINK.
IT'S BETTER TO TAKE IT SLOW.
ONCE SOMETHING GOES WRONG, YOUR WHOLE BODY'LL SHUT DOWN.

READ THIS WAY

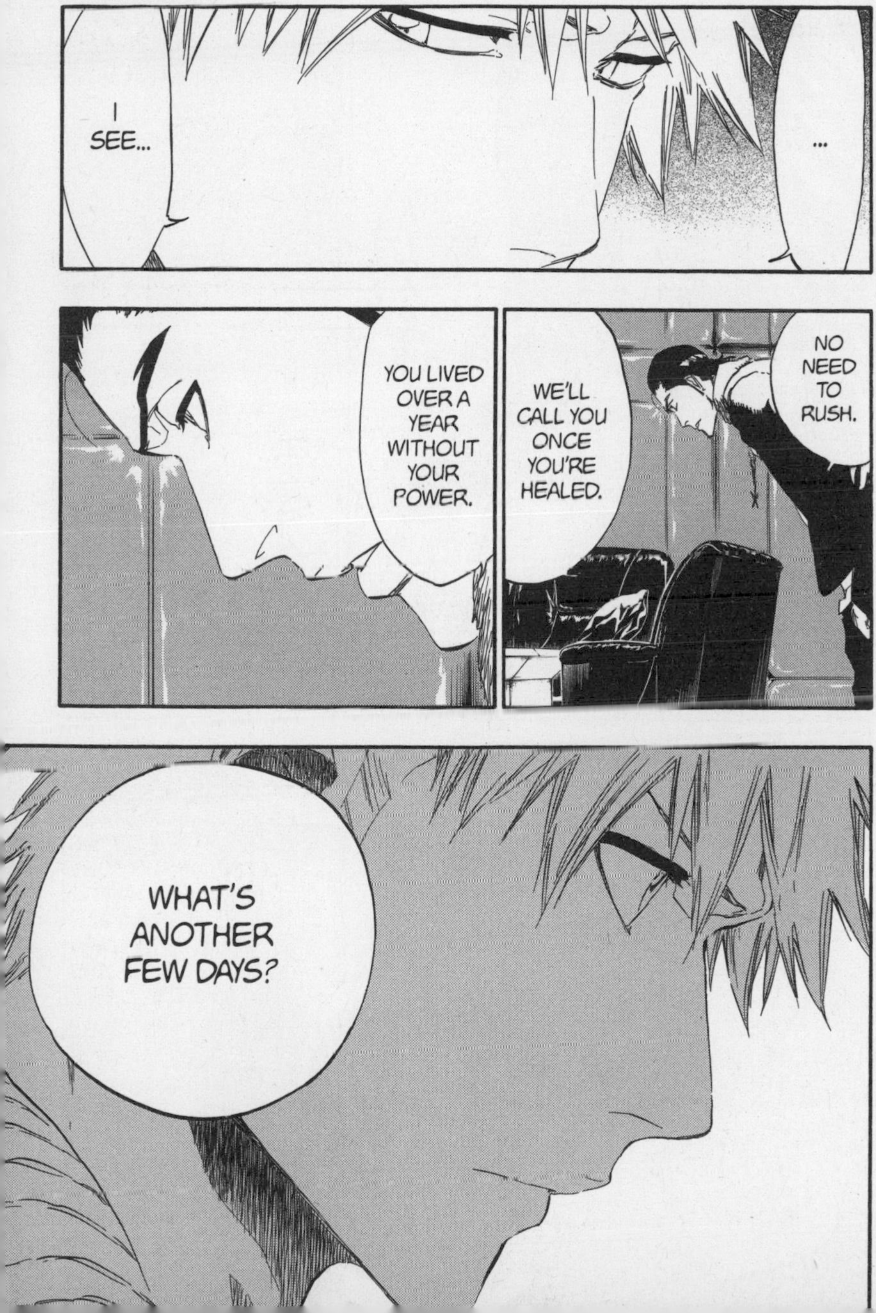
...
I SEE...
NO NEED TO RUSH.
WE'LL CALL YOU ONCE YOU'RE HEALED.
YOU LIVED OVER A YEAR WITHOUT YOUR POWER.
WHAT'S ANOTHER FEW DAYS?

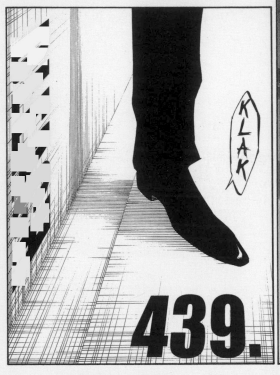

KLAK

439.

...ARE
YOU...?

WHO...

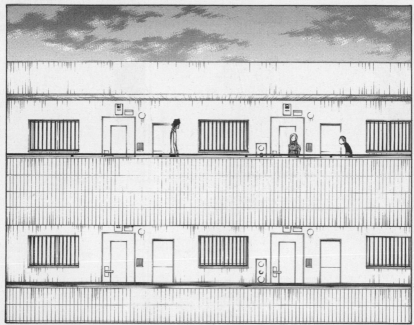

KEEN MARKER

SHUKURO TSUKISHIMA.

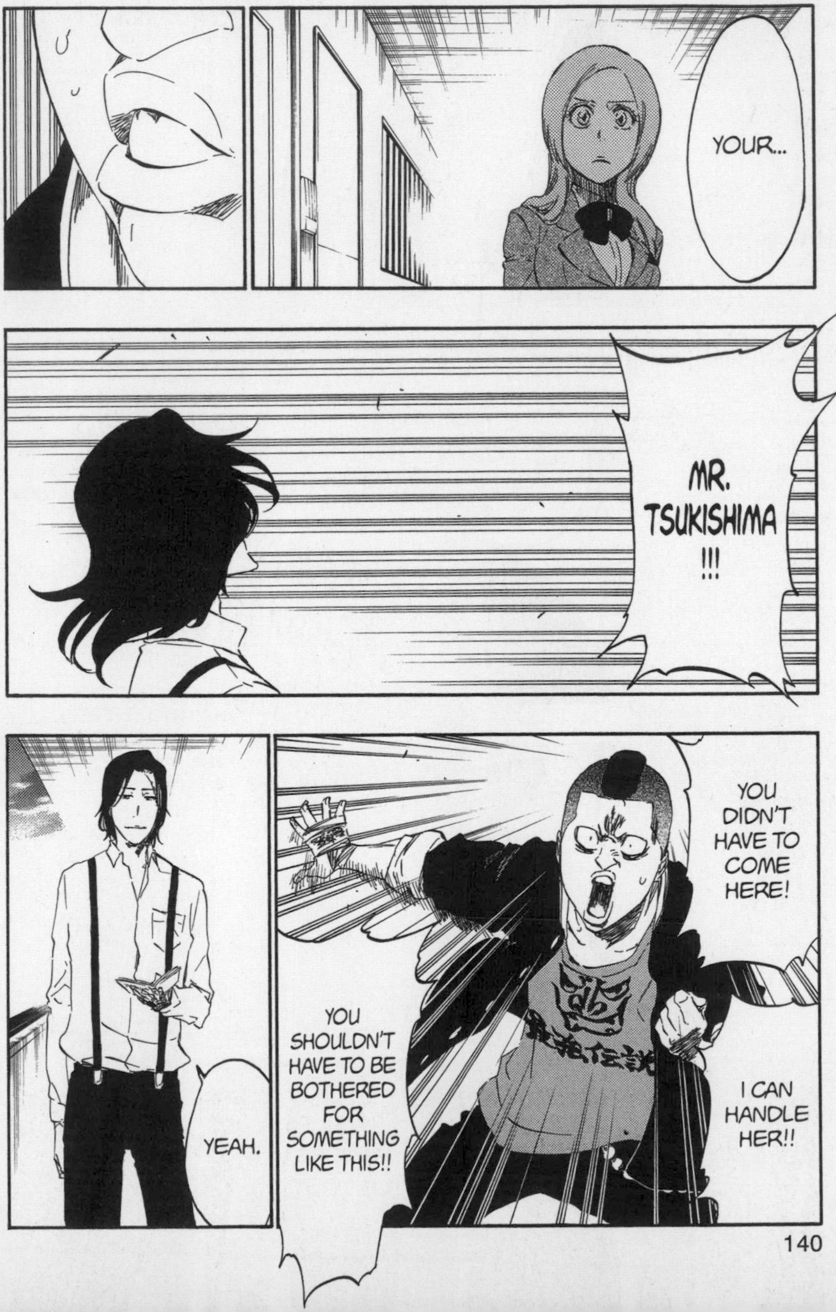
YOUR...
MR. TSUKISHIMA!!!
YOU DIDN'T HAVE TO COME HERE!
YOU SHOULDN'T HAVE TO BE BOTHERED FOR SOMETHING LIKE THIS!!
I CAN HANDLE HER!!
YEAH.

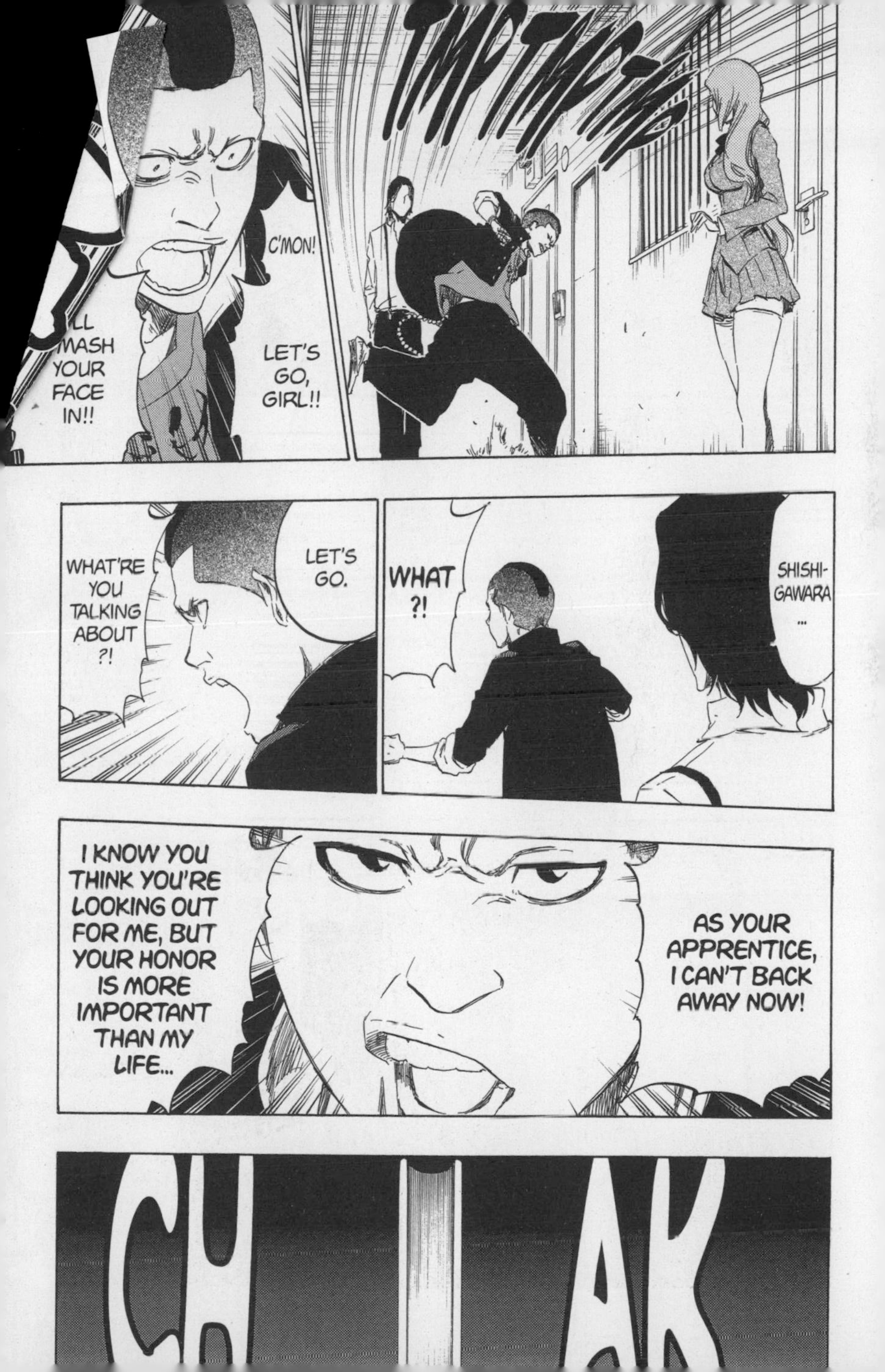
TMP TMP TMP
C'MON!
LET'S GO, GIRL!!
LL MASH YOUR FACE IN!!
SHISHI-GAWARA...
WHAT?!
LET'S GO.
WHAT'RE YOU TALKING ABOUT?!
I KNOW YOU THINK YOU'RE LOOKING OUT FOR ME, BUT YOUR HONOR IS MORE IMPORTANT THAN MY LIFE...
AS YOUR APPRENTICE, I CAN'T BACK AWAY NOW!
CH AK

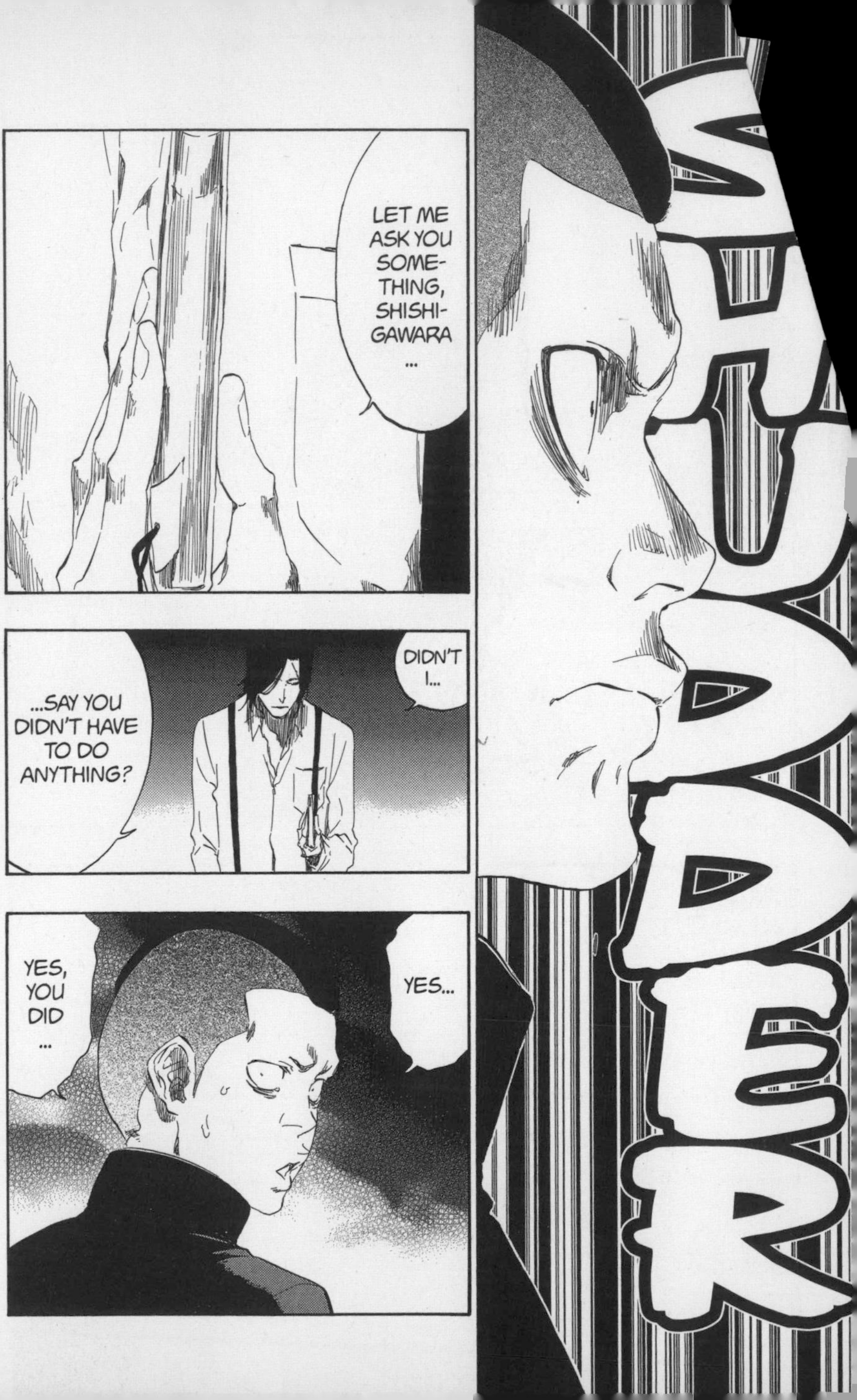
SHUDDER
LET ME ASK YOU SOME-THING, SHISHI-GAWARA ...
DIDN'T I...
...SAY YOU DIDN'T HAVE TO DO ANYTHING?
YES...
YES, YOU DID ...

FSH

WHAT ARE YOU DOING HERE?

THEN...

NOW I LOST TRACK OF HOW FAR I HAD READ.

OH NO.

TO HELP YOU...

TO...

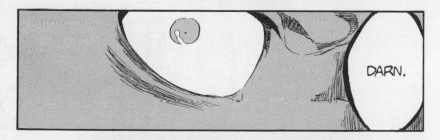

DARN.

SHISHI-GAWARA.

HEY...

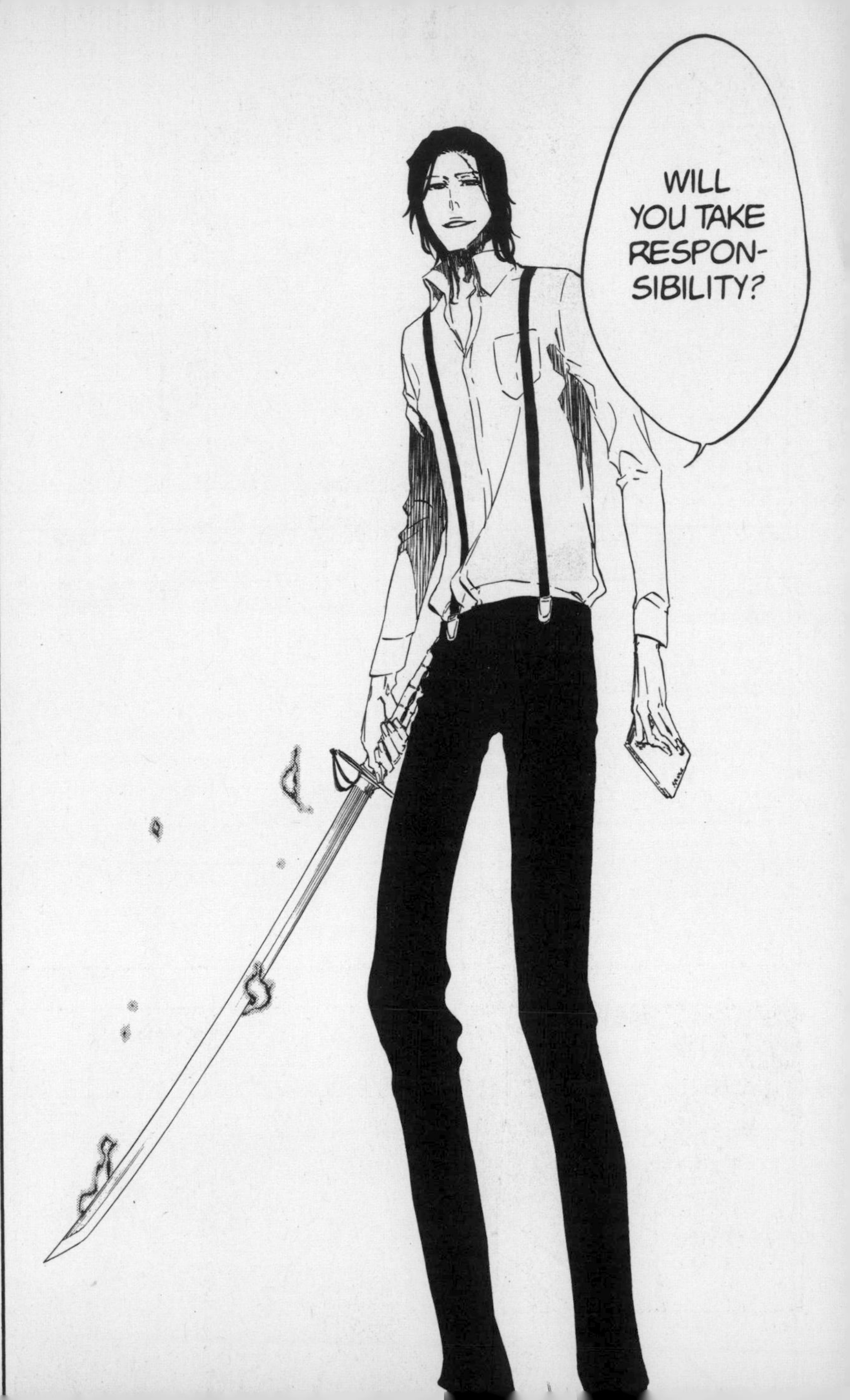
WILL YOU TAKE RESPON-SIBILITY?

HIS BOOKMARK TURNED INTO A SWORD...?!

WHAT... WAS THAT ...?!

WH...

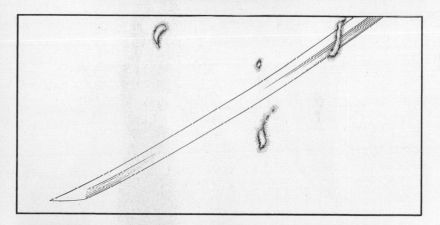

MM?

...A ZANPAKU-TŌ...?!

IS THAT...

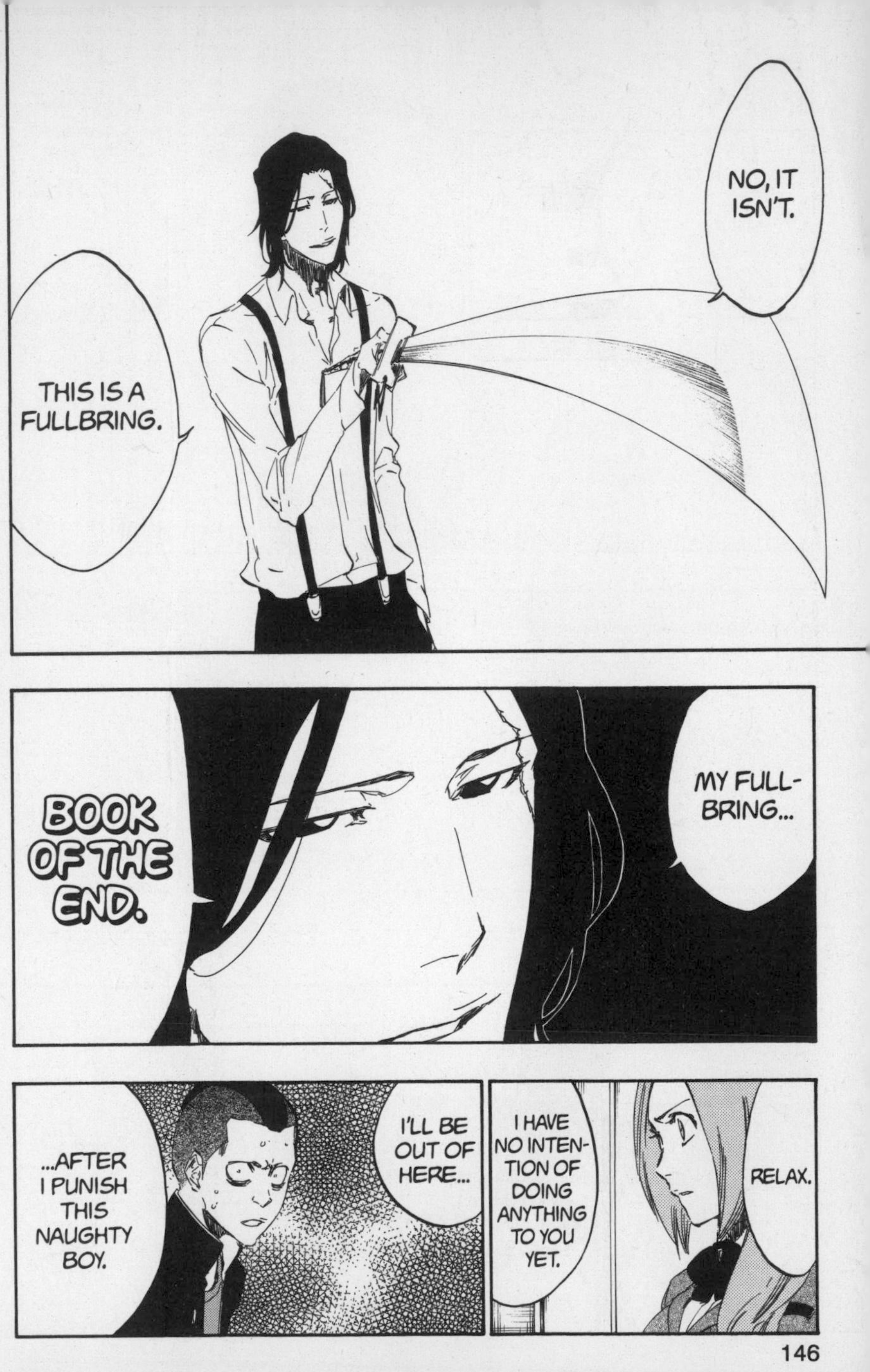
NO, IT ISN'T.
THIS IS A FULLBRING.
MY FULL-BRING...
BOOK OF THE END.
RELAX.
I HAVE NO INTEN-TION OF DOING ANYTHING TO YOU YET.
I'LL BE OUT OF HERE...
...AFTER I PUNISH THIS NAUGHTY BOY.

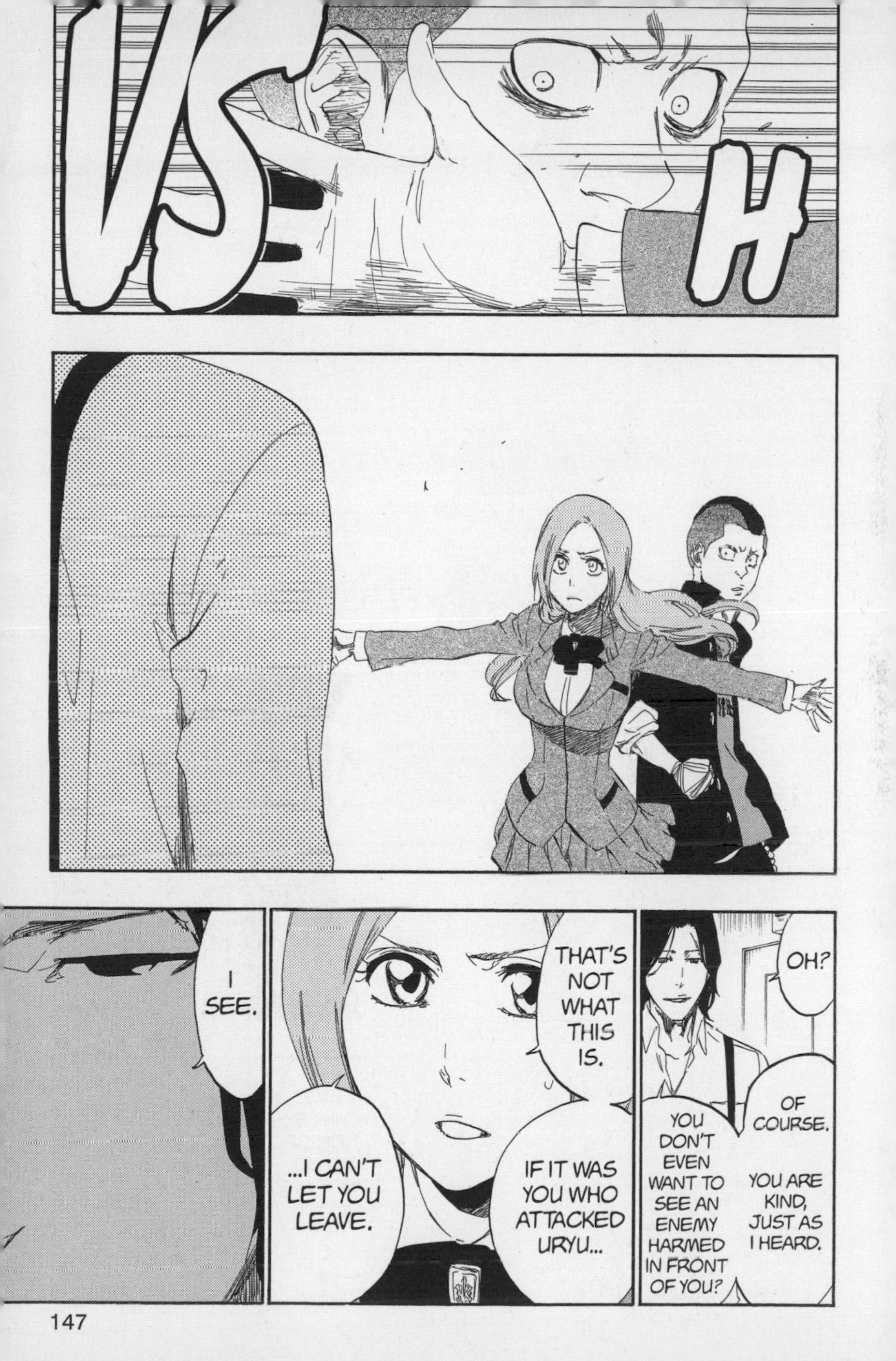
VSH
OH?
OF COURSE.
YOU ARE KIND, JUST AS I HEARD.
YOU DON'T EVEN WANT TO SEE AN ENEMY HARMED IN FRONT OF YOU?
THAT'S NOT WHAT THIS IS.
IF IT WAS YOU WHO ATTACKED URYU...
...I CAN'T LET YOU LEAVE.
I SEE.

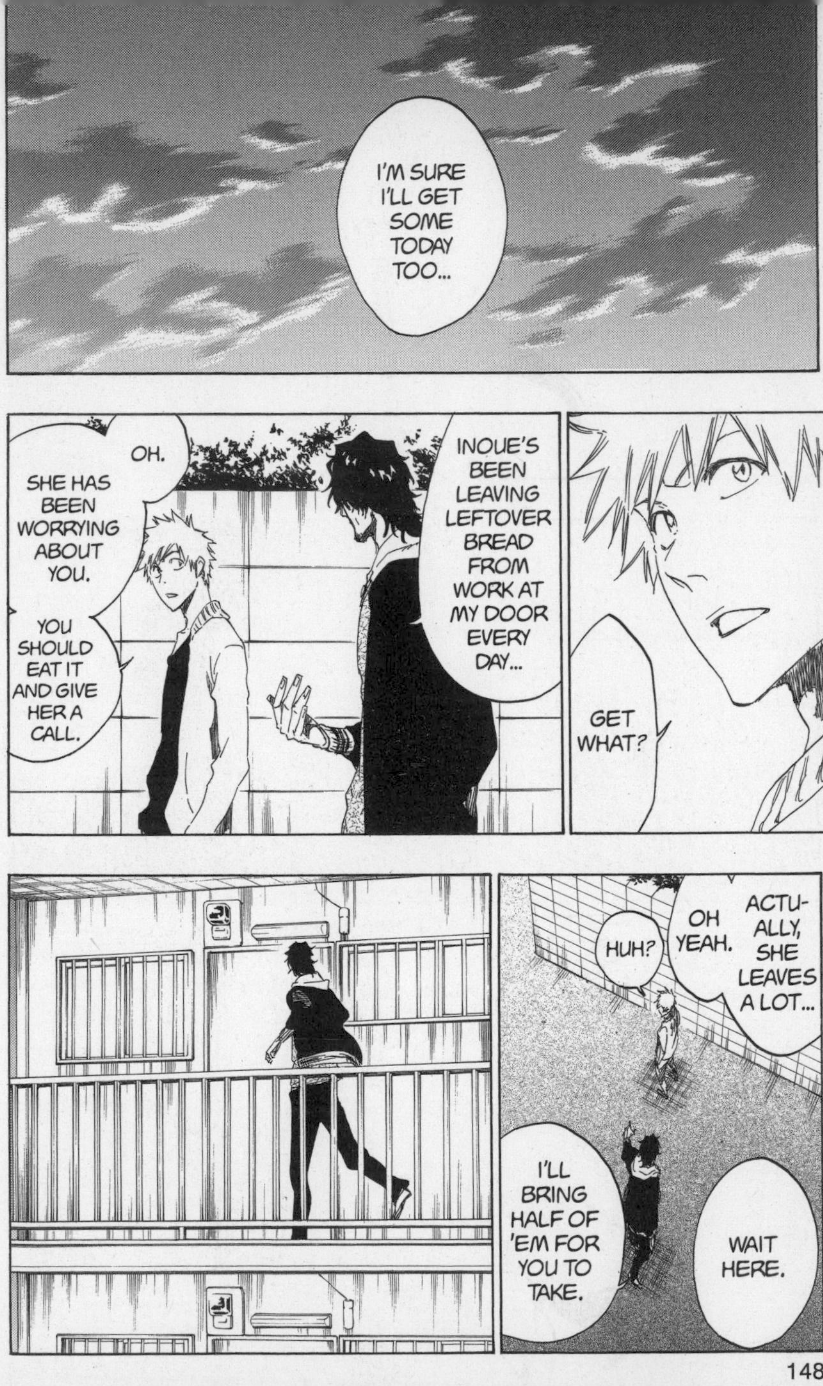
I'M SURE I'LL GET SOME TODAY TOO...
GET WHAT?
INOUE'S BEEN LEAVING LEFTOVER BREAD FROM WORK AT MY DOOR EVERY DAY...
OH.
SHE HAS BEEN WORRYING ABOUT YOU.
YOU SHOULD EAT IT AND GIVE HER A CALL.
ACTU-ALLY, SHE LEAVES A LOT...
OH YEAH.
HUH?
WAIT HERE.
I'LL BRING HALF OF 'EM FOR YOU TO TAKE.

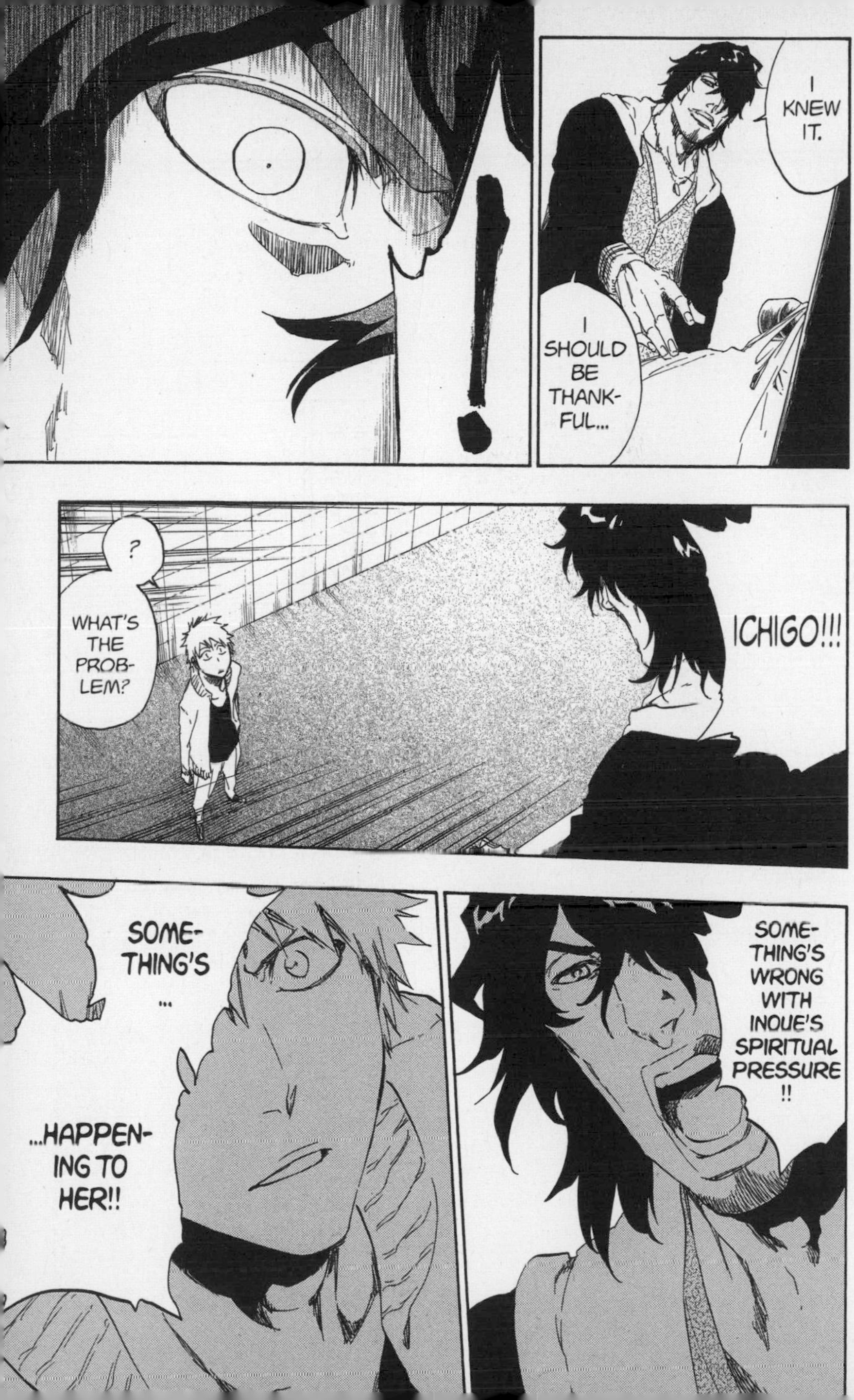
I KNEW IT.
I SHOULD BE THANKFUL...
ICHIGO!!!
?
WHAT'S THE PROBLEM?
SOMETHING'S WRONG WITH INOUE'S SPIRITUAL PRESSURE!!
SOMETHING'S...
...HAPPENING TO HER!!

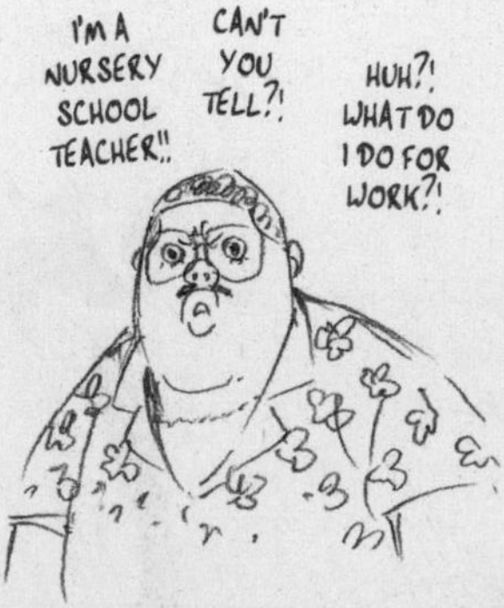
HUH?! WHAT DO I DO FOR WORK?!
CAN'T YOU TELL?!
I'M A NURSERY SCHOOL TEACHER!!

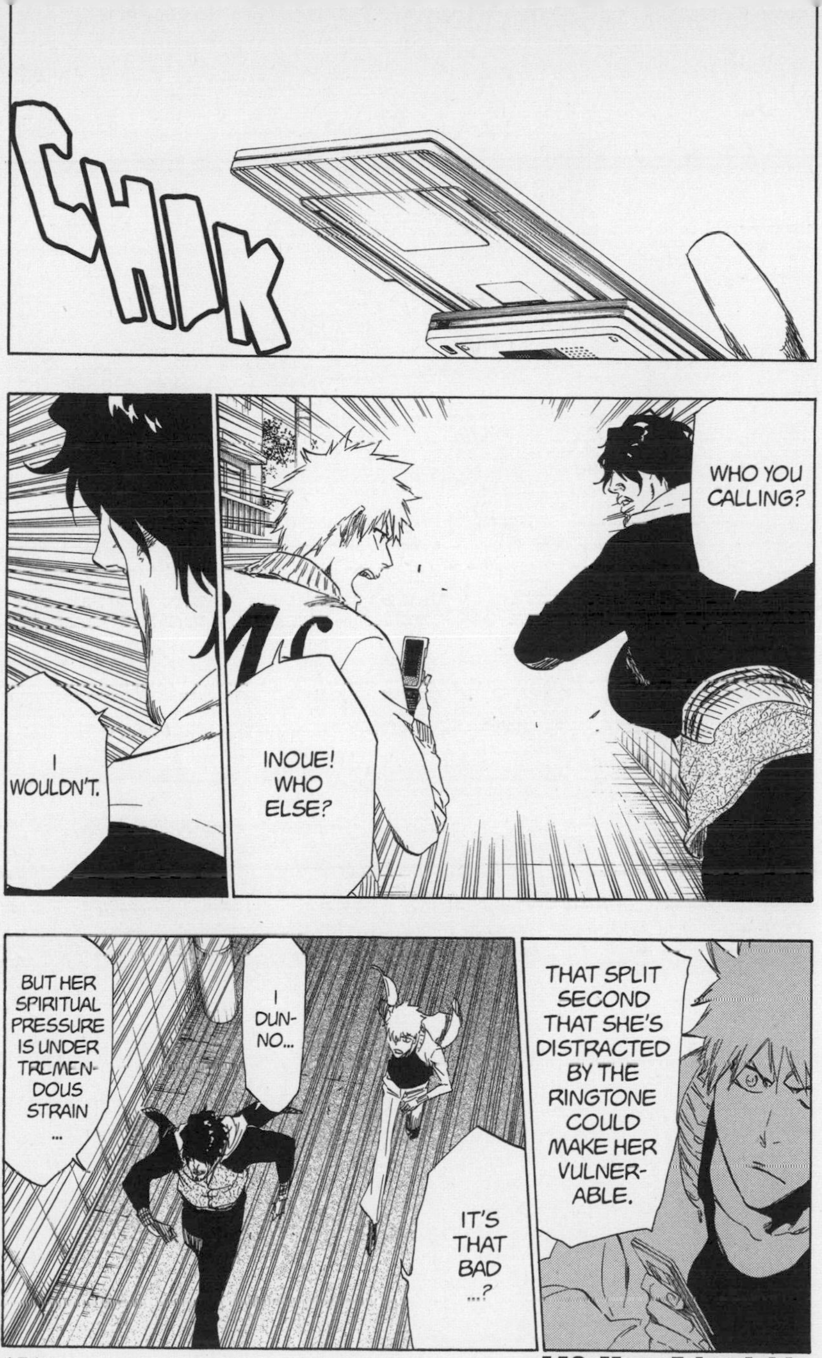
CHIK
WHO YOU CALLING?
INOUE! WHO ELSE?
I WOULDN'T.
THAT SPLIT SECOND THAT SHE'S DISTRACTED BY THE RINGTONE COULD MAKE HER VULNER-ABLE.
IT'S THAT BAD ...?
I DUN-NO...
BUT HER SPIRITUAL PRESSURE IS UNDER TREMEN-DOUS STRAIN ...

440. Mute Friendship

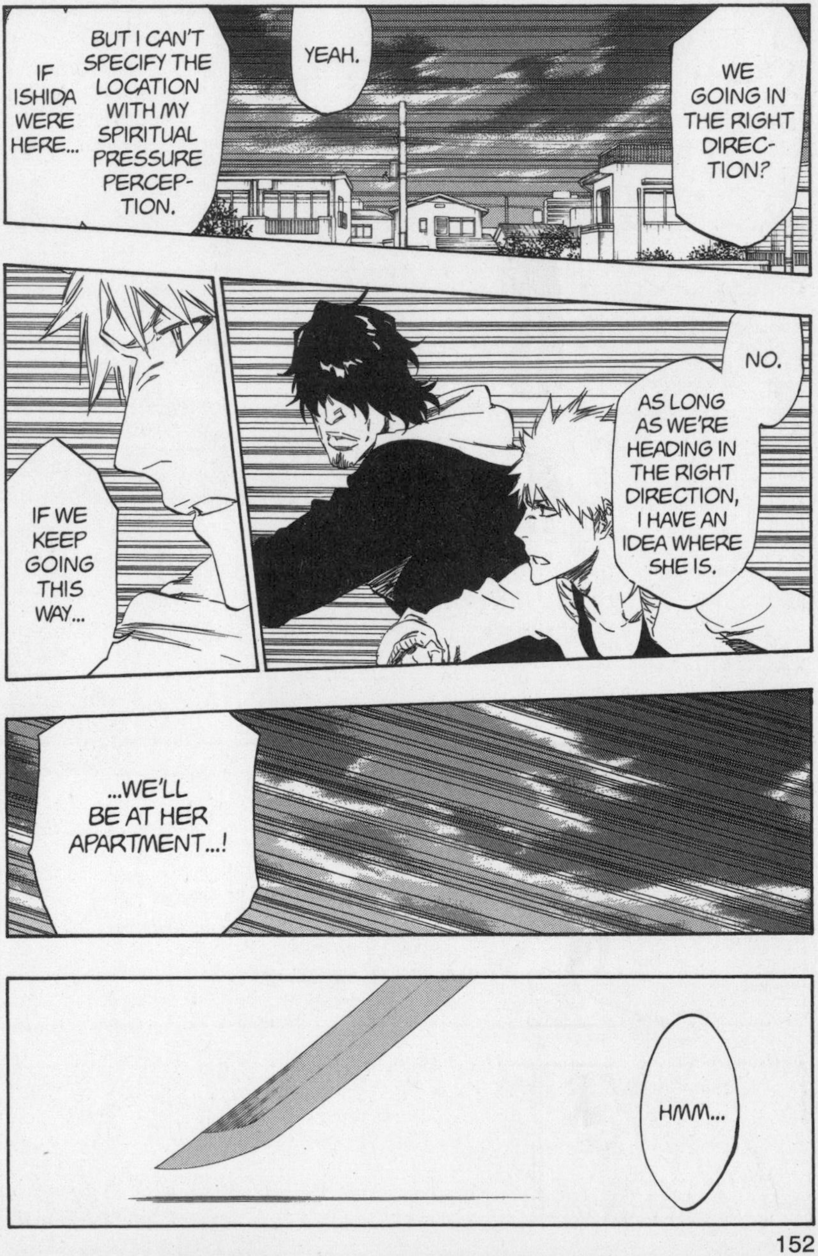
WE GOING IN THE RIGHT DIREC- TION?
YEAH.
BUT I CAN'T SPECIFY THE LOCATION WITH MY SPIRITUAL PRESSURE PERCEP- TION.
IF ISHIDA WERE HERE...
NO.
AS LONG AS WE'RE HEADING IN THE RIGHT DIRECTION, I HAVE AN IDEA WHERE SHE IS.
IF WE KEEP GOING THIS WAY...
...WE'LL BE AT HER APARTMENT...!
HMM...

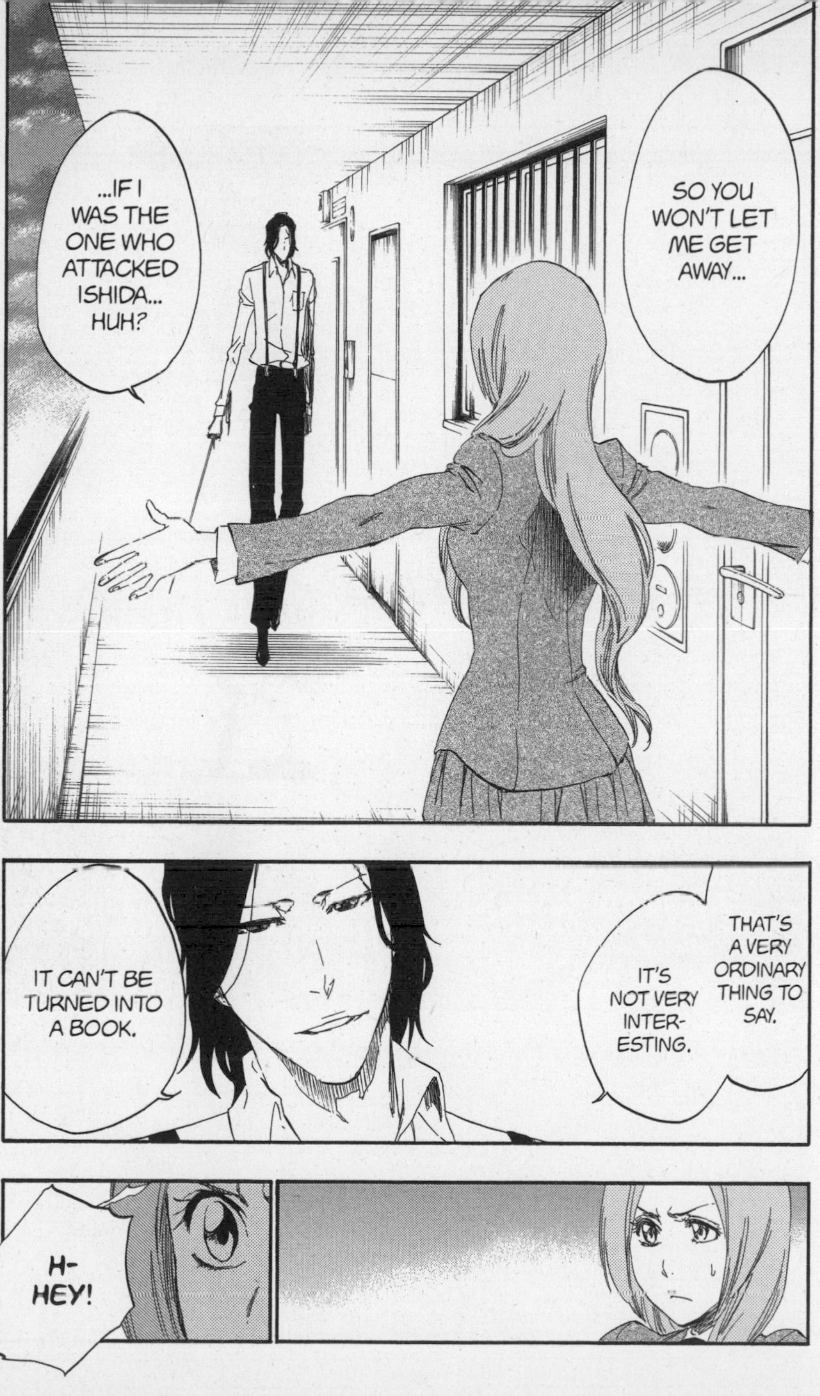
SO YOU WON'T LET ME GET AWAY...
...IF I WAS THE ONE WHO ATTACKED ISHIDA... HUH?
THAT'S A VERY ORDINARY THING TO SAY.
IT'S NOT VERY INTER-ESTING.
IT CAN'T BE TURNED INTO A BOOK.
H-HEY!

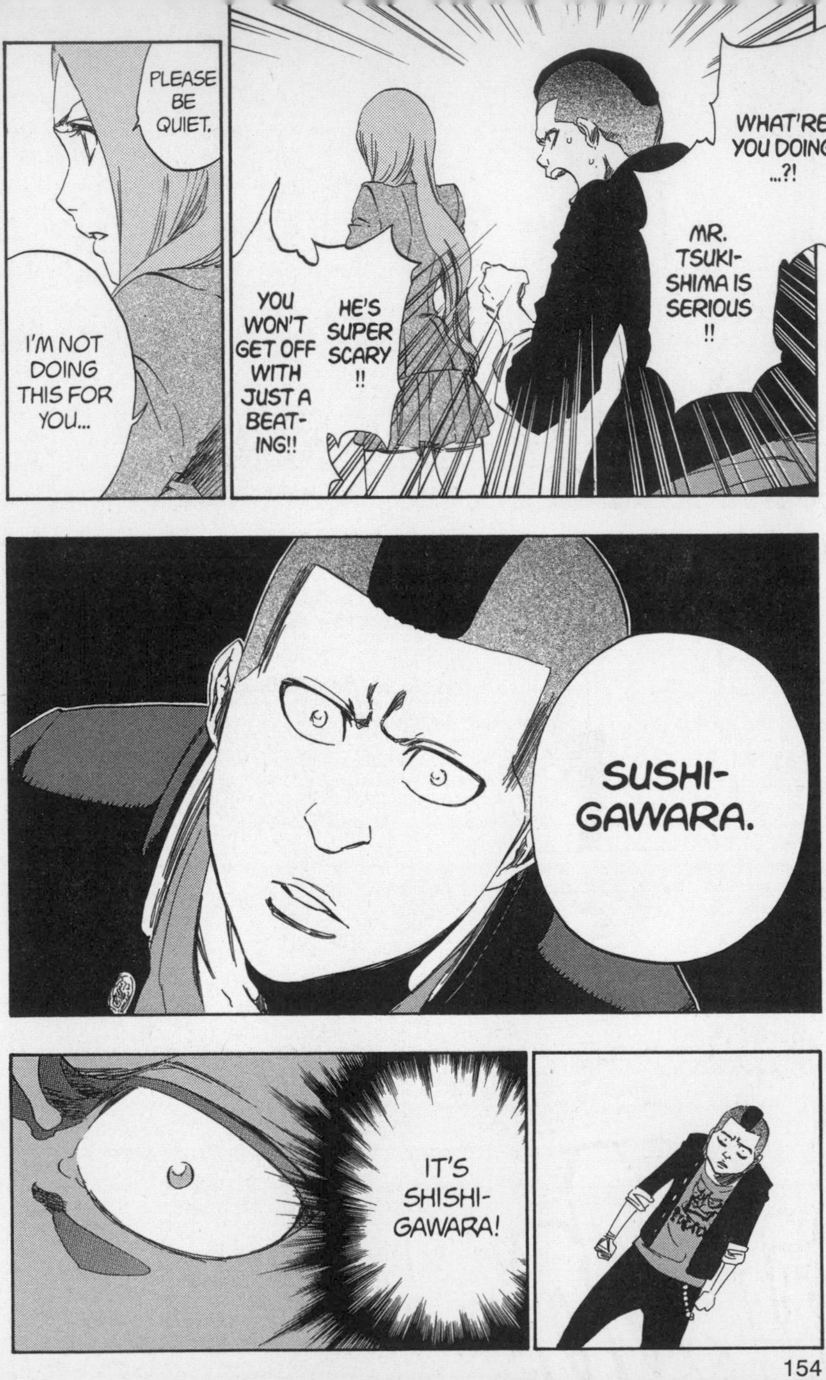
WHAT'RE YOU DOING ...?!
MR. TSUKI-SHIMA IS SERIOUS !!
HE'S SUPER SCARY !!
YOU WON'T GET OFF WITH JUST A BEAT-ING!!
PLEASE BE QUIET.
I'M NOT DOING THIS FOR YOU...
SUSHI-GAWARA.
IT'S SHISHI-GAWARA!

READ THIS WAY

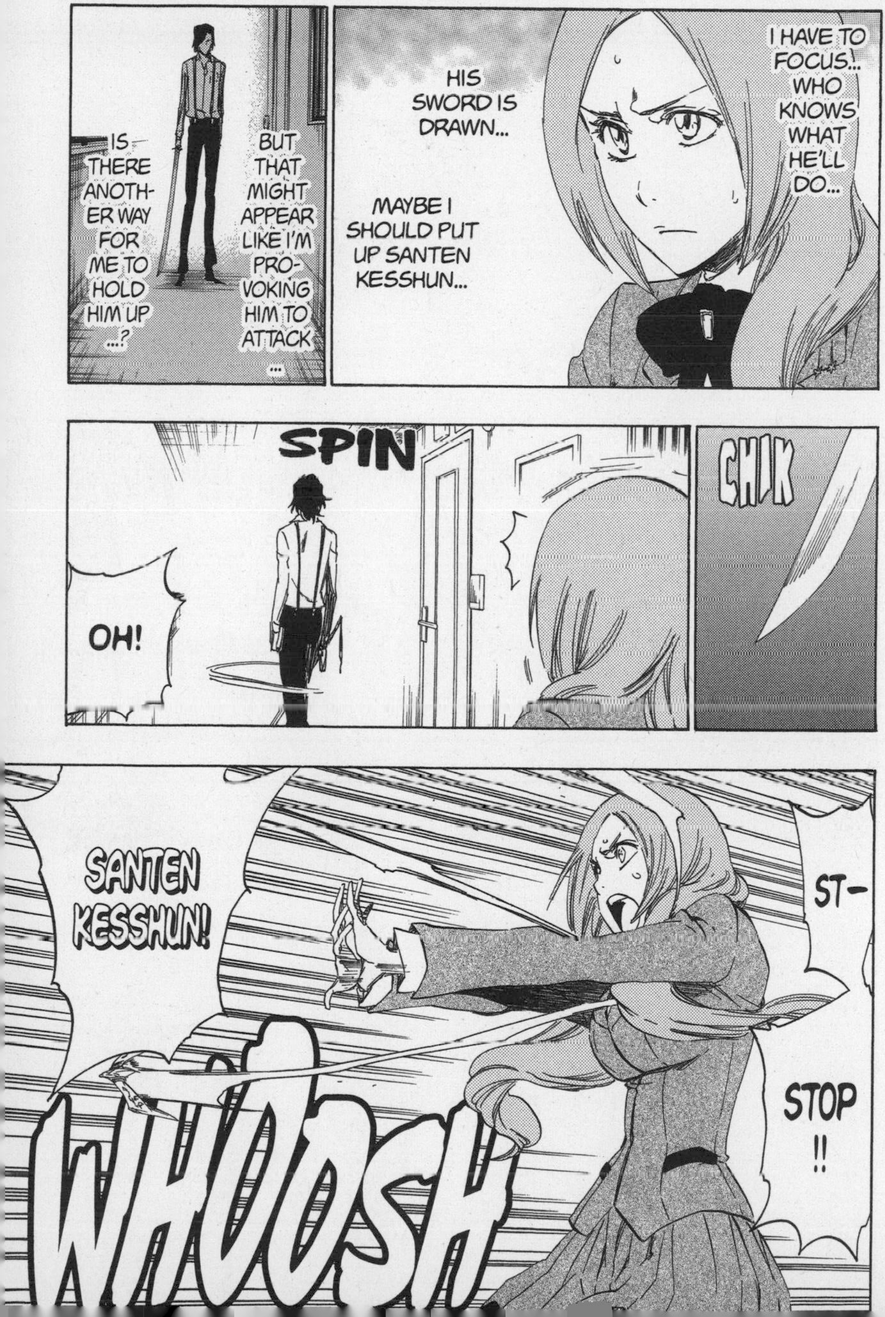

I HAVE TO FOCUS!... WHO KNOWS WHAT HE'LL DO...
HIS SWORD IS DRAWN...
MAYBE I SHOULD PUT UP SANTEN KESSHUN...
BUT THAT MIGHT APPEAR LIKE I'M PRO-VOKING HIM TO ATTACK ...
IS THERE ANOTH-ER WAY FOR ME TO HOLD HIM UP ...?
CHIK
SPIN
OH!
ST-
STOP !!
SANTEN KESSHUN!
WHOOSH

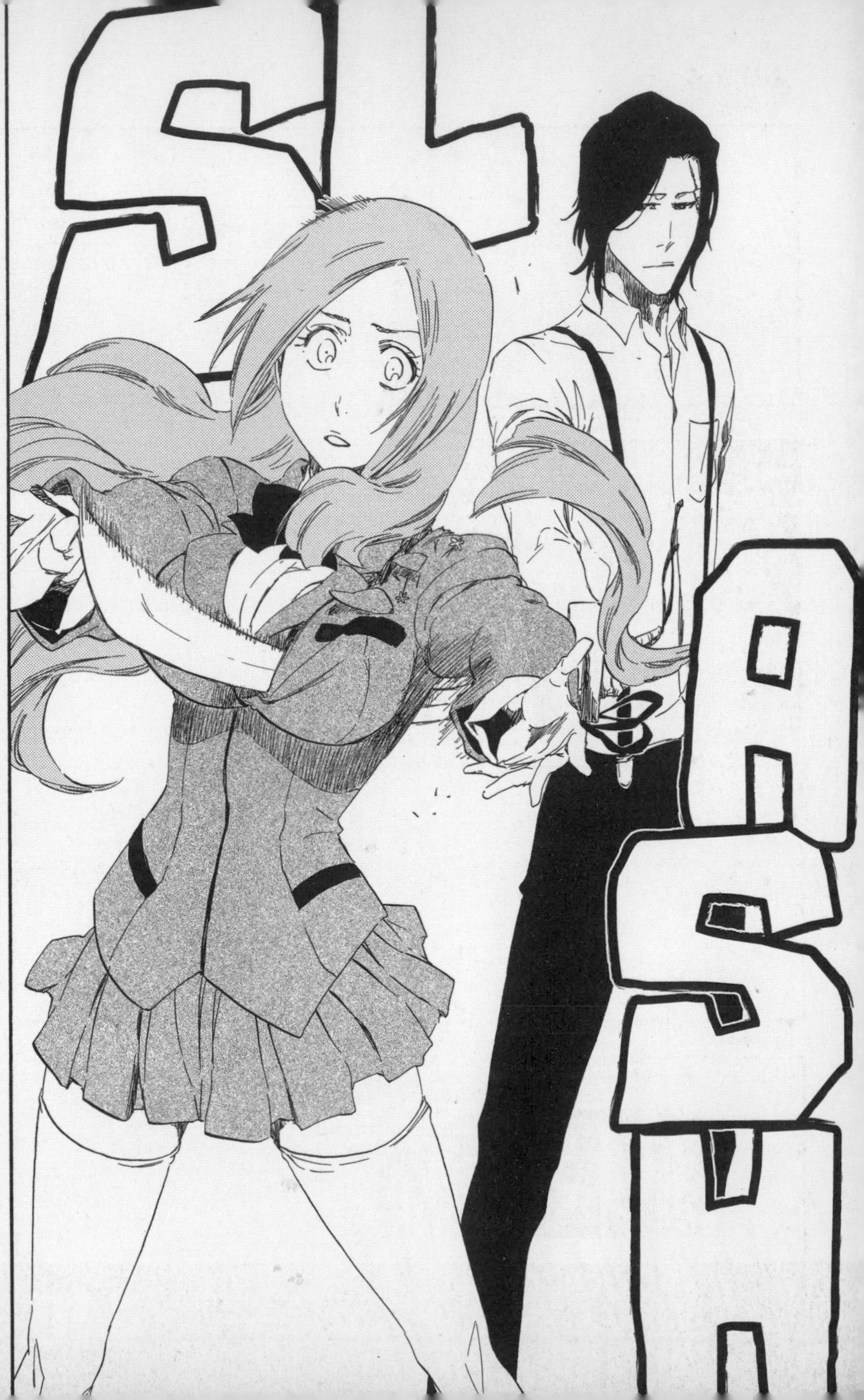
SLASH

READ THIS WAY

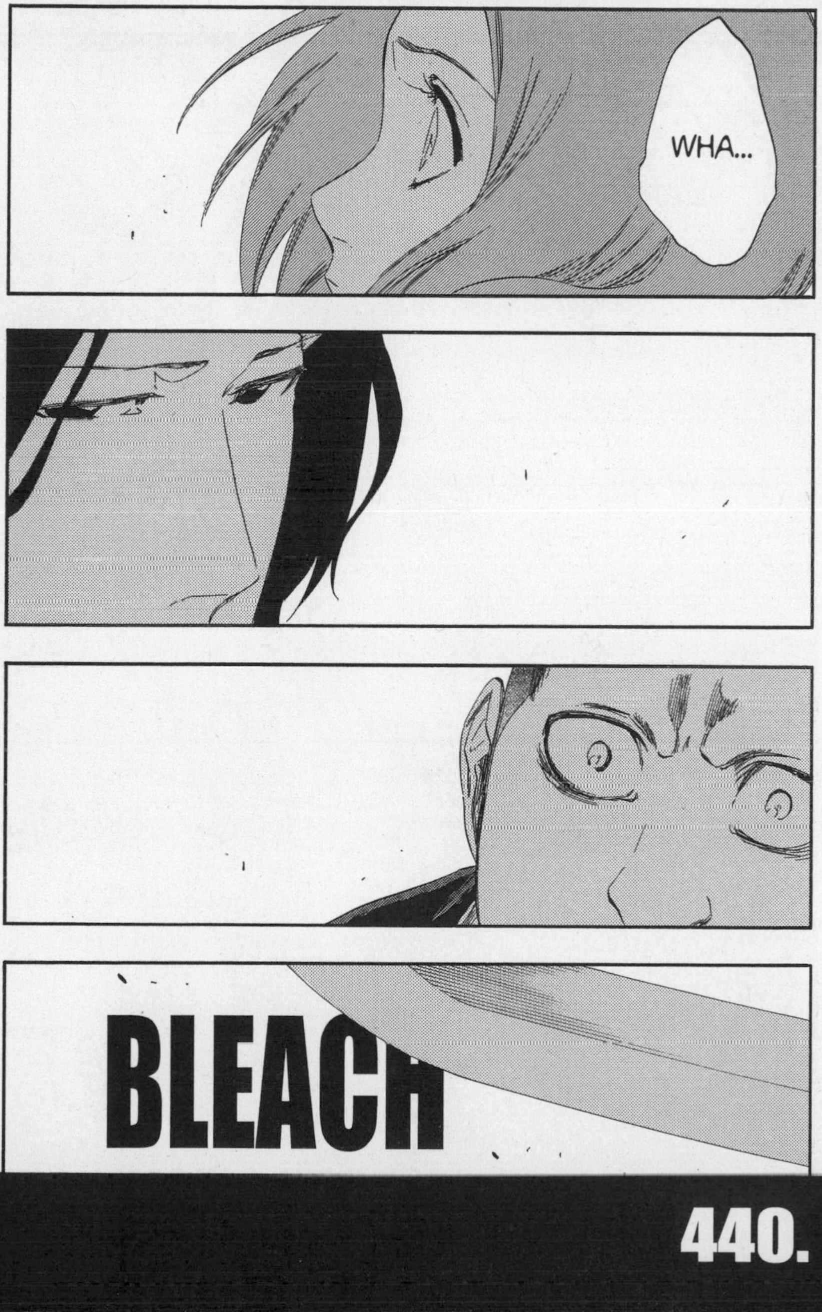
WHA...
BLEACH
440.

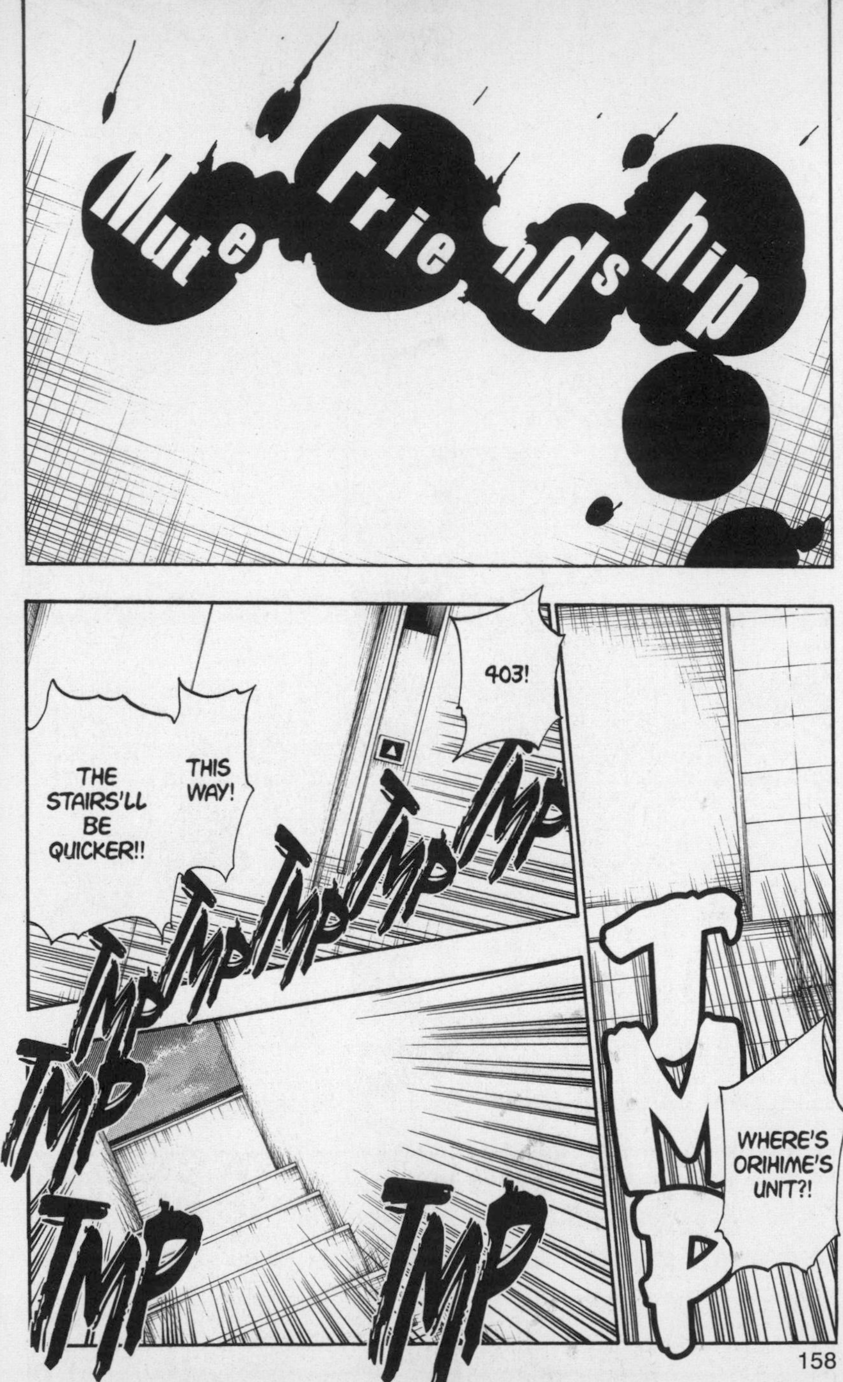
Mute Friendship
WHERE'S ORIHIME'S UNIT?!
TMP
403!
THIS WAY!
THE STAIRS'LL BE QUICKER!!
TMP TMP TMP TMP TMP TMP
TMP
TMP
TMP

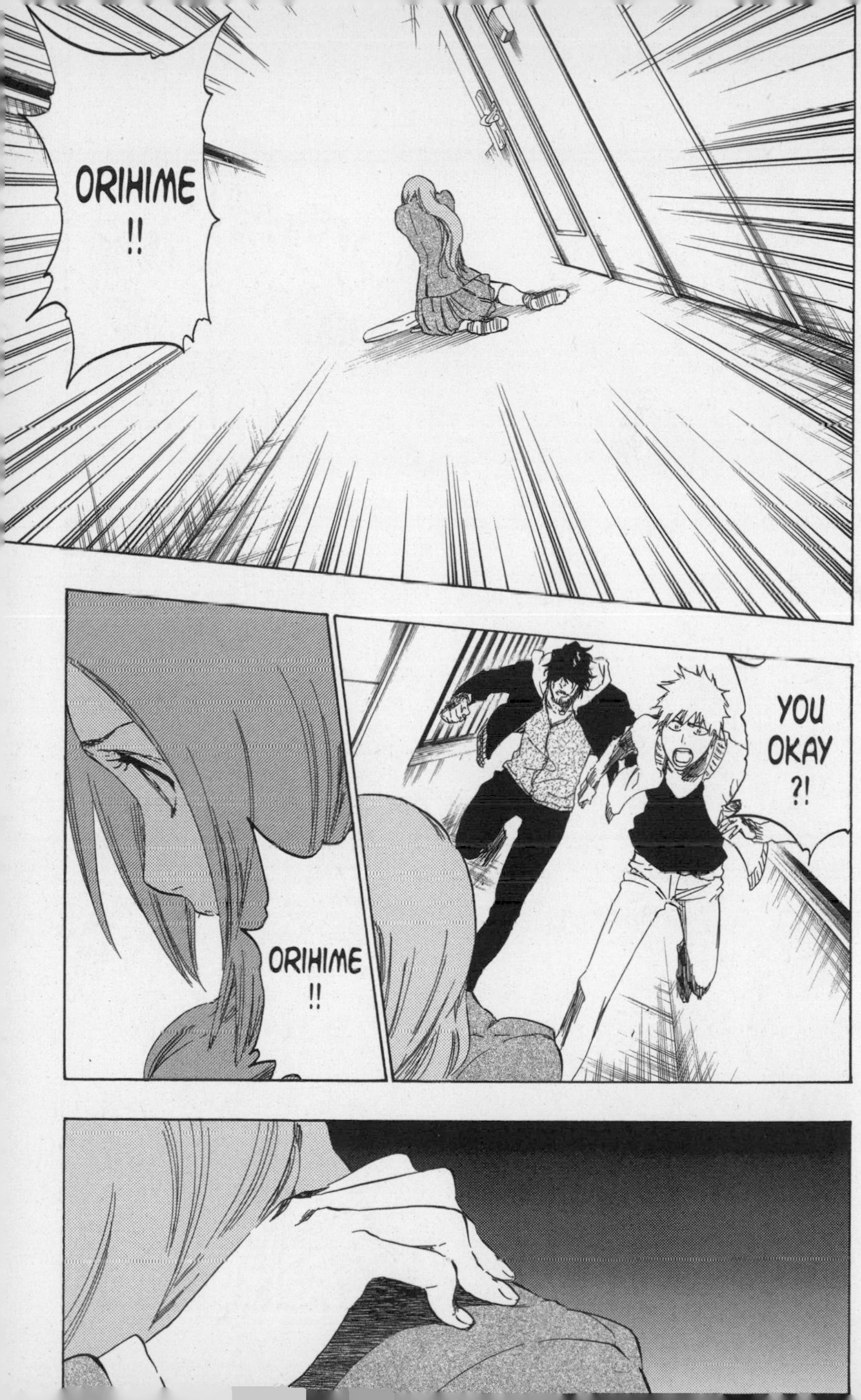
ORIHIME !!
YOU OKAY ?!
ORIHIME !!

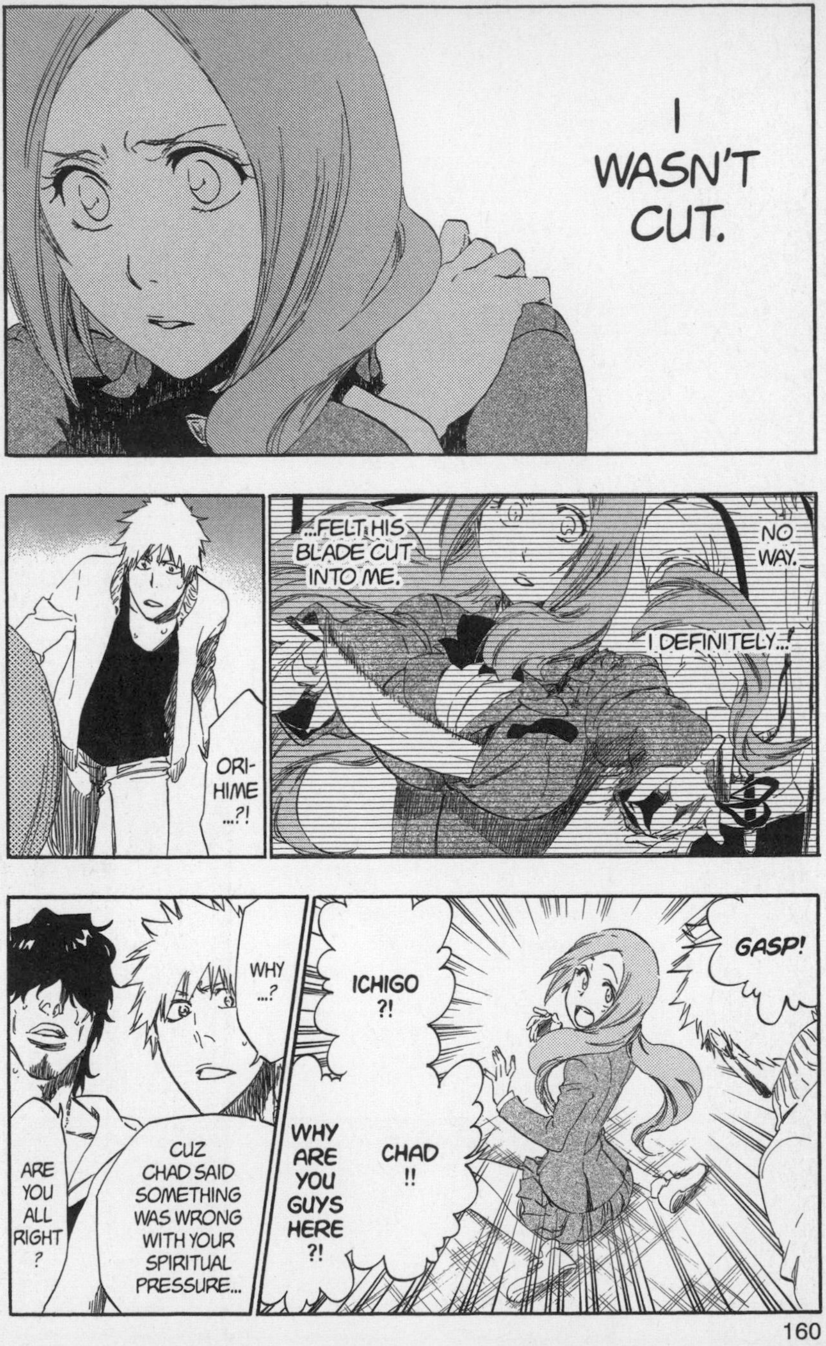
I WASN'T CUT.
NO WAY.
I DEFINITELY...!
...FELT HIS BLADE CUT INTO ME.
ORI-HIME ...?!
GASP!
ICHIGO ?!
CHAD !!
WHY ARE YOU GUYS HERE ?!
WHY ...?
CUZ CHAD SAID SOMETHING WAS WRONG WITH YOUR SPIRITUAL PRESSURE...
ARE YOU ALL RIGHT ?

READ THIS WAY

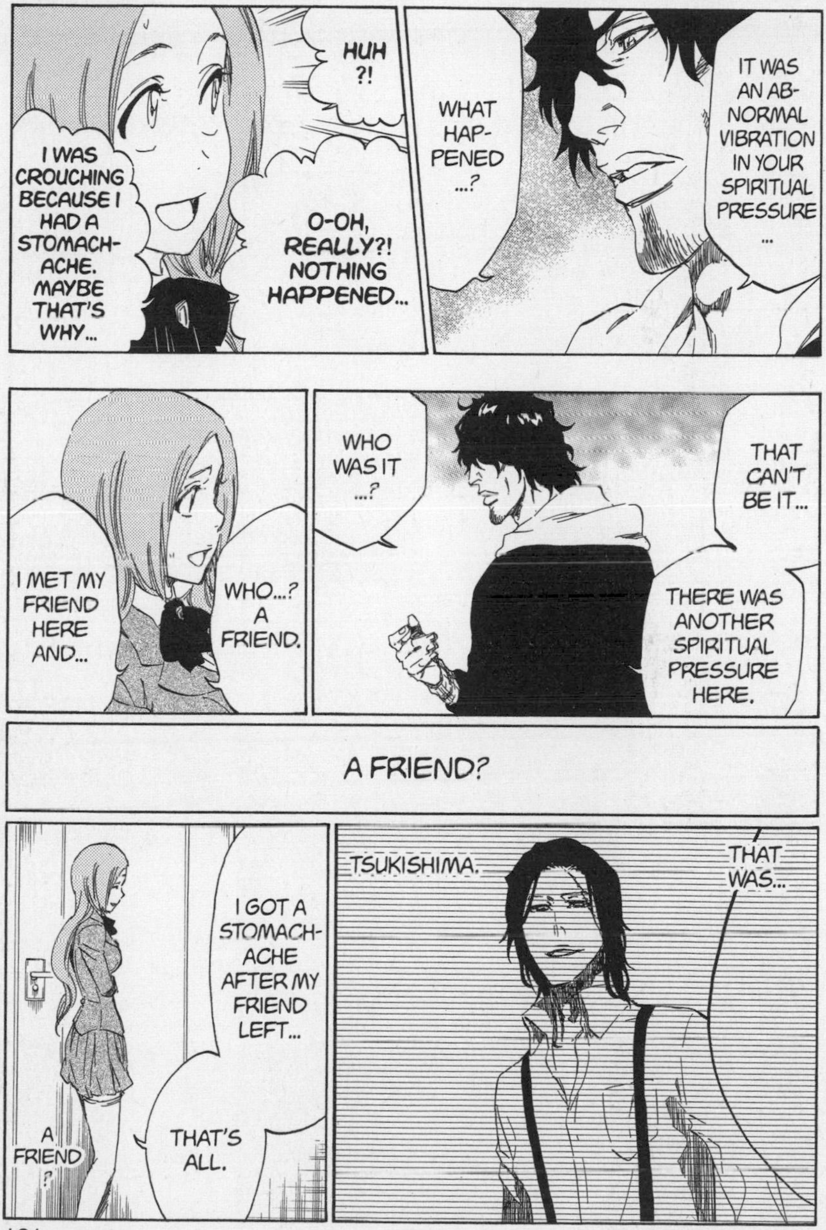
IT WAS AN ABNORMAL VIBRATION IN YOUR SPIRITUAL PRESSURE...
WHAT HAPPENED...?
HUH?!
O-OH, REALLY?! NOTHING HAPPENED...
I WAS CROUCHING BECAUSE I HAD A STOMACHACHE. MAYBE THAT'S WHY...
THAT CAN'T BE IT...
WHO WAS IT...?
THERE WAS ANOTHER SPIRITUAL PRESSURE HERE.
WHO...? A FRIEND.
I MET MY FRIEND HERE AND...
A FRIEND?
THAT WAS...
TSUKISHIMA.
I GOT A STOMACHACHE AFTER MY FRIEND LEFT...
THAT'S ALL.
A FRIEND?

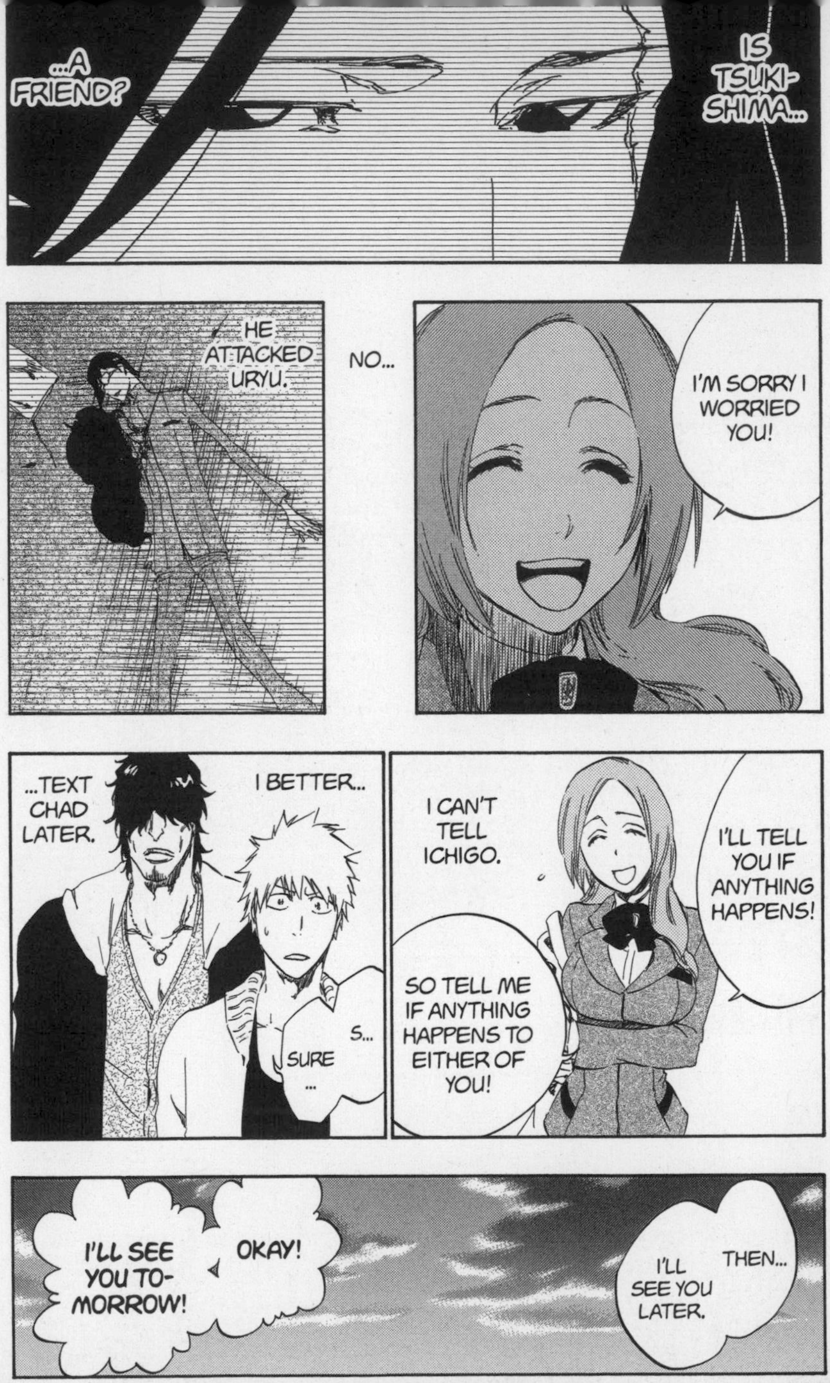

IS TSUKI-SHIMA...
...A FRIEND?
I'M SORRY I WORRIED YOU!
NO...
HE ATTACKED URYU.
I'LL TELL YOU IF ANYTHING HAPPENS!
I CAN'T TELL ICHIGO.
SO TELL ME IF ANYTHING HAPPENS TO EITHER OF YOU!
I BETTER...
...TEXT CHAD LATER.
S... SURE...
THEN... I'LL SEE YOU LATER.
OKAY!
I'LL SEE YOU TO-MORROW!

READ THIS WAY

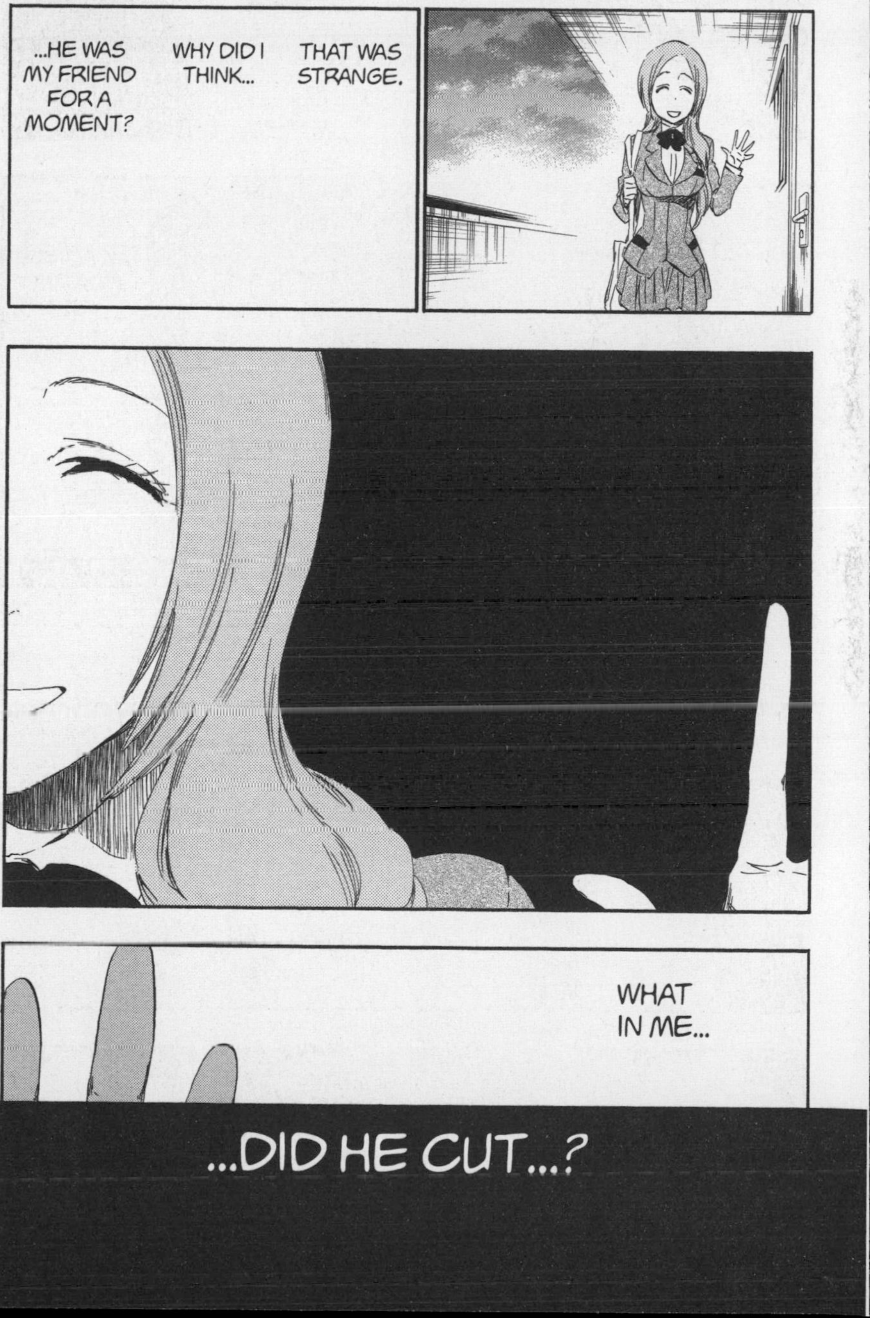
THAT WAS STRANGE.
WHY DID I THINK...
...HE WAS MY FRIEND FOR A MOMENT?
WHAT IN ME...
...DID HE CUT...?

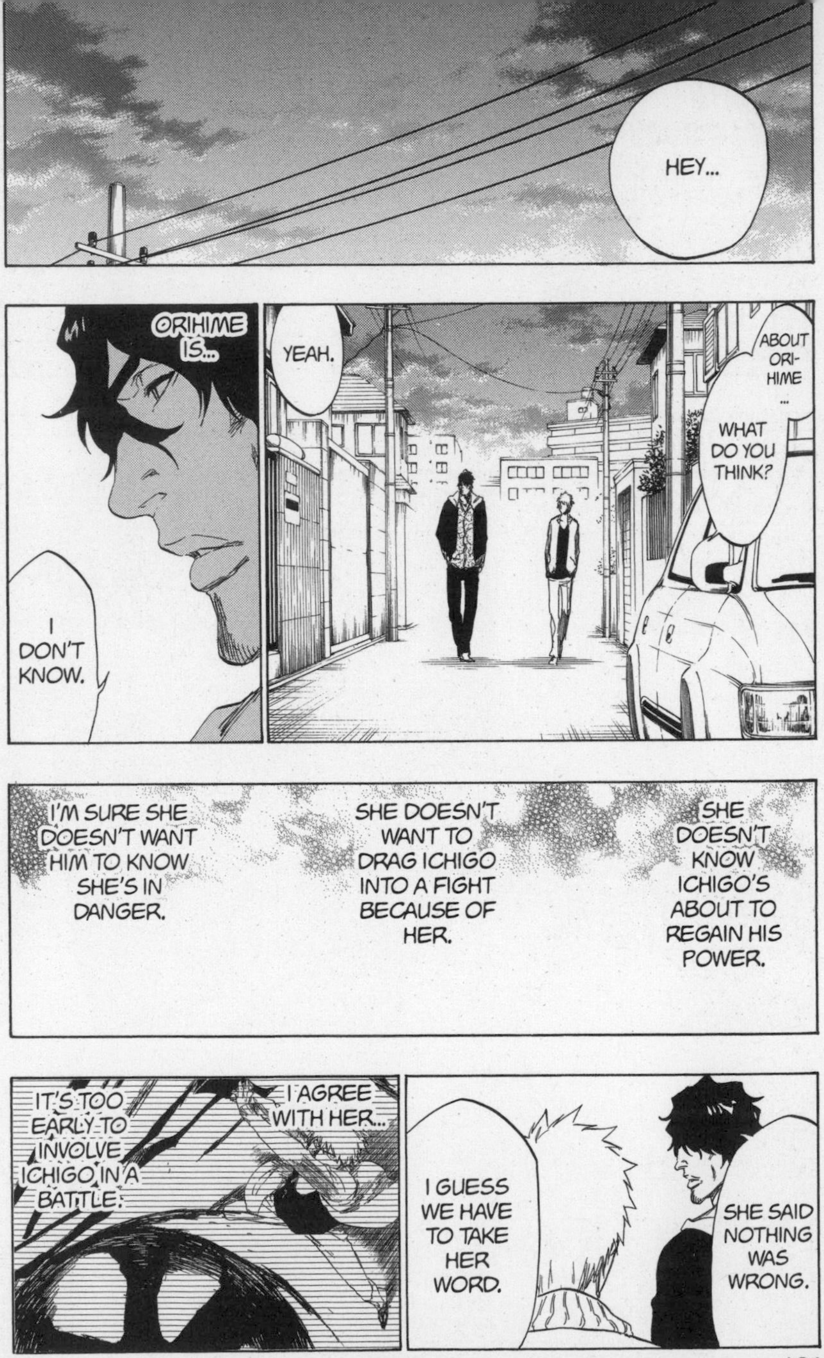
HEY...
ABOUT ORIHIME... WHAT DO YOU THINK?
YEAH.
ORIHIME IS...
I DON'T KNOW.
SHE DOESN'T KNOW ICHIGO'S ABOUT TO REGAIN HIS POWER.
SHE DOESN'T WANT TO DRAG ICHIGO INTO A FIGHT BECAUSE OF HER.
I'M SURE SHE DOESN'T WANT HIM TO KNOW SHE'S IN DANGER.
SHE SAID NOTHING WAS WRONG.
I GUESS WE HAVE TO TAKE HER WORD.
I AGREE WITH HER...
IT'S TOO EARLY TO INVOLVE ICHIGO IN A BATTLE.

READ THIS WAY

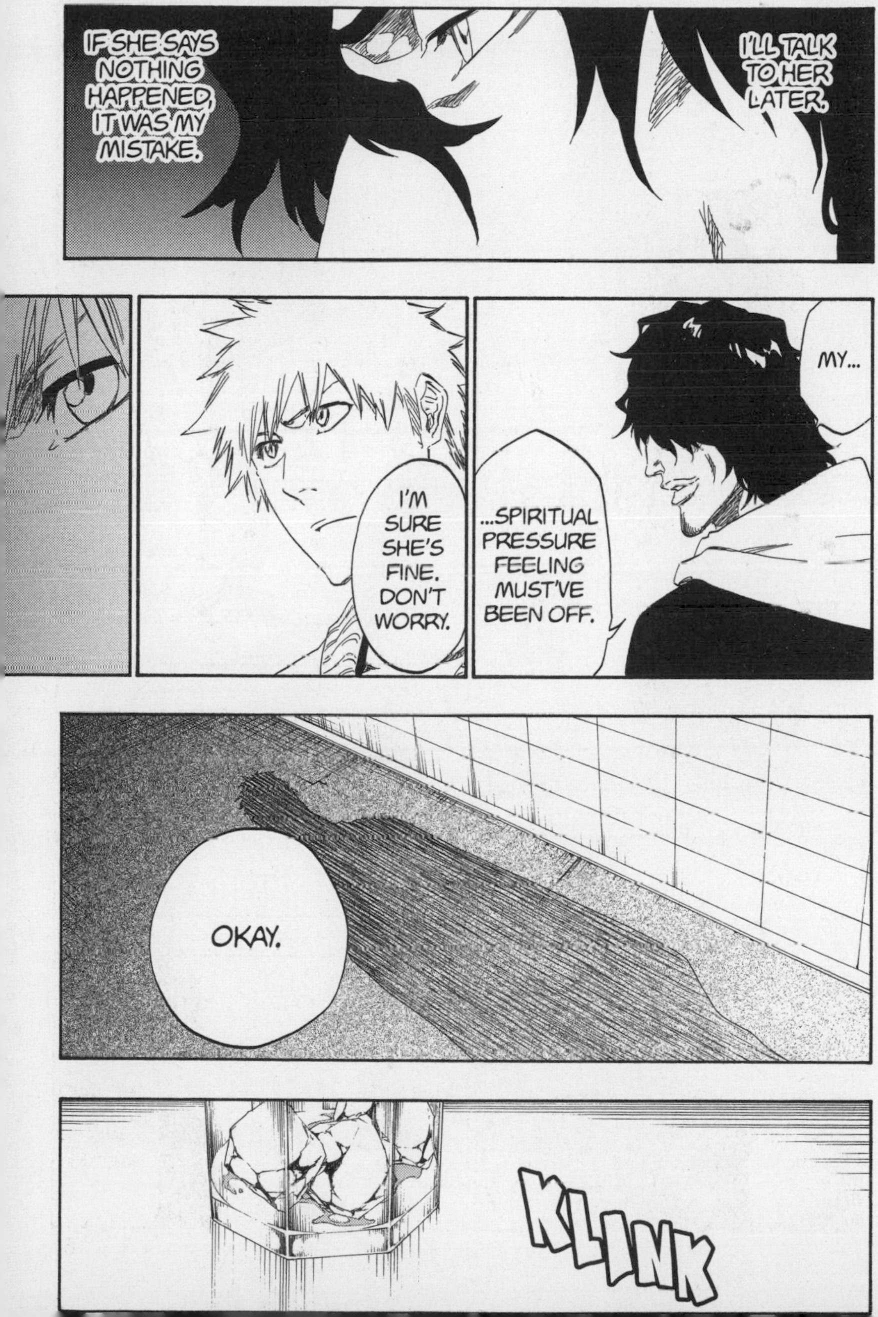

I'LL TALK TO HER LATER.
IF SHE SAYS NOTHING HAPPENED, IT WAS MY MISTAKE.
MY...
...SPIRITUAL PRESSURE FEELING MUST'VE BEEN OFF.
I'M SURE SHE'S FINE. DON'T WORRY.
OKAY.
KLINK

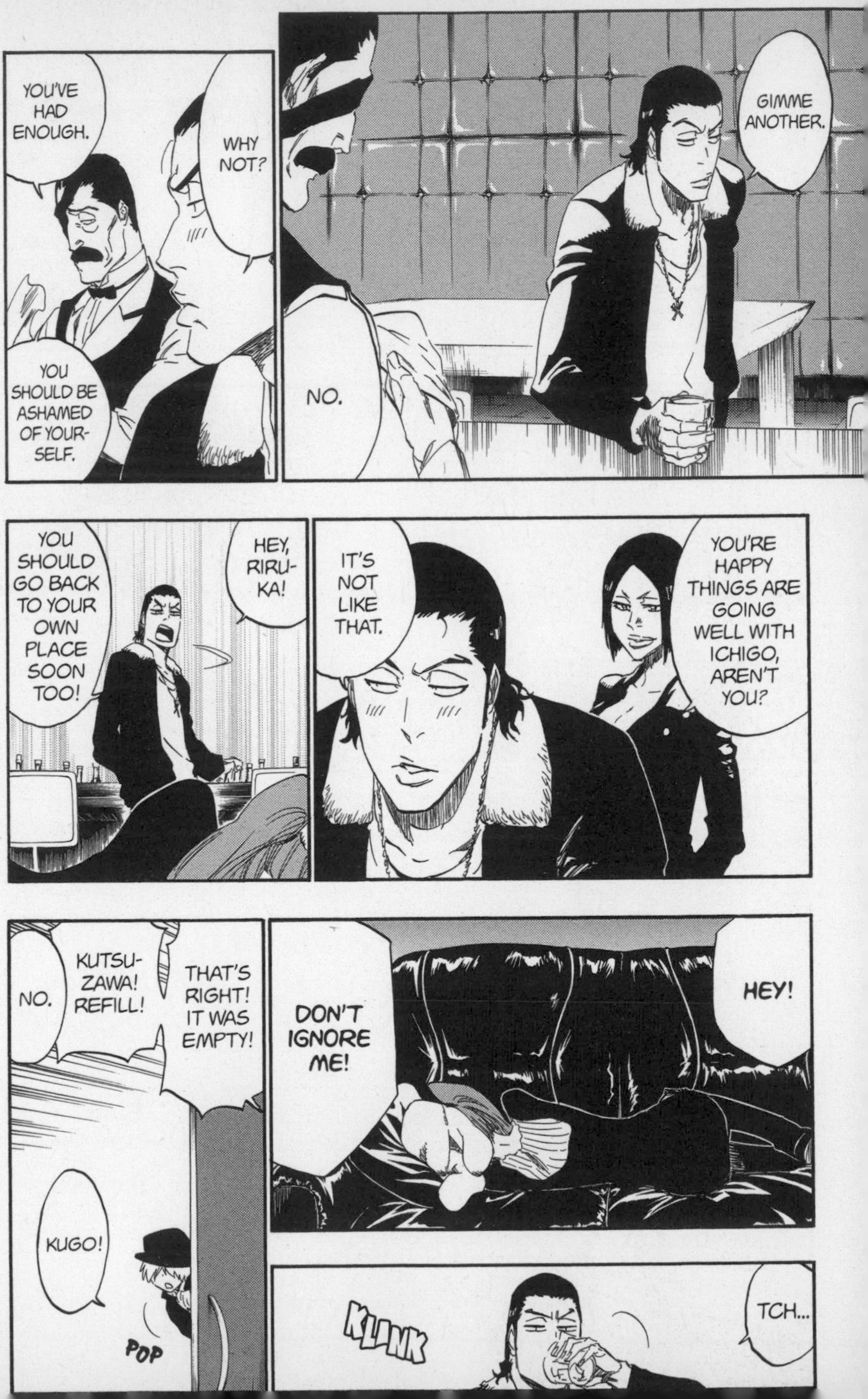
GIMME ANOTHER.
NO.
WHY NOT?
YOU'VE HAD ENOUGH.
YOU SHOULD BE ASHAMED OF YOUR-SELF.
YOU'RE HAPPY THINGS ARE GOING WELL WITH ICHIGO, AREN'T YOU?
IT'S NOT LIKE THAT.
HEY, RIRU-KA!
YOU SHOULD GO BACK TO YOUR OWN PLACE SOON TOO!
HEY!
DON'T IGNORE ME!
TCH...
KLINK
THAT'S RIGHT! IT WAS EMPTY!
KUTSU-ZAWA! REFILL!
NO.
KUGO!
POP

...IS RING-ING.

YOUR DIRECT LINE...

BRRIIING

BRRIIING

BRRIIING

WHO IS IT?

...

KLATCH

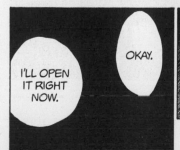

I'LL OPEN IT RIGHT NOW.

OKAY.

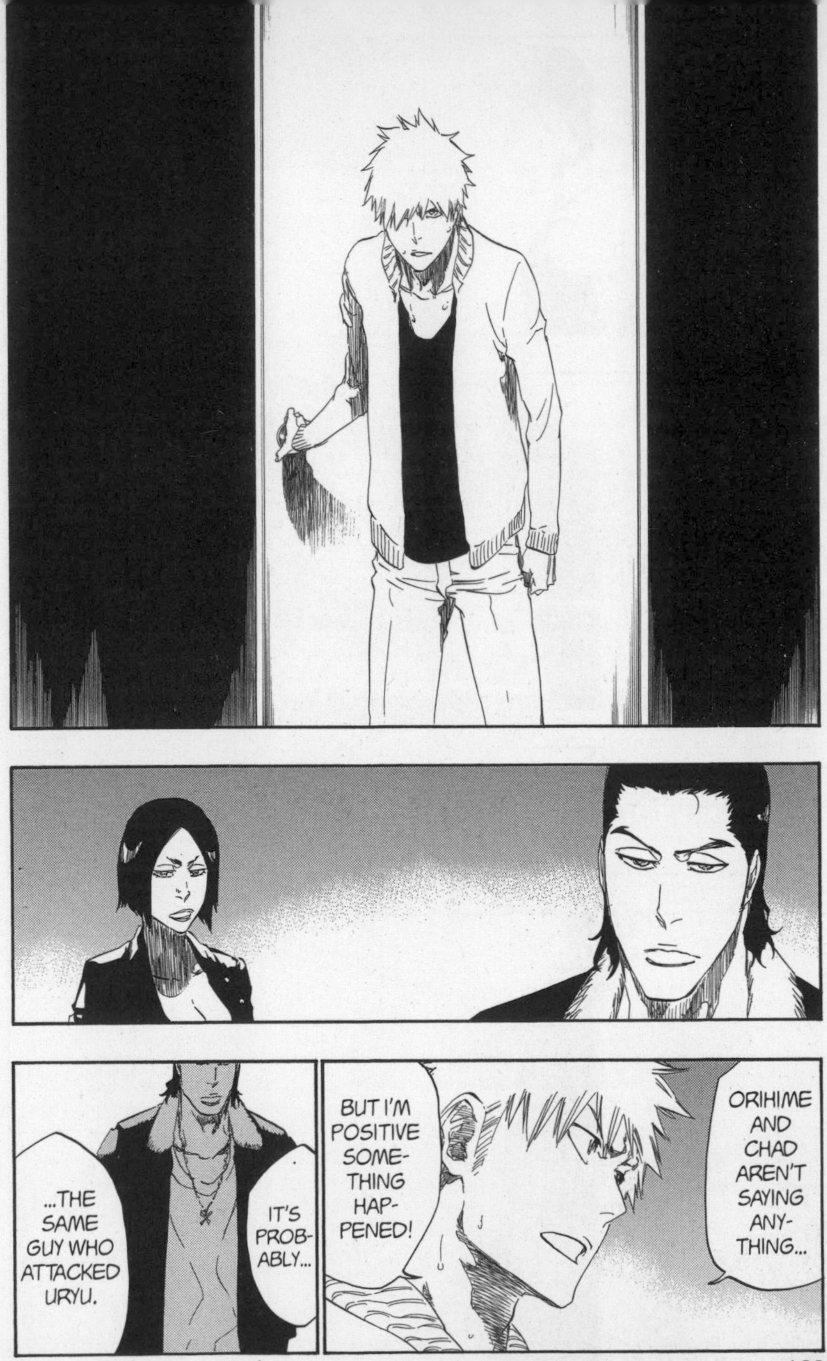
ORIHIME AND CHAD AREN'T SAYING ANY-THING...
BUT I'M POSITIVE SOME-THING HAP-PENED!
IT'S PROB-ABLY...
...THE SAME GUY WHO ATTACKED URYU.

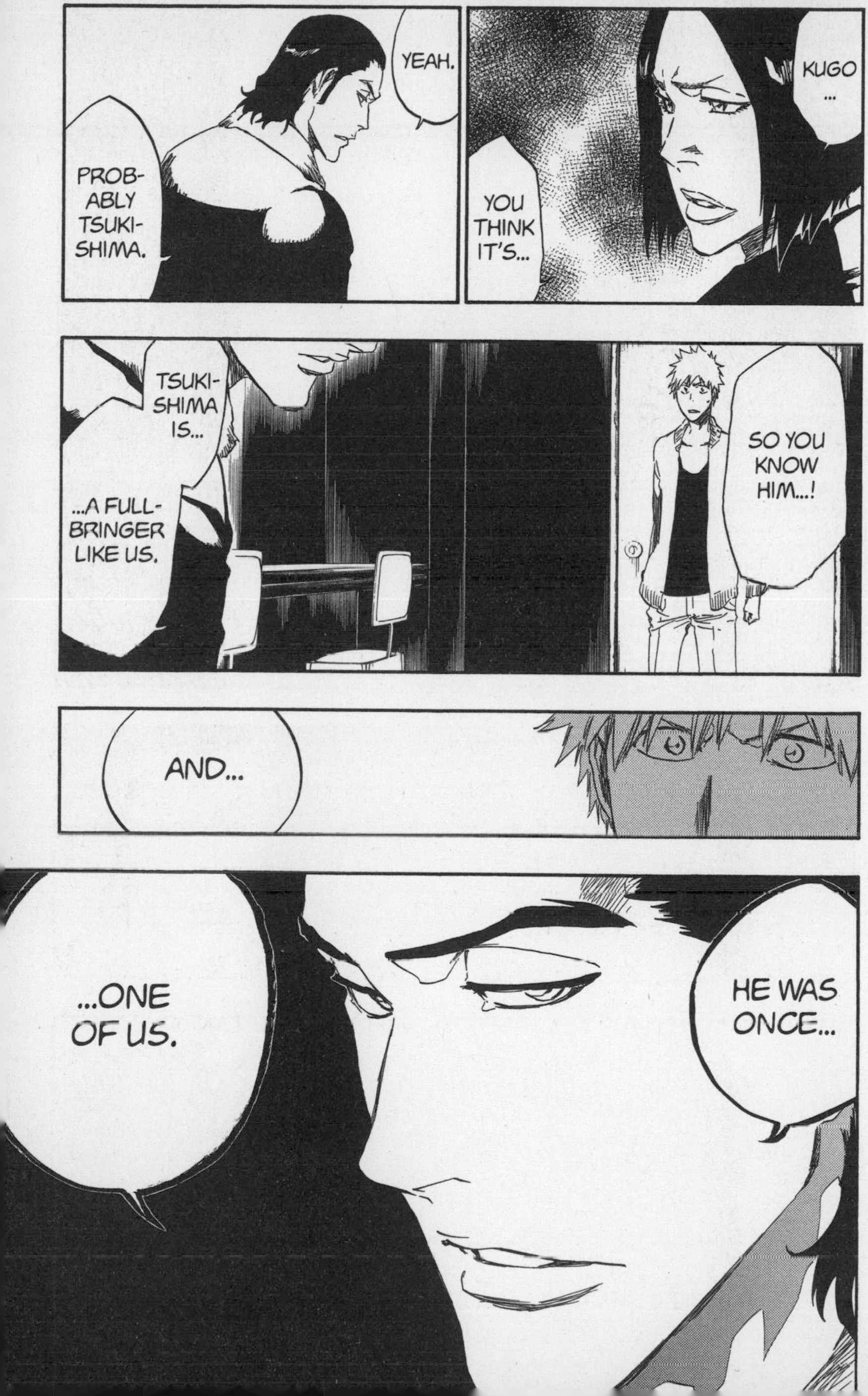
KUGO...
YOU THINK IT'S...
YEAH.
PROB-ABLY TSUKI-SHIMA.
SO YOU KNOW HIM...!
TSUKI-SHIMA IS...
...A FULL-BRINGER LIKE US.
AND...
HE WAS ONCE...
...ONE OF US.

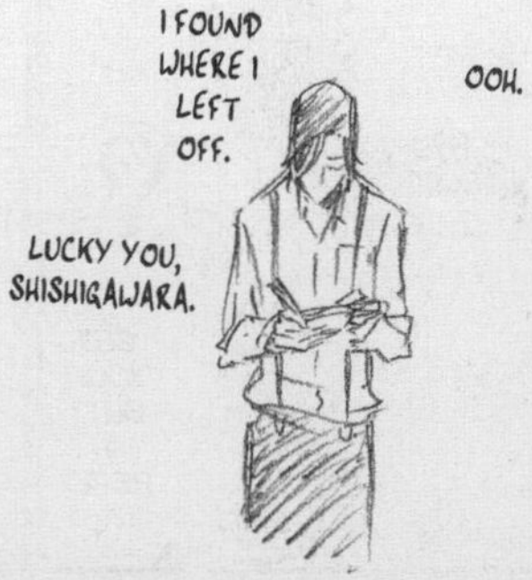
I FOUND WHERE I LEFT OFF.
OOH.
LUCKY YOU, SHISHIGAWARA.

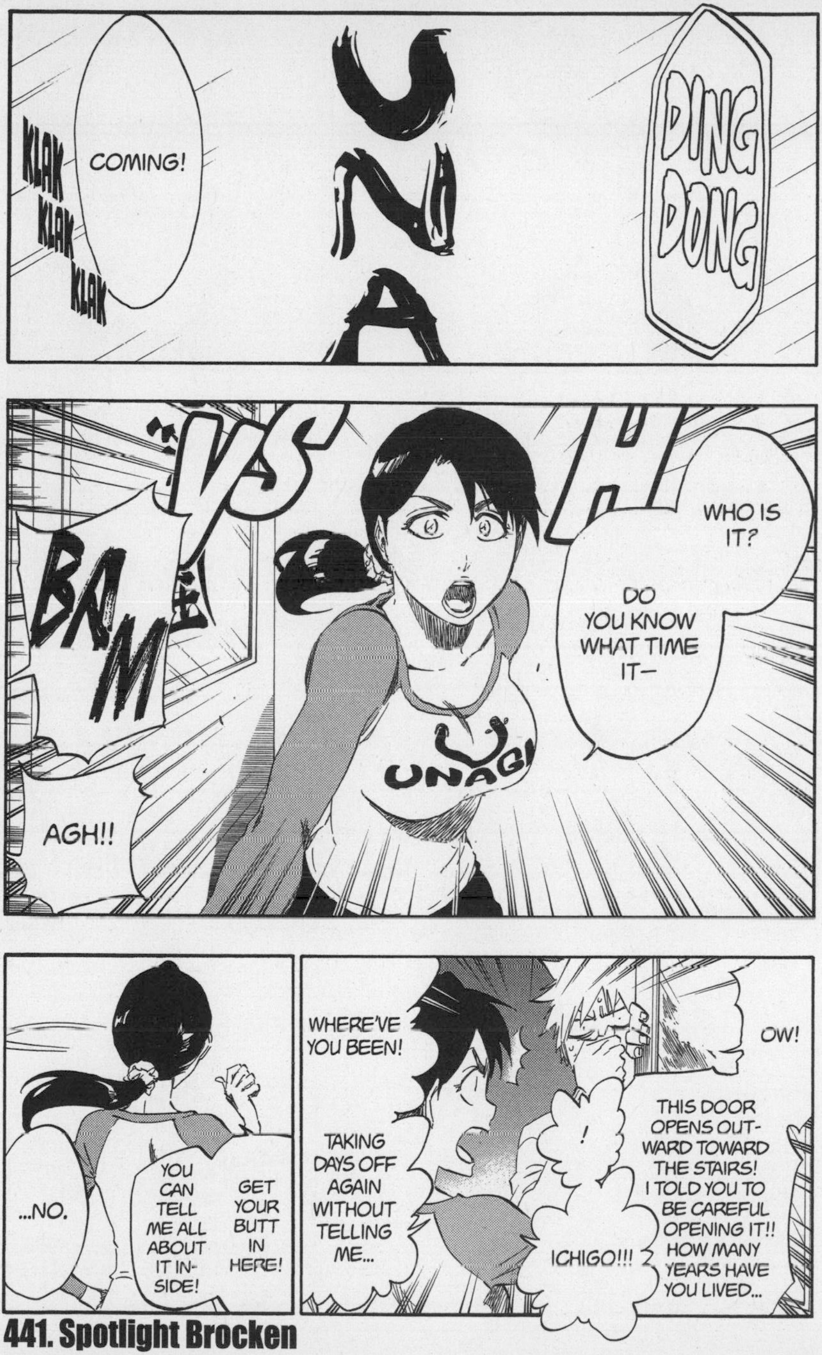
DING DONG
COMING!
KLAK KLAK KLAK
WHO IS IT?
DO YOU KNOW WHAT TIME IT–
BAM
AGH!!
OW!
WHERE'VE YOU BEEN!
THIS DOOR OPENS OUTWARD TOWARD THE STAIRS! I TOLD YOU TO BE CAREFUL OPENING IT!! HOW MANY YEARS HAVE YOU LIVED...
TAKING DAYS OFF AGAIN WITHOUT TELLING ME...
!
ICHIGO!!!
GET YOUR BUTT IN HERE!
YOU CAN TELL ME ALL ABOUT IT INSIDE!
...NO.

441. Spotlight Brocken

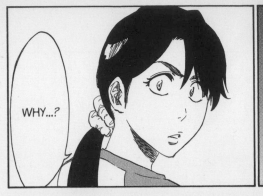

I'M FINE RIGHT HERE.
WHY...?
HUH?!
YOU WANT SOME TIME OFF?! ARE YOU CRAZY?!
YOU'VE ALREADY TAKEN DAYS OFF!!
HOW MANY DAYS DO YOU NEED?!
ARE YOU LISTENING TO ME?!

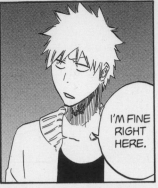

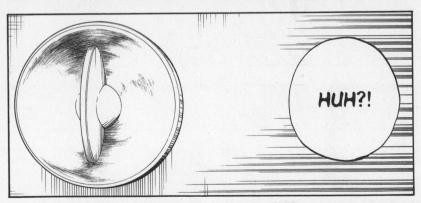

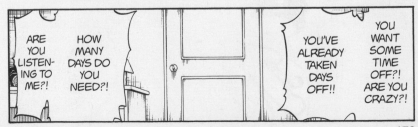

HEY... THAT'S ALL I WANTED TO TELL YOU...

WELL...

HUH?!

I'M SORRY.

ICHIGO!!

HOLD ON!

CRP

KREE

LISTEN...

I DON'T KNOW WHAT YOU'RE GOING THROUGH, BUT...

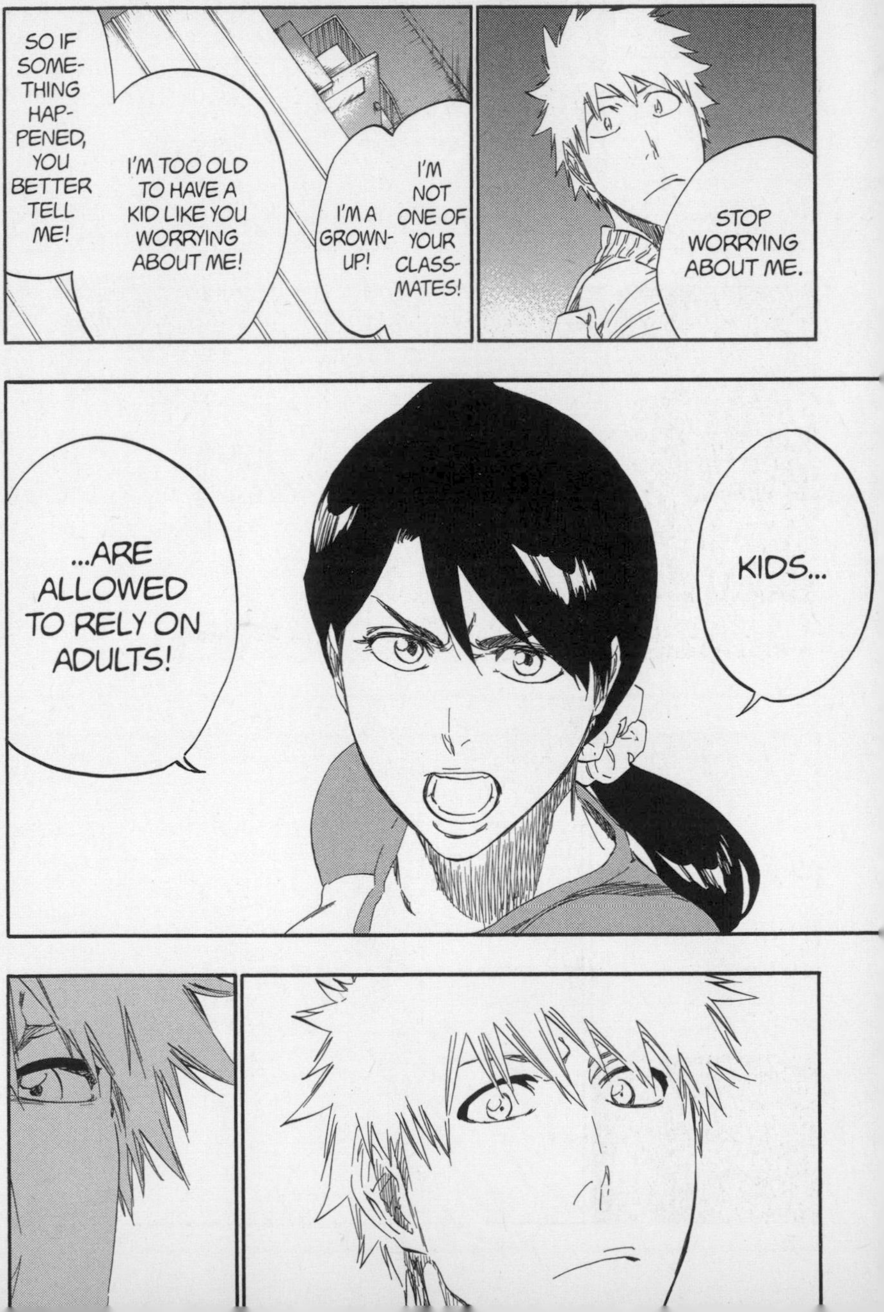
STOP WORRYING ABOUT ME.
I'M NOT ONE OF YOUR CLASSMATES!
I'M A GROWN-UP!
I'M TOO OLD TO HAVE A KID LIKE YOU WORRYING ABOUT ME!
SO IF SOMETHING HAPPENED, YOU BETTER TELL ME!
KIDS...
...ARE ALLOWED TO RELY ON ADULTS!

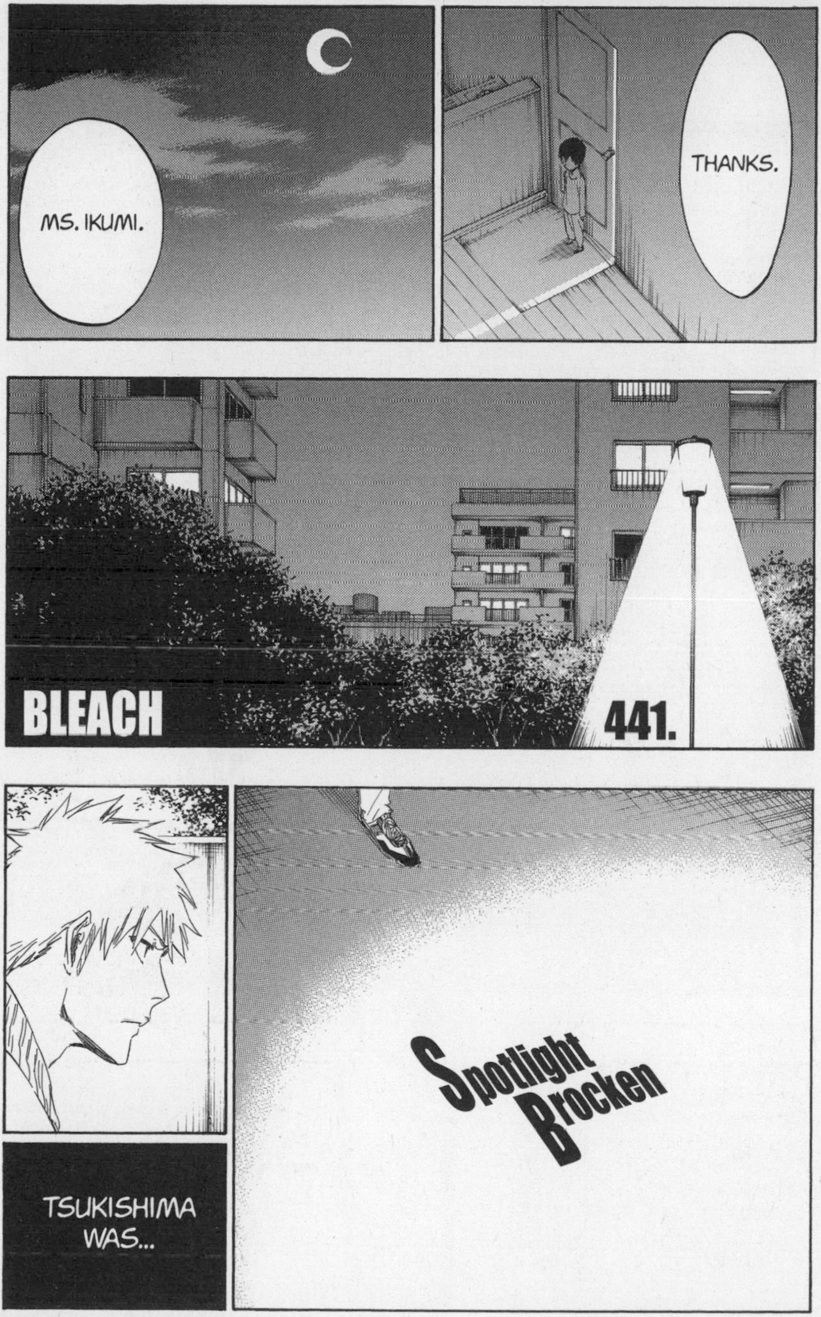
THANKS.
MS. IKUMI.
BLEACH
441.
Spotlight Brocken
TSUKISHIMA WAS...

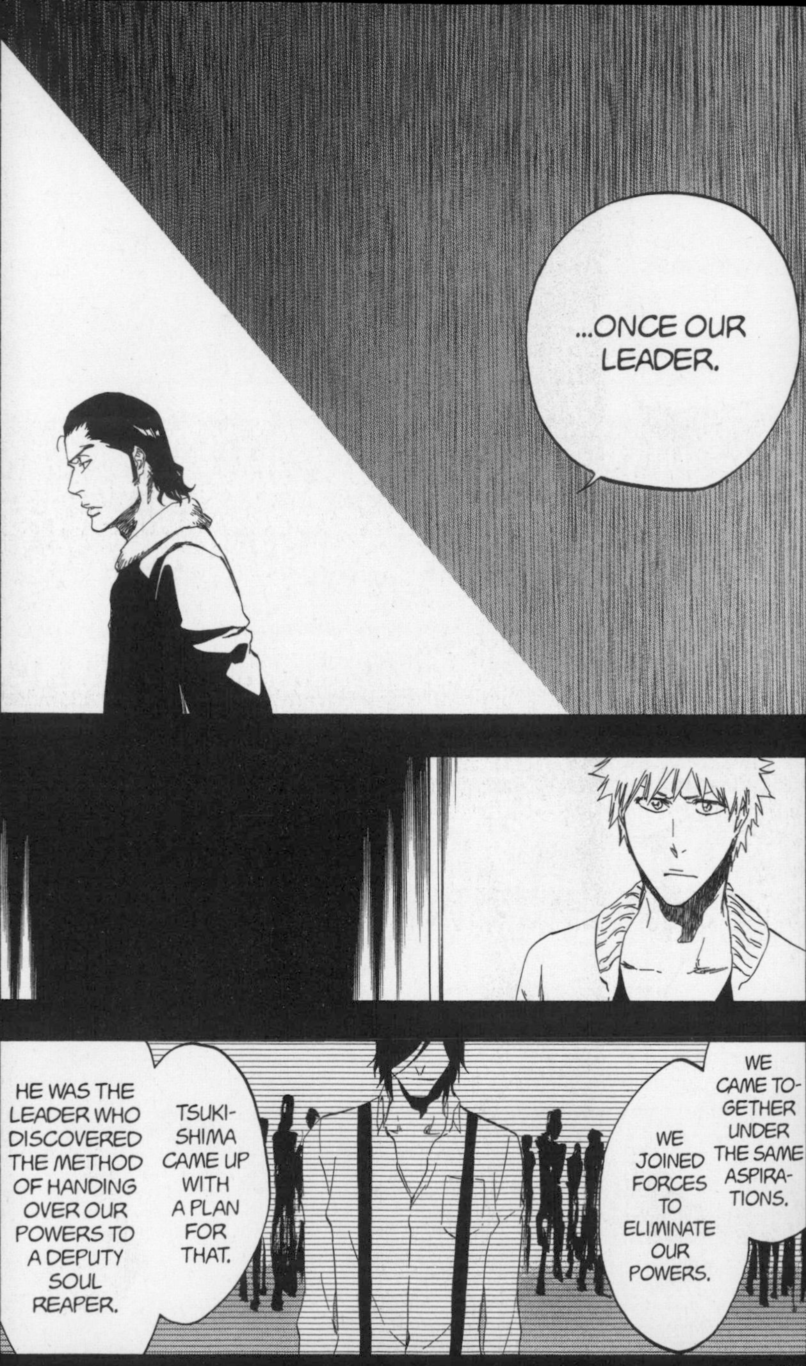
...ONCE OUR LEADER.
WE CAME TOGETHER UNDER THE SAME ASPIRATIONS.
WE JOINED FORCES TO ELIMINATE OUR POWERS.
TSUKISHIMA CAME UP WITH A PLAN FOR THAT.
HE WAS THE LEADER WHO DISCOVERED THE METHOD OF HANDING OVER OUR POWERS TO A DEPUTY SOUL REAPER.

READ THIS WAY

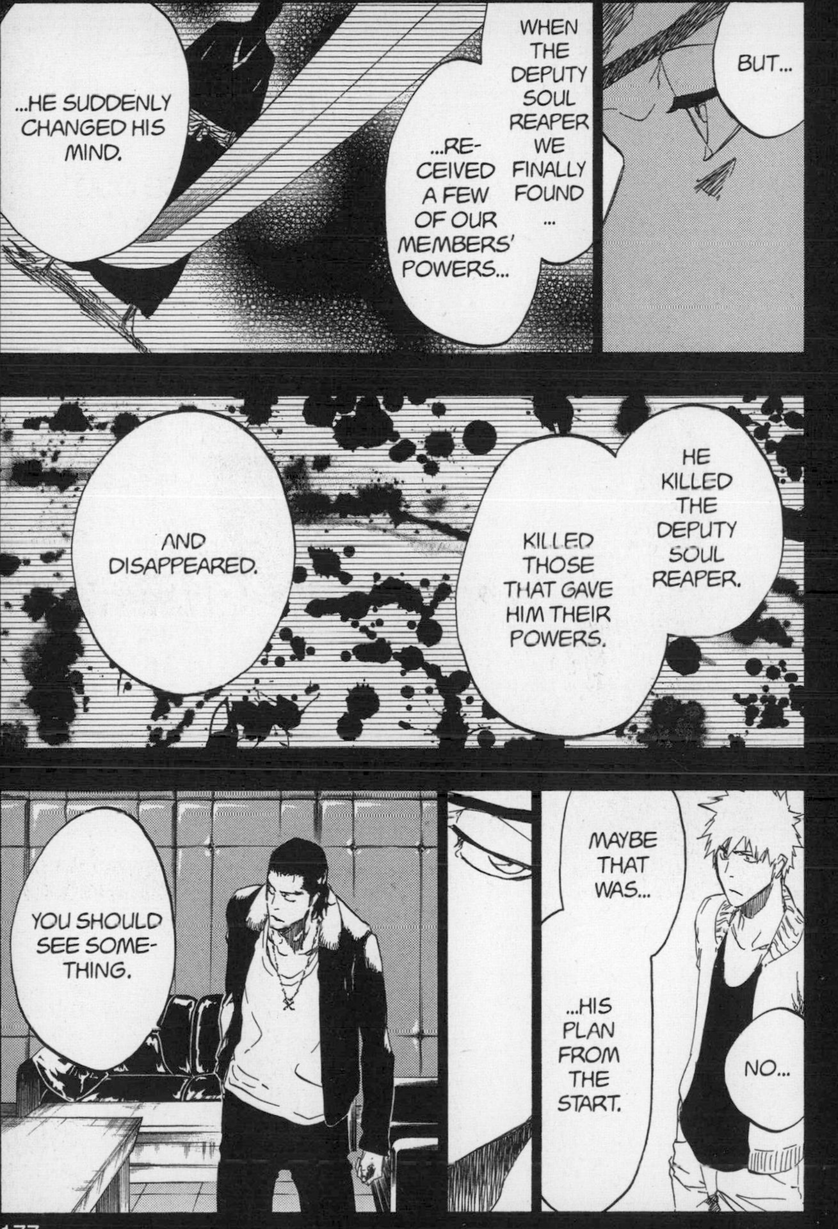
BUT...
WHEN THE DEPUTY SOUL REAPER WE FINALLY FOUND...
...RE-CEIVED A FEW OF OUR MEMBERS' POWERS...
...HE SUDDENLY CHANGED HIS MIND.
HE KILLED THE DEPUTY SOUL REAPER.
KILLED THOSE THAT GAVE HIM THEIR POWERS.
AND DISAPPEARED.
MAYBE THAT WAS...
...HIS PLAN FROM THE START.
NO...
YOU SHOULD SEE SOME-THING.

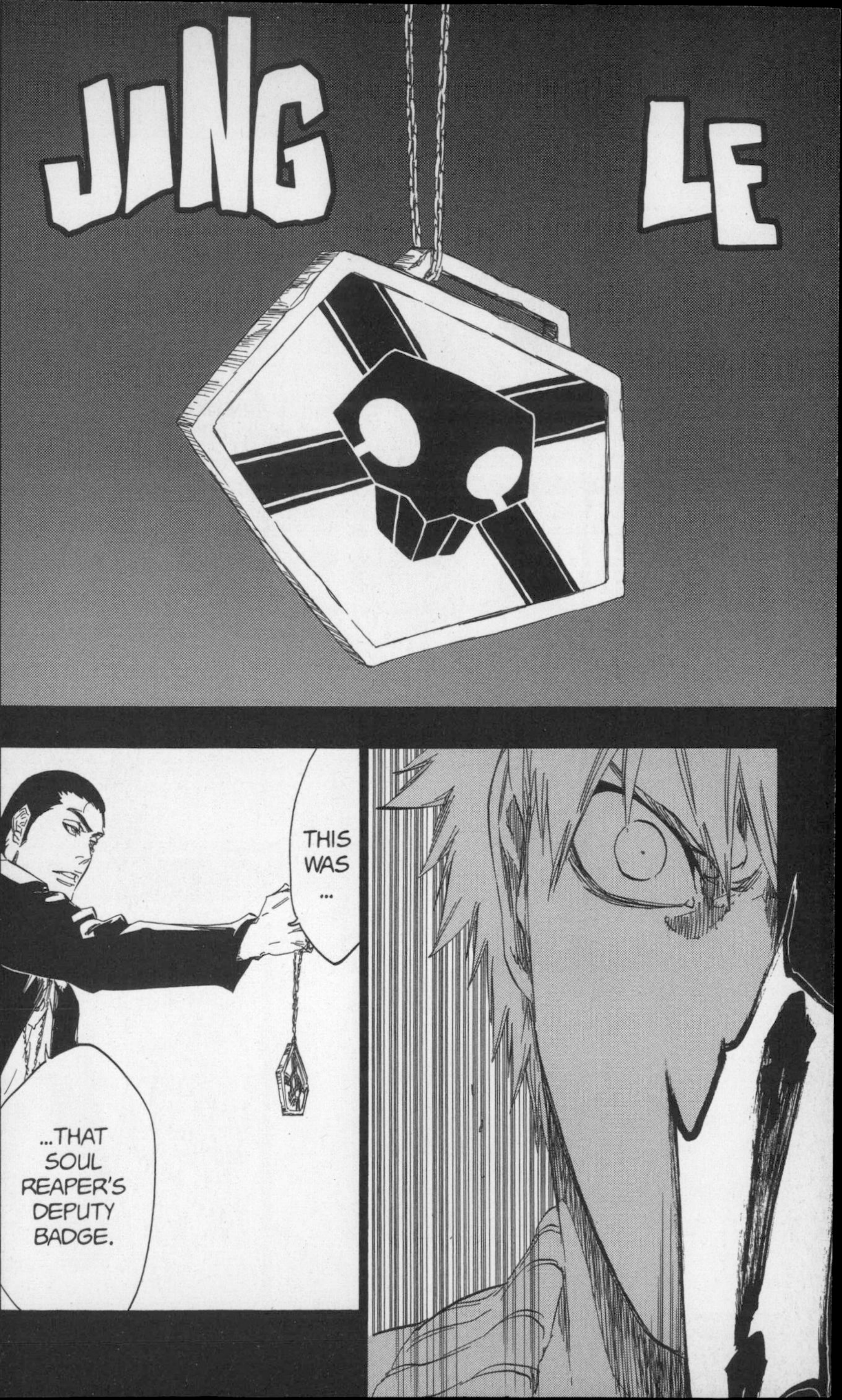
JINGLE
THIS WAS ...
...THAT SOUL REAPER'S DEPUTY BADGE.

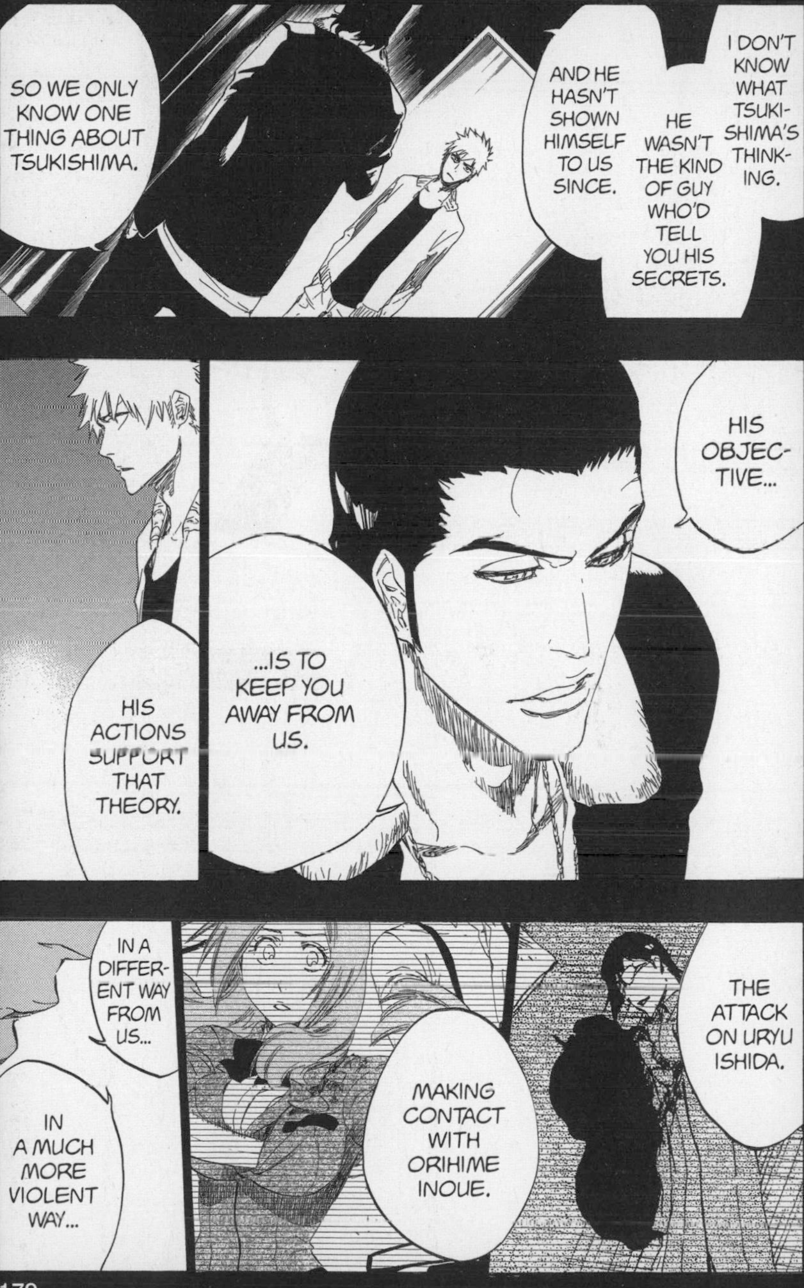
I DON'T KNOW WHAT TSUKISHIMA'S THINKING.
HE WASN'T THE KIND OF GUY WHO'D TELL YOU HIS SECRETS.
AND HE HASN'T SHOWN HIMSELF TO US SINCE.
SO WE ONLY KNOW ONE THING ABOUT TSUKISHIMA.
HIS OBJECTIVE...
...IS TO KEEP YOU AWAY FROM US.
HIS ACTIONS SUPPORT THAT THEORY.
THE ATTACK ON URYU ISHIDA.
MAKING CONTACT WITH ORIHIME INOUE.
IN A DIFFERENT WAY FROM US...
IN A MUCH MORE VIOLENT WAY...

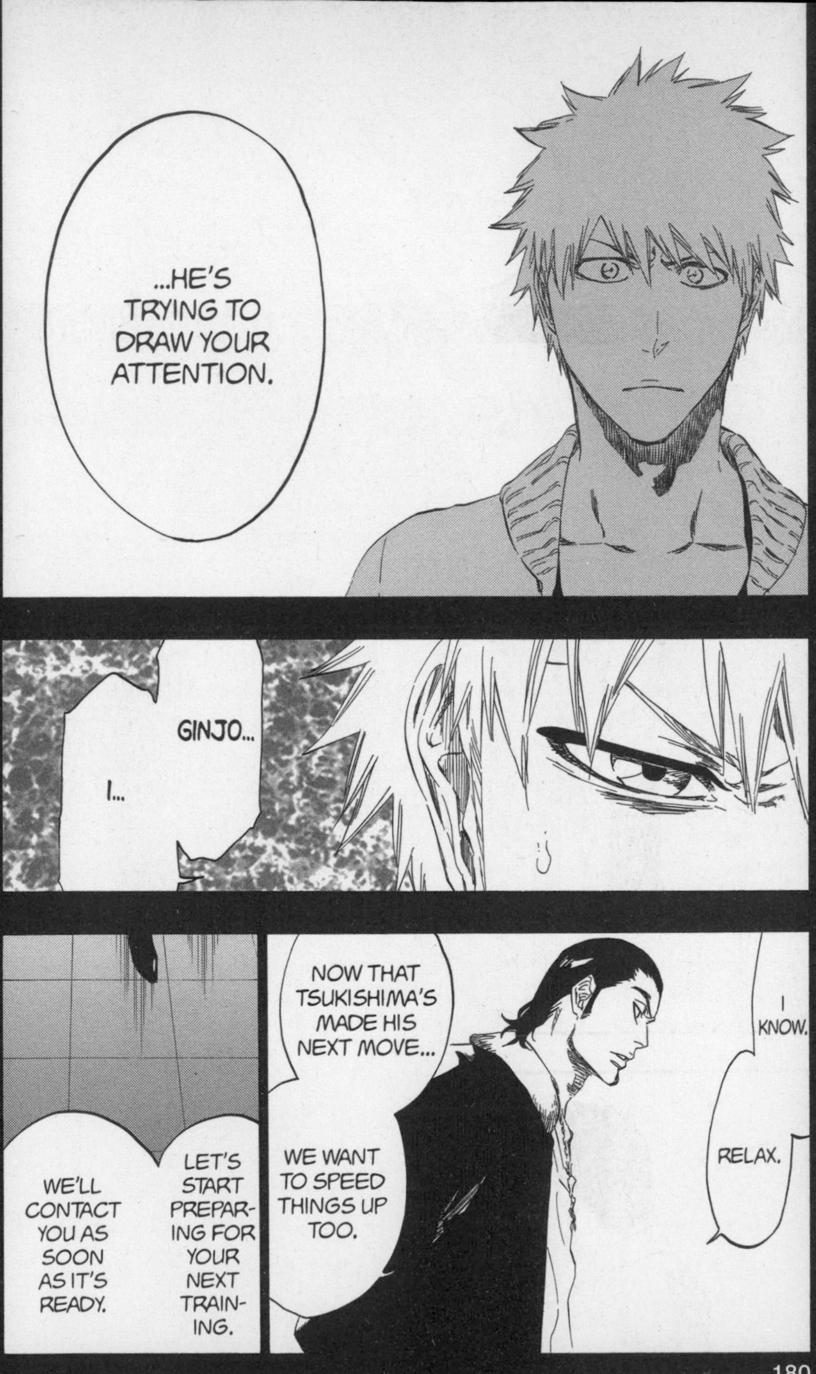
...HE'S TRYING TO DRAW YOUR ATTENTION.
GINJO...
I...
I KNOW.
RELAX.
NOW THAT TSUKISHIMA'S MADE HIS NEXT MOVE...
WE WANT TO SPEED THINGS UP TOO.
LET'S START PREPARING FOR YOUR NEXT TRAINING.
WE'LL CONTACT YOU AS SOON AS IT'S READY.

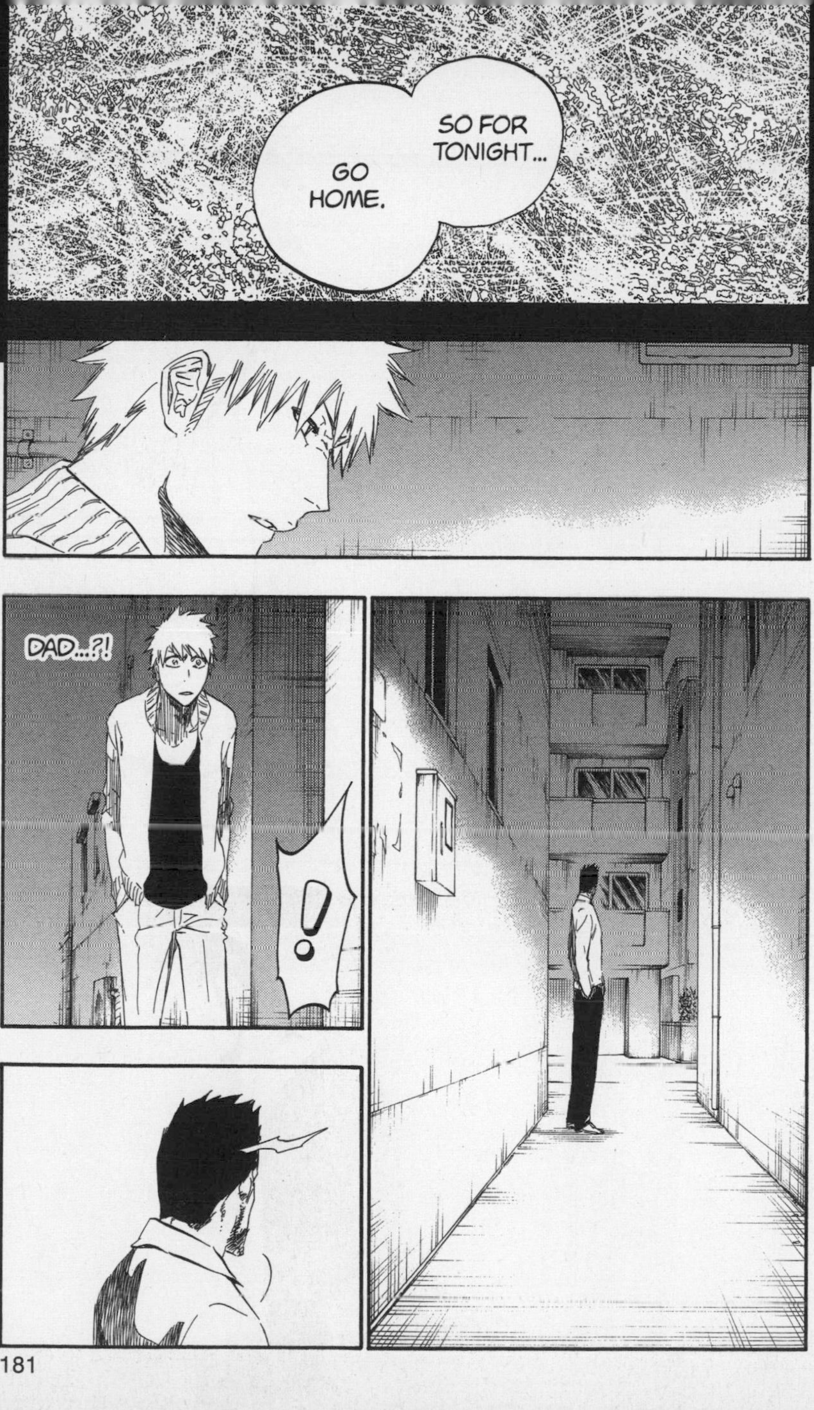
SO FOR TONIGHT...
GO HOME.
!
DAD...?!

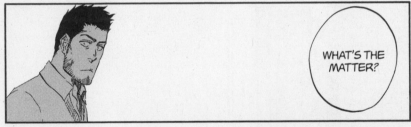

WHAT'S THE MATTER?

OH... NOTH- ING.

KLAK

READ THIS WAY

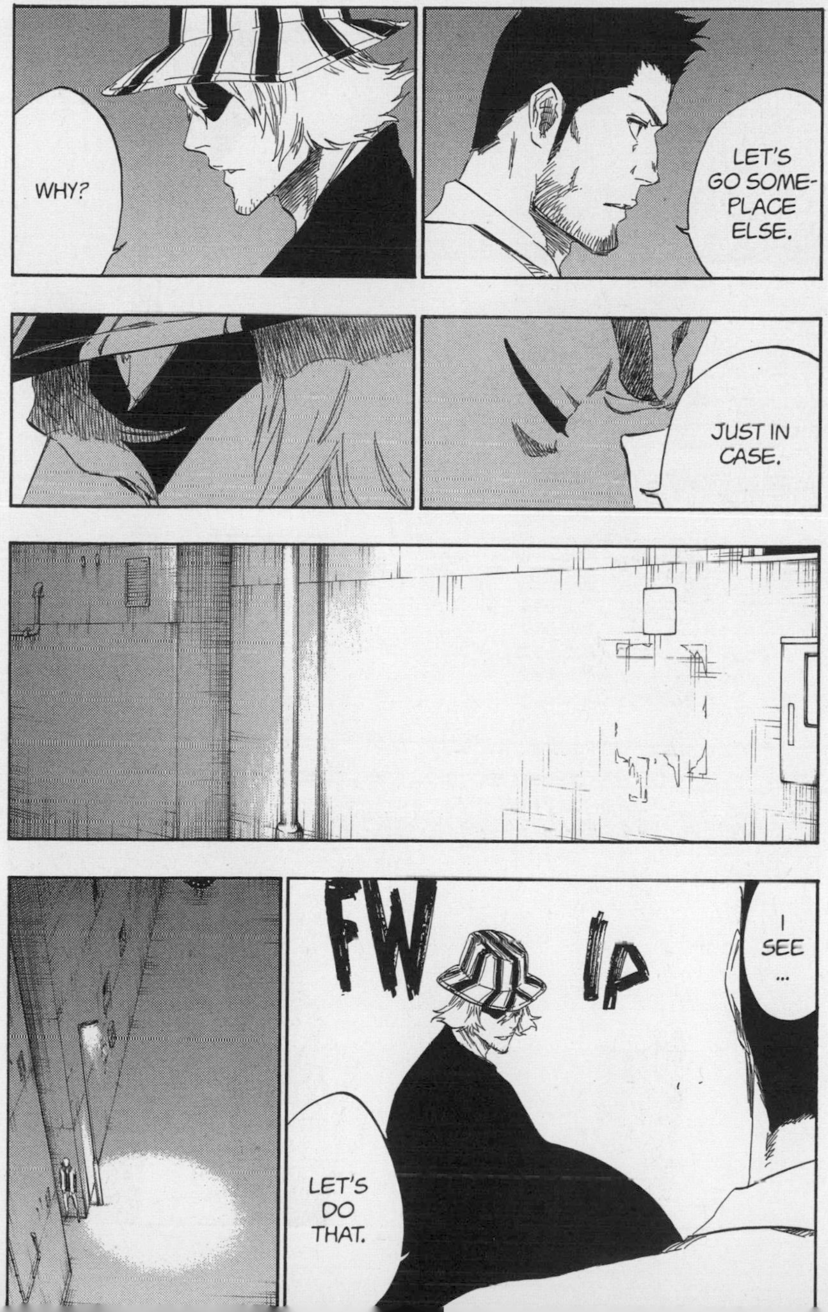
LET'S GO SOME-PLACE ELSE.
WHY?
JUST IN CASE.
FWIP
I SEE ...
LET'S DO THAT.

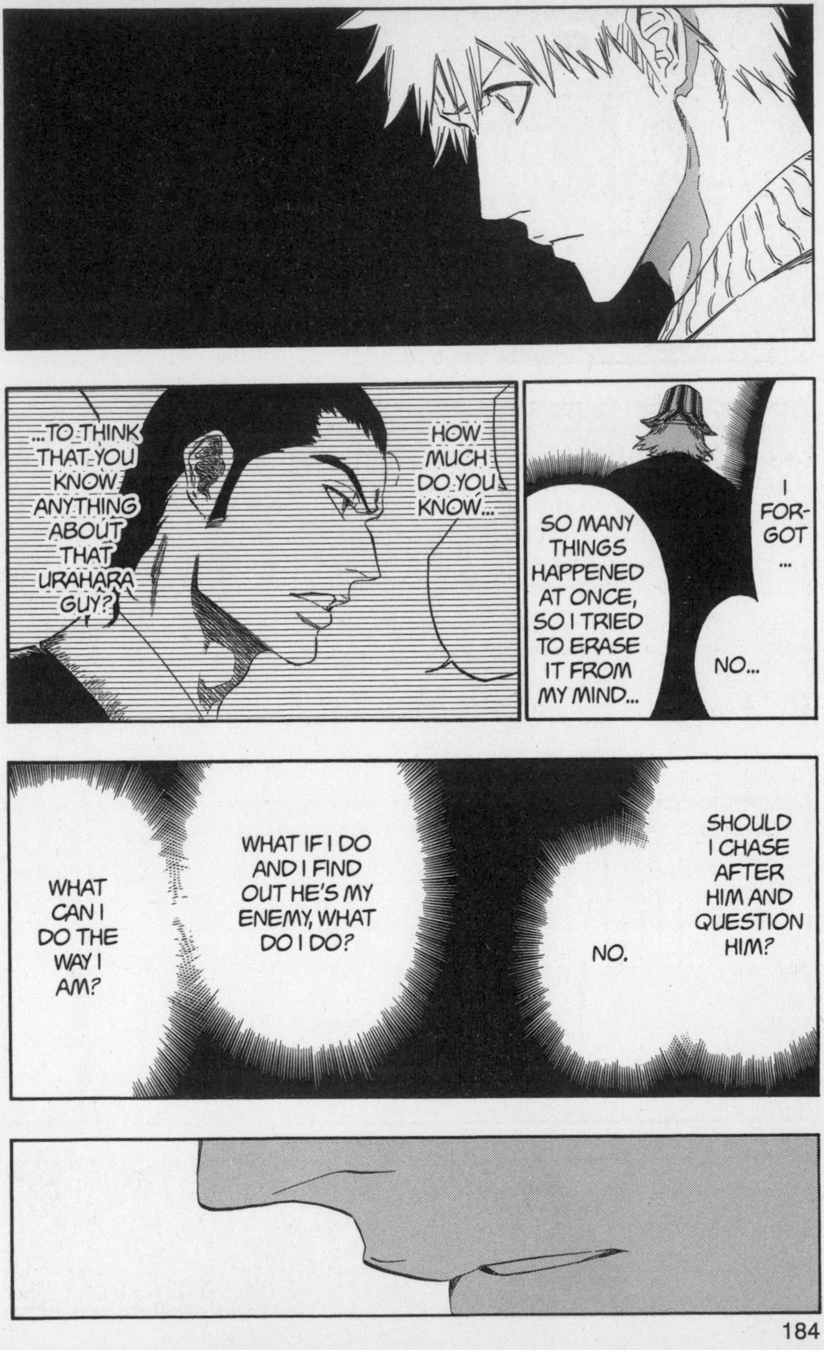
I FORGOT...
NO...
SO MANY THINGS HAPPENED AT ONCE, SO I TRIED TO ERASE IT FROM MY MIND...
HOW MUCH DO YOU KNOW...
...TO THINK THAT YOU KNOW ANYTHING ABOUT THAT URAHARA GUY?
SHOULD I CHASE AFTER HIM AND QUESTION HIM?
NO.
WHAT IF I DO AND I FIND OUT HE'S MY ENEMY, WHAT DO I DO?
WHAT CAN I DO THE WAY I AM?

NO...

I GOTTA REGAIN MY POWER AS SOON AS POSSIBLE...!

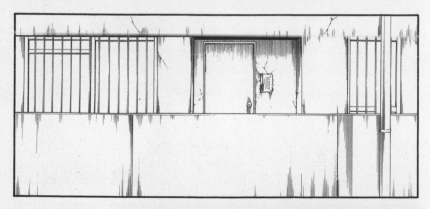

PLOP

YOU'LL BE ENTERING THIS FISH TANK!

ALL RIGHT!

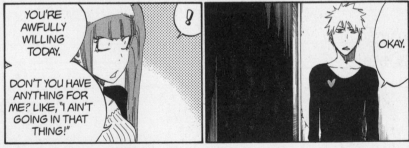

YOU'RE AWFULLY WILLING TODAY.

DON'T YOU HAVE ANYTHING FOR ME? LIKE, "I AIN'T GOING IN THAT THING!"

!

OKAY.

JUST DO IT.

NO.

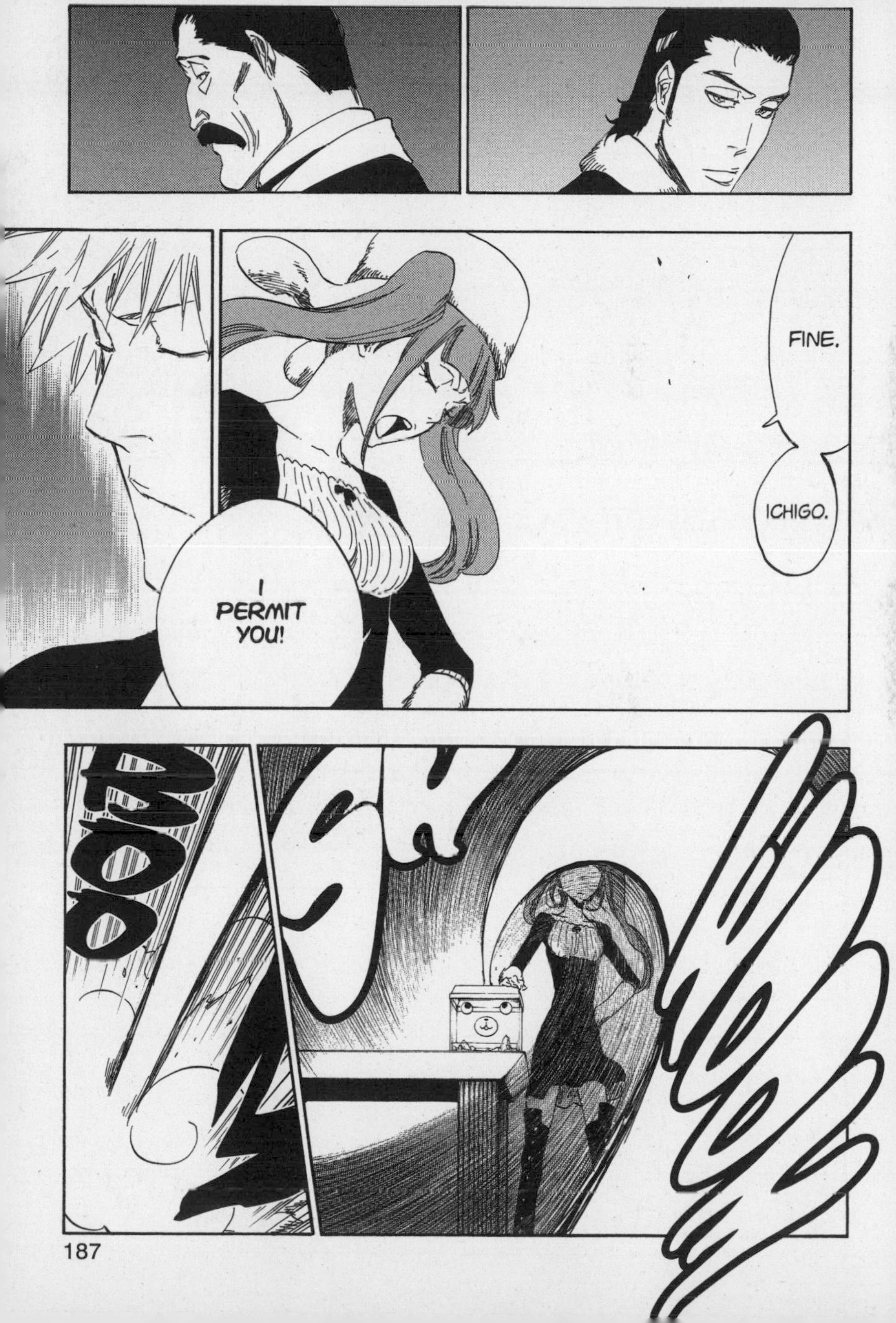
FINE.
ICHIGO.
I PERMIT YOU!

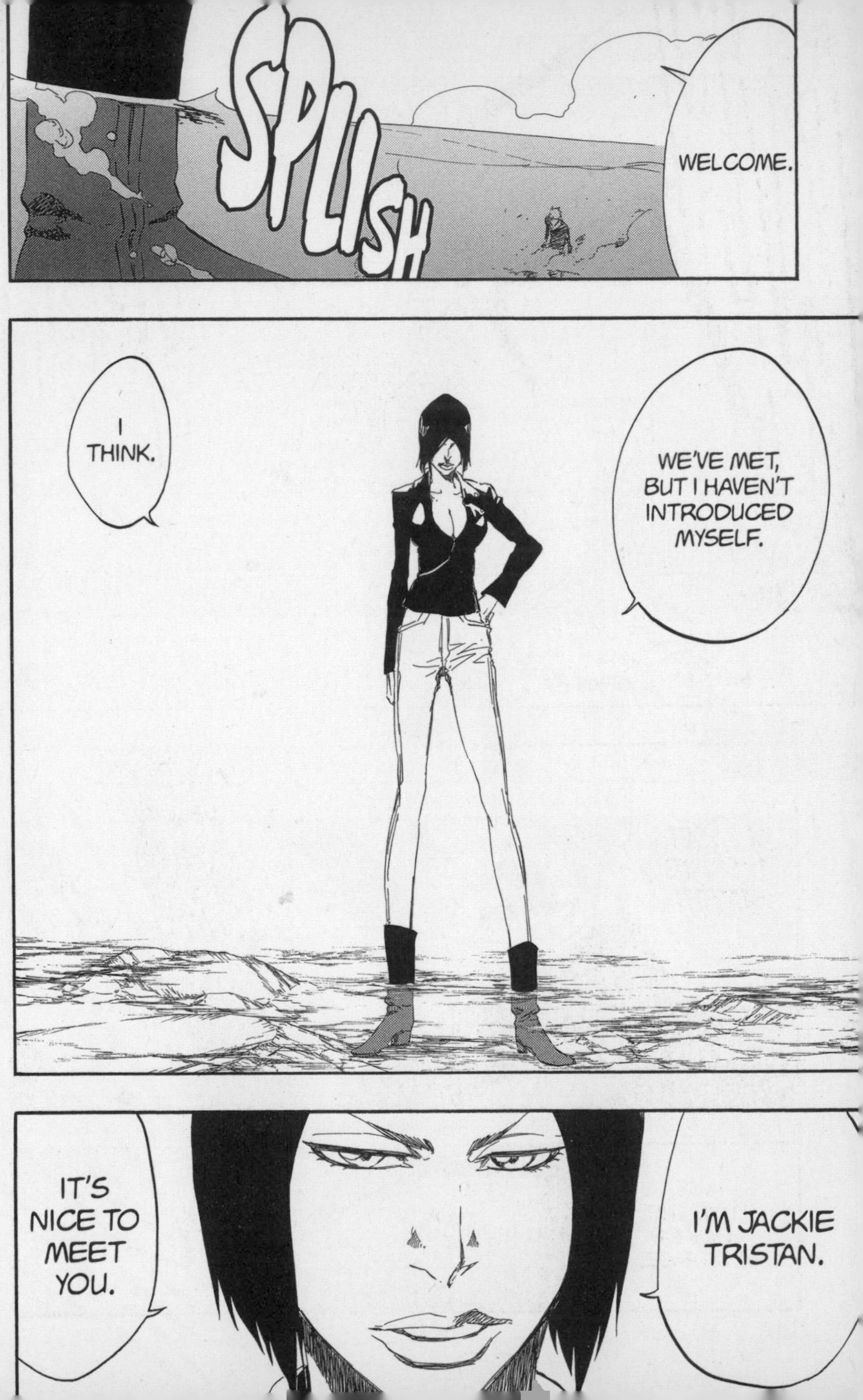
WELCOME.
SPLISH
WE'VE MET, BUT I HAVEN'T INTRODUCED MYSELF.
I THINK.
I'M JACKIE TRISTAN.
IT'S NICE TO MEET YOU.

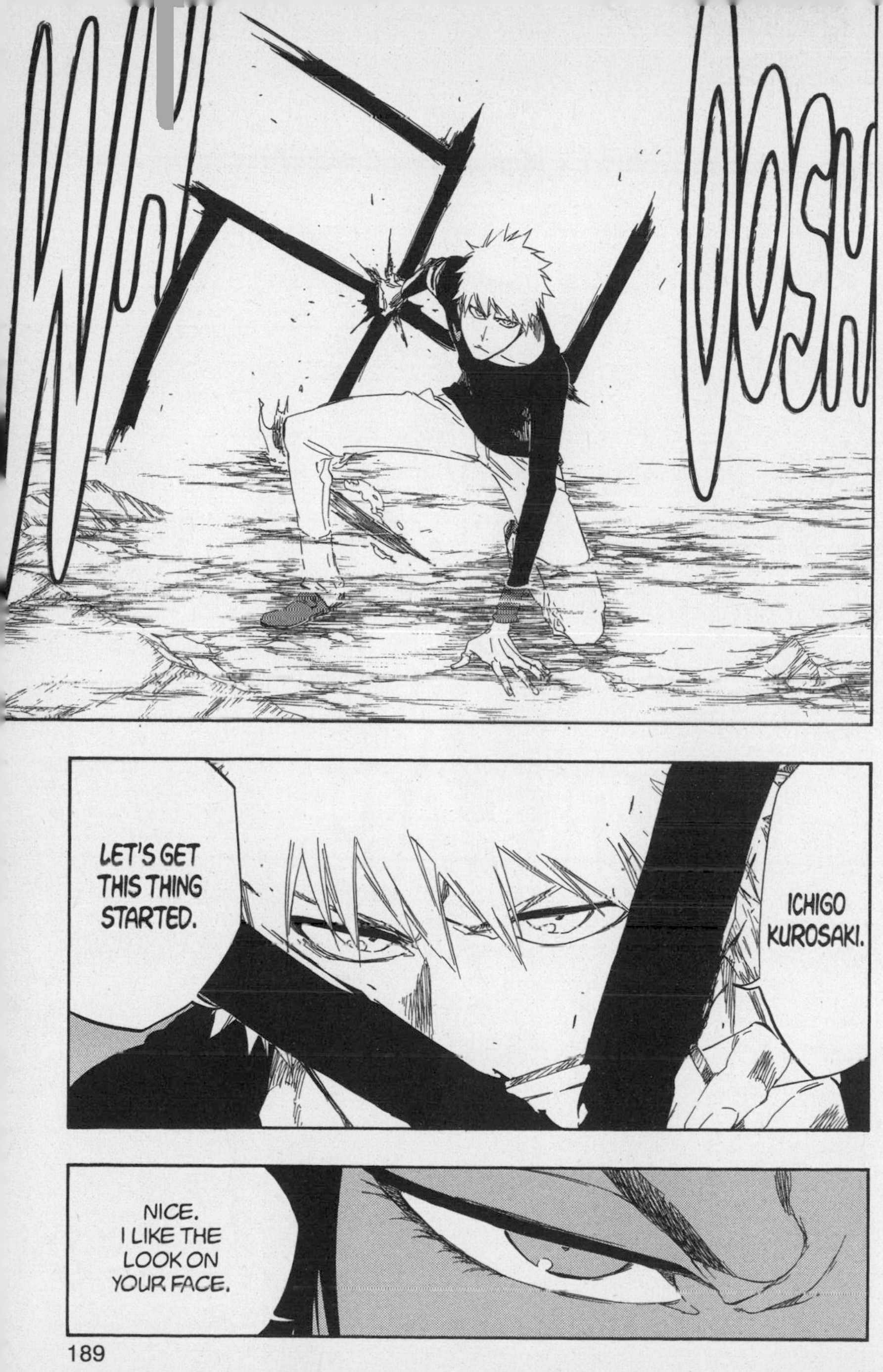
WHOOSH
ICHIGO KUROSAKI.
LET'S GET THIS THING STARTED.
NICE. I LIKE THE LOOK ON YOUR FACE.

CONTI
NUED
IN
BLEACH
51

Next Volume Preview

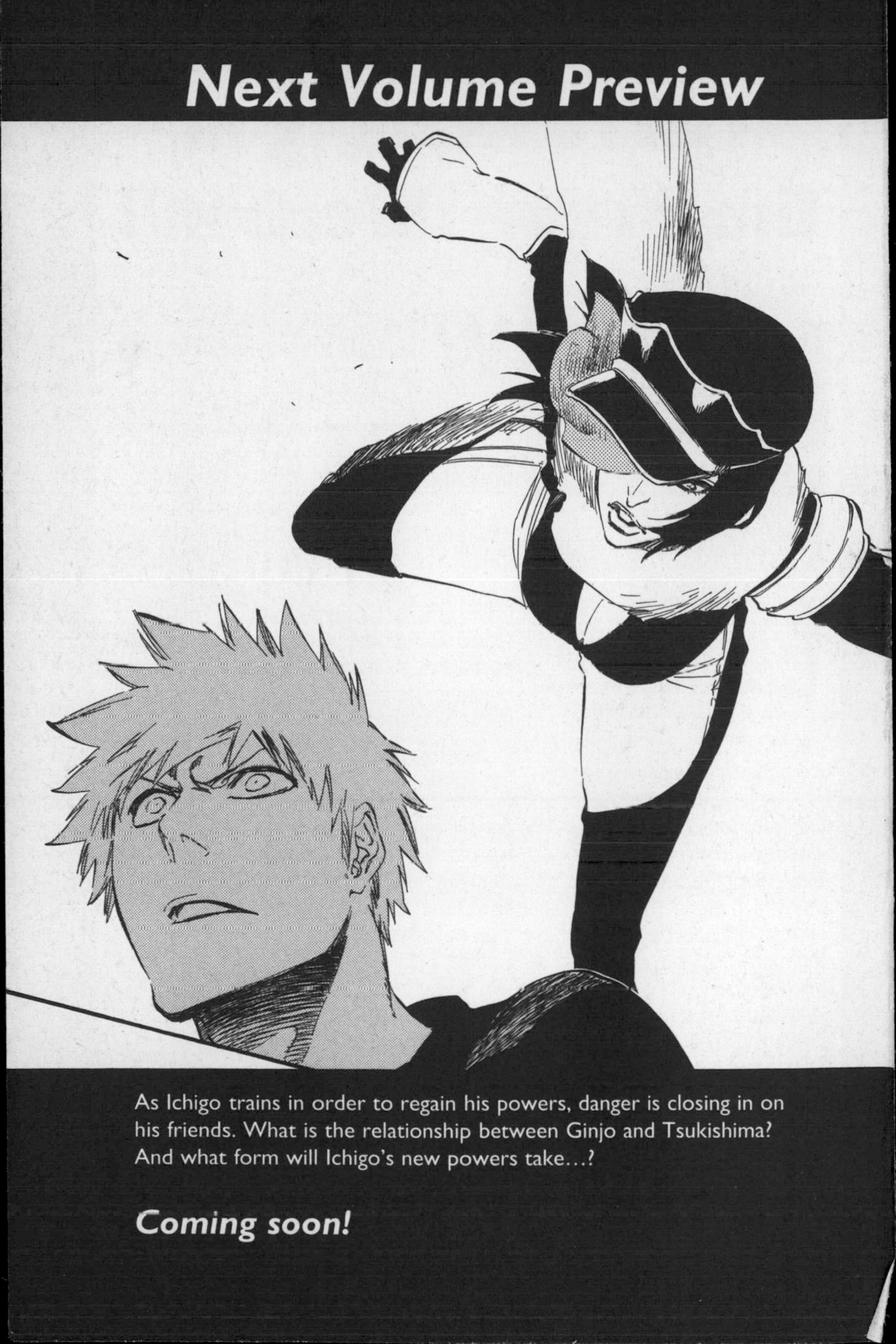

As Ichigo trains in order to regain his powers, danger is closing in on his friends. What is the relationship between Ginjo and Tsukishima? And what form will Ichigo's new powers take...?

Coming soon!

You're Reading in the Wrong Direction!!

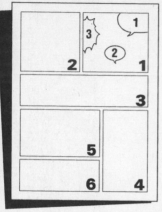

Whoops! Guess what? You're starting at the wrong end of the comic!

...It's true! In keeping with the original Japanese format, **Bleach** is meant to be read from right to left, starting in the upper-right corner.

Unlike English, which is read from left to right, Japanese is read from right to left, meaning that action, sound effects and word-balloon order are completely reversed... something which can make readers unfamiliar with Japanese feel pretty backwards themselves. For this reason, manga or Japanese comics published in the U.S. in English have sometimes been published "flopped"—that is, printed in exact reverse order, as though seen from the other side of a mirror.

By flopping pages, U.S. publishers can avoid confusing readers, but the compromise is not without its downside. For one thing, a character in a flopped manga series who once wore in the original Japanese version a T-shirt emblazoned with "M A Y" (as in "the merry month of") now wears one which reads "Y A M"! Additionally, many manga creators in Japan are themselves unhappy with the process, as some feel the mirror-imaging of their art skews their original intentions.

We are proud to bring you Tite Kubo's **Bleach** in the original unflopped format. For now, though, turn to the other side of the book and let the adventure begin...!

—Editor